REA

The Gate of Light

SARA F. YOSELOFF MEMORIAL PUBLICATIONS
In Judaism and Jewish Affairs

This volume is one in a series established in memory
of Sara F. Yoseloff,
who devoted her life to the making of books.

The Gate of Light

Janusz Korczak, the Educator and Writer Who Overcame the Holocaust

Adir Cohen

Rutherford • Madison • Teaneck
Fairleigh Dickinson University Press
London and Toronto: Associated University Presses

Associated University Presses
440 Forsgate Drive
Cranbury, NJ 08512

Associated University Presses
25 Sicilian Avenue
London WC1A 2QH, England

Associated University Presses
P.O. Box 338, Port Credit
Mississauga, Ontario
Canada L5G 4L8

Library of congress Cataloging-in-Publication Data

Cohen, Adir.
    The gate of light : Janusz Korczak, the educator and writer who overcame the Holocaust / Adir Cohen.
        p.   cm.
    Includes bibliographical references and index.
    ISBN 0-8386-3523-7
    1. Korczak, Janusz, 1878–1942. 2. Educators—Poland—Biography.
3. Authors, Polish—20th century—Biography. 4. Holocaust, Jewish
(1939–1945) I. Title.
LB775.K6272C63   1994
891.8′58709—dc20
[B]   92-55108
                                                                       CIP

PRINTED IN THE UNITED STATES OF AMERICA

Contents

6 *Contents*

Introduction

"When the sun goes out and grows cold, man shall be his own light and warmth, man shall be his own sun . . . "
—Janusz Korczak (according to Vaslav Nalkovsky)

When the sun went out in Treblinka and Meidanek, in Auschwitz and in Dachau, and throughout the smoke-shrouded kingdom of incinerators, man seemed beyond redemption. When hearts were cold, and blocks of ice lay locked within those who rejoiced the fall of man and the trampling of all virtue, and the beast of blood was the only true reality, it seemed that all hope was lost for man's salvation.

And then from the mountains of ash rose the phoenix, the human voice that restored hope and faith to mankind and carried the vision of man as light and warmth for himself, as his own sun. The death chambers of Treblinka could not quash Janusz Korczak's creed of love, and resurrected, it returns to give us life and hang a new hope in our blackened firmament, a hope for the rebuilding of a better world, a world rebuilt by a child. This is the only chance of happiness for mankind.

Among the educators who have shaped education in the last century, the Jewish-Polish Janusz Korczak stands out as an exceptional man, a noble teacher, philosopher, and educator who in his institutions applied his philosophy and vision, his long experience as a physician and as a teacher, his great love of children, and his conviction of the child's right to liberty. He sacrificed his own personal happiness for his work, for his teaching, and for the happiness of his students; his educational creation ended when his soul united with those of his students in the last and deepest of human ties—that of death, as they all took their last journey together, when Korczak and his children were transported to the gas chambers of Treblinka in August 1942. He refused Nazi offers of liberation and clemency and chose to die with his orphans.

Anyone wishing to understand Korczak's philosophy of education must acquaint himself with the secrets of this educator's life—full of hesitation and crises, pain and sacrifice, transcendence and purity. His was a life of great love, sanctified by a brutal death, which he proudly faced.

Korczak neither affiliated himself with any particular educational

7

school, nor identified with any recognized method. His approach to children and his views on matters of education were always original. He did not record his thoughts and educational experiments in any orderly way. Rather he chose to summarize his ideas and experiments in diaries, in notes of his experiences as an educator, and in sketches of his teaching methods. His written appraisals of his projects and his many notebooks and loose notes enable us to summarize his teaching, appraise its main features, and point out its timeless elements. We may also examine its internal contradictions, illuminate the many excesses of his practical teaching, and grasp the great sincerity and truth in Korzack's teachings.

Janusz Korchak was not only a great educator, but also a gifted author whose literary writings gave voice to his vision of man, to the distress of human society and to the horrors of the last days of the Warsaw ghetto. He even foresaw the Nazi madness in his play *The Senate of Madmen*, which serves as a warning even today as people continue to gather about the flag of enmity and hate.

Korczak's writings for children remain to this day some of the best children's stories ever written, reflecting a rare blend of his knowledge of education and children, his humanistic and social message, and his wonderful creative ability.

A martyr in death, Janusz Korczak was a legend in his own lifetime. Legends tend to thrive on imagination and emotion. Irrelevant details are emphasized, and basic principles are sometimes obscured. The vision may be clouded with such sentimentality as to obstruct a clear view of the true importance of the work and the philosophy of the protagonist.

Some twenty-five years ago, I was urged by my friend Dr. Chaim Ormian, now deceased, to devote myself to the reading and study of Korczak's educational accomplishments. Thus did I begin an exciting and painful, yet at the same time comforting, adventure of research which, more than a quarter of a century later, is not yet ended. At the time, I published a first summary of my findings in the form of a short treatise intended for instructors. This treatise was followed, six years later, by a book on Korczak based on more extensive research of his writings and on archival material that was available at the time.

Over the past fifteen years, the Korczak archives have grown as a great deal of new material has been uncovered and published. Much of our previous Korczak research and our perceptions of the man have become obsolete. Issues accepted as fact have been proven inaccurate. Descriptions and assessments of major Korczak biographers have turned out to be politically and sociologically biased as researchers made conscious attempts to model Korczak as an atheist supporter of Jewish assimilation, as indifferent to the Jewish people and their problems, or as a loyal Pole.

These new revelations have not only altered the study of Korczak's life, but also our perception of his educational accomplishments at his orphanages and summer camps, our understanding of the principles of his educational teaching, and our appraisal of his literary writings. This book constitutes an attempt to re-examine Korczak's life, philosophy, literary creation, and educational accomplishment, which have a relevance to the humanist mission of education everywhere. Let us become more closely acquainted with this faithful educator, with the vision of his soul and the great scope of his mind, as reflected in his creation. Let us examine his teachings and try to learn from the educational endeavor of a man whose whole life was devoted to the educational calling, as he envisioned it, felt it, and realized it.

The Gate of Light

1

Life As a Calling

Were we to sing of the laughter of children, the mirth of flowers, the chuckles of birds and the smile of a poet and doctor—it would be Janusz Korczak we would be singing of.

—Stephania Nei[1]

Heinrich Goldschmidt, who came to be known by the pen name of Janusz Korczak, was born on the 22nd of July, 1878 in Warsaw, then the capital of Congressional Poland under the sovereignity of tsarist Russia. Poland was enjoying a period of prosperity and economic and industrial expansion. New markets opening up in the Russian empire brought wealth and financial stability to the bourgeoisie, while at the same time leading to the growth of an urban proletariat and an increasing social inequity.

The economic boom was accompanied by a process of "russification," as the Russian language slowly became the main language of instruction at universities and schools. This was also a period of great agitation against Russian rule as national feelings stirred, and the first intimations of the harsher class struggles were felt—struggles in which the socialist parties were to play an important role.

Janusz Korczak's great-grandfather was a devout, God-fearing Jew, a glazier who wandered among villages. Korczak wrote of him:

I know that he had been a glazier in a small town. Poor people did not have glass panes in those days. My great grandfather would wander about the courts, install glass panes and buy rabbit skins. I like to think that my great grandfather fixed glass so that there shall be light, and bought skins—from which furs were made—to bring warmth. Sometimes I think of my great grandfather walking great distances from one village to another, resting awhile in the shade of a tree, or hurrying home before dark and the beginning of the Sabbath.[2]

His grandfather, Zvi-Hirsh Goldschmidt, was a renowned physician, the director of a hospital, and a respected scholar. Although he chose to

13

receive a Polish education, he retained an affinity with his Jewish heritage and culture, perhaps as a result of the traditional education he had been given in his parents' home and at various institutions of Jewish learning.

Zvi-Hirsch's son, Joseph, recounts an interesting tale about his father's university days at the school of medicine. He tells how one evening there was a great debate between the medical students as to whether medicine was a fitting profession for the character and tendencies of a Jew. Some of the Jewish students claimed that medicine was perfect for anyone who had studied the Bible and the Talmud in his youth, since they, too, are closely connected with care for man's health and well being. Some quoted Maimonides, a great physician of world renown. Another group of students claimed that a Talmudic education develops a Jew's *legal* sense, and that the most appropriate profession for a Jew is thus the law. One student claimed that a Jew is seized with anxiety when confronted with death and is, therefore, not suited to the medical profession. Zvi-Hirsh Goldschmidt, a proud and aware Jew, contested this assumption and stated his willingness to disprove these baseless accusations by sleeping in the morgue. Moreover, he would lie down with a corpse and sleep by its side. The students placed bets on this boast, and Zvi-Hirsh entered the morgue, lay down beside a corpse and fell asleep. Suddenly the bodies began to move, lifting their hands and kicking their feet, as the students manipulated the corpses with strings in an attempt to frighten Zvi-Hirsh, who ignored it all and won the bet.[3]

This story, if true, is an excellent illustration of the depth of Zvi-Hirsh's Jewish identity. He completed his studies in Lvov, passed his examinations, and set up practice in Poland. Unlike other doctors, he did not change his Jewish name. He lived in a Jewish neighbourhood and mainly treated Jewish patients. Zvi-Hirsh was deeply involved in the founding and operation of the Jewish hospital, for which he raised contributions and enlisted Jewish public opinion.

Heinrich's own father, Joseph Goldschmidt was a successful and respected lawyer in the capital. Although his home was secular with Polish cultural leanings, Joseph Goldschmidt retained an affinity for Jewish culture and history, like his father before him.

Joseph (born in 1844) and his brother Jacob (born in 1848) studied Judaism in their father's home and acquired a general education at the pre-gymnasium of Harobishov, the town of their birth, and later at the Lyceum in Lublin. In their father's home they read the Jewish periodicals *Juczenke* and *Israelite*—two publications written in an intellectual spirit that sought a greater proximity to Polish culture, identified with the local population, and encouraged Polish patriotism, while stressing the preservation of Jewish uniqueness rather than preaching atheism and assimilation.

Of particular interest is an article, published by Joseph Goldschmidt in the *Israelite* of 6 September 1866, which indicates the deep interest Jewish education held for Korczak's father and his care for the wretched and impoverished day centers that had been set up for poor girls in Lublin. In this article Korczak's father harshly criticized the Lublin politicians who did nothing for the day centers and advised the rehabilitation of the centers, the collection of funds, and making the education of the unfortunate girls the responsibility of the community.[4]

Joseph Goldschmidt published four books on Jewish history and an article titled "The Peddler's Daughter" in which he described the 1867 plague of Warsaw, and his own role in saving unfortunates among the Jewish poor. During the same period, he also began publishing a series of articles titled "Portraits of Renowned Jews," the first of which was dedicated to Moshe Montifiore. He edited Jewish historical studies that had been published in Western Europe, and even wrote a penetrating treatise on the staging of William Shakespeare's *The Merchant of Venice* at the Polish theater. The main idea of the treatise was that "Shylock is a victim of the enmity and evil which characterize the attitude of Christian society toward the Jews."[5] Joseph was sensitive to any slight to Judaism and fought against such disparagement. An excellent illustration of this is a story titled "Helena," published in the Polish periodical *Tigudnick Illustrobani*, where the Jewish prayer and its form are mocked and described as raucous loudness accompanied by bizarre movements. The story emphasized that the Jew "prays for himself and his people, and could a Jew pray for anything else?"

Although Joseph Goldschmidt wished to react to the story, the editor of *Tigudnick Illustrobani* refused to print his response, and he was obliged to publish it in the *Israelite*. He attacked the author of "Helena" for his derogatory description and ended his article with the words: "In a man's conversation with his creator, form is unimportant. If the distorted prayer of the ignorant is sincere, then it must win our respect.[6]" He also rejected the author's contention that the Jew prays only for himself and his people and presented excerpts of Jewish prayer which clearly indicate a universal spirit, an appeal for the well-being of all people, and a view God as the God of all living.

Joseph Goldschmidt published a considerable number of articles on diverse issues of Jewish education such as a demand to found a day center for Jewish boys, education for the poor, the education of girls from impoverished families, and the education of Jewish women. The articles show a liberal orientation, a deep educational and social involvement, and a progressive view of education. Korczak's father's major work was his comprehensive book *A Presentation of the Laws of Divorce in Accordance with the Traditions of Moses and the Talmud*. This affinity to the

Jewish world, however, did not lead him to adopt a Jewish life-style in his own home. Although Jewish holidays were still commemorated, the Goldschmidt household was run along wholly Polish lines; the servants were Polish Christians, and the customs were local, devoid of any sign of Jewish tradition.

Heinrich was mainly educated by his mother, who lacked any affinity for the Jewish world or tradition. Polish was spoken at home, and the Polish culture was the only one she acknowledged and to which she fostered Heinrich's identification. Heinrich only discovered his Jewishness by accident at the age of five. He wrote of the incident in the 1942 diary from the Warsaw Ghetto.

It seems that already then, in my earliest childhood, I revealed to Grandma, in an intimate conversation, my daring plan to change the world. No more and no less than to do away with money. How I would get rid of it, and where I would dispose of it, I did not know, nor what to do after it was gone. But I must not be judged harshly for I was only five years old and facing a most difficult problem: What to do so there would be no more dirty, tattered and hungry children, those children with whom I was forbidden to play in the yard. That same yard where, beneath the acorn tree, Mati, my beloved canary, was buried in a shroud of cotton wool, encoffined in a tin box of sweets. His death evoked the mysterious question of religion. I wanted to put a cross over his grave, but the maid said that was forbidden because he was a bird, which is far inferior to man, and that it was even a sin to weep over his death. Thus the maid. But matters were made far worse by the son of the porter who said that the canary was Jewish, and that I, too, was Jewish, while he was a Polish Catholic. He would go to paradise, while I, if I did not talk dirty and would not obediently bring him the sugar which I pinched from home—would go after to a place, which though it was not hell, was very dark. And I feared dark rooms.[7]

It is almost inconceivable that Korczak was totally unaware of his Jewish roots; that he had absorbed nothing of the heritage of his father, who was so involved in Jewish issues; that he had heard nothing of his family history, or that he had experienced no Jewish religious rituals.

Paolina Apanshlak, an assimilationist far removed from Judaism, writes in her biography of Korczak that his family placed a fir tree in the children's room on Christmas. On Sundays the Christian nursemaid took the children for a walk to the Church of the Three Crosses, where they would make the sign of the cross and shiver in fear when she told them of the bones entombed in the cellars. Apanshlak writes:

The mind would grow a little dizzy from the aroma of the incense. On the altar, the lights flickered so that the statue of the Holy Mother, in a light blue gown, seemed to come alive. In a harsh voice, the priest would recite the Latin verses at length, then the Organ player would begin to play and the choir sing, and it seemed as if the angels themselves were singing.[8]

Besides the Christian experience that deeply impressed them Apanshlak notes that Jewish holidays were also celebrated in the Goldschmidt family home and that care was taken to observe religious ceremonies. During the Jewish holidays the Christian nursemaid was sent back home to her family. Apanshlak describes the night of the Seder when matzos were eaten and four glasses of wine were drunk. She also writes of Yom Kippur, the Day of Atonement:

That day was well-remembered by all the children. Heinrich wore a new sailor's suit and a round cap which he was forbiddent to take off in synagogue. He stood by his father and looked wide-eyed at all that was taking place. The remains of candles which had been lit the night before continued to burn. His grandfather seemed like an Oriental king, very pale and in his beautiful white praying shawl, whose edges were embroidered in black and silver. The men were red eyed, and their feet were shod in slippers. From the women's gallery above, he could hear the crying of the women. . . . Once he began attending the gymnasium his father stopped taking him to synagogue and his ties to Judaism became truly invisible.[9]

In his long conversations with Yerachmiel Weingarten, a tutor at the orphanage he directed, Korczak often referred to his Jewish memories. One of his strongest memories was a tale told by his grandmother about his great great-grandfather. This story shocked him and was deeply embedded in his soul. Although he understood it only partially, it would occasionally haunt his dreams at night.

His great-great-grandfather was named Joseph and had been orphaned at an early age. Charitable people in his small town took care of the orphan and provided him with a small attic in which he could live. Each day he would eat at a different home, at the tables of generous people. He studied at the "Cheder," and found various odd jobs in an attempt to earn his own living. At fourteen he was nominated as water-carrier for the town's Jews. He was given a yoke and two buckets and would lift water from the well and carry it to the Jewish homes. He supplied free water to the synagogue, to the house of the rabbi, and to the houses of the poor.

On Saturdays he was the guest of the rabbi, eating at his table and learning wisdom during the hours of rest. At the rabbi's house there lived an orphan girl called Sarah, who helped the rabbi's wife in her store and with the housework. At that time, Jewish boys were sometimes kidnapped for service in the army of the Russian tsar. Each Jewish community was obliged to provide a number of boys for recruitment. When the head of the community wished to send Joseph, who had no family and no one to protect him, the town rabbi hastily wedded Joseph to Sarah, in the graveyard. During the marriage ceremony the rabbi explained to the gathered crowd that it is a great virtue to marry orphans in the cemetery where their parents are buried, and because of this virtue, any plague which threatens the townspeople is thwarted and dangers are prevented. (And indeed, such weddings were often conducted in times of plague or minor edicts. They were called "black weddings" or "cholera weddings.") With the wedding gifts which they received from the community, the orphans rented a small apartment. Sarah began to sew clothes for the town's women, and Joseph learned the art of tailoring, so that between them they clothed the whole town.[10]

Little Heinrich often woke during the night with nightmares of a black wedding in a graveyard. He was chilled whenever he heard or remembered the concept of a "cholera wedding," and he often thought of his great-grandfather the water-carrier and tailor, his grandfather the glazer, and his other grandfather the physician.

The essential experiences of Korczak's childhood hold the key to his complex personality, and constitute the primary source of the wonderful passages on children, dreams, and education that fill his pedagogical writings and children's books.

Despite his family's affluence, the comfortable living conditions, the beautiful furniture, the expensive ornaments, and the other luxuries that filled the house, Korczak's childhood was difficult. His father was mentally unstable, and his behavior was often strange and fickle. The relationships between his father and his mother, Cecilia Gambizki, were tense. Their attitudes toward the children were radically different, and they often quarreled. The tense atmosphere at home, and his father's frequent illnesses severely affected his mental and emotional development. Korczak's conservative parents did not understand their dreamy and sensitive son, who was often lonely and bored, feeling himself a prisoner in a glorious jail. He would express his dreams, sorrows, aspirations, and prayers in writing or find release in many hours of daydreaming. At a very young age he had already composed a special, personal prayer he called *A Prayer for the Ability to Pray*, which he would repeat every evening.

My Lord
I come to you with humble spirit
To ask you for the greatest grace required by man:
The ability to pray with an innocent heart.
Let all that is not you disappear from my sight and thought
Let nothing distract my mind.
Teach me, my Lord, to pray to you in hope and faith.[11]

This prayer is not directed to the Hebrew god, but to the god of hearts. He did not know his father's god. The language, culture, and customs of his parents' home were Polish, and there were few childhood experiences which were different from those of a Christian child of this period.

His book *The Drawing Room Kid*, written many years later, contains numerous autobiographical elements, and faithfully expresses his sad childhood, his sorrow, and the gloomy thoughts of his loneliness and self-made seclusion. "I was a child who played many hours by himself. A child who one does not notice. I received building blocks when I was six, and stopped playing with them when I was fourteen".[12]

Korczak wished to examine everything, to see, to think, to ask the essence of the matter, not from any particular wish to research or find solutions, but out of an inner urge to ask and continue asking, as if the fact of posing the question, the very fact of seeking, held the possibility of life, of a deeper affinity with the essence of things.

I asked my building blocks, I asked children and adults, who they are. I did not destroy toys, and I did not care why the doll closes its eyes when it is put down, it was not the mechanism but the essence—the thing for itself and in itself, which interested me.[13]

Korczak's relations with his father were special and complex. Sometimes they presented a united front against the women who ruled the house (mother, sister, grandmother, cook, housemaid, and nursemaid). At other times, his father would neglect and ignore him, becoming totally involved in his legal work and personal affairs. Occasionally his father would taunt him and call him derogatory names such as lazy, stupid, crybaby, or no good after which he would take him on long walks, and they would plan adventures and pranks. Korczak's mother would often berate his father for his capricious relationship with his son as well as his lack of responsibility in dragging Heinrich to theater plays in the middle of the frozen winter and then feeding him ice cream and cold drinks.

Korczak suffered greatly from the frequent quarreling of his father and mother, but he still loved to go out for those winter walks with his father. He was captivated by the theater, and enjoyed participating in his father's pranks. His father, bursting with laughter, would colorfully describe how Cecilia would react when they described their adventures. Most of all he loved the spring and summer outings on the river Visla, and some of his warmest memories are connected with these trips.

When he was eight years old, he entered a private primary school of the old tradition where discipline was severe, and students were commonly beaten. At school, he isolated himself and did not befriend his peers, rejecting even those who sought his company. The school was gloomy, the lessons boring, and the teachers tired and baleful. Students counted the minutes to the recess bell. Written papers were a nightmare and examinations a horrifying prospect. The school was like a prison in which the teachers and the headmaster were jailers who inspected their student-prisoners from the height of their podium. Korczak's school days were engraved in his soul like a bad dream, and when he came to recall them in his book *When I Shall Be Little Again*, he wrote:

> There were no good schools in my day. Nothing but strictness and boredom. Nothing was allowed. Alienation, cold and suffocation. So that even years later, when I would dream of school at night, I would wake up covered with sweat and full of happiness that it was only a dream.[14]

Indeed the school that Korczak attended showed no consideration for the child's mental needs, for his special world, his interests or talents. Physical punishment, which was freely applied, frightened and depressed Heinrich. The mechanical learning by rote and the lack of free thinking made him detest learning, and when he saw his parents' eagerness for good grades, and their joy over any seeming success, he felt that hypocrisy ruled and external appearances and affectation were of the essence.

Korczak's school was an institution in which the dialogue between man and God had been stifled; where all communication between a child and beauty or knowledge had been severed—a contact that Korczak the child longed for and which he would, in his loneliness, seek with himself, his building blocks, people in the park, or even with inanimate objects. When the hero of *When I Shall be Little Again* is asked to draw a school, he paints a triptych. In the central picture, *Recess*, children are running about, and one unruly child is being punished by a teacher who pulls his ear and strikes him while other children stand with bowed heads, saying nothing out of fear. In the right panel, he draws a class in which a teacher is beating shoulders with a ruler. In the left, he portrays a real lashing, where the bearded spelling teacher lifts his hand and strap. It is a drawing as gloomy as a prison, of which Korczak writes, "When I was eight years old, I went to this school."[15]

In his essay "Confession of a Butterfly," Korczak described his horrifying school experience:

It is hot in class. Thirty students. The sixth lesson of the day. The tired teacher sits on the podium and calls a student to read the lesson. He hardly listens and the student therefore chats with his peers. The students are tired after six hours of sitting in one place. Outside there are sunshine, birds, freedom, while here inside, it is a prison, chains. Poor teachers. Is it any wonder that they are nervous, nasty, unjust? We suffer this burden, hoping and dreaming of the day of liberation, and they? They teach generations who grow up and leave, while they are condemned to a life of boredom and degeneration.

I dreamt: I was at the gymnasium, sitting on the podium. The teacher suddenly entered and stared at me. Such a stare as one only sees in nightmares: mute, mad and black. The stare of a tiger about to pounce. I began moaning and crying aloud, and I woke up.

The next day, I got a good question. I was asked about everything for more than half an hour. The worse my replies, the more indifferent I became. Let them give me what they will, I thought, so long as they let me go. The headmaster entered and I felt my energies return. The teacher whispered something in his ear. I thought—wait, you bastard, and began to answer vigorously and to the point. The teacher stared at me with hate. Our angry gazes cross. The headmaster had already said—"enough" twice, but he, nothing. And so, I pass. I proceed to the next grade.[16]

It is in this depressing world that love began to flower in the heart of Korczak the child. It is a love that he kept locked within his heart, that he dreamed of, and that illuminated his lonely world and lit some of his most beautiful hours. In his memoirs he wrote:

From my seventh year to my fourteenth, I was constantly in love. Always with a different girl. It is interesting that I remember most of them. Two sisters from the ice-skating rink, Stach's cousin, the one with mourning clothes, Zusha Kalhorn, Aneilke, Irenka Mnalanchov—Stefacia, for whom I picked flowers by the fountain in the Saxian garden. And here is a young juggler, for whose fate I bitterly wept: I loved for a week, a month, sometimes two, three at a time. I wanted one to be my sister, the other my wife, my sister in law.[17]

When he was eleven, Heinrich's world was shattered, and his family collapsed. His father succumbed to severe mental illness, and, until his death, was hospitalized a number of times in institutions for the mentally insane. The sight of his mentally deranged father depressed Heinrich. When his father was seized by bouts of madness, he would closet himself in his room or run out of the house with a breaking heart. The impressions of those days were deeply engraved in his soul and became basic traumas of his life. In his memoirs he wrote:

> When I was seventeen, I even began to write a suicide story. The main figure began to hate life for fear of madness. I was scared to death of the mental institution where my father was hospitalized a number of times. I am the son of a lunatic and the weight of heredity is thus upon me. Although many years have passed, the thought periodically torments me.[18]

Korczak was to carry this fear throughout his life as the possible experience of madness followed him like a shadow. Thoughts of death always accompanied him, and he wrote in his diary:

> For many years I kept mercury, chloride and morphium tablets at the bottom of my drawer. Once, I would take them with me only when I went to visit my mother's grave, but since the outbreak of the war I carry them in my pocket all the time. . . . If I constantly postponed my plan, which was calculated to the last detail, it was because always, at the last moment, some new dream would rise within me, which I could not forsake without realizing.

It is interesting to note that at a later stage in his life, when he began directing the orphanage, he had his father's old writing desk transferred to the attic where he lived. It was at this desk that he wrote many of his works. Yet in all his writing, including his memoirs, there is no reference to his father's literary, historical, and scientific work, nor does he mention his father's contribution to the study of Judaism or his legal work. It seems that in his early youth he suppressed the memories of his father's mental illness and forced himself to forget those bitter memories, and that with them he also supressed the Jewish traditions of his father's home, the memory of holidays, and everything else that was associated with his miserable childhood.

Yerachmiel Weingarten tells of his first visit to Korczak's room at the orphanage: "The walls—between the bookshelves and the files—bore a number of photographs of Korczak's family (*I do not think I saw a photograph of his father among them*) as well as a large picture of the pedagogue he admired from his youth—Freidrich Froebel."[19] This offhand remark testifies strongly to Korczak's inability to cope with his father's memory. He could not keep his image before him, and seems to have decreed that his father with everything connected to him be forgotten.

It was only in the last year of his life that he returned to the image of his father, as if closing a circle. In that return there is a note of regret as well as a sense that without consciously admitting it he had used his life to realize the traditions of generations and the purpose of his fathers. He wrote in his diary: "I was forced to devote much to my father: in my life I have actualized the essence of his aspirations, the goal towards which my grandfather strove in great agony, for many years."[20]

The father's prolonged illness, the high fees required for hospitalization in mental institutions, and the lack of any other source of income for the family, quickly depleted the family savings and brought the Goldschmidts to the brink of poverty. The large, attractive apartment was exchanged for a smaller one in a poor district, and the lovely furniture was sold in a public auction. Valuables went for a song, the family was declared bankrupt, and poverty began to gnaw at his mother and at the two small children. From this point onward, young Korczak's life was hard and depressing indeed.

He began studying at a state high school, which obliged its students to study Russian and look down on Polish. The methods of instruction used at the school were old-fashioned, very authoritarian, and lacking in any consideration for the child, his needs, or his interests. The curriculum was based wholly on senseless learning by rote, repetitious exercises, and exhausting examinations.

In order to earn some money, Korczak combined his studies with hard work, tutoring slow students, and thus, with enormous effort, he succeeded in completing his high school studies. "I was rich as a child, and then poor, and I know both affluence and poverty. I know that one can be good and decent either way, and that it is possible to be rich and very miserable." And, indeed, Korczak had experienced changes, struggles, and suffering, and this rich life experience was a constant model for his literary work and educational accomplishment. Korczak's many books for children reflect and enlarge on his childhood dreams, his world of secret fantasies and aspirations, and his life plans. He always considered dreams to be life plans, and cautioned young teachers to be "always careful in their actions, but daring and bold in their dreams." Korczak was a great dreamer who dreamed of man's redemption and happiness. While in his youth he had sought an interesting world in legends of far places and in dreams of the future, as an adult he found this world within his own heart. "No longer is the interesting world behind me. Now it is within me. I do not exist so that people should love me and respect me, but so that I myself may act and love. My environment is not obligated to help me, but I am obligated to care for the world, and man."[21]

At the age of fifteen he was seized with a great craving for books, and would lose himself for many hours in the wonderful worlds he found within their pages. He noted in his diary: "I was seized with a madness for reading. The whole world would recede until only the book existed."[22] The more he read the more he felt a growing urge for self-expression, and he began writing original stories and poems. He wrote a great deal and devoted most of his spare time to the task, evoking criticism from the members of his family who reproved him for wasting his time on a task more suitable for sentimental girls than for men. But Heinrich ignored their jibes and taunts and continued to write. In his pursuit of inspiration he would walk for long hours on the banks of his beloved Visla, drinking in the sights and allowing his soul to merge with the world of many secrets that unfolded before him.

In "Confession of a Butterfly," Korczak described his daily schedule: "School in the morning, and then tutorials combined with meals, sleep, and . . . dreams. The dreams saved me from a year of desperation, and I owe them my life."

He was a closed and secluded person whom no one accompanied on his lengthy evening walks; he was alone with his sad thoughts and great longings for a different, more pure and beautiful reality. He did not show his notes and rhymes to anyone, and one time when his sister Ania peeked into his poem book, he raged at her and refused to forgive her for what he called a trampling of his emotions. He talked of his writings only with one young girl—the lovely Adila—to whom he bared the secrets of his soul. His meetings with her were the only moments of joy and happiness in his desolate life, and he became distraught when he heard that Adila had married another. He rejected the explanations of her acquaintances that her parents had lost their wealth and that Adila was used to a life of luxury, that she could not resist the great pressures exerted on her to marry a rich man who would provide her with diamonds and lovely clothes, a horse- drawn carriage, and a well-furnished five-room apartment. This great disappointment wounded Korczak deeply, and he felt himself surrounded by lying and deceit, pettiness and baseness.

When he brought the first flowers of his poetry to the editor of a well-known Polish periodical in Warsaw, the man riffled through the poems and rejected them with ridicule. Deeply hurt, Korczak refrained from writing poetry thereafter, and devoted himself exclusively to literary and philosophical writing.

Igor Neverly recounts Korczak's humorous description of that meeting with the editor who sealed his fate as a poet:

I wrote for quite a few years during senior high school, sometimes whole rhapsodies, and always in secret. At last, I grew bold, and approached the editor of "Pravda," which was the most serious social-literary perodical of the time. I was received by Schweinatochovsky himself—you know, Alexander Schweinatochovsky, the main editor, a brilliant writer, the author of "spirits" in three volumes. In a word: the so called representative of progressive thought . . . so, the representative himself, brilliant in both style and manner, listened to me while I stood and he sat. No, I am sure I would not have read them so excitedly if I were sitting. I read, then, my elegy. He listened quietly and when I'd finished with the words: . . . "allow me not to feel, allow me not to be, allow me to descend to the grave" he said: "I allow you." Well, that was it. I wrote no more poems.[23]

In the year 1896, Heinrich's father died, and he increasingly withdrew into his inner world with his writing and his thoughts.

Responding to family pressures, Heinrich began studying medicine at the Warsaw university immediately after completing his high school studies, yet he did not stop his intensive literary work.

As a student of medicine he devoted a great deal of time to the "Free Reading Halls of the Warsaw Society of Charity," where he worked with children. He introduced them to the wonderful world of books, told them stories, had conversations with them, and encouraged them to unburden their souls, tell him of their lives and speak their hearts. He discovered that he had a wonderful talent for establishing intimate relationships with children. They would surround him, avidly drinking his words and sharing their cares and dreams with him. He devoted many hours to teaching them Polish, geography, literature, and history, combining everything with stories and long discussions into the night.

Helena Bobinska, who worked with Korczak at the reading halls, wrote in her diary:

During the winter of 1897, I distributed books in the library on Cipla street. I was joined in this work by a senior year medical student—Heinrich Goldschmidt, a blonde with a red beard, a pleasant smile and a wise look in his sapphire eyes. On Saturday nights the reading hall was usually full to bursting with lively and boisterous youths, and Heinrich had an amazing ability to control the youngsters without raising his voice. It seemed as if he had known each of them for a long time, and knew everything about them. . . . I myself was subjected to the extraordinary influence of this pedagogue. Every Saturday afternoon, children from the whole surrounding area would gather in Heinrich Goldschmidt's room on Heldona street (the room was on the ground floor and opened out onto a yard). He would organize games and I would assist him in this.[24]

In 1898 Heinrich participated in the Padervsky literary competition held by the *Warsaw Herald*. He handed in a play of four acts, entitled *Where To?*, which he signed with the pen name of Janasz Korczak, a name gleaned from the hero of Kraszavsky's book *The Adventures of Janasz Korczak and the Daughter of the Beautiful Knight*, a book much loved by him. His play won acclaim, and when it was published, the name Janasz became distorted to Janusz. Heinrich accepted this distorted version of his pen name and made it into his permanent literary pseudonym.

This play, which Korczak wrote as a young man, has not survived, though the newspapers of the period had published its contents and even noted the influence of Ibsen on the playwright. The theme of the play seems to have been taken from Korczak's life and the atmosphere in his father's home. Itzchak Perlis, who followed the newspapers of that period, described the main issues of the play:

> It is a tragedy of a family in which the father, a mentally disturbed man with weak nerves, forces his whole family to act according to his whims. As a result, one of his sons is a pervert and criminal, his second son, though a talented author, is tubercular and awaits his death at any moment, and the daughter has become a radical rationalist. The oppression of the fickle father casts its shadow on the whole family and the house is filled with fighting and tension. The play closes with the father's madness and the dissolution of the entire family.[25]

It was a difficult period for Korczak. The university studies were intensive, and he devoted whole nights to the study of anatomy and physiology. From the university he would rush to the homes of his slow pupils, and it was only with great difficulty that he managed to support himself and to aid his mother and family who had been left penniless. Because Korczak was forced to work for his living and support his mother and sister, his medical studies extended over a protracted period, during which he also became involved in patriotic public activities and taught the Polish language—a virtually subversive act under the rule of the Russian tsar. He established ties of friendship with prominent figures of the radical Polish intelligentsia, such as the geographer, educator, and reporter Vaslav Nalkovsky; the psychologist and experimental pedagogy pioneer, Yan Vladislev David; the patron of political prisoners and organizer of the underground enlightment movement in Warsaw—Stefania Sempolovska, and others.

In 1900 he began contributing to the humor and satire weekly *Koltza* edited by Alexander Paievsky, and, in 1901, began writing a weekly sketch, which he signed Hein-Rich. During the same year Paievsky published Korczak's first book, *The Street Children*, which was based on his close acquaintanceship with the children of the impoverished classes and the knowledge he had gained through his volunteer educational activities among the Warsaw poor. For about a year Korczak lived in a tiny room in one of the poor quarters, Solz, where he befriended the unlucky and the oppressed, the utterly destitute, the drunkards, and the thieves.

In his treatise on Korczak, Gdalia Alkoshi rightly stressed that the literary importance of this book was slight. The critics ignored it, and even Korczak eventually came to disregard it. However,

> In the context of Korczak's spiritual biography this composition has a very special place, for it is the first expression of Korczak's deep mental attitude to the oppressed child, and constitutes the first signpost on the way of thorns which he was to tread as the educator and patron of the children of poverty.[26]

During the final years of his medical studies at the Warsaw university, he drew very close to the socialists, and though he did not join the party, he contributed to the leftist paper *Gloss* in which he wrote of social problems and of the severe social injustices in Poland. He was arrested for a short period by the tsarist police in connection with leftist activity in the reading halls of the Warsaw society of charity, where an anti-Semitic newspaper editor falsely charged that atheism and radical ideas were being propounded.

It should be noted that in addition to his contributions to the weekly *Kultza* (Thorns) and the leftist newspaper *Gloss* (The voice), Korczak also published a great number of articles, sketches, and compositions in a variety of other periodicals. Suffice it to note but a few of the periodicals to which he contributed during this period, to show the depth and extent of his involvement in the social, medical, and pedagogical issues of the time. These periodicals covered such subjects as pedagogy, medicine, and pediatric medicine, as well as social issues. He also contributed to various periodicals of the left such as: *The Light*, *The Knowledge*, and *New Life*, which were edited by the well-known leftist activist Thedeush Rachnivetzky.

His contributions to the newspapers of the left were the product of Korczak's intense involvement with social issues. The political issues interested him far less than the conditions of human beings, the oppression of the lower classes, and the social injustices. He favorably mentions the short period that he spent in jail on account of this involvement, because as fate would have it, he chanced to share a cell with the important Polish sociologist, Ludwig Katzivetsky, who influenced him greatly and who provided him with an important tool for his educational work—that of statistical research which he later applied to his work at the orphanage.

Igor Neverly tells how after his release from jail, thanks to the intervention of the mother of one of his pupils, the wife of the Russian general Gilchenko, Korczak continued his activities in the underground Polish college, then known as the "Flying University." He became friends with Stefania Sempolovska, who was the living spirit of this "college" and one of the founders of the underground enlightenment movement in Poland. Stefania Sempolovska fought for the independence of the Polish school and its liberation from the dictates of Tsarist rule. She was a patron of Polish political prisoners and did much to foster original Polish culture.

According to Neverly:

Korczak taught young children at Sempolovska's large apartment, which was also a place of gatherings and meetings, and a kind of headquarters. . . . The main focus of Stefania Sempolovska's and Heinrich's public activities were the open reading halls (free of charge) of the Warsaw Charitable Society, and the Flying University. The period, at the close of the last century, during which Korczak worked with Stefania Sempolovska was one of great prosperity for the Polish underground enlightenment movement, when many people, both youths and adults, worked with great dedication to mislead the authorities and spread knowledge in the national language.[27]

At the same time, it should be emphasized that Korczak's activities were never political. He wrote: "I have never been a member of any political party, though I have had close ties with many underground politicians."[28]

Korczak was close to the social-democratic party of the Polish kingdom, (the SDCPL), which was deeply involved in social struggles and much less in national ones. Korczak viewed the class struggle, the constant battle for the liberation of the working man, as the main issue, and being far less perturbed by national barriers and aspirations, he saw a chance for friendship between nations and for the liberation of man in the idea of internationalism.

Korczak broke off his contacts with the party after its leadership leveled accusations at the important Polish author Stanisalv Bjojovsky, whom Korczak esteemed as a friend and guide, and whose books he very much appreciated. Korczak viewed the accusations as treason and baseness on the part of the narrow-minded leaders of the party bureaucracy. It was already evident in those days that Korczak's way would not be that of party struggles, for he did not believe in a violent revolution and detested any show of violence. Rather, as Itzhak Perlis remarked, Korczak believed in "Education as an antithesis to revolutionism."[29]

Nevertheless, Korczak's many meetings with persons active in various areas helped expand his knowledge of education, sociology, philosophy, economics, and politics. Moreover, these encounters sharpened his perception for the suffering of children and their plight in the context of social struggles and the battle of the classes.

Even before Korczak completed his studies at the University of Warsaw and qualified as a physician, he had already chosen to specialize as a pediatrician. In 1903 he received his first position as a house physician in a little children's hospital named after Bauman and Breson, where some of the best pediatricians worked and to which many patients came from all over Warsaw, including many Christian children. For Korczak this position was an important material achievement, and for the first time after a long period of poverty he wanted for nothing. In his memoirs, he wrote:

> As an in-house physician, I received an apartment, and an extra two hundred rubles for four lessons. My honest mother was able to run the household on fifteen rubles. From my medical practice I received one hundred rubles per month, and for writing articles—a few more pennies.[30]

Korczak not only excelled in his knowledge of bodily ills and his ability to cure them, but also in his perception of the child's mind. He knew that a small boy who enters a hospital is still a child who wishes to play in order to dissipate his fears and boredom. He would bring his young patients dolls and toys and would invent various games for them himself.

Korczak's fame as a doctor grew. Although Jewish doctors, except for the most famous ones who resided on the main streets, did not have Christian patients, Korczak was called on by many Christians who offered him a great deal of money. He did not succumb to the lure of money, and did not wish to accumulate wealth or build himself a brilliant career. He treated the children of socialists, teachers, young lawyers, and poor people for free. He noted in his memoirs:

> As the old doctors do not like to bother themselves at night, especially where the poor are concerned, I, who am young, must give this nightly assistance. Do you understand? Speedy help. Can it be otherwise? For what will happen, should a child not live to see the light of day?[31]

In 1904, when the Russo-Japanese war broke out, Korczak was recruited into the Russian army, where he experienced all the horrors and terrors of war and acquired a painful scar on his sensitive soul. He was discharged from the army at the end of 1905, and returned to Warsaw to resume his work as a doctor at the Jewish children's hospital. He then traveled abroad twice to France and Germany, for advanced studies in Western hospitals; he also visited England and Austria.

Of his advanced studies in the West Korczak wrote:

> The Berlin hospital and the German medical literature taught me to re-consider our accomplishments and to progress slowly and methodically; Paris taught me to think of what we do not know and wish to know, and what we must know and will know in future. Berlin was a day's work full of worries and tiny efforts, Paris was the celebration of a future of lovely premonitions, lively hopes and unexpected successes. Paris gave me the power to want, the pain of not knowing, the joy of the search; Berlin taught me the technique of parsimony, the unveiling of little things, the organization of details. It was in the Paris library that I thought of the child's great synthesis, as with a glow of excite-ment I read the wonderful writings of the classic French clinicians.[32]

And indeed he spent a whole year in Berlin, six months in Paris, and a month in London. Apart from his hospital work he visited orphanages, prisons, schools of special education, and institutions for delinquents. He wished to learn all aspects of child care and the physical and mental re-habilitation of children.

His book *Straw and Stubble* was published in 1905 and contained an anthology of thirty three of his *Kultza* articles, in which he satirized the Polish bourgeoisie, challenged manifestations of nihilism in Polish society, and discussed the confusion of Polish youth.

His third book, *The Drawing Room Kid*, was published in 1906, and Chana Mordetkovitz-Ohlatchkova claimed that it "bravely and extensive-ly embraced the many problems of a child's emotions and aspirations, and knew how to suffuse its irony, with the blood and tears of true suffering".[33] In this book Korczak attacked bourgeois society for its de-generate life-style, assailed the hypocrisy of educators, and took up the struggle for the hurt and suffering child. His medical practice contributed greatly to his future educational enterprise:

> Medicine has shown me the wonders of therapy and the incredible sur-prises of discovering the secrets of nature. It helped me discover many things; how a man dies, and with what merciless power the embryo sunders the womb of its mother and bursts out to life and the world, like a ripe fruit, to become a man. It is medicine which taught me to link separate details and conflicting phenomena into one plausible di-agnosis, so that, enriched with empirical knowledge of the enormous power inherent in natural laws and in the genius of investigative human thought, I stood now before that unknown: the child.[34]

Korczak would frequently visit the shabby houses of the poor in order to examine sick children, and not only did he refuse any payment, but he occasionally even left a little money at the patient's house in order to buy medicine or food for the children. His many encounters with the poor slowly taught Korczak that the main causes of childhood diseases and of the worst illnesses are none other than neglect, oppressive poverty, lack of proper care, and the absence of understanding on the part of adults. Consequently he began devoting a great deal of his time to the neglected child and eventually completely forsook the hospital in favor of educational care.

Korczak believed that "to fix the world, means to fix education," and he committed himself to this struggle, devoting himself to the child both as a doctor and an educator. Thus, when the "Company of Children's Camps" offered him the position of supervisor and educator for poor Warsaw children at a summer camp in Michelovac, he accepted willingly.

The Company of Children's Camps had been founded in Warsaw in 1882 by the physician and politician Dr. Stanislav Markevitz. As a student, Korczak had already instructed in this camp during one summer, and in autumn the camp's children had visited his home. He now viewed his work at the camps as an educational mission, and it influenced him greatly and increased his sense of calling as an educator. He expressed his experiences with the first group, which was comprised of poor Jewish children, in his book *Mushkim, Yoskim, Srulekim*[35] and his experience with the second group, comprised of Polish-Christian children, in his book *Josekim, Yashkim, Frankim*.

In 1904 Korczak described these summer-camp experiences in articles that he wrote for the Polish Language newspaper, *Israelite*. These articles revealed his sharp eye for detail, his deep empathy, and his great affinity with the Jewish child. Rather than a spiteful assimilationist, as the prejudiced distorters of his image would wish to present him, Korczak is revealed as a man with deep feelings for the Jewish fate, who aches over the humiliation of Jewish children, and suffers from their vilifications at the hands of arrogant gentiles and such hostile stereotypes as "Jewish cowardice," "Jewish filth," etc. As a man whose ears were open to their Yiddish folk songs and who carried the melodies in his heart, he wrote:

Seventeen of thirty children had not seen a forest before; thirteen had never played with a ball; only a few know that potatoes grow, and none have seen the sun rise. They lie cramped in bed, cramped to the point of pain . . . their living conditions cramp the body by night and the soul by day.

They are not afraid of the cold water. Before jumping in they cry "Gewald Mama Tate!" which seemingly expresses their cowardice as

presented by the humoristic gentlemen. . . . Oh, gentlemen of morality: "the Jewish filth!"

In none of them have I found the "Jewish cowardice" ascribed to
them. They were not afraid of dogs, and knew how to work and sweat
and even "fight." In their cramped homes and closed yards they were
sad, but here they showed their strength and were as lively as all children . . . these children love to sing to the point of pain. I discovered
that song was the only poetic element in their grey lives. Singing holds
the true sorrow of this wandering people, the true catharsis of their
pain.

I heard them sing in Yiddish "Slowly Mercy," the popular song
"Oifen Prifetchik" and various cantor's songs.[36]

The experience of working at the camp increased Korczak's desire to
devote more and more to the education of the child. In 1908 Korczak
joined the Jewish association "Orphan's Help," and in 1910, he was
elected to the association's board of directors, where he was party to the
decision to build a special orphanage in place of the existing orphanage
building on 2 Franzishkanske Street, which was outmoded and in-
appropriate for its function. The Jewish public contributed to the construction of the new building, and at the end of 1912 the orphans were
moved to a new building on 92 Krochelmane Street. Korczak was elected
director of the orphanage, and Stefania Vilenczika vice-director and
housemother. From this time on, he was to devote his entire energies to
the child in need of assistance. He would know no private life, would never have a home or family of his own, and he would sacrifice everything
for that child. The fear that his father's illness was hereditary may have
contributed to his decision not to build a family or have children. In a letter to his student M. Zilbertal he wrote:

> I remember the moment when I decided, somewhat ceremoniously and
> naively, that I should not establish a family of my own. Later I felt that
> this decision had been suicidal. I managed my seemingly disorderly life
> with great force. Alone and alien, I have adopted, as a son, the idea of
> serving the child as his matters are my mission.[37]

Korczak's decision to leave the hospital and devote himself entirely to
the work of the orphanage was accompanied by moments of regret. He
wrote in his memoirs:

> Throughout the many years which have gone by since then, I am
> haunted by the unpleasant sensation that I have deserted, betrayed the
> sick child, betrayed medicine and the hospital. A false pretention

swept me off my feet: Doctor and scultptor of the child's soul, his soul no less. (Oh, old idiot you have missed life and missed the mission! You deserve your punishment!)[38]

And in another place in the same memoirs he wrote:

Now, that I know that I do not know, and why I do not know. Now, when it is in my power not to harm a patient, as is required by the first commandment, I leave to sail unkown waters. The hospital has given me much and I, ingrate, gave it little. Life has punished an ugly desertion.[39]

From 1912 onward Korczak spent most of his life at the Jewish orphanage on 92 Krochlmane Street, where he lived, wrote, and educated with great love and dedication. Twenty-four hours a day, he lived the lives of the children of the orphanage and wrote his impressions, experiences, and educational methods. He devoted his entire soul to his mission. The architect who designed the Krochlmane Street orphanage building consulted with Korczak and tried to meet his requirements. In its time it was considered one of the most advanced and beautiful orphanages in Europe. The building included two main floors, a cellar, and a high loft. The cellar contained a laundrette, a kitchen, washrooms, and a changing room. At the center of the building was a dining and leisure hall, which was two stories high, and from the gallery of which one could view the activities in the hall. On the first floor were the educators' rooms, and on the second floor were large bedrooms for the boys and girls that were separated by the housemother's room and the service rooms. Above the building there was an attic intended for the director. Over the years Korczak came to severely criticize the design of the building and particularly that of the dining and leisure hall, where the children spent most of their day, as well as the gallery that surrounded it. Chana Mordetkovitz-Ohlatczkova wrote:

The gallery from which it was possible to see what was happening below, seemed to indicate a lack of trust in the child and a lack of respect for his sanctified secrets, serving as proof of the weakness and inability of the educators.

Korczak himself told Yerachmiel Weingarten of his objections:

Many praise the building, in which the architect Mr. Heinrich Stiepelman and myself have invested much effort and thought. I see its drawbacks from a perspective of 12 years. Today I would have built a different building. I would have given up the large bedrooms and built small rooms, a few children to each room. In this way it is possible to develop brotherhood and friendship among the children.[40]

Not all the orphaned Jewish children in Warsaw could be accepted to the orphanage. David Zilber, a former educator at the orphanage, explained that:

Because of the secular character of the orphanage and the Polish language spoken there, only the students of the "Hasabatovkut" (sovereign primary schools for Jewish children) were natural candidates for the institution. However, the Jewish quality of the "Hasabatovkut" was marked by no more than the fact that crucifixes were not hung on the classroom wall, that there were no studies on Saturdays and the Jewish high holidays, and that a lesson of "religia" was given once a week, instead of the prayers and religious instruction given at the Christian schools, which lesson usually comprised various Bible passages in Polish translation.[41]

During its first year, the orphanage on Krochlmane Street was the home of eighty-eight children. The atmosphere at the orphanage was that of an intimate family as Korczak strove mightily to expunge any taint of a gloomy institution based on strictness, stern order, and harsh discipline. He aspired to create a sense of home, in which he had assumed the role of the father. His attitude to the orphans was one of honor, faith, and respect for their wishes and desires. Throughout the day, he was constantly and personally involved with his protégés. He cut their hair, weighed them, and measured them, and precisely noted their development. He thought deeply about them and studied their world. He observed them as they slept at night, and, retiring to his room, he read the writings of other educators, reaching his own conclusions as to the development and education of his orphans.

Even when he was occupied with his literary and educational writing, his door was always open to protégés, who could sit in an armchair opposite the window that opened out onto the world, or join their mentor in feeding the sparrows which flocked to receive their groats on a special board that Korczak had installed along the window. Korczak had the glazier cut out a piece of the external windowpane, so that the sparrows would be able to eat between the two panes and warm themselves a little in winter. In summer the windows remained open and the sparrows would enter the room and sit on the flower pot. One day Korczak had entered the room suddenly and frightened one of the sparrows who, afraid, could not find the window and was badly injured. After this incident Korczak always knocked on the door before entering his room.

Children were permitted to enter his room at any hour of the day or night, but only if they kept their voices down or were completely silent. He kept a small chair, an armchair, and a stool for his little guests, and children were able to look out through the low window. When he took the seats away from the window, the children always found their way to it. Korczak stressed that "The child requires movement, air and light— there is no disputing that, but he needs more than that: A view of space, the sense of freedom—the open window."[42] When he began his work at the orphanage, Korczak was full of enthusiasm and believed that with the new building and the new conditions, the children would quickly respond to his care, come to accept the new rules of their life, and enjoy the relative prosperity. But he was mistaken for the children declared war before he could even assess the situation. They refused to accept the new reality into which they had been thrust. Korczak believed that his camp experience would help him cope with the children and easily solve any problems that might arise. But he was wrong on this count, too. He wrote:

For the second time, I now met with children as a powerful mob before which I stood helpless . . . as to our demands—the children were so totally defensive that no talk could overcome their resistance, while coercion gave rise to resentment. The new home of which they had dreamt for a whole year was becoming hated. It was only after quite a long time that I understood the children's liking for their previous lives. In the disorder they had lived in, the gypsy poverty of conditions and the almost non-existent means, there was a great deal of room for free initiative, for the flight of short, strong, isolated efforts, for free-ranging imagination, for the valour of a strong act, for the need to sacrifice something of oneself, and for indifference as to what the morrow shall bring. Others would suddenly, by force of authority, bring order. But only for a short time.

Here, however there must be permanent order born of an impersonal necessity, and it is because of this that the very children on whose help I relied the most have suddenly paled and dissappointed me. It seems that the educator forced to work in the midst of chaos, with little means, should not too avidly long for order and comfort—for these bring great difficulties and many dangers.[43]

From the very beginning of his work at the orphanage, Korczak was faithfully and devotedly helped by Stefania Vileczinska. Born in Warsaw in 1886 to a rich assimilationist Jewish family, Stefania studied at a Warsaw high school, took pedagogical courses at Farbel's school, and advanced studies in Switzerland and Belgium. On her return to Poland, she devoted herself to child education. She was only twenty-five years old when she joined Korczak at the orphanage on Krochlmane Street. Joseph Arnon wrote of her:

> Stefa was always there. To the children she seemed big, strong, quick of movement, appearing everywhere and always a safe haven. Her deep emotions and fiery temper aroused a sense of awe in the children (and the young educators) and they were always afraid lest she lose her temper and grow angry, yet at the same time she also evoked a feeling of security, for she knew how to share their joys. Her big, black, beautiful eyes, fixed in an otherwise unattractive face, reflected sadness and gentleness. She was always dressed in black and unadorned, her feet shod simply, but her sure footsteps were never far away.[44]

While Korczak was the spiritual father of the orphanage, the philosopher and planner, Stefania Vileczinska was the executor of his ideas and the direct caretaker of the children. The institution's protégés reported how they considered her, rather than the doctor, to be the authority, even in medical matters. She was directly available to the children at all times and seemed to be "all-knowing."

Korczak did not abandon his literary enterprise in those first days of the orphanage. He wrote *Bobo*—a work dealing with man's childhood; "The Confession of a Butterfly"—the notes of an adolescent boy on the conflicts of adolescence, and *An Unlucky Week*—a satirical criticism dealing with the alienation and suffering of the school child. In all three works, Korczak focused on the world of childhood and managed to penetrate to the very soul of his characters and expose adult alienation from children. He fought for the right of the child to self-actualization and a life of his own.

Some of the critics did not like these books especially his book *Bobo*. The critic W. Razimovsky wrote scathingly in the newspaper *Pravda* (The truth):

> Adulthood holds no interest for Korczak, who sees it as a ruin left over from flowering childhood . . . the moment you have outgrown your childhood, you lose all worth, you have nothing to innovate, you have only one thing left to do: to listen to the words of babes . . . because every child is a poet, each is a creator, each a potential genius. Among adults you shall discover one Columbus every thousand years while among children each and everyone of them is considered to be a world-discoverer.[45]

At the close of 1914, following the outbreak of the first world war, Korczak left his orphans for active service as an army doctor in the Russian army. He participated in many battles and had a close view of the slaughter. Listening to the screams of the wounded and the thunder of guns, Korczak dreamt of a better man, of redemption for all suffering children. It was in the military tents of the field hospital that he wrote his important educational creation—*How to Love Children*, in which he summarized his experiences as a child-physician and his observations on the lives of his protégés at the orphanage and the summer camps.

Korczak told of how he wrote the book to the sound of booming guns, and how, especially in those terrible hours he felt an inner urge to write. He wrote as if possessed, as if to save his sanity, as if to provide himself with a human hold on a world that had lost its humanity, and become monstrous. He wrote whenever he could, even during short stops, in the late night hours, and at the expense of his meal times.

Later in the war, when Korczak's regiment arrived in the vicinity of Kiev, the capital of the Ukraine, Korczak served as the physician in charge of a shelter for Ukrainian children, organized an orphanage in Kiev, and served as the physician of three other orphanages in the vicinity. He also became very active in the children's home for Polish refugees, run by the Polish educator Mariana Palska née Rogovsky.

An active member of the leftist movement, Mariana Palska was an educator and cultural activist, who, following the death of her husband and of her only son, had dedicated her entire life to poor and unfortunate children.

Work at the children's shelter on Bogoautovaska street was not easy, as Mariana Palska was unable to control the grown boys in her charge, who had become wild during the war and who refused to accept any sort of discipline. It was Korczak who succeeded in finding a way to the hearts of these children, when he asked to give them a form of self-rule, including their own court, civil constitution, and newspaper. He had some bitter arguments with Mariana Palska, who tended to prefer strictness and authority, but whom he eventually convinced, so that she worked to put his ideas into effect.

The First World War was very hard on the Warsaw orphanage, and Stefa struggled valiantly to keep the institution open. Prices rose from day to day, food rations were cut, and the deficit in the institution's budget increased inexorably. The patrons of the orphanage had left Warsaw at the beginning of the war so that Stefa was left to fight her difficult battles alone. The difficulties increased sevenfold when the management decided to accept twenty-five additional orphans, the sons of soldiers who had died in battle, and the number of children in the institution grew to two hundred and fifty. A typhoid plague struck the orphanage and claimed many victims among the young children—among them Estherke, Stefa's beloved protégé-helper. Estherke had been sent by Stefa to complete her education in Belgium, and when the war broke out and Korczak left for the front, Stefa had asked her to return to assist at the orphanage. Thus Estherke came back to help Stefa, but she contracted typhoid and died. Stefa's pain over the deaths of the children was terrible, and she was to mourn Estherke, who had been like a daughter to her, for the rest of her life.

In 1918, having been away four years, Korczak returned to direct the orphanage at Krochelmane Street. In that same year, Mariana Palska also returned from Kiev, and founded "Beitenu," a home for the orphaned children of Polish workers. Korczak cooperated with her from the first, spending two to three days a week in her institution where he introduced all the educational methods he had developed at the Jewish orphanage on Krochelmane Street.

Conditions were extremely difficult in Beitenu during the first years. The budget was small and limited, the place was crowded, and the rooms were unheated. The cold was terrible, and the food was very little and never enough. In her diary Mariana Palska notes that for many years not a penny was spent on clocks, on handicraft materials for the children, or on any form of entertainment. For many months they ate fresh bread only once a week.

Despite this the children received a great deal of motherly care from Mariana and the other workers of the institution. Mariana notes in her diary that all of the children bore their poverty in good spirits, and although there was no bread, there was never a lack of laughter, jokes, and games.

Korczak knew how to recruit philanthropists from among the rich Jews and the heads of the Christian Polish government. The Jewish orphanage would not have existed at all were it not for the help of some wealthy Jewish philanthropists such as the banker Cherchevsky, the Drs. Issack Eliasberg and Maximilian Herz, and a number of others. They provided most of the financial resources for building the Jewish orphanage and maintaining it. However, so as not to go against Korczak's educational principles, the patrons understandingly submitted to his instruction prohibiting any visit to the orphanage which he had not approved in advance.[46]

The orphanage lay beyond their influence, and they had no say in its actual operation, for Korczak worked hard to prevent a patronizing attitude toward the institution or its protégés. He adopted the same approach to the Christian orphanage Beitenu and the Christian authorities who supported it, and Igor Neverly relates how Korczak told Alexandra Pilosodsky, the wife of a wealthy Polish patron, that he did not approve of the entry of her car and the cars of her entourage into the orphanage yard, as their appearance smacked of exhibitionism. It is as if they were announcing: "Here we are, the generous wealthy, we have come to visit our dependents." Korczak refused to accept such exhibitionistic gestures of patronization. The chastised philanthropists were obliged to park their cars far from the institution, and their tour of the place was always factual and concerned with administrative requirements and issues.

Despite their cooperation, there were also many arguments between Korczak and Mariana Palska. She supported the idea of involving the orphans in the urban life surrounding them, of a greater openness of the orphanage toward the environment and of diminishing the greenhouse atmosphere, while in many respects Korczak wished to dissociate the orphanage from its surroundings. He wished to provide the orphans with an atmosphere of love, reinforcement, and personal satisfaction that lives its own harmonious life and is less aware of the outside. Though the orphans studied at the city's schools, the rest of their lives were entirely concentrated between the walls of the institution itself.

Another important point of disagreement revolved on the issue of religion within the orphanage. Korczak believed that children should be given a chance, if they so wish, to pray and keep religious ceremonies. He claimed that each child should be allowed some time for silence, contemplation, and personal prayer, and when designs were begun for the new building of Beitenu, Korczak attempted to convince Palska to include a room of prayer, to serve as a chapel or a place for seclusion and meditation. Mariana Palska objected vigorously to this conception and began an all-out battle against Korczak until he was forced to back down and give up his plan. In a conversation with Yerachmiel Weingraten on this issue, Korczak told him that during his discussions with Mariana Palska a strange idea had entered his mind that here "sits a tough *anti-religious nun* . . . who lacks fairness in her approach to the child's freedom of choice . . . and he, the Jew, would look like a fanatic Don Quixóte were he to continue his struggle for a prayer chapel in a Christian institution."[47]

Those were difficult times for the Jews of Poland. Between 22 and 25 November 1918, the Polish army surrounded the Jewish quarter of Lvov, with its fifty thousand Jewish inhabitants, and conducted a three-day planned pogrom of robbery, arson, and murder. Seventy-two Jews were murdered, and 443 were wounded.

Anti-Semitism was on the rise: Itzchak Greenbaum relates how a command was issued to discharge all Jewish officers and men from the Polish army and imprison them in the Yavlona labor camp near Warsaw on the pretext that they were Bolsheviks. Great protestations and much wheedling were required to convince the representatives of the government and the army to withdraw the edict.[48]

Such events were not limited to the government and the army, as hatred had begun percolating into the streets, and into the life of the towns and cities. Korczak was gradually exposed to the Polish anti-Semitism, the hate for the Jewish child, and the suffocating atmosphere of the relationships between Jews and Gentiles. Hana Mordetkovitz-Ohlatczkova recounts how "Attacks on the street, curses, invectives and blows were part of the sad reality of the Jewish orphans. Korczak became sombre when he thought of the fate of his little Yosekim and Srulikim to the point that when a co-educator expressed his fear lest the camp children should drown in the river, Korczak responded with an infinitely sad smile and a bitter question: "Is that what's worrying you? And what if they drown? Is this not the best solution for the situation of the Jewish orphan?"[49]

In 1919 Korczak was re-enlisted in the Polish army and was obliged to serve as a physician at the military hospital for contagious diseases. During that same year, he also began lecturing at the institute of special pedagogy and at the Wolna Waczachnitze University. He also contributed to a number of periodicals. Fearing to transport the germs of the severe diseases he treated at the hospital, Korczak lived with his mother rather than at the orphanage, and would go to her place in the evenings. At some point, Korczak contracted typhoid fever and his mother nursed him in his illness. Then she herself contracted the disease and died. Korczak, who was seriously ill, did not know of the tragedy that befell him, and was only told of her death after his recuperation. He sank into a deep depression, blaming himself for her death, because he had not taken the necessary precautions, and had transferred the germs of the disease to her. Often wishing to put an end to his life, he always carried poison when he went to visit his mother's grave. His book *Face to Face with God* or *The Prayers of People Who Do Not Pray*, was written as a consequence of this deep mental trauma. (The book was translated into Hebrew under the title *With God I Shall Converse*.)

Meanwhile the range of activities at Korczak's orphanages widened as a summer shelter named Roziska, after a wealthy donor's daughter, was opened for the children in Gutzlaback, in 1921, and winter and summer holidays were organized.

In 1923 Korczak founded the Burse. This was a dormitory for boys aged fourteen and over who wished to complete their professional training. These children lived and ate at the orphanage in exchange for a few hours of work at the institution. Most of these boys were former protégés who could no longer remain at the orphanage because of their age, yet they could not be independent as they had no professional training.

The Burse solved a whole series of problems and importantly contributed both to the boys and to the orphanage. It provided the boys with an opportunity to complete their high school and occupational studies and acquire a profession, and it also served as an excellent framework for the training of select youngsters as educators. Indeed Korczak gave precedence to boys who were interested in educational work, and closely followed their progress. He helped those who seemed to him good educator material, to complete their higher studies, and found them a place at the orphanage. Additionally the work of the boys at the institution, which amounted to about four hours a day, allowed considerable savings in the employment of paid labor.

At a later stage, most of Korczak's Bursists were drawn from among poor university students, who, in exchange for three hours of teaching or some other educational activity, received food and shelter and a wonderful opportunity for guided and controlled educational experience. Korczak demanded that these students keep precise notes, follow the behavior and reactions of the protégés, and write down their observations. These notes later served as the basis for educational talks that Korczak held once a week.

Thus Korczak gave many of his former protégés a chance to develop into educators and men of science.

In 1923, when the new independent Zionist newspaper *Nash Pshgelund* (Our survey) was founded, Janusz Korczak began contributing to it regularly along with Professor M. Balaban, Florian Sokolov (the son of Nahum Sokolov), and others. According to Abraham Levinson, a historian of Warsaw's Jews, the influence of *Nash Pshgelund* on the Jewish population was quite considerable, for while it was pro-Zionist, it also supported the Polonization of the Jewish public, thus appealing to the tastes of a varied audience. The paper also published some of the best Hebrew and Jewish literature in sequels (Mendele Mocher Sfarim, Optushu, Singer and others).[50]

In 1926 Korczak founded *Mali Pshgelund* (The little survey), a newspaper in the Polish language intended for Jewish children. This was a weekly supplement to the daily *Nash Pshgelund*, in which Korczak actualized some of his ideas for a children's newspaper, which would be written and edited by the children themselves. This weekly also allowed Korczak expression as a talented and original author, with a place of honor among the authors of Young Poland.

It was during this period that the Jewish National Fund asked Korczak to sign a special manifesto that the Fund was preparing for Lag Ba'omer (the traditional celebration of the Jewish rebellion against Roman rule). This manifesto had already been signed by such Jewish notables as Shalom Asch and Ytzchak Grinbaum, and the Jewish National Fund believed that Korczak's signature would rally some of the Jewish intelligentsia in Poland, who until this time had always shied away from the matter of Palestine and did not cooperate with Zionist elements. In conversation, Korczak told Weingraten that:

> It would be wonderful if Lag Ba'omer could be declared a national holiday, a holiday for all children, without reference to their faith, and everyone would go out on joint trips on this day, and spend it in song and dance in the country. It is hard to tell when such a dream may come true. In the meantime Lag Ba'omer is needed for the Jewish children who are so far from green grass, flowers and skies.[51]

Korczak signed the manifesto which was a call to all members of the free professions to donate their income from the day of Lag Ba'omer to the Jewish National Fund, and which also mentioned the Zionist idea and the contribution of the Jewish National Fund to the land of Israel. Ten prominent Jewish notables signed their names to this manifesto, and it was published in *Nash Pshgelund*, the Jewish paper in the Polish language, where it aroused great sympathy among the Jewish intelligentsia. It should be noted, however, that an anti-Semitic Polish newspaper used the manifesto's publication as a pretext to attack Korczak in a short and offending note:

> Anyone who thought that the author Janusz Korczak is a Pole—has now lost his last illusion, for yesterday the truth became known to us: His name is Heinrich Goldschmidt, and he is busy gathering money for his Jewish brothers in Palestine.[52]

Korczak corresponded with his students who had immigrated to Palestine. Among them was his friend Esther Bodeko, who was the sister of the famous Jewish painter Joseph Bodeko, who, an immigrant himself, had served as the director of the Bezalel school of art in Jerusalem for seven years. Esther had studied with Korczak for one year in order to prepare herself for educational work on a kibbutz in Palestine. She had been accepted for work at the Warsaw municipal "Asuphim" nursery, where she took care of deserted and neglected babies under conditions of great neglect. Throughout the period, she kept in constant contact with Korczak, and would visit with him at the orphanage on Saturdays. He wrote to her at Kibbutz Ein-Harod and expressed his views on the difficulties of adapting to the new country:

The attempt to reunite the two ends of a string which had been cut two thousand years ago, is a difficult one: History dictates that it shall succeed, but how much effort and suffering . . . it is very easy to die for an idea, such a wonderful scenario: The hero falls with a bullet in his chest, a small pool of blood in the sand—and a flower-strewn grave. It is far harder to live for an idea, day in day out, year in year out.[53]

Yet, as for himself, Korczak was not ready to make the move, claiming that

The life remaining to me is too short for me to devote ten years to spiritual and physical adjustment to new conditions of breathing, digesting and seeing. Does not the eye too have to adjust to the glare, perhaps the dust?

Moreover he did not believe that the problems of the child had been solved in Palestine, and was convinced that there, too, the child was ill-understood and subject to suffering and oppression. And Korczak's main concern was always the child rather than the Jewish problem:

The problem of man, his past and future on earth—seems to me to eclipse the problem of the Jew. I have chosen the child as the focus of my work and I am not deceived by all the flowery rhetoric as to the great wonders of the child in Palestine. No! He suffers there too. For there too, the adults, the strangers, do not understand him.[54]

Before long Korczak became painfully aware of the fact that though his vision of man was great and important, the status of the Jew was slowly crumbling in the meantime. With the rise of Hitler in Germany, the traditional hatred of Jews in Poland was acquiring new force, as legislative measures were taken to force Jews out of all areas of the economy, to limit their practice of the free professions, to diministh their numbers at the universities, to abolish their rights, and to remove Jewish thinkers from the mainstream of Polish culture.

The Polish economy was badly hit by the great world economic crisis that began in 1929. As unemployment increased to the point where a quarter of the population was without work, there was a consequent rise in hunger and crime, violence and aggression, as well as severe anti-Semitism.

The Jews were doubly maligned for while they too were badly hurt by the economic crisis, the unemployment, and the breakdown of trade, they also suffered from the hate of the Polish population which, in accordance with ancient anti- Semitic tradition, blamed the Jews for the great crisis in

Poland. The "Orphan's Help" association, which had supported the Jewish orphanage, was badly crippled and Korczak wrote that:

> Clouds cover the horizon. Again we think only of tomorrow. No longer do we think of expansion, but only of preserving what we have. The twenty fifth year of the orphanage is drawing to a close with great anxiety, and the question—will we be able to withstand this shock or will this be our last anniversary?[55]

The difficulties involved in maintaining the orphanage grew daily in severity. Stefa, who had in the past managed to find administrative, secretarial, cleaning jobs and the like for the institution's graduates now ran into a wall of hate and refusal to accept Jewish girls. She wrote her friend Feiga Lifshitz Beiber in Kibbutz Ein-Harod:

> The national and religious relations here are becoming more difficult every day. It is a disgrace which slowly spreads over everything, and is even worse than the economic crisis itself. Everywhere it is the same, and there is no escape from this rot.[56]

In 1930 Korczak's helper and right-hand woman, Stefa, visited Palestine and was captivated by its educational enterprise especially in Ein-Harod. Through her Korczak became increasingly aware of the central importance of Palestine, but was still dubious and reluctant. In a letter to his student and friend Joseph Arnon, dated 15 May 1933, he wrote:

> If fate had wished it and I came to Palestine, I would not come to the people but to those thoughts which would have been born within me there . . . the world does not need work and oranges, but a new faith. The faith in a future life must be connected with the child, as the source of hope. . . . I forsee much suffering and a great burst of enthusiasm. I delude myself that I would have many things to say at that moment. One must wait. But at my age, the thought that I shall not have the chance, is close.[57]

However, some months later, greatly depressed by the increase of anti-Semitism in Poland, he is more willing to consider a visit to Palestine, though he is afraid lest his illusion of finding a better world there should also be shattered. On the 27th of November, 1933, he wrote Joseph Arnon:

> For many years I have been looking at sensitive children, at their helplessness and silent sorrow, and at the insolent dance of the beasts of

prey. I fear, that . . . this is but a senseless destruction of all that is good and pleasant—the devouring of the lambs by the wolves. I have no illusions—it must be the same in Palestine too. Therefore, under alien conditions, without ties, without a language, far from people—I would find there my hermit's cell.[58]

After many postponements and deliberations, Korczak finally arrived at the port of Haifa on the 24th of July 1934 for a three-week visit. He spent most of his time at Ein-Harod, having turned down invitations to visit other places because of his wish to closely and methodically observe the communal educational practices in the kibbutz, and because of feeling it would be better to focus his observations in one place. And indeed Korczak not only wished to see everything but also to involve himself in direct human contact. Thus he worked at the kibbutz during the day, sharing in the various tasks of the members, then, during the evenings he met kibbutz members, talked with them, and lectured them on the health and education of the child.

One of the main reasons why Korczak chose Kibbutz Ein-Harod was the fact that Feiga Beiber, Stefa's close friend, his student at the kindergarten teachers seminary, and a veteran educator at "the orphanage," resided there.

Ada Hageri (Poznansky) has collected some interesting material about Korczak's visit to Ein-Harod, through a questionnaire she gave everyone who had been with him in those days.

David Simchony received Korczak at the port of Haifa and they walked to the train which was to take them to Ein-Harod. Full of his characteristic energy and curiosity, Korczak wanted to try some sweets sold by an Arab boy, and finding them far too sweet and greasy gave them to another Arab boy he met on the way. As was his wont, Korczak's very first steps in Palestine were already concerned with children. Well aware of the importance which children ascribed to sweets, Korczak told the kindergarten teacher at Mishmar Ha'emek: "To count the sweets given to a child—madness."

On the first Saturday of his visit Korczak rose early, and evading his hosts, was later found peeling potatoes with the older Kibbutzniks in the kitchen. When asked what he was doing, he replied: "I want to earn my Saturday."

Korczak wrote almost photographic observations on bits of paper which he kept in his pocket. He described the children's walk over rocks: "They place their feet down in two rhythms—first they check with their toes to see if the earth is level, and only then do they place the whole of the foot and step forward." He also provided a more general description of the Israeli child: "If you bump into, or taunt a European—he will cry out in fright: 'Mother!' but an Israeli child will grumble or call you 'Idiot!' " (Impressions of Israel).

When visiting the children in their class, Korczak would not tolerate a "Stuffy" atmosphere, as Shoshana, the class educator recounts: "When Korczak entered the class for the first time, he shouted: 'Sheket!' (Silence!—which was almost the only word he knew in Hebrew) and the children were a little scared, but then realized it was a joke and became themselves. Korczak then walked among the tables and looked at the drawings they were making. He took a pen out of his pocket and added small details to the children's drawings: Some buttons here, a few pockets . . . the children were delighted. One of the children agreed to give his notebook to Korczak as a momento."[59]

On the ship, on his way back to Poland, Korczak wrote to his friends at Ein-Harod:

I wanted to congratulate you and thank you for some things, but also to apologize. To apologize for having not believed you. Yes. I came in order to discover the measure of falsity in your truth, the truth in whose hands you have put your fate and your grandchildren's fate— because on every grain of honesty there must be some hint of fraud; that is the law of the world; such is man.

Korczak is again revealed in all his honesty and penetrating truthfulness. He is not hastily sentimental, but rather doubts, examines, weighs, and masterfully analyzes. Yet his first impression of the social, educational, and human enterprise of the kibbutz is great indeed, and he perceives that despite the great daring and the social vision things have been kept in proper human perspective and are very far from the melee and stink of "sanctity."

Your efforts and your aspirations are as pure as your cares, your confusion and your disorder are human. Your "home" is honest; there is nothing to conceal from the eye—your valour is real, for without experience it strives, reaches for labour—does not exceed the limits of human capability, *does not aspire to sanctity*.[60]

Korczak's educational teaching is characterized by a number of elements that also comprise his philosophy of life: 1) the strong emphasis on eternal longing, on aspiration as a precondition to creative life, on the island of creative experience which is the only chance for development, change, improvement; and 2) his emphasis on a *We*, which is not just the social or international *We*, but the natural, ecological *We* that embraces both man and the whole cosmos.

On his return to Poland, Korczak devoted himself once more to his work at the Krochlmane Street orphanage and at Beitenu. In 1935 he was invited by the Polish radio to broadcast a number of short talks, which won great acclaim all over Poland and acquired an enormous audience. Rife with anti-Semitism, the radio's management did not allow Korczak to reveal his name, and the lecturer was presented as "The Old Doctor." Hana Mordetkovitz-Ohlatczkova wrote:

At the set hour, thousands of people all over Poland would switch on their radios and listen to the quiet, thoughtful words, spoken with seeming reluctance. They were enchanted by the noble and melodious voice and the clear Polish language, beautiful in both expression and form, and novel and daring in its abbreviations. This voice entertained children and made them laugh, enchanted and troubled adults, and moved anonymous people everywhere—though it too remained anonymous and nameless.[61]

Ascribing greater importance to his ability to reach and influence the wide public, Korczak did not demand that his name and identity be revealed. He talked of this to Yerachmiel Weingarten, and with his characteristic humor called his anonymous radio broadcasts: "My work in the radio underground."[62]

Ian Piotrovsky, editor of the Polish radio magazine *Antena* described Korczak's broadcasts thus:

The old doctor did not read monotonously, did not hasten, did not speak in beautiful and empty phrases. He did not make an effort to joke. His humor was natural. Seemingly, he talked to children, but adults were also mesmerized . . . the Old Doctor emphasized that only love could tie both young and adult man with the world . . . he was the greatest intellectual and humanist on the Polish radio. He talked with us humbly, quietly, caringly, hesitatingly. He would look at us, watching our suffering, our pain, our poverty and doubts. Seeing and understanding us, but still examining, holding his stethoscope to the heart and the soul—and then, carefully, giving his diagnosis . . . before you could even feel it, he had already left you. Disappeared and gone. Gone is the Good Old Doctor, and he has left you a prescription and money on your desk, because he knows that you the patient are poorer than he.[63]

Though the radio authorities guarded Korczak's anonymity fanatically, and even forbade Ian Piotrovsky from publishing Korczak's conversations in a book, he managed to circumvent the prohibition in 1939 by publishing his book *Amusing Pedagogy*, in which he collected a few of his talks.

Korczak knew that the prohibition on publishing his name stemmed from anti-Semitic hate, and the fear of radical organizations that would not permit a Jew to broadcast on the radio. When this hate increased and the management of the radio eventually refused to broadcast his talk on Christmas so as not to mar the sanctity of the holiday with the talk of a Jew, Korczak quickly resigned. As more of his projects were canceled because of this rising anti-Semitism, Korczak began longing for Palestine. He wished to believe that there it would be possible to realize his dream of protecting the child and fostering him faithfully. He wrote to Joseph Arnon:

> I have vowed and I wish to stand by the child, look after his affairs: but now only a prayer or a blessing is possible for his hasty and insecure steps. And where is the place most suitable for reprimanding the wayward, for commanding the strong and protecting (by speech!) the small and weak—if not in Palestine? This I miss.

In his letter of the 27th of July, 1936 to Joseph Lichtenbaum, he planned a visit that would last at least six weeks and no more than ten weeks, during which he would like to study the life-style of the settlements, examine the lives of the guards, and visit Nazereth and Jerusalem.[64] And indeed, Korczak embarked on his second visit to Palestine that summer, during which, beside revisiting Ein-Harod where he had formed deep ties of friendship, he also visited settlements, villages, and various towns. He traced the development of the Jewish settlement, and absorbed the landscape, and the wish to come and settle in Palestine slowly grew in his heart.

He visited Jerusalem, Nazareth, Tiberias, Haifa, and Tel-Aviv, and he lectured at a number of kibbutzim. Moshe Zertal, who accompanied him on many of his trips, describes Korczak's enthusiasm for the landscape and his realization that only on this second visit did he begin to properly comprehend the Bible.[65] Zertal relates how Korczak kept emphasizing that everything in Palestine was totally new to him and that he therefore did not dare advise or instruct.

One of the things that captivated Korczak's interest was the method used to educate the children. He believed that Palestine held infinite possibilities for the renewed cultivation of the Jewish person, for a radical change of values in the concept of education, for the growth of a new type of person living within nature, free of the diseases of the diaspora, liberated in body and soul. Yet, when Zertal offered him a post at the educational institution in Mishmar Ha'emek, he immediately replied that he was too old, and would not be able to free himself from the bonds of his routine. Moreover his presence would only disturb the young educators and he did not wish this to happen.

Korczak's meeting with the land, its landscape, and people, was a deep experience. In his many tours of the country he seemed to wish to unravel its secret, the secret trapped within both its stones and its people. In a lecture based on his impressions from Palestine, he stressed:

Palestine has many stones. Now I know, one must decode and comprehend not only the sky, the wind, the wild grass, the braying of the donkey and its stare, the call of the cock, the insect, but also the mountain, the stone and the star—the night.[66]

His contacts with Palestine had touched hidden recesses of his spirit until he felt as if a screen of forgetfulness had melted to reveal the spiritual birthplace lying within him. Although at first everything seemed strange and amazing, he had quickly felt himself merge with the country that met his eyes and presented its riddles.

Experience had taught Korczak to regard political and social revolutions with skepticism. He described the Russian revolution as "a tragic and bloody attempt to change man," and he claimed that he had "no curiosity as to counterfeit Austria, nor tragic, helpless France." Yet his attitude to the Jewish revolution in Palestine was different. It was more open, involved, and perhaps even intimate because "One must view Palestine, even through a chink, even through the slats of a rail coach, as an attempt to revive the land, the language, the man, his fate and faith."[67]

In the same way as he approached any issue, so he seriously observed the wonderful attempt to rejuvenate the country and the people, and with his discerning eye he also perceived the points of weakness, the problems, and the difficulties. Thus he immediately sensed the acuteness of the Jewish-Arab clash, and quoted a picturesque Arab phrase he had picked up:

The Arabs and the Jews are pulling on the same rope, each in a different direction, and are slowly nearing each other. When they are close, there comes an Englishman and cuts the rope so that they won't meet.[68]

But Korczak was not so naive as to blame the Englishman. Rather, he felt that this opposed rope pulling would not stop for he had inadvertently heard an Arab friend of Jewish settlement innocently reveal that he had already chosen a home to live in after the deportation of the Jews.[69]

Despite his deep impression, and his belief in the possibility of a renewed and healthier growth for the Jewish people, Korczak was not captivated by slogans and was unwilling to blind himself with emotional national festivities. He wrote:

Jewish Palestine should not fear the truth, . . . it merits not being treated as a child prodigy who is told: wonderful, simply wonderful and then gets an indulgent pat on its cheeky mouth. . . . That is why the propaganda films we have seen up until now, which are so full of pretence, seem to me extremely damaging. Yes, everything that is shown is true, and even more beautiful than the truth, but it is a shallow perception. True, there are oranges, but there are also thorns. There are briars, thistles, prickles, thorns and many others.

The question: "Is it worthwhile?", is a serious and difficult one.

One must have a right to emotion. One must present evidence of the great treasure of efforts, if not sacrifices, which has been invested, and of everyone's share in the work.

One must know the stone and the mountains of stone as well, a bane which might end in disappointment.

There are temperate and comfortable mountains, forgiving, good, blessing and contemplating—and there are serious, indifferent and sublime mountains—as well as somber, threatening, evil, cruel and vindictive ones. Perhaps one should start with these? For, they, in any case, are easier than man. I did well in that I only looked at the mountains of the Gilboa during my first visit.[70]

Korczak saw the communal education of the kibbutzim as an important chance for the proper education of the child and a possibility for realizing his own educational teaching. In a letter to M. Zartal he noted:

It is only through the child that one can grow into the land. Even the kibbutz is a child. . . . This enterprise of yours shall not be destroyed by fire, nor by locust or earthquake; eternal is each sign, each drop of sweat or blood, each laugh and tear, thought and emotion.[71]

On returning to Warsaw after his second visit, he could find no rest. Hitler's rise to power and his political and military conquests caused Korczak much agony. He felt that Poland was slowly sliding into an abyss, and he began planning his immigration to Palestine. He wished to go to Jerusalem, settle there for a year and study Hebrew, then make his home in one of the kibbutzim. He believed in the Jewish enterprise and in his letter to Joseph Arnon he stressed:

> History is moving quickly; indeed, this situation cannot go on for long. The evil had not yet reached its peak: In the next five, or perhaps ten years—storm or flood; you shall see the beginning of a new order. Our generation has gone through a chunk of history and failed. We have seen age old religions destroyed, good and evil ground to dust. We are facing yesterday, you tomorrow; we—are each of us alone, you—together; we—tombstones and graves, you—cradles. The eyes of children are now filled with awareness and action. There are so many days in the illusions of our lives.[72]

Korczak would never realize his plan of immigrating to Palestine, for he ultimately viewed such an act as a desertion of his responsibilities in Warsaw. He felt that in those venomous times especially, when the world had gone mad, he must remain with his Jewish and Polish orphans:

> I feel myself obligated to the child, that I would like to serve him, that I have tied my life's work to him. I feel guilt because not only do I leave the world in great disorder and was unable to protect the child, but I have not even found an attentive ear to the method which—though perhaps I delude myself—I have discovered. To base the organization of children on mutual sympathy and justice, to separate them in time from the evil of adult affairs; to provide them with years of selfhood, peaceful years . . . not to oppress, not to burden, not to neglect, not to harm. I claim that I did it for the few at the orphanage. Despite the difficult conditions this is an oasis, which to my sorrow is now covered with the evil sands of the desert surrounding us.[73]

Korczak continued his educational work and inquired into the possibility of resuming his talks on the Polish radio, but the Polish authorities would not permit it. Well aware of the great influence that the Korczak talks exerted on thousands of listeners, the authorities had realized how, under the guise of amusing and bright words, Korczak presented noble ideas of love between men, of progress and fraternity. He was too humanistic, too advanced for the liking of Poland's rulers, and besides, he was a Jew.

During that same year (1936) Korczak was also forced to resign from his position at the Polish orphanage Beitenu, where he had worked for fifteen years. Although it is difficult to precisely pinpoint the reason for terminating his work at Beitenu, it is known that he fell out with Mariana Palska, the manager, because of serious disagreements over the educational method at the institution. Pressure was doubtless also exerted by government circles on which the institution was financially dependent. Korczak, in any case, refused to explain, and Mariana Palska also kept her silence.

Throughout the years Korczak and Mariana Palska had had many differences, both over the goals of education at the orphanage and over its means. When matters came to a head, Mariana Palska wished to establish cooperative activities between the orphans of Beitenu and the children of the Bialani district where the institution was located, believing that the orphanage could become a center that influenced all children in the area. Korczak had objected to this idea, believing that it would expose the institution to undesirable influences, disrupt his educational principles, and serve as an opening to politicization. Mariana Palska had not forgotten Korczak's arguments in favor of religious education at the institution, and she now also viewed him as a Zionist who had sinned by visiting Palestine twice. The anti-Semitic atmosphere in Poland must have left its impression on her, and thus their mutual cooperation came to an end.

The termination of his work in Beitenu left Korczak stunned as he helplessly watched many of his plans collapse. Believing in his educational methods and not wishing to restrict his experience to the education of Jewish orphans alone, he had hoped that one day it would be possible to attain full cooperation between the Jewish and Polish orphanages, thus breaking national and religious barriers and placing the care of the child at the center of concern. This was now not to be.

Forced into a closed and narrow framework, he felt increasingly isolated from the Polish world. His spirit broke over the loss of his general and public educational influence, which he viewed not only as a personal hurt, and the destruction of his life's work, but also as a sign of the failure and bankruptcy of humanistic ideals. In a letter to Esther B., he wrote:

> I have never felt myself to be in close contact with life—it seems to have passed me by. From the dawn of my youth I have felt myself to be both old and unnecessary; is it any wonder then, that this feeling is now greatly intensified within me?[74]

In the same period he also wrote to Jacob Kutelczok:

> I strangle these truths, which I cannot express aloud, within me. Perhaps in Palestine, which now seems to me the promised land; Unfortunately, I lack those forty years which I must spend in the desert—I

would rather not write about myself and the orphanage. It is not happy.—Perhaps I trusted too much in my own powers, perhaps I was carried away by ambition or delusion, yet the balance of my life is disappointing—if not a total bankruptcy, then an almost total one when compared to what has been achieved.[75]

The lives of the Jews in Poland became increasingly difficult. The successors of Pilsodsky found it hard to staunch the rise of the "Andanczia" with its open anti-Semitic policies. In the course of that year (1936) there were pogroms among the Jews in sixty towns and cities. Jews were being gradually pushed out of their sources of income, and the government had adopted an anti-Semitic ideology which draconically restricted them and left them only one way out—emigration.

Korczak's vision of Polish reality became clearer and more sober, and recognizing that there was no future for Polish Jewery, he called for the emigration of Jews out of Poland. His vivacity and great educational faith would not let him completely despair. He could not but at least believe in the future. In a letter to Moshe Zilbertal, he wrote:

Despite everything, I believe in the future of humanism, of the Jews and of Palestine. The brave commanders, who have no conscience, are parceling out the world and handing out roles. As the situation now stands, it cannot go on for long. That is the only consolation—not the madness of the world, but more its cruelty. Can it be otherwise?[76]

Korczak began a penetrating soul search during that period, and he wrote his friend Moshe Zilbertal:

Dearest Mitak! It is good, that you have a child. I remember now when I decided not to make a home for myself. With what ceremony and warmth. It was in the garden-city of London: "The slave has no right to a child: A Polish Jew under Russian rule." And then I immediately felt it as a form of suicide. I have managed my seemingly orderless life forcefully, alone and a stranger. I have adopted the idea of child care as my son. It seems I have lost. They have the might and I the right; they have the power and they rule the day.[77]

Of his present situation he wrote:

Today, in Poland I can be nothing but a consumer: I read what others write and reminiscence of my own worth. I am not allowed to walk about carrying stifled truths. Perhaps Jerusalem will give me the strength—exile, longing—such an impersonal life. As if I were already looking from the next world on the satanic comedy of this present reality.[78]

Yet, as had already happened in the past, Korczak underwent a deep personal crisis over his possible journey to Israel. In a letter to the Simchoni family at Ein-Harod, he wrote: "I beg you, please believe me that I want to come, but mustn't come lest I become a burden. You have enough rocks in your fields and your lives."[79] This was not his main difficulty; rather, despite all the disappointments and the pain, Korczak remained tied to his country and its children. To leave Poland and its orphans seemed to him to be treason. He wrote Moshe Zilbertal:

I do not want to, because I cannot sever my contacts with the Polish reality, I shall remain open to every call, every sound. I wish to relate what has been to what will be. It is difficult. But I cannot act otherwise"[80]

Eventually he forsook his plans for leaving Poland. He felt responsible for the enterprise that was his life's work. His heart was given to the child, both Jewish and Polish, and he wished to serve them both: "The Yosekim and the Yahsekim are both close to me. . . . To leave and come to you? . . . —to breach a trust—that is wrong and shameful, I became afraid at the last moment."[81]

An indication of the depth of Korczak's humanistic feelings and his true sensitivity to the pain of man everywhere is the fact that he even touches on the question of the Arab's place in the Jewish Homeland, and the problem of the Arab child. He wrote:

I have not spoken of it, but the Arab child nevertheless worries me. The port of Tel-Aviv means the death of the port in Jaffa. Here, I am capable of reading the complexities of life. There, I shall be forced to guess at them, here, my eyes are wide open. There, I do not know if I shall be able to close them.[82]

Korczak devoted himself to his work at the Jewish orphanage, to tours of Jewish towns in Poland, and to literary work. In 1937, he published his book, *The Stubborn Boy—The Life of Louis Pasteur*, of which he told Zrubavel Gilad:

We must help all children expose the beautiful and the sublime which they carry within them. I intentionally wrote the book, *The Life of*

Louis Pasteur, now, when tyranny and spiritual slavery rule all, when this madness called "Hitler" is everywhere—so that the children growing up now will see that there are other people in the world, who are devoting and have devoted their lives not to the destruction of men, but to their salvation and liberation—in order to enrich the human world and beautify it. This was Louis Pasteur's greatest dream![83]

The conditions of Polish Jewry continued to deteriorate. The children of the Jewish orphanage were harassed by their Gentile neighbors and graffiti vilifying Jews appeared on walls. Zrubavel Gilad recounts how, when encountering a large and colorful poster that screamed, "Jews to the Ghetto" in large red letters, Korczak fell silent a long while, and finally said:

Not good, my friend. Not good. I come from the shelter for Czechoslovakian refugees who have been banished from Germany. What these people tell is almost inconceivable! And mainly—man's image is slowly being obliterated.[84]

Korczak strengthened his ties with the Jewish Zionist youth movements and lectured in seminars for their instructors. He became a member of the non-Jewish section of the Jewish Agency and felt himself a partner in the Jewish enterprise. He told Zrubavel Gilad:

After Hitler, Europe will face a terrible spiritual emptiness, such as it has never known before. And then . . . well, well, I do not wish to prophesy, but I am certain of it. I have both dreamt of it and thought of it a hundred and one times: The land of the prophets, the land of the prophets revived! Actually, this is the special meaning which Zionism holds for me.[85]

Korczak also began contributing to the newspapers of the Zionist youth movements. Thus he wrote for the newspaper *Zeirim* of the Akiva youth movement, published articles in the *Young Guard* newspaper, and commencing from January 1938, consistently contributed to the newspaper, *The Young Vanguard*, where he published stories and articles dealing with education and instruction.

In August 1939, Korczak met Itzchak Greenbaum, who was then a member of the Jewish Agency, in Warsaw, and consulted with him about his plans for immigrating to Palestine, and the possibility of joining one of the kibbutzim.[86]

The anthology of his radio talks, *Humorous Pedagogy*, which was published during that period, ends on an optimistic note and a call for cooperation and effort:

> Give a hand, and put your shoulder to it—less of talk—pull! Hard, heavy—better, for greater is the effort—because a tongue which talks with a hand which doesn't help—that is a terrible thing . . . terrible![87]

This optimistic tone of cooperation was completely without basis, since on 1 September 1939, the Germans invaded Poland and the Second World War broke out. Korczak donned his major's uniform and reported for service in the Polish army. He was, once more, called to speak on the radio, and he tried, in his talks, to rally the Polish people to armed resistance against the German invaders. He encouraged the defenders, emphasized valor and love of country, and attempted to instruct children as to how they should behave in the difficult days of the war. Between broadcasts, he roamed the streets to help the wounded, especially the wounded children.

On the 27th of September Warsaw surrendered, and the Germans moved into the city. The population of Korczak's orphanage swelled. The welfare association "Orphans' Help," which had supported the institution, was now disbanded, and the entire responsibility for the institution fell onto the shoulders of Korczak and Stefa. Korczak would wear out his feet, walking among the houses of the wealthy Jews and collecting contributions of food, clothes, and other donations. Taking full personal responsibility, he published a leaflet that called on the Jews of Warsaw to aid the orphanage which now housed one hundred and fifty children. In the leaflet he wrote:

> He who runs away from history, history shall overtake him.
> Extraordinary conditions necessitate an extraordinary effort of thought, emotions, will-power and action. The orphanage has withstood these tragic weeks with honor. Seven shells, two attempted robberies. This is not the time for words. It is past now. God has saved. We are lost for lack of immediate help. I demand:
> A loan of 2000 Guldens.
> It shall be repaid sooner than you think.
> It is the fourth war and the third revolution which I have not only seen, but actively participated in. I know how to read the pages of war.
> It is not the orphanage for which we are all responsible, but the tradition of helping the child. We shall be villains were we to deny it. Vile, were we to turn our backs on it. Dirty, if we should soil it—this

tradition of two thousand years! We must preserve our honor in our plight![88]

His visits to the homes of the wealthy Jews and his incessant attempts to collect the means to sustain the orphanage were difficult and arduous, and he was often forced to shout, reprove, beg, and lose his temper. Frequently he set out on this painful mission at dawn and returned to the orphanage late at night. He wrote in his diary:

It cannot be otherwise, but it causes one much anger, desperation, fear and disgust that a good and sensitive man becomes the enemy of the family, of himself and of other people. I wish my hands were empty so that they could see with their own eyes that I am totally destitute, so that all this should end. I came back exhausted from my "tour." Seven visits, conversations, stairs, questions. The results: Fifty Gulden and a declaration of monthly payment of five Gulden. One can support two hundred souls![89]

At the end of November, 1939, the German authorities issued an edict obligating every Jew to wear a white ribbon and a blue Star of David. Korczak refused to follow this edict and also refused to take off his Polish officer's uniform. Moreover, in order to emphasize the Jewishness of his orphanage and his belief in youth's promise of the revival of humanism, life, and growth, he decided to give his institution a flag. One side of the flag was a blossoming chestnut tree on a green background, while the other side displayed a blue Star of David on a white background.

As the flow of refugees into Warsaw increased and the economic situation deteriorated, Korczak's institution ran into severe difficulties. Korczak continued to plod from one Jewish institution to another, from one benefactor to another, to ask for help. Adam Czerniakov, who was the head of the Judenrat, wrote of Korczak's untiring work for his orphans and his wonderful ability to save both himself and those about him from depression through his great store of humor. Thus, for example, he wrote of how Korczak proposed that stamps should be pasted to the notes that people threw onto the graves of saints, and the income from which should be devoted to welfare.[90]

This unceasing work of Korczak took its toll, and he began displaying signs of fatigue and illness. Dr. M. Lansky, a physician who examined him, wrote:

He was weak and running a fever. It was difficult to persuade him to have his lungs X-rayed. He was very thin, his cheeks were covered with red spots and his eyes shone. The X-ray revealed pulmonary fluids. Dr. Korczak remained unmoved, asked after the level of the fluid, and when told that it had not yet reached the fourth rib, gestured with his hand, as if saying that the situation was not so bad and that he was not yet permitted to stop working and lie in bed.[91]

Through his unceasing efforts and many labors, Korczak managed to enlist help and influence the heads of the orphan care organization to send the Krochlmane Street orphans to summer camp. In June 1940 they left for the country at Roziczka, where they were joined by boys and girls from a number of other orphanages and children's shelters, all of whom Korczak agreed to care for. Dr. Zufia Shimanska (Rosenblum), who visited Korczak at the summer camp, wrote:

> In his room, I found three children ill in bed. He explained with some embarrassment: "I do not trust the practical caretaker to wake up to the child's call at night. It is but a small matter—they must be helped at night, they are feverish and wish to drink . . . apart from that, the caretakers are too soft, they wish to do everything themselves and the children cannot be taught independence." And so the old doctor goes to a lot of trouble to teach four year old Yojo how to use a certain utensil, or three year old Leo how to unbutton his shirt.—"Yes, yes my son, one must learn how to get along in life without help, and it is never too soon to learn!" On the nearby lawn, children chased each other, played with a ball and frolicked. Every once in a while, one could hear a peal of happy laughter. The sun, in its magic, brought a flush to the pale faces. The doctor's sad eyes lovingly caressed the playing children.[92]

During the same period the ties of Korczak and Stefa with the Zionist youth movements became even closer. Zvia Lubetkin testifies how:

> Korczak and Stefa were the only ones among us who had ever been to Palestine and thus became the experts on the subject. In seminars and talks they would tell us about it, the children, the kibbutz, etc.[93]

On the Day of Atonement (Yom Kippur) of the year 5701, (12 October 1940), the German authorities used megaphones to announce that the Warsaw Jewish population was to be concentrated inside the ghetto. Since the orphanage on Krochlmane Street lay beyond the boundaries of the ghetto, Korczak made great efforts to have it included. His efforts failed, and he was obliged to exchange places with a Polish high school situated within the ghetto. During the move to the new place, the Germans confiscated a load of potatoes that Korczak had managed to obtain for his children after a great deal of effort, and he ran to the German headquarters to complain of the robbery. The Germans interrogated him, and when they saw that he did not wear the stigma, sent him to prison, where he remained jailed for a number of months. He was finally released for a ransom of 3,000 Gulden, which was collected by a number of his former protégés. Throughout his months in prison, Korczak kept his proud spirit and preserved his honor as a Jew and a human being. Once freed he immediately returned to the orphanage within the confines of the ghetto.

The orphanage building on 33 Cheldona Street was large and roomy, and Korczak and his helpers strove to keep up a normal life-style. Jona Buchian, whom Stefa Vileczinska accepted for work in 1939, worked in the institution until its very last day, and described its life in her memoirs.[94]

She wrote that the protégés were scattered in groups in the wide central hall. In one group they read a story, in another they played a game, in a third they held a conversation, while at the far end of the hall they held court with the participation of one of the educators. Korczak walked among the children without interfering in their affairs, but his presence was felt. The children would occasionally turn to him with questions, and he would answer factually and seriously. Korczak would pass through the dormitories and look over the sleeping children, caress the brow of a child moaning in his sleep, and cover those children whose blanket had fallen to the floor. Occasionally he would take children who could not sleep or who were troubled by nightmares into his own bed to calm them. In his diary he wrote:

How fast the hours fly. It was just midnight and already it is three in the morning. I had a guest in my bed, little Mendeli. He had dreamt something. I brought him to my own bed, he caressed my face and fell asleep. He whines. He is uncomfortable—are you asleep?—I thought that I was in the dormitory. He looks at me wonderingly with those black ape-like eyes of his.—I was in the dormitory. Do you want to return to bed?—Do I disturb Sir?—Lie on the other side, I will bring you a pillow.–O.K.[95]

On Saturday mornings the educators and employees of the institution would meet with Korczak. After the meeting, Korczak would tell the children a story of their own choice. In the afternoon the children left the orphanage to visit their relatives. When the Nazis shut down the Jewish schools, Korczak began teaching the children reading, writing, and arithmetic at the orphanage. Studies were mainly self-directed and based on worksheets prepared by Korczak, graded according to difficulty and the age of the children.

A great deal of the orphanage school's time was devoted to talks, meetings with invited guests, hobbies, and art education, which included a puppet theater, plays, reading, a choir, music, and concerts.

In order to enrich the curriculum, Korczak invited members of various professions to the orphanage, among them grocers, paperboys, and shoeshiners as well as theater actors, authors, and artists. It was especially in this difficult period that he felt a need to show his students the various facets of life in the ghetto as part of the survival effort of a people struggling for life.

Roman Lilian-Lilienstein, a survivor of the Warsaw Ghetto, tells of a concert program that Korczak prepared for the children before the Passover of 5701 (1941). The program included Passover songs in Hebrew and Yiddish, a lullaby in Yiddish, and a number of classic melodies by Mozart, Brahms, and Moniescu.

> The house was clean and orderly, and to this day I am haunted by the smell of poverty which permeated its halls and corridors. Like ourselves, the children were also dressed for the occasion, and were sitting full of tense expectation, under the all-seeing eyes of Stefa Vileczinska. Dr. Korczak spoke a few opening words before the concert, which was sufficient to establish an atmosphere both ceremonious and calm. The children's attention was extraordinary. We, the artists, were simply hungry and it seemed to me that our young listeners too, were not satiated. I shall never forget the excitement and the look in the one hundred pairs of eyes which were turned to us. It is very hard to explain what such a concert meant to both artists and children in those days.[96]

In October 1941 the orphanage was transferred from the building on Cheldona Street to another building at the intersection of 9 Szliske Street and 16 Szanan Street. This building did not suit the needs of the orphanage, and difficult conditions prevailed. The protégés were all huddled together on the first floor, in which there was a large central hall with rooms on both sides. Most of the life of the orphanage was concentrated in this central hall, which served as both dining room and a place for educational activity. Some furniture was used to create a few corners that served for reading, handicraft, study, sewing, and so forth. At night the hall doubled as a dormitory, divided between the boys and the girls. Korczak slept in the little isolation room with the sick children, and Stefa Vileczinska slept in the office. The second floor was reserved for social activities, plays, and concerts.

The difficulties of maintaining the orphanage increased, and Korczak shouldered the responsibility with the last vestiges of his strength. At the same time, he remained sensitive to more than his protégés' plight. Realizing that the shelter for abandoned babies had been transferred to 39 Djalne Street in the ghetto, and that the children were not receiving proper care in that institution and were hungry and dressed in rags, he applied to the Judenrat for a post in that institution, thus acquiring an additional burden and serious responsibility, which he bore with all his customary seriousness and devotion.

The conditions at the shelter were abominable, and it was appropriately called "The House of Death." Children died there every day from starvation, lack of care, and diseases. Most of the shelter's employees did not cooperate and tried to sabotage Korczak's work. They protested against the placing of the shelter under the jurisdiction of the Judenrat, and claimed that it infringed their rights. In protest they stole equipment, blankets, clothes, and food, and the orphans were left almost totally destitute.

Korczak struggled to "get the criminal characters on the staff at Djalne, who only remained at their posts because of habit and cowardice, to resign of their own free will" and strove mightily to correct the terrible evil that was being done to the children. Thus, Korczak was saddled with serious worries and the care of hundreds of starving children, in addition to his own orphanage's protégés. The following description by Stefa Aliasberg illustrates the terrible difficulties that were involved in supporting the orphans while hunger raged in the ghetto, and food was nowhere to be found:

Only those who have suffered through it can possibly understand the plague of lice and starvation which raged in the Ghetto. Walking to my work at the hospital, at nine in the morning, I would see starving children and adults on the stairs and on the pavements, thin and weak. They did not even have the strength to beg. When I returned from work at three in the afternoon, I would see the bodies of the same people, the adults and the children, covered with sheets of paper, until the corpse-wagon should arrive to transport them to a mass-grave. The hunger grew so intense, that the hungry would attack people carrying food parcels in the Ghetto and consume the stolen food while escaping. Neither the robbed person, nor the other people on the street, dared pursue the robber.[97]

It was Korczak's good fortune that he was assisted by the Judenrat, which was headed by the engineer Adam Czerniakov who was his close friend and who was involved with the orphanage and sympathetic to

Korczak's enterprise. Czerniakov was one of the directors of the Association for Care of Jewish Orphans—Czantos—which provided Korczak with part of the food required as a minimum for the sustenance of the orphanage.

Yet this was truly the bare minimum, and hunger left its imprint among the orphans. In his terrible distress, Korczak did not abhor any means and any way of obtaining food. So much so that he even went to 13 Shano Street, where sat the hated Laganczweik and his band of collaborators who cooperated with the Germans. Korczak suppressed his disgust and aversion for these collaborators and accepted bread and potatoes for his orphans. As head of the judenrat, Adam Czerniakov received this radical act in anger and protest, unable to accept any cooperation with collaborators.[98]

Emanuel Ringelblum also acknowledged the shock that spread among the leaders of the community when they heard of Korczak's act. Korczak, however, once more emphasized that for his orphans he was willing to ask bread even from the devil himself.[99]

Korczak also managed to convince the heads of the Judenrat to give the children's institutions those food parcels which arrived at the ghetto in such a torn condition that it was impossible to decipher the address, or parcels addressed to people killed by the Germans, or who had been sent to the camps, or who had died in the ghetto, or who had managed to escape.

John Ouerbach, who was then a postman in the ghetto, wrote of this arrangement:

> The Doctor was but one of half a million tormented Jews. True: He did not come to ask for himself, but for a bunch of starving children, whom he said were his protégés. Yet there were plenty of starving children on the streets, no less than there was dirty melted snow—and Korczak's forty or fifty or even one hundred children, were they so special? Was their hunger not of the ordinary kind? He would take a few half crushed parcels, the wrappings of which bore completely obliterated addresses, because of rough handling, and which had been marked "Cannot be Delivered," or parcels for addresses which no longer existed—parcels containing half-rotten food. He would put all these in a sack and bring them to the children, his children. And who the hell made him responsible? Who, indeed, could be responsible for them? Can a person here be responsible for any other human being? On whose behalf, on whose orders? How can a person define his own desire to survive, which places his "self" and his needs above all? The postmen respected him, for the man had a look of supreme tranquility and solid strength.[100]

He goes on to describe how he had arrived one day at the orphanage in order to deliver a parcel:

The sound of heavy footsteps came from the darkness of the corridor and Korczak appeared at the entrance. I gave him the sheet to sign, and while he wrote his name, I suddenly smelled the sharp odor of Vodka. He seemed to immediately sense that I had noticed the smell. He straightened and we stood thus staring silently at each other for a long moment. The he stepped toward me, put his hand on my shoulder and said: "We must . . . we must try to live despite everything . . . somehow . . . and he gestured with both of his hands as if to encompass the world, time, life and his hungry children . . . open hands directed at me, which said more than a thousand words. Then he vanished.[101]

In his distress Korczak occasionally found refuge in the bottle. As his failing health deteriorated, drink also seemed to somehow fortify him, allowing him to carry on a while longer without breaking.

During May–August 1942, up to August, the eve of his transfer to the death camp, Korczak kept a diary that included notes, memoirs, thoughts, ideas, dreams, and observations on life. In some passages he raises childhood memories, while in others he contemplates old age and death. At the beginning of his diary, he wrote:

When coming to dig a well, one does not begin the job from the deep bottom. First one widens and breaks up the upper layer, removes the earth, shovel by shovel, without knowing what one will find down below, how many entangled roots, what barriers and faults, what number of hard, uneven and heavy objects, what stones buried there by oneself and others. . . . I seek to find subterranean springs, to find the cool, clear force of water, exposing and revealing memories. . . . Here, one must work alone. None can help, none can do it for you. We can do everything else together, if you still believe in me and do not despise me, but this last task of mine—only I alone can do.[102]

In the face of death, his dreams and long-range plans are of special interest. He fantasized about the building of a large orphanage in the mountains of the Lebanon which would have:

Large dining rooms and large dormitories, but also small "houses of seclusion." On a flat roof, I shall have one small room with transparent walls, so as not to miss even one sunrise or sunset, and so that I shall be able, while writing at night, to look at the stars now and again. The young Israel is toiling with great effort and dedication to come to terms with the earth. But the sky's turn shall also come, for if not, it will be a misunderstanding and a mistake.[103]

Korczak sensed that the cruel end was near, and he wished to prepare the children for approaching death. A few months before he and his protégés set out on their last journey, he prepared the presentation of *The Post*, a play by the noble Indian poet Rabindranath Tagore, in which, Amal, a dying Indian boy, bids his life farewell. His adoptive father, the farmer Mashawa, loves him with all his heart, but must accept the fact that his days are numbered. Little Amal dreams of the moment when he may leave his bed and walk out of his small and suffocating room to wander the great and wonderful world, to climb the high mountain peaks beckoning over the horizon, to sing with the sunlight and the chirping of birds, to kiss the flowers and jump distances like a wind. His step-father and friends assure him that he will soon receive a letter from the king, nominating him to be a postman who travels all over the country and brings letters to people who are full of longing. In this promised illusion of freedom, the child falls asleep and his spirit, which so thirsted for the wide spaces, leaves his wracked and tormented body. The play shocked many of the children in the audience, who deeply identified with its main character. Hana Mordetkovitz-Ohlatzckova wrote:

> Little black-eyed Abrasha played the part of the dying Indian boy, Amal, with great inspiration and talent. The soft passage into death, while illusion and hope quietly succumb to sleep, was acted by the boy with such fascinating and prophetic truthfulness, that the audience wept . . . the face of the listening Korczak changed its expression through an excess of emotion and paled. When asked why he chose that play in particular, he replied that he wished to teach his children to peacefully receive the angel of death.[104]

And death, indeed, was coming nearer. On the eve of his sixty-fourth birthday, on 21 July 1942, Korczak wrote in his diary:

> To be born and to learn to live, these are difficult labors. I have a far easier task left to me: to die. It is possible that after death things will be once more difficult, but I do not think of that. This is the last year, or perhaps month, or perhaps hour. I would like to die with full awareness, with a clarity of mind. I do not know what I will say to the children on parting. I wish to tell them that they are given full freedom in choosing their way.[105]

Sensing what was about to happen, Korczak and Stefa prepared the orphans for their last journey. They explained that the Germans must not be allowed to humiliate Jewish children or gladden their hearts at the sight of tears, screams, and whimpers. One should face them standing tall. In the next few days, the Germans would probably take them on an extended nature trip, and they must be glad and not afraid at all. A satchel with food and a water bottle was prepared for each child. The children were calm because they knew that Korczak and Stefa and the entire orphanage staff were going to accompany them and would not forsake them. They were ready for what was to come.

On 5 August 1942, the S.S., Ukrainian troops, and policemen from the ghetto police surrounded the orphanage. Korczak and his protégés were required to exit. Carrying the institution's flag, they came out in an orderly way. There were 192 children and eight adults besides Janusz Korczak, Stefa Vilenczinska, and a few of the institution's workers. Joshua Perla described this terrible journey in his article, "The Destruction of Warsaw":

A miracle occurred: Two hundred children did not cry. Two hundred pure souls, condemned to death, did not cry. None of them escaped, none of them hid. They only leaned, like sick swallows, on their teacher and educator, their father and brother, Janusz Korczak, to protect and preserve them. . . . Janusz Korczak, hatless, wearing a leather belt and boots, bent low, holds the hand of a child and steps forward. He is followed by a number of nurses in white aprons, and following them are two hundred children dressed in clean and orderly clothes, led to the slaughter.[106]

Eye witnesses report that the ghetto policemen halted in their tracks and saluted this march toward death. Igor Neverly, the writer, who was Korczak's friend and close helper for many years, related how a German officer who had read Korczak's book, *Little Jack*, wished to allow him to get off the death wagon, but Korczak refused and returned to his children.[107] The description of the death march of Korczak and his children is legendary; how they marched carrying their green flag—the symbol of growth and life, the banner of their institution, which they had sworn to live and work for in the spirit of love, truth, and justice. They walked to their death as one family, and their educators went with them.

Korczak's friend, the poet Vladislav Shlangel, wrote of the last journey of Korczak and his protégés:

The children entered the wagon as if they were heading for a Lag-Baomer outing. It was then that I understood that Europe did not give a damn for what was happening here . . . indeed, at this moment Korczak is writing the most wondrous page of valor . . . for in this Jewish war, in the terrible ignominy of it, the helpless chaos, the struggle to save one's life without heed for the cost, in the confusion of treason and baseness, the nightmare dance—Janusz Korczak was the single lonely soldier who protected the orphaned child.[108]

In his article "Saint, Martyr or Hero," Nachman Blumental quoted a Polish underground fighter who had objected to the wisdom of Korczak's decission to obey the German's orders:

For, knowingly or unknowingly, he led his children to death. If, for example, instead of leading them all, without exception, to the "transport," he had told them to scatter or hide, each child to a different place, there is no doubt that some of them might have remained alive! While, in this way, all of them were killed, both children and educators.[109]

Such activist initiative did not constitute a part of Korczak's world. He did not belong to those who carried on an active Jewish struggle, but in bearing the flag of life to the gates of death, equipped with his infinite optimism and great faith in the victory of man, he conquered death and opened gates to eternity.

2

With God I Shall Converse: Religion and Religious Education in the Teaching of Korczak

Silence, Sorrow, On a black wave a coffin rocks.
Black moths such black dew of black flowers.
No more shall man sing, no more shall babies smile.
The last bell has burst, the world's clocks are stopped.
The last tower has toppled, the last star has gone out last night—
Who shall see its glow? . . .
Such sadness, God, such sadness.
No color, no tone, God, God, no tone, no color, no tear.[1]

Immersed in silence and sorrow, and surrounded by pain and solitude, Korczak felt a deep need for faith. His direct and prolonged contact with worldly sorrow gave birth to a deep religiosity. As early as 30 March 1937 he wrote to Yosef Arnon: "You mention worldly sorrow. It lies within all men. In all lifetimes and throughout history. Hence the need for faith and a search for God."[2]

Yet if we are to examine the question of faith and religion in Korczak's world, we must first differentiate between two kinds of religion; the institutional-ecclesiastical and the personal—the essence of which is an inner religiosity.

While Korczak hated institutionalized religion and its priests, ceremonies, and churches, by his very nature he was a man of faith. Religion, for him, was a private and personal experience that abhorred any taint of institutionalism, any pervasive system of injunctions, and any holy vestibules serving as intermediaries. This religiosity, which is a willingness to come into contact with the infinite, rebels against any attempt to bend the spirit and rejects dumb submission. It is not the theological creed which is at the center of this religiosity, but rather the unique individual with all his feelings and experiences. The religious longing is for that which is forever beyond human ken: perfect justice, the absolutely moral, the infinite, and the irrational. Korczak stressed that each man made his own

67

way to God. As God lies within the soul of every individual, there is an infinity of ways to reach Him. Each man must discover his own way within himself.

The old man in Korczak's play, *The Senate of Madmen*, speaks of an empty world despite the human multitudes, of darkness despite electricity, and of cold despite central heating:

> Men get bored without God and prayer . . . rather than have faith, they study and research it . . . the priests are going from bad to worse . . . our churches and their bells are still in place, but God is meted out sparingly . . . our priests are to blame: they have commanded that we fear God rather than love Him. Yet, He is not so terrible—as people have discovered—He is forgiving, kindhearted, smiling, patient and bright. Are man-made evils and punishments not enough? There were times when people would call Him when in danger, but now that vaccination has been invented and there are no plagues, only the many lonely and sad all over the world are in need of faith.[3]

Proximity to death and a realization of the finality of life drew Korczak to converse with God. Korczak blamed himself for his mother's death. He felt that by carrying home a contagious disease he had been the instrument of her demise. While his emotions were in turmoil and thoughts of suicide raged in his heart, a prayer and challenge broke from between his lips—"The Prayer of People Who Do Not Pray." In a little booklet, *With God I Shall Converse*, Korczak collected his conversations with a God whose face is hidden:

> How have I sinned, oh God, that you have chosen this moment to forsake me. When my feet were pierced with thorns and my hands and heart shed blood, I cried: People! Not a sound. I cried, mother! never an answer. It is my last cry: God! and what? Nothing. Alone.[4]

This sensation of being all alone, with no one to depend on but himself, as well as the encounter with death and the morbid thoughts of doom that frequently troubled Korczak from his early youth finally brought him to an existentialist-religious experience. Wishing to save his very being and escape his own uncommunicative loneliness, he sought to find some point in which to anchor his life, some bridge between man's existential loneliness and God, so as to alleviate his orphanhood. In this, Korczak is very close to religious existentialist philosophers such as Kierkegaard and Martin Buber. In the introduction to "Eighteen Prayers for Those Who Do Not Pray," which forms part of his treatise *With God I Shall*

Converse, he speaks of the relationships between man and his gods and says of prayer:

> Into the prayer sequence, I have blended the whispered secrets of the soul, which a man speaks to himself alone, I knew that every being must involve his life in a greater world through God, and in God through his own self. I knew, I am sure. May God help me and provide for me.[5]

The prayers gathered in *With God I Shall Converse* are those of a mother, a youth, a frivolous woman, a little girl, an old man, a maiden, a scientist, an artist, and even some anonymous miserable person. They are prayers of anger, rebellion, mutiny, introspection and reconciliation, and of happiness and fun. To each is his own prayer which expresses his own soul in his own spirit, and not in the collective-communal-uniform-canonical tongue of the established liturgy.

Through these noninstitutionalized liturgies, these "unofficial" prayers express their personal longing for a God who is neither in heaven nor on earth, neither in synagogue nor in church, but is everywhere. "You are not only in man's tears, but in the fragrance of the lily, not only in heaven but also in a kiss." By creating these prayers and giving them expression, Korczak exposed that hidden side of his world which shied fearfully from the public limelight, that part of himself which, refusing to express itself in any generality, would not even formulate individual "rules of prayer." Korczak was willing to formulate "rules of life," and "rules of education,"[6] but never rules of prayer. Thus his prayers are phrased in direct, primary speech reflecting the intimate relations of discourse represented by the Buberian "I and Thou," which can never become the institutionalized, formalized, utilitarian, repetitive, "I and It." The very essence of Korczak's experience of prayer is that of communication and contact.

Despite the deep individual expression of his prayers, and though God is neither defined nor delineated, He yet remains a haven, a presence felt, though not defined.

All of the conversations with God, intended for people who do not pray, are very intimate, and the knowledge of God expressed within them is first and foremost a knowledge of affinity. Their humanizing element never vulgarizes the encounter with God, but rather transforms it into a real, human experience of almost total directness.

Thus it is especially the intimate, extremely sensual, and earthy words of the frivolous woman that give us a taste of this direct encounter with God:

Please sit yourself, my sweet old man, here beside me—very close. Do not be afraid, I shall not harm you,—only if you yourself should want to sin. Such an unholy thought . . . what a pity I cannot see you! I would cling to you, and stare delightfully into your eyes. And you would softly smile and say: "Silly One." Is this not so?[7]

From this intimate conversation, the prayer shifts to such empathy, to such a deep human warmth directed at God that in this affinity the roles seem to shift until the frivolous woman would entertain Him or enliven His soul:

You are to be pitied, my kindly grandfather. More than once have I wished to come to your aid, to lighten your burden, bring you happiness. And truly, how difficult it is to always think of nothing but poverty, justice and mercy, and of orphans.[8]

The conversation of the frivolous woman is not the fixed ritual or liturgy intended for some definite event. Rather it is an everyday coversation—a moment of spirit in the flood of secular events. It is a moment of great religious power that breathes God into life itself rather than out of it, and it is close and intimate rather than detached, aloof, and exteriorized. Between appointments with men she finds a moment to converse with God.

My beloved God, it has been a long time since I last spoke to you. Perhaps I do not pray much because I do not like to kneel. Well, I shall put aside my cigarette, perhaps I shall sit on the sofa and look at the flowers. You will not take offense for you are a good and beloved God.

She entertains God at home, on her sofa, in intimacy. And when the bell suddenly rings and a man announces his presence, she stops the conversation: "Oh, the bell . . . it's him . . . I'm sorry . . . please do not be angry . . . you are Lord of all . . . goodbye, my God, thank you, it was so good to be alone with you."[9]

The same seemingly self-evident natural ease in conversing with God can also be seen in the prayer of the young boy who, though he knows the empty injunction that it is not proper to make demands of God, cannot help himself, for God is the only all-powerful address to which he can turn. Although aware of the general convention that views God as a deity of trial and judgment, his true inner knowledge tells him that God is not a pedantic accountant constantly tabling the balance of sins and punishments, registering every sin and every whim and collecting bills of punishment. He knows that God understands and that he is a God of forgiveness who is capable of properly evaluating the weight of a sin and sweeping aside those heavy weights which people ascribe to sins in order that they be heavy enough to tilt the balance of judgment.

> Forgive me my sins. They are many, very many. I have eaten jam out of the jar. I have laughed at the sight of a hunchback, I have said that my mother lets me stay up until whatever hour I fancy—which was a lie; twice, I have smoked cigarettes and used dirty words, but you are good and forgiving, so forgive me everything, for I regret my sins and would mend my ways.[10]

This close personal attitude to God allows one to complain bitterly, to accuse Him, to ask Him difficult questions, to contend against Him. A mother afraid of abandoning her baby to Him castigates Him in such fashion: "For you take babies from their mother's lap and mothers from their babies. Please tell me: Why such mischief? I am not accusing you, God, just asking."[11]

It is especially in this context of prayers by people who do not know how to pray that the prayer of a mother who praises God for having taken her son and killed him for the sake of the country seems oddly out of place. For a moment, it seems as if Korczak's nonconformist call is stilled, and the prayer of the individual can no longer be heard over the hum of the multitude, the national anthems, and the trumpeting of the collective. Reading the first prayer of the mother who appeals to God we expect Korczak to challenge the false God of state who has consumed the son.

> Please forgive me my God, for my love for my child is greater than my love for you. I have given him life, but then so have you, my God! We bear a shared responsibility for his fate as we have both given him life—and already he suffers. We must protect him.[12]

Yet he disappoints us, and his personal statement is replaced by that of the false God. Even though we are mindful of Korczak's Polish patriotism and the active role he played in the Polish army and its wars, still the mother's prayer sticks out like a sore finger among the prayers of people who do not pray, whose words are spoken by Korczak. And even when we realize that this prayer is deeply rooted in Korczak's world, still it stands oddly different from the other prayers which are so valiant in their firm resolve to reject, to disagree, to protest, to make their silent voice heard, a voice that cannot be stilled by the din of hymns sung by God's forgers, who have crowned themselves his blood-drenched representatives on earth.

Forgive me God, for having complained.

I have said: my son has been killed, the country has taken my son. He has sacrificed his life. I did not understand. I thank You for having enlightened my soul.

I say: You have called my son to You, the country has adopted my beloved son as its own, and has given him—given, not taken—a beautiful death.

I shed tears of happiness and pride knowing that I shall stand before You as Your closest soldier and declare:

At Your command, my Lord.

The country has given him a beautiful death.

I thank you for having enlightened my soul.[13]

And when we read this prayer on the backdrop of Korczak's other prayers for people who do not pray, the prayers of those who will never be able to say, "at your command, my Lord," and those whom the very concept of "a beautiful death" would choke into silence, we wonder if we have indeed perceived this prayer properly? Perhaps we have missed its tune? Perhaps its very tone belies the assurance of the sacrifice that it expresses? Perhaps its obverse is the truth? According to Korczak, the way to God involves breaking through the barriers and masks of those who forge his image, of the pimps who purport to represent him, and the false creeds that would supplant him:

And this is the worst of all: the shadow of your false translators has blinded my eyes to your brilliant image. I have had to make my way through a dark gang. Their charade: straight-fall-shake-up-right!, their tasteless incense—powder and smoke and candles of terrible miracles—their threats and trespasses—brown, grey—their encouragements and promises—slates of stone and poisonous gasses.[14]

In order to break through to his own personal God, the God of truth, the individual must pass through the huge charading armies of God's would-be representatives: the pimps, the executioners, the priests, and the parsons, who would lead man astray from God, who furnish man with idols, masks, and dead creeds instead of the Living Word, who freeze man's lively, dynamic, ever-changing dialogue with God and replace it with slogans, commands, and lifeless verses, which hide God from the individual and surround him with walls and curtains, screens and covers. And when a man returns to God, desperate after having been in the hands of those who make a sham of God, the hands of the false prophets, he does not crown God with the empty pompous and impersonal epithets of "Great," "Just," "Good," but only calls to him directly: "My God!" I say "my," and "I trust."[15]

Korczak scorns the pseudo-prayer, the endless repetition of lifeless chants and psalms, the daily intoning of an externally ordained rote of liturgy that has become a straitjacket to suffocate all feeling and true intention. This practiced, ceremonial prayer only drives man farther away from God.

> And if I pray no more than seldom, believe me—it is their fault. Their prayer is the thoughtless mumbling of phrases, or a cunning wish to mislead you, to cheat you, and to extract from you something for moans and a red nose.[16]

Korczak believed that self-awareness is a precondition to dialogue with God, for in his prayer a man must be honest with himself. An empty person would find it impossible to adopt such a stance before God, as would someone who had not tried to understand himself.

> And it seems to me, that before a man can know you, God, he must first know himself well, and find himself. And I am lost, I do not understand, and only try to decode myself like a puzzle, like an extremely difficult algebraic problem.[17]

And it is especially because of this need for self-knowledge, for removing the veils that hide the self, for daring to stand exposed and unmasked before God, without artifice and without resort to the various implements of holy service, the incense and the scents—that it is appropriate to examine and overcome the various intermediaries, the external commands, the obligations, and the rules, the slogans and the crutches, the directions and the instructions in order to meet God from the heart.

Like Erich Fromm, who views the meeting with "God" as the peak of humanistic experience and defines his personal position as "Mysticism without Theism"[18] so Korczak's religiousness is also rooted in human experience. It seems that the essence of his religiousness can be found in this wonderful passage where he describes the free human encounter with God:

> Totally unexpectedly, we shall suddenly meet. I do not know where, how or when. Suddenly, I shall see You. I shall blush, my heart shall beat strongly, and I shall believe. I shall believe that You are *different*. That You do not befriend them, that You do not wish to be with them because they bore You, because You look down on them for

You know them. And I shall believe that You wish to seriously and openly converse with me. You shall say to me: "I know that they have uglified Me, when you did not wish to believe what they believed." You will say: "I know that they are cheating Me and lying to Me." You will say that You are lonely, forsaken and ashamed, and like me, full of yearning and free. Free as a bird! And we shall make a pact of friendship between us: You and me. And we shall burst out laughing right before their eyes, we shall hold hands and run as far as our breath holds out. They will call to us, they will be angry and say we are not polite. So we will stop for a moment, listen to them once, and both of us, You and me, shall stick out our tongues at them. And while we laugh to bursting we shall disappear from their view and begin eating handfuls of snow.[19]

Korczak's experience of God is the epitome of creative experience. It is sensual-mental-spiritual and free. In this, too, it is similar to Erich Fromm's conception of "God" as an expression of the ultimate humanistic value.[20] Like Fromm, Korczak holds the sanctity of man as a key concept, and his writings strongly stress the idea that, by nature, man is a rebel and a vessel of potential holiness: "and within me—there is no submission, no adoration, only rebellion. . . . I am proud, I stand tall, I do not plead for grace and I am not afraid of punishment."[21] Fromm strove to show that as a man develops he is gradually freed from God's ascendancy and is capable of resembling Him. Every additional development in the concept of God diminishes His role as the owner of man. Thus Fromm emphasized that the act of eating of the tree of knowledge was not in itself a sin; but to the contrary, later religious development made the ability to distinguish between good and evil a most important virtue to which man must aspire. Man's likeness to God, as expressed in his ability to know good and evil, endows him with a measure of independence and perfection, and instills humanism with a dimension of sanctity.

Korczak added an experiential dimension to this essence of rebellion. On the surface of it, man is but "a few buckets of foul water; sewage clothed in skin," yet his body has winged thought and imagination. Man can rise to the heavens and be as God. The forgers of God have locked the gates of heaven and posted a guard who lets pass only those servants who admire God submissively. It is against these that Korczak's hero declares: "I am a slave who has rebelled . . . my own spirit is a part of You, so that You have rebelled against Yourself. I, the god, call you God as one equal to another."[22]

Because of man's sovereignty, his meeting with God is not one of abasement, submission, or fear, but rather, a happy encounter. In this Korczak holds similar views to those of the Chassidic movement in Judaism, which upholds that God should be worshipped with joy. The saying of Rabbi Nachman of Bratslav, "Joy will bring your prayer into the king's palace," would have probably been to Korczak's liking, as he was also close in spirit to some of Rabbi Nachman's other prayers which view the entire world as participating in the encounter with God—"every blade of grass sings the praise of the Lord and what better than to pray in the field and sing with the whole of creation."

Korczak's God is a pantheistic one, embracing the entire world. There is a certain affinity between the Kabbalah's concept of God and Korczak's conception in that the Kabbalists emphasized that God was not only revealed on Mount Sinai, but also in each of the six days of creation, and that He will continue to be revealed until the Millennium, so that His acts of creation are His central revelation. Yet Korczak makes no generalizations, and develops no divine gospel. Rather than any formulated philosophical theory, his pantheism is illustrated by his poetic portrayals of God.

The revelation of God in the whole of creation and man's perception of Him, both in nature and within his own heart, is the essence of Korczak's pantheistic religious philosophy. This wonderful combination of feeling alive with God, discovering Him, conversing with Him and rebelling against Him, is not without the pain of God's silence and the feeling of having been abandoned by Him. Thus Korczak's hero complains:

> I started my journey with You. Am I condemned to go on alone, abandoned? And I am tired and weary and cannot find my way. . . . I was led astray in a gloomy hour of dusk and God went away to some far place. He has abandoned me to my fate. I have hung my anger on the necklace of tears which I wear on the table of my heart. You are to blame, my God.[23]

And from Korczak's pantheistic experience we are drawn to his shrouded attempt to formulate religious issues in *Confession of a Butterfly*, where he wrote:

> I no longer wonder over the fact that God has no beginning and no end, for in him I see the harmony of an infinity of stars. It is creation which testifies to the existence of the creator, and not the priest. I have created a new religion for myself, it has not direction yet, but it is the manifestation of spirituality.[24]

The experience of personally discovering God avers any accepted terminology or conventional concept of God. It is a stranger to such concepts as "God is angry," "God punishes," or "God forgives." There is no place in its world for genuflections and curtsies, for the burning of incense and the mumbling of prayers, for sermons and preaching and moral castigation. It is so completely focused on the experiential dialogue with God that it even shies away from the conventional terminology, which, so used and abused, is no longer capable of expressing a unique personal experience:

> Full of wisdom is the prayer in an unknown language. Ula Tel Solt Min Kioso Vit Derto, Vack Robo, Vack Rista, Kin Bra-Ole. . . . I would choose the most bizzare words of all languages, and I would spread them, grind them, blend them, and create a prayer incomprehensible to human beings, incomprehensible to myself. Ula Tel Solt Min Kioso Vit Derto, Vack. The words have no meaning but I cannot have it otherwise, I cannot. . . . Ababa, Adaba, Ababa.[25]

On the one hand, God is so close, personal, and open to everyday conversations, so soothing of all fears, that little Zusia tells him she has peed her pants and her mother is angry and hits, and in places where people are angry and hit everything is ugly: "Mother is ugly, doll is ugly, puppy is ugly, beautiful puppy is ugly. Listen doggy of mine, here is the pot, do it for me. Zusia is nice, don't hit me mother. . . . Zusia loves God."[26]

On the other hand, this is no simplistic anthropomorphism, but a unique horizon of intention and aspiration. Korczak's God never becomes something that one can get hold of. He continues to exist as the perpetuation of a wish, as an address for eternal wishes. This concept of Korczak's is close to that of Fromm, who wrote:

> God is a horizon, which places limits on our field of vision. To the uninitiated, the horizon seems tangible, attainable, yet any who attempt to reach the horizon strive to grasp an optical illusion. We move and the horizon moves with us: if we climb a hill, even a small one, the horizon expands, but still remains as it was—a limitation. It will never become a thing of substance, which can be grasped.[27]

Erich Fromm discusses the biblical prohibition on concretizing God, as expressed in the interdiction against making an image of God. According to Fromm, this prohibition emphasizes the idea that God is a symbol of all that is in man, while at the same time He is a symbol of all that man is not. The symbol is of a spiritual reality, which we may aspire to actualize within us, but which we shall never be able to describe or define. Korczak's characters talk to God, appeal to Him directly, and speak from the heart, yet they do not define Him, do not make an image of Him, and do not limit the horizon of yearning.

On parting from some of his students who left the orphanage to live their own lives, Korczak told them:

> We did not give you God, because you must look and find Him within yourself. We did not give you love of country because your heart and reason must dictate your own choice. We did not give you love of man, because love comes from forgiveness which must be discovered through effort. We gave you one thing—a longing for a better life, a life of truth and justice which you must build for yourself. We hope that this longing will lead you to God, to Country and to Love.[28]

Although Korczak's characters do not know the proper order of the liturgy, their personal prayer comes from the heart. They are all on their way to God. He describes a great march of all created creatures striving to discover the secret of secrets—God. At their head, march the poets, the undisciplined novitiate-priests, the rebels against all institutionalized orders, the vanguard of aspiration, seeking, soaring high, and dreaming. After them come the accountants who calculate everything: number, define, weigh. For these the sun and a grain of sand are one and the same. One is the weight of a tear and the weight of a rock, one the measure of a smile and of a road. The astronomer who pokes at the heavens does not heed the singing of the stars, he only registers them as points on the maps of space. The chemist catalogs the smell of roses and the smell of rot. The physicist studies the forces and oscillations of the cosmos.

According to Korczak, all of us are on the way to God, and by the struggles of our stormy lives, in our diverse and different acts, in our tireless forward striving, in our incessant search, in our joys and sorrows, and especially in our hours of great loneliness, we confront God face to face.

During certain periods in Korczak's life, and especially in times of depression, disappointment, or deep spiritual anguish, Korczak's way to God was opened. At these times, he became religiously sensitized, expressing deep religious longings and experiencing a mystical awakening. He prayed devoutly in the midst of nature, staring into the secret and the mystery contained in the whisper of silence, removing the barriers between himself and the absolute. His point of departure was in disappointment, a profound loneliness in a blind and evil world, and his solution was an awakening of the sensation that human life is not a lonely life, but rather, as Buber described it, a permanent dialogue with God. Thus, during Korczak's most difficult hours in the ghetto, while everything collapsed about him, he spoke with God, prayed to Him, and thanked Him for the multihued sunsets and the fresh breeze, for the smell of flowers and the twinkling of fireflies, the song of the lark and the blaze of stars in the firmament.

As his distress and suffering grew, Korczak's lips often whispered words of prayer to the God who had hidden His face: "Out father who art in Heaven . . . this prayer was shaped by hunger and bitter fate. Our daily bread. Our daily bread. The bread."[29]

In his book, *The Drawing Room Kid*, which includes many auto-biographical elements, Korczak dedicates some passages to the desire to pray to God directly, without outside interventions or excessive delibera-tion:

> My Lord! I submissively appeal to you, God, to bestow upon me the greatest grace possible to man, that of pure and warm prayer. . . . May you grant that prayer shall remove from visions and thoughts all that is called in Your great name, that no evil thought shall take my mind off You, God. Oh teach me, God, to pray before you in faith and hope.[30]

The ultimate embodiment of a prayer, which was forged in pain, distilled and pure, free of words, of unmitigated intention, devoid of all mediation or conventional formulation or even existing words, was the pain-filled cry that Korczak directed at God during the last Seder he held for his proteges at the orphanage. Hana Mordetkovitz-Ohlatchkova describes this last "Seder" of Korczak and his orphans:

> The invited guests stared in amazement at Korczak's uplifted arms, spread in a desperate gesture as he cried for the help of the deaf heavens. He lost his clear mind in the pervasive feeling of great help-lessness and the nearing storm, and all the formulations of prayer were compressed on his lips at one and the same time, so that one could not tell which held the keys to salvation and which were but empty sounds.[31]

Korczak knew that a child requires faith and the sensation of a great, all-powerful father watching over his world. By nature, the child's world is a violent one, and he believes in mystery and wonder. If a child is not told of God, he creates Him for himself. God fills him; the prayer of a child is in his laughter and his tears. Hence the educational conclusion which Korczak reached is that "one can educate children without religion, but not without God. How can we explain birth, death and the past gen-erations? The child requires God, let him create Him for himself."[32]

Korczak is well aware of the loss of God in our world:

> The true God has slowly evaporated from man's thoughts, actions and time. Perceiving that He was no longer needed, that men were tired of Him, He has wandered off, become lost. The true God, I mean.[33]

God, however, continues to live within the heart of every child, so that he can turn to Him and talk to Him in joy as well as in pain and sorrow.

And, indeed, Korczak emphasized the importance of religious education in his institutions. This was not an education aimed at observing the practical commandments, but rather a religious education through public singing, prayer, moments of solitude and silence, etc. Those children of the Jewish orphanage who expressed their wish to pray were taken to synagogues in the vicinity. In the orphanage itself there was a special hall that was called the "Hall of Silence." It was a big hall, decorated with pictures and containing a large aquarium with various fish. The children came to this hall at any hour when they felt a need to be alone with their thoughts or to pray alone. Absolute silence was the rule at all times, and anyone breaking that silence was liable to be tried by the court of students. A Jewish teacher named Gutman regularly visited the orphanage in order to teach religion and Hebrew. These lessons were not obligatory, and any who wished to participate could do so.

Yerachmiel Weingarten related how, during his first visit to the orphanage, his eyes were drawn to the messages posted on the wall. He read them with great concentration and was surprised to discover one message bearing the following announcement: "If you intend to pray every morning during this month—please sign your name. Even after you have signed you are not obligated to pray, if you decide to change your mind."[34]

On Saturday, before breakfast, Weingarten entered the hall where the prayer was held. Despite the fact that the praying children all gathered together, the prayer was not a public one. There was no cantor, and each child prayed alone. The main prayers were marked in the books, and the children could choose any prayer they wished and read it at their own pace until the time for prayer was over. Weingarten also reported that Korczak also participated in the prayers, and when the time for prayer was over:

> Korczak would get up and place his right hand over his closed eyes. The children also rose. Korczak's lips would move, but no sound was heard, and when he finished he would say, "Gut Shabess" (Good Sabbath) to the children and exit the room.

When Weingarten asked the children if Korczak prayed, they did not know, but they related that at the end of the prayer period he always got up, covered his eyes with his hand—and said something softly. The children were sure that he said 'Kaddish' for the souls of the orphans' parents.[35]

When the new Christian orphanage Beitenu was built, Korczak demanded that a small prayer chapel should be included in the building. He felt that an orphaned child, lacking the love and care of a mother, bereft of the warmth and protection of a loving father, must have some place in his painful life where he can think, cry alone, complain, express his sorrow, and have very intimate personal, face-to-face conversations with God. Mariana Palska, who was a total atheist, objected forcefully, and no chapel was built.

Korczak ascribed great importance to prayer, through which a man speaks to his creator. He viewed prayer as an excellent means of catharsis, a way of giving vent to all the pressures and the pain, the disappointments and the dreams, a perfect tool for fostering a sense of belonging through affinity and for unburdening the heart. It was a way of increasing self-confidence through the recognition that there is someone to turn to. In a wonderful play that Korczak wrote for Chanuka, he included a conversation between a Chanuka candle and a girl who asks it: "What is this prayer?"

> *The candle*: Prayer is like old wine, which turns to fire once you drink it, passing from your lips to your head and your heart. . . .
> *The girl*: I do not understand. I have never drunk wine.
> *The candle*: There are some stones which are grey and very hard. If you polish such stones they become agates. Every word of prayer is a grey stone, but men have repeated each word many times. They have spoken it so many times that it has become polished by their lips—and turned into an emerald.
> *The girl*: I do not understand. I have never seen an emerald.
> *The candle*: Prayer is like a forest. Its words are the trees. Many storms and tempests have struck the forest; lightning and thunder have assailed it, yet the forest continues to grow and flourish: the trees shall be warmed by love and faith, which are like the sunshine on the leaves.
> *The girl*: I have never been in a forest.
> *The candle*: Prayer is like bread. You eat bread every day. Every day it is the same bread, but every day it is different.
> *The girl*: I know what bread is. I think I understand what you mean.[36]

When Korczak was once asked why he held prayers in his institution, he answered that many of the children came from simple devout homes where they saw their family members pray. Their families taught them to respect religion, and he wished to bring some of the atmosphere that prevailed in their parent's homes into the institution.

In his institutions Korczak devoted special attention to the celebration of religious holidays. It was especially on holidays, when families tend to come together, that the sensation of being orphaned, destitute, and lonely became especially poignant and depressed the young souls who had no home or family. Korczak saw to it that the holiday spirit would be felt in his institution by providing many games, ceremonies, and festive meals, thus attempting to instill an atmosphere of sanctity and true unity.

Korczak once said that the two religious holidays he liked most were Chanuka and Passover. The reasons he gave for his preference of these two holidays was that both demonstrate that the weak and the right shall triumph in the end, that both are connected with a struggle for liberation, that both are full of light, and both have many songs for children and impressive ceremonies.[37]

Passover was ceremoniously celebrated at the orphanage. Korczak prepared a special Haggadah for the children, written in Polish and Hebrew. Rather than the complete Haggadah, it was an abridged version suited to the children's ability to absorb and concentrate.

He also created a lovely new practice for the "Stealing of the Aphikoman." He liked this tradition because it had elements of suspense and fun, surprise and light adventure, and it also made the Seder more colorful. Since it was impractical to allow so many children to disperse throughout the hall in search of the hidden Aphikoman, Korczak began a new tradition, which did not include "theft" or cause a great uproar. At the orphanage kitchen, the cooks baked special dumplings. Inside each dumpling they hid a nut, and the number of special dumplings was identical to the number of tables where the children sat. Each table was served one such dumpling with the other dumplings in which there were no nuts. The child who discovered a nut in his dumpling was the winner and would receive one of the gifts which had been especially prepared for the occasion. Korczak and Stefa Wilenczinska personally distributed the gifts to the winners.

One passage that Korczak deleted from the Passover Haggadah and from the orphanage Seder was that of "Spill Thy Wrath on the Gentiles." He told Yerchamiel Weingarten:

The words are terrible. There are some people who love us, and some who do not love us. But how can one use such words to curse even those who hate us? I cannot hate, and I will not teach our children to hate.[38]

In the last Passover Seder which was celebrated at the orphanage in 1942, Korczak's lips were already whispering: "Spill Thy Wrath" while he and his protégés cast their arms up high and cried their terrible anguish to the unheeding heavens.

3

To the Sun: The Summer Camps

In Warsaw, there is no sunset, but at the hour of twilight, there comes a man bearing a long stick and lights up ugly, yellow lanterns. The man's clothing is dark and drab, and his face cannot be seen in the shadow. It is he who ushers in the city's night. But at the summer camp in Michaelovka, it is the sun, in purple splendor, which brings the day to a close and ushers in the night. The sun slowly descends, sinking beneath the earth and disappearing by stages.

Some say—already.

—Not yet.

There! Its light is now no more than that of a star. A tiny spark.

. . . .

Perhaps we shall not return to Warsaw at all? Perhaps we shall take up flags, sign a song and march off?

—Where to?

—The Sun.[1]

The opening lines of this chapter are the closing lines of Korczak's book *Moshekim, Yosekim, Srulekim* on the experiences of poor Jewish children from Warsaw at the country summer camp in Michaelovka. Although it is apparently a simple diary of the summer camp, a notebook of daily experiences, and an educational report, it is written with such great sensitivity that many passages are elevated to the level of poetry.

Can the phrasing of any report more aptly express the feelings of an educator for his students than the following excerpt that portrays the summer-camp protégés Charansky and Krok?

There are two kingdoms in life. One—the kingdom of entertainment, of drawing-rooms and fancy clothes, where reside the richest hereditary princes, who have the merriest laughter and who have worked little in their lives. And there is another kingdom, a much larger one—the kingdom of cares, of hunger and grueling work. The aristocrats of this kingdom know the price of a pound of bread from childhood. They take care of their younger brothers and work hard with their parents.

Charansky and Krok of the summer camp are princes in the kingdom of sad thoughts and coarse bread. They have been princes since the time of their forefathers. The prestigious title of nobility was given them in ancient days.[2]

Korczak was conscious of the Jewishness of the Moshekim, Yosekim, and Srulekim, and he devoted another book—*Josekim, Yashekim, Frankim*, to the Christian summer camp and to the things that distinguished it. This book, too, is full of sincere emotion and great empathy; both books taken together are a testimony to the great faith that Korczak had in the child *qua* child, and to his great initial optimism which became sorely corroded over the years as he became increasingly aware of the Jewish fate.

In this context, his words on the natural and spontaneous language of children reverberate and echo:

Here, in the country, the Polish tongue smiles at them from the green trees and the golden wheat, here the Polish speech flickers in starry pearls, breathes in the gusts of river breezes. Like wild flowers, the Polish idioms are lined in gay meadows or borne aloft, pure and radiant like the sinking sun.

No one teaches the boys to speak here. There is no time for that, and we do not even correct the mistakes they make as they speak. We teach them the Polish countryside, the skies of Poland. . . .

Even Yiddish sounds pleasant here, for it is not the screeching, coarse argot of squabbles and curses, but rather the alien tongue of youngsters at play.

Yiddish, too, has expressions full of longing, touching to the heart, the expressions of a mother as she lulls her sick child to sleep.

And the silent, grey Polish word—sad, is the same in Yiddish: Sad. And when a Polish or Jewish child is feeling miserable—he uses the same idiom when he thinks of his sadness.[3]

In truth Korczak's first actual encounter with educational work and his first experiences of educational care were gained in the course of his work as an educator-supervisor during these two summer camp cycles of poor Warsaw children. It was there that he first met large groups of children, and, through trial and error, learned the basics of educational work.

As a young physician who had devoted many hours to volunteer educational work among neglected youth, and who had tirelessly cared for the sick children at the Jewish hospital for children on Shliske Street, Korczak was closely acquainted with the children of the poor, and he had even attempted to express their woes in a literary creation. He saw a great challenge in going out to the country with a group of needy children in order to bring some light and sun, some natural beauty, and the joy of play into their harsh lives. He wrote: "I aspired to make those four weeks in which the children of cellars and attics were gathered in summer camp, into one long holiday. One joyous day without a tear."[4] He came to this task with many illusions and little experience, sentimental and young, innocent and full of faith in his success. He did not even know how to properly prepare for this task, concentrating on irrelevant matters rather than serious and important issues. He took care to find a gramophone, a magic lantern, colorful fireworks, games, and the like, and it seemed to him that these were sufficient.

His lack of experience and knowledge made his first attempt a failure. Analyzing his mistakes, Korczak considered his basic error to have been his educational approach. Believing that children should be given total freedom in everything and that his role was to treat everyone equally. Korczak found this principle of uncontrolled liberty a great disappointment, and he eventually reached the conclusion that his basic definition of freedom had, in fact, been wrong. His initial concept of liberty had been that everyone should do as he liked, that there be no order or regular procedure, and that anarchy be permitted. Only later did he understand that freedom is derived from the basic right of the child to be treated with respect, while his previous conception only led to the infringement of other persons' rights. Order, definite procedures, and organized frameworks were not intended to rob the child of his freedom, but rather to enable him to realize himself, to realize his inner freedom, to protect him against any infringement of his rights, and to prevent total anarchy, which can only hinder the realization of personal freedom. Korczak wrote:

> I was disappointed on the way to the summer camp. When the first child got off the wagon, because he was tired of travelling, I should have ordered him to get back on again. I did not do so, and the result: The children disembarked with wild whoops, in a disorderly ruckus, losing their bags and prayer books, and pushing each other.[5]

The issue of going to sleep at night was another case in point, for when Korczak allowed the children to freely choose their beds in the dormitory, disorder, pushing, noise, attacks, weeping, and total bedlam were the results. He finally gave up his original intention and dictated the children's sleeping arrangements by means of a preprepared list, thus achieving relative quiet. He understood then that the freedom to choose a bed was no more than an illusory external liberty, of no real consequence. When he had offered them such freedom, he had pushed the children to aggressively realize a totally external side of their freedom, ultimately causing frustration and disappointment to many children who were crushed by the sterile struggle between the strong and burly and the weak and timid.

Once the children realized that there were no established rules, no clear procedures, and above all—no strong authority that could support their own personality, they increased the disorder and began taking liberties at the very lowest level of freedom—the freedom of the impulses. They littered the forest, they destroyed the porch, they tore bricks out of pillars, and they wasted precious water. In short, they ran wild, made a terrible row in the dormitory, and even armed themselves with sticks in order to attack Korczak if he should try to control them. Not stopping to think, the shocked Korczak grabbed one of the children, pinched his ears, and threatened to throw him out onto the porch where the dog had been let loose for the night. This lapse into physical punishment greatly tormented him later. The rebellious children opened his eyes to the negative aspects of extreme freedom on the one hard, and of physical punishment on the other. He began to understand that instead of allowing external liberty and then attempting to order it by means of an external police authority, it is better to get the children themselves to cooperate. And, indeed, on the next day, he no longer lectured to the children but rather talked to them. He made no further speeches on what he wished them to become, but rather attempted to learn what they wished to become and what they could become. He summed up his attempt, saying: "For the first time, I realized that one can learn a lot from children, that they, too, have demands and that they have a right to posit their conditions and express doubts."[6]

Moreover Korczak understood that one of the most important qualities of the educator is his ability to admit to a mistake, to explain his actions and even criticize them. Speaking to the children in the dormitory the night following the incident, he told them:

I have hit the boy. I have done a bad thing. I threatened that I will take him out onto the porch where the dog will bite him: that was very ugly. But who is to blame for these two evil deeds which I have done? The children who purposefully made a terrible noise and mess in order to infuriate me are to blame. Perhaps I have punished an innocent, but who is to blame: those children who availed themselves of the dark in order to hide . . . that is your fault. I am very much ashamed that I have been unjust, but you too should be ashamed. I have admitted my guilt, it is now your turn to admit yours. There are good boys and bad boys. Every bad boy can better himself if he so wishes, I will gladly help him. But you too must help me, so that I can continue to be good, so that you do not spoil me.[7]

Korczak attributed great importance to conversations with children, and took great care to prepare these talks in advance.

When the second summer camp cycle arrived, Korczak had already gained experience and developed his own methods. He understood the great importance of becoming acquainted with the child, and learning his name and nickname. He attempted to memorize the children's names right from the first encounter. Armed with a notepad and pencil, he also wrote down everything that drew his attention during his first contact with a child. A plus, a minus, or a question mark noted beside the child's second name, served to evaluate his first impressions. He now gave special attention to precise planning, down to the last detail, the various procedures and routines of the summer camp, and the distribution of food, water, clothes, and equipment as well as the ordering of sleep, postage delivery, seating arrangements, and so on.

Korczak carefully watched how the children's society organized itself and having learned some important lessons from his observations of the children of the first cycle, he now implemented his new understanding with the children of the second cycle. He was convinced that children were blessed with a natural public spirit and that though certain innovations may be received with initial displeasure, because the children had lost their faith in adults, or because they had not understood the issue thoroughly, they will quickly show their pleasure if everything is carried out with their participation. He organized the routines of the summer camp with the cooperation and help of the children. He insisted that the educator must never forgo the help of the children so long as such help was received with constant and meticulous criticism and that the helpers were rotated. He wrote:

> Only thus can one prevent the domination of the young helpers. Power corrupts! One should carefully explain that the role of duty officer does not carry any special rights, and that it is only an honorary post.[8]

He nominated duty officers for the dining room, for making the beds, for putting toys in order, for cleaning the yard, etc.

Through his methodical observation of the children's socializing processes, Korczak came to realize that positive elements among the children require help, support, and protection from aggressive, domineering, or wild individuals. He wrote:

> If the duty of government is to protect the public from robbery and the treachery of harmful elements, it is the duty of the educator to protect children from violence, threat and humiliation, guard their personal posessions from robbery (even if it is merely a pebble or small stick),

and to safeguard their organization (whether it is a ball game or a sand castle). Once this central task is carried out, light supervision will suffice in order to prevent deviations.[9]

Despite his great belief in the role of education, Korczak was also aware of its limitations. He wrote:

Quickly and miraculously, under the influence of the country and the pleasant educational methods, depressed souls are awakened to the beautiful and the harmonious, first in surprise and fear, but later with growing faith and joy. But there is a limit to educational possibilities, which no miracle can change. A rich and sensitive soul, whom only the circumstance of life have caused to tire, shall awake; but the child whose soul is depleted and spent, will, with great difficulty, twist his lips into no more than a sickly smile.[10]

Korczak devoted a great deal of thought to the question of whether retardation, lack of progress, disturbance, or abnormal behavior were the result of an educational-biological limit that cannot be breached, or of environmental circumstances which can be changed, thus freeing the thinking and behavior of the child from their bonds or disturbance.

He noted that in any group of children there must be some singular characters—anti-social children and bullies, children who are angry, selfish, no-goodniks, sickly, aggressive, and the like—to whom the attention of the educator must be directed, both for their sakes and for the sake of the group as a whole. Korczak stressed that:

Without this, the work would have been dull, monotonous and lifeless. In fact, these special children provide us with the richest material for thought and contemplation, and teach us how to improve. Were it not for them, how easy it would have been for us to fall into the self-illusion that we have attained our ideal! And who is so unwise as to ignore the chance that beyond the relative good, there exists the possibility of attaining something even more sublime?[11]

4

To Be a Home: The Orphanage as a Home and House of Education

I kiss these children with a glance, a thought, a question: who are you, the wonderful secret, and what shall you bring with you? I kiss you with an effort of will: How can I help you? I kiss as the astronomer kisses the star, which was, is and will be. This kiss must find an intermediate place between the enthusiasm of the scientist and the humble prayer; yet this wonder will not be felt by the man who in seeking his liberty has barely lost his God.[1]

Korczak's words seem to encapsulate in a kiss the whole idea of the orphanage that he founded, directed, and fostered throughout most of the years of his educational activity. His fundamental questions about his protégés were basically these three: *1) Who are You?* What makes you unique? What are your personal needs? What is your inner world? What does your soul need? *2) What do you bring with you?* What is your personal heritage? What are the memories you bring with you, the commandments of your original home, the experiences of yesterday? What is the burden of pain, sorrow, destitution, and poverty that you carry? *3) How can I help you?* And this is perhaps the main question that Korczak poses, for his entire life was distinguished by the care of children, by responding to their needs, both as individuals and as a group, and by his total devotion to raising and educating them.

Before founding his orphanage, Korczak toured Switzerland, Italy, the Netherlands, and Denmark in order to study the work in orphanages in these countries. Wishing to study the most advanced methods, his disappointment was great, for all the orphanages he visited were alike in one important aspect: they had all succumbed to routine and conformity, and seemed to him like prisons for children. Describing one of these orphanages, he wrote:

The orphanage has been built without faith in children or staff. Everything must be seen, known, prevented. A huge recess-hall is nothing less than an open square, a market. A sharp-eyed person can encompass all. The same goes for the huge, barrack-like dormitories . . . there is not one quiet corner in the building. Noise, turmoil, shoving and pushing, the children rightly complain.[2]

Blind discipline and total obedience were the basic commandments of these institutions whose educational methods were based on the use of force and the enforcement of discipline. The children were subjected to an atmosphere of constant fear, lies, and betrayal, and there was no cooperation at all between them and their educators.

The feel of a prison was amplified by dark and oily wall paints, and small windows set in high walls. Thus, in April 1912 when the cornerstone for the building of Korczak's new orphanage was laid at 92 Krochelmane Street in Warsaw, Korczak took care to have big windows set in its walls.

In planning his orphanage, Korczak favored the hotel method, with a corridor and small rooms, but stressed that in addition to individual rooms, it is necessary to provide the children with a place where they may stay when they do not feel well. He wrote, "His foot hurts, his head aches, he cannot sleep, he feels angry—find him a quiet corner, where he can be alone, or with a friend."[3]

The living quarters of the director of the institution were also an important issue. The tendency to house him away from the children's quarters so as to provide him with better living standards and some peace in order to concentrate, seemed to Korczak both wrong and anti-educational. He stated that this:

Removes him from the essential area of educational influence. He can supervise the secretaries and the accountants, represent the institution and correspond with the authorities; but he will then be a guest rather than the proprietor of the boarding-school, for the whole of the boarding-school is comprised of "little strips," and one must not forget it. The architect must house the director in such a way as to force him to be an educator, so he will not see and hear the child only when he comes into his study by invitation.[4]

Korczak's children's institutions were full of light and air, and life within them was organized in such a way as to leave room for equality and freedom. Korczak totally devoted himself to the fostering and raising of his orphans. Each child constituted a whole and very complex world. Although they all wore similar uniforms, Korczak knew that beneath the costume, different hearts were beating, each with its own conflicts and woes, each with its own past and characteristic difficulties. Even when the first adjustment to the life of the institution had been accomplished, when the children were clean and their clothes in order, and they had learned some tentative manners and acquired a little knowledge, Korczak did not delude himself into thinking that their sad memories and bitter experiences had been obliterated. He knew that a very long time would be required before they could be free of their festering wounds, which require lengthy and patient care. Bad influences would stay with them for a long time, and even after thorough and prolonged care, some scars would always remain—scars that could easily become malignant wounds once more. Korczak knew his orphans intimately because he lived their lives for twenty-four hours a day.

In the introduction to his book, *How to Love Children*, Korczak wrote:

I became privy to the secrets of the lights and sounds of the boarding house. I became acquainted with the dormitory, the showers, the playing hall, the dining room, the yard and the lavatories. I am not facing children in their neat school uniforms, but rather in their naked daily lives as they are.[5]

Korczak did not believe in accepting children to his orphanage in a wholesale manner or without prior evaluation. He objected to any pressures applied for the acceptance of a child who did not fit, and demanded that an educational and psychological screening be instituted. Although he wished to provide children with the right to rehabilitate themselves, he recognized the fact that a minority of children would not only fail to benefit from the orphanage but might also be a destructive factor. He wrote:

A child who has been designated inappropriately will not benefit at all, but will cause damage to everyone. Coercion cannot be allowed, nor any pressure on the educator to keep a child in his institution despite his better judgement. It is essential that the educator have the right to say: 'This child is harmful.' We must believe him. We must ensure that the educator has many rights, for the work of the orphanage is hard, and in matters pertaining to education his opinion is the decisive one.[6]

Korczak took personal care of the children who were accepted into the orphanage. He playfully and jokingly cut their hair and trimmed their nails, usually refusing to delegate these tasks to his helpers lest they hurt the child through carelessness. He would receive the new child with great warmth and simplicity and attempt to lighten his entry into his new life.

Korczak recognized that a clear, simple means of communication must be established in order to operate the orphanage properly and prevent hopeless turmoil. One such important tool of communication, which was so elementary as to seem of no importance, was the notice board. In a prominent place, and not too high, so as to enable all children to read the notices, Korczak placed a board onto which instructions notices and advertisements were tacked. According to Korczak, life in the institution without the notice board would have been full of suffering, endless arguments with the children, misunderstandings, complaints, and evasions. He wrote:

> In the rush of things, an educator is forced to give sudden instructions, which have not been calculated and arranged and are, therefore, faulty. He is forced to decide quickly, and the decision is, therefore, dependent on his mood and clarity of mind. And, always, at the last moment, something unexpected is bound to crop up. The notice board forces him to always think out the plan of every action in advance. It is a great mistake on the part of the educator when he does not know how to correspond with the children. Even in a place where most of the children have not yet learned to read, I would post a notice board: Even when they do not know the letters, they will learn to know their names, they will feel a need to read and will recognize their dependency on children who can read.[7]

Notices, requests, and other messages and communications were tacked onto the notice board not only by the educators but by the children themselves. Some would pass on a personal message, others include an important news item from the newspaper. One recommended a reading book, a second posted a riddle or a crossword, a third offered some item for exchange. The doctor published a list of the damages caused by fights, or tables of child development, and thus the notice board became an object of interest, stimulation, information, and even formentation.

Korczak was acquainted with the "gang" mentality that children may adopt. He both warned and advised the educator to act very gently in situations where children unite against him as one. Korczak described the difficulty of such a situation for the beginning educator, who may be slowly wrenched from his self confidence in the face of this tremendous force of the children's group:

> The thought of your strength is already well entrenched, when suddenly you feel small and weak. A huge crowd, with enormous public weight and a great deal of experience, sometimes unites in stubborn solidarity, sometimes splits into tens of pairs of feet and hands—heads, each of which conceal different thoughts and the mysteries of different demands.[8]

Korczak recognized both the negative and positive aspects of the fraternity of children. The negative fraternity meant going with the crowd. It was the result of avoiding effort and "unnecessary thinking" in controversial situations. It was an accidental and lazy fraternity of disorder and uninvolvement. Every educator at the institution knew that even if he were to discipline someone who was not favored by all—immediately, as if to spite the educator, many "defenders" would be found, and a united group of consolers and advisors would gather about him, attempting to lighten the punishment. In contrast, the positive fraternity was one that stems from cooperative efforts, from groups that unite in order to attain a common purpose and achieve a common creative goal.

Korczak explained to educators that if they wished their educational work to succeed, order must be preserved. Educators can create order and keep it with the help of the children, but if they are incapable of availing themselves of the help of the children, the latter would institute their own order. He wrote:

> Sometimes you cannot help them, and at the same time are unwilling to accept their order, and then a battle breaks out, a war. Any war causes disorder and damages. Do not forget for a moment that they are a throng, and the throng is a giant—many hands, feet, eyes, ears. You cannot win this war. Their power immeasurably exceeds yours. Your chances of victory are small, and what seems to you as a victory is often an illusion.[9]

He also clarified the strategy by which order can once more be achieved, and explained to the educator that he must always take care to have allies among the children. Those children who love order must be on his side. His advisors and helpers must be the honest children, the truthful and well-mannered ones. When dealing with a problem, one must never become angry, but rather seek reasons and explanations. Anger at the whole group can only cause damage. Anger at an individual is permitted, but with great care. According to Korczak, "An ambitious statesman issues edicts, an educator tests and examines."[10]

The educator must understand social relationships, the processes by which individuals join a group and the special psychology of the group, and its reactions and its behavior.

> One child—a huge, wide world. Two children—three worlds: The world of each child separately and of both together. Three children are not one plus one plus another one, for in addition to the three we have the first and second together, the first and third together, the second and third together, and on top of that—the world of all three together,

and we have seven worlds. Reluctance, friendship, hostility, happiness, sorrow; the worlds within ten, twenty, thirty children are beyond calculation. Many and difficult worlds. On your own, without the children's help, you will not get to know these worlds and your educational work shall fail.[11]

In the institution Korczak wished to direct social solidarity into the patterns of a large extended family. Korczak understood the great importance of the family for the mental growth of the child and the shaping of his character; and since the orphan had been deprived of his natural family, Korczak wished to create a kind of social substitute for the extended family. Joseph Arnon, who was Korczak's helper and friend, noted:

> There were many elements of the large extended family in the structure of Korczak's children's company, and these served as the background for the education of the orphans. There were the big brothers, who served as role models . . . and there were the younger brothers whom the older children strived to better. The child wished to attain the achievements of his older brother, and the older brother made an effort to prove his maturity to the younger child—all according to the norms and value system of the children's company. The directors of the two educational institutions served as a substitute for the attentive father who understands and forgives (Korczak) and the mother, the demanding caretaker, who keeps track of everyday things and who is alternatingly angry and loving: at Krochelmane, Stefa Wileczinska, and at Bielany, Marina Palska. Although the two women and Korczak did not raise families of their own, they knew well that nothing can replace a father and mother.[12]

Korczak also took care to preserve whatever ties the child had with his natural family—a parent still living, uncles or aunts, and the like.

Before the child was accepted into the orphanage, a committee would visit the family at home, and examine its material situation and the quality of the ties with the child. Contact with the family was preserved after acceptance into the orphanage. Once a week, on Saturdays, all protégés visited their families without any limitation, and permission could be granted to stay with the family for longer periods during the holidays. While their friends went out to visit their families, those who were orphaned of both father and mother, and who had no relatives, stayed at the orphanage. Korczak took special care of these children, and would take them to the zoo, feed them cakes and sweets, and often accompany them to the cinema.

To some extent, the families were also involved in the life of the in-

stitution. Twice a year family members were invited to meet the educators. Families were notified of particularly severe transgressions, were
obliged to sign report cards, and were invited to plays staged at the institution. Korczak stressed that the institution did not wish to compete
with the natural family, but only to complete and extend it when it disintegrated, providing the child with an extended family, within which warm
and close relationships prevailed. Korczak was often concerned with the
issue of these home visits, for as much as the children loved to live at the
orphanage, Korczak knew that the child's ties with his parental home,
even a disintegrated, poor and often abusive, violent, and even rejecting
home, were essential. And, indeed, those children who had a living parent or some other natural kin remaining in their extended family, found
it important to preserve that tie.

David Zilber, who was deeply involved in the life of the orphanage as
an educator, wrote:

> Every Saturday afternoon, it seemed as if all the goodness they had re-
> ceived at the orphanage had been washed from memories in the flicker
> of an eye, and as if even the warmth of the doctor's fatherly manner
> had somehow cooled. Lunch, which throughout the week was sched-
> uled to fit the time at which the children returned from school, was
> taken earlier on Saturdays and every table with its eight young diners
> became a land-mine of excitement and tension. Everyone was dressed
> up in the finest Saturday garments and ate quickly as if awaiting the sig-
> nal to leap outside. Once the meal was over, a silence quickly settled
> over the house, which was suddenly emptied of all its little inhabitants
> at once. . . . Usually toward supper, a number of children returned
> from their visit in great disappointment; they were somewhat bedrag-
> gled and dirty and often sported some cuts and bruises on their faces.
> The family members, for which the child's soul had yearned, quite
> often simply ignored him, out of fear that he should wish to stay with
> them and not return to the orphanage, or insulted him out of jealousy
> for his "sleek" and "satiated" condition. This scene of the return of the
> vanquished and humilated from the adventure of a visit, repeated
> itself on many Saturdays, but never diminished that unknown power
> which impelled them all from the orphanage on a Saturday and cast
> many of them into the bosom of a cruel family which refused to accept
> them.[13]

Although David Zilber may have exaggerated somewhat, it is true that
most of the orphanage children went out on visits that quite often involved pain, frustration, and humiliation. It seemed as if this outing,
though far from pleasant, was in the nature of a statement, made both to

themselves and others, that they remained unique, that they were not only a part of a general body, sympathetic and accepting as it may be, but they also had personal affiliations. It was statement that their presence in the orphanage was not the result of rejection by the family, but in many respects, an act of choice, and that their new lives had an affinity with an individual past which was totally their own for good or bad.

The sitting arrangements in the orphanage dining room reflected Korczak's attempt to establish an extended family atmosphere. A mixed group of children sat beside each table—both boys and girls, of varying ages, and an instructor. Korczak and Stefa themselves also sat and ate with the children. The meals were served at fixed times, with great observance of order, beauty, and comfort. A diagram of the seating arrangements in the dining room was posted on the notice board, and every child was entitled to register himself in a seat and state beside whom he wished to sit. Seats could be changed once every three months. In contrast to other institutions where total silence was demanded during meal times, Korczak encouraged free conversation between the diners, believing that it added spice to the meal, so long as everything was done with good manners, in a plausible tone, and in proper order.

The dining room duty officers asked each child whether he wished a small, large, or medium helping in order to prevent waste of food. Yerachmiel Weingarten, who was an educator at the orphanage, relates how the duty officers:

> Walked down two empty aisles between the tables. In one aisle moved the distributors of food, and in the other aisle the removers of cutlery and utensils. This arrangement prevented damages and accidents. The utensils and the food were concentrated on both sides of a long table placed beside the wall. The kitchen (on the ground floor) was joined to the hall (on the first floor) by means of a small manual dumbwaiter, which opened out in the wall beside the table. The children in charge of the task would pull on the ropes and bring the food into the hall. In this way, they also removed the plates, the pots and the cutlery to the kitchen after use.[14]

Korczak preferred a manual elevator over an electric one in order to avoid the dangers inherent in a fast elevator. He even considered the fact than many children loved to "ride" the elevator, and to avoid temptation he would occasionally declare a day of supervised riding in which those children who were interested could avail themselves of the services of the elevator.

Korczak placed special emphasis on the personal hygiene of his protégés and on educating for cleanliness. Here, too, he did not use authoritarian means, but a method of gradual education combined with help, encouragement for personal efforts, and prizes intended to foster motivation for cleanliness. Thus, for example, clean children who were very careful with their hygiene and the cleanliness of their clothes received pretty woolen clothes; children whose cleanliness was satisfactory received pretty but washable clothes, while children whose personal cleanliness was unsatisfactory received clothes capable of withstanding rough laundry that were less attractive as a result of the many launderings.

Korczak also devoted a great deal of attention to sleeping arrangements. In order to provide the children with a sense of security, one of the educators slept in the dormitory, and a light was allowed to remain in the lavatories throughout the night. Ana Cohen Ronen relates that:

> Korczak was of the opinion that since in the houses of the poor, family members slept together in a single bed, upon arriving at the institution, children are afraid of sleeping alone. Korczak found an appropriate compromise for these children. Moveable screens, only slightly higher than the beds, were set up. Any two children who wished to do so, could move their beds together, with only the screen to separate them (so that they will not breathe into each others faces). The children were able to reach out and touch each other with a sense of security. If they woke up at night, they could sense the proximity of their neighbour and continue to sleep in peace.[15]

In the evenings Korczak would tell the children stories out of an intentionally limited repertoire, for he knew how the children liked hearing the same story over and over again. He was aware of the fact that he was actually telling a "lull-a-story." His voice was calm and placid and brought sleep to the children.

In his fatherly manner Korczak attempted to lighten the daily lives of his orphans and to ease their anxieties. There was not one aspect in the lives of the children that went unnoticed by his penetrating eyes and his devoted care. Dozens of examples can be found in the testimonies of his protégés and his helpers. He traced the physical development of each child and took care to have special diets for underweight children, whom he encouraged to eat more by means of games and competitions between tables. He would calculate the daily or weekly weight gain of the table's occupants and then give a prize to the winners. He would keep track of the preparation of homework by those of his protégés who studied in the city, and frequently he helped them. He held competitions of reading speed and fluency among the children whose reading was retarded, thus encouraging the protégés to make a greater effort.

In order to dispel the monotony of life at the orphanage and to provide as many opportunities as possible for relaxation and merriment, Korczak took care to celebrate holidays with great festivity. He even increased the number of occasions by stipulating special days devoted to various subjects, and he provided opportunities to raise the morale. His protégés and helpers tell of many such days, like "The first day of snow." "A day on which it isn't worthwhile getting up" (the shortest day of the year), "A day on which it isn't worthwhile going to bed" (the longest day of the year), and so on. These were days of general uproar, play, and practical joking in which Korczak's role was not inconsequential.

Wishing to instill color and light into the life of the orphanage, Korczak supported Stefa when she decided to dress the girls in flowery custom-made gowns, a stark contrast to the uniform that was common in most orphanages. On this issue both he and Stefa had a major argument with Mariana Palska, the director of Beitenu, who considered that the uniform and grey clothes were essential and important as they obliterated the differences between the children and provided a sense of equality in the children's community.

Korczak ascribed great importance to aesthetic education. He took care to introduce beauty into his institutions and to foster the creativity of his protégés, and to provide music and enrich their lives with color, sounds, and dreams. He adopted an extremist position against the Russian policy which would limit any artistic creation that was not egalitarian, that did not conform, that did not portray by prescription, and that did not yield to the rules of socialist realism. Yerchamiel Weingarten quoted him as saying:

Did not Chagal return full of enthusiasm from Paris to Russia at the outbreak of the war in 1914? Did he not paint the most wonderful pictures in Weitabsk, did he not create at the beginning of the revolution the most fantastic illustrations for Gogol's play as directed by Meirhold? Did he receive recognition? Was he not recently forced to leave Russia and return to Paris?[16]

Korczak was attentive to the complaints of the children and was opposed to the opinion of other educators that it was "Not nice to complain." He wrote:

Whoever sanctified that assumption? Did the children inherit it from bad educators or did the educators inherit it from bad children? For this assumption suits only the bad and the evil. The quiet and helpless will be exploited, deprived and blocked, and then be forbidden to call for help and demand justice. The tramplers shall rejoice and the deprived shall suffer. The conscienceless, inept educator finds comfort in not knowing what happens among the children, because he scorns their interests and does not know how to wisely judge them.[17]

According to Korczak, most children complain only rarely and reluctantly, and if some children complain frequently, the reasons for this must be examined. He stressed: "You shall never get to know children, if you belittle their complaints".[18]

Of special interest is the arrangement Korczak implemented in his institutions whereby he would correspond with the students. There was a special mailbox into which the children could insert letters expressing their wishes, doubts, views, conflicts, fears, problems, and the like. Sometimes they would even complain about the educators or about Korczak himself, and occasionally they would release some tensions or latent aggression through curses and invectives. Korczak either responded in writing or invited the child for a talk. To those who objected that correspondence seemed an excessively formal and estranged form of communication, Korczak responded that frequently the letter is but a desirable preparation for a face-to-face talk, besides its many other advantages such as the delayed response. The need for immediate reaction often involves a lack of proper consideration and attention, and may even cause an important matter to be ignored because of an inopportune situation or because the educator is busy with something else. By contrast, however, the educator reads the letters at a convenient hour, when he is free and able to seriously consider them. Letter writing was also very important for the child, who learned to differentiate between fleeting, momentary issues and more durable problems. Children were also given a chance to learn to formulate, weigh, and express their thoughts with clarity.

Besides the notice board and the mailbox, a shelf was provided for various reference books: dictionaries, encyclopedias, city maps, calendars, game collections, newspapers, and the like. The shelf also held notebooks written by the children themselves, collections of their poems, jokes, riddles, dreams, and independent creations. There were leaflets edited by the children and duty officers' reports, and it was here that one could also find the educator's diary.

Korczak believed that the educator's diary should not be concealed, for by revealing his dissapointments and difficulties, his mistakes and his joys, his successes and his failures, it played an important role in establishing authentic cooperation with the children, and sharing the educator's experiences and thoughts with them.

Korczak emphasized the importance of a balanced tempo of work and rest, study and play, and gave particular recognition to the great value of play in the life of the child. He noted that it was very easy to learn a person's traits and character through his play. One person is revealed as domineering and abusive, another a leader, a third a cheat, a fourth a whiner, and so on. Group play binds the children together and instills respect for regulations and fair play, while solitary play serves for the catharsis and expression of the individual.

> It's not what you play with which is important, but how you play with it, and how you think and feel while you play. One can play wisely with a doll, and play chess foolishly. One can play cops and robbers, train, hunters or Indians with great interest and imagination and one can read books without thought or interest.[19]

Indeed, Korczak's institutions left much room for games, trips, marathons, and sports events. Korczak himself participated in the children's games. He would jump on one foot, and from time to time he was not above indulging in some wild prank or practical joke. No barrier of formality existed in his attitude to the children of the orphanage. One could find him sitting on a small study-bench beside a reading child or listening to the noisy conversation of a group of children or encouraging a friendly wrestling match between two small children.

The children loved Korczak. Ya'akov Zuk relates how

> The doctor would sit in the orphanage yard under the shadow of the trees, in order to watch a competition or the play of the children, and the poor souls would immediately surround him. One of the toddlers climbs onto his knees, caresses his beard, presses against his chest, puts his head in his lap and falls soundly asleep.[20]

Korczak's orphanage had none of the stifling feeling that characterized other orphanages, nothing of the sense of a harsh regime, of charity and sanctimoniousness combined with spiritual oppression and the absolutism of educators. Korczak wished to liberate his orphans from the bonds of slavery, to provide them with as much self-rule as possible, and to develop their own world. The social organization of the institution could be likened to the organization of a democratic republic. The children's company had its own governmental institutions that included a court of law, a parliament, a legislative committee, a sports committee, a committee for the organization and distribution of work, a newspaper committee, and a committee that determined the grade of citizenship. Daily life was meticulously organized by duty officers, supervisors, and the like. Membership in the institutions was structured in levels, and the child had to progress from one level to another.

Each new arrival was assigned a guardian from among the veteran children who would advise and protect him for a period of three months. The guardian was obliged to keep detailed notes of his protégé's behavior, the important events of his life, and any virtues and shortcomings he found. The guardian served to lighten the entry of the newly arrived protégé into the life of the institution. He explained the rules, acquainted him with the procedures, the customs, and the regulations, and instructed him how to behave properly. He spoke for him, represented him in the self-administrative institutions, and protected him during the first week.

This help of a young guardian was very important for a new child, who could draw confidence in his first encounter with a new society. Although weak children ran a certain risk of becoming dependent on the guardian and postponing their adjustment to the new situation, this risk was somewhat tempered by the fact that the position of the guardian, as defined by his role, was a blend of proximity and distance, help and supervision, intimacy and appraisal. This process of assimilation into the life of the orphanage had important implications for the wider process of the child's becoming socialized into the group, for the guardian's role ensured that the group could not remain indifferent or alienated from the new protégé, and through the representative guardians, the child became an active partner in the whole process. The educators, too, found this assimilation process to be extremely helpful, for with the help of the guardian, they could keep careful track of the new arrival, and the guardian's diary taught them a great deal about the new child, the guardian himself, and the entire group.

Ada Poznansky-Hagery interviewed former protégés of the orphanage and asked them to describe the role of the guardian in their assimilation. One of the protégés related:

> I came and they shaved my hair off. I cried for a week and did not want to go home, because I was ashamed. . . . Sabinka, a big girl, an angel, brought me a sandwich. She sat beside me until I fell asleep. . . .
>
> On the second day, they appointed me a guardian. A lovely child. She tried to explain what I was doing here, what they were going to teach me, in short—everything. There were all kinds of things which I did not want to tell Stefa or the doctor but only my guardian. She documented my behavior in a diary. I was in constant contact with her—I loved her greatly.[21]

Israel Zingman (Staszek) also tells of the calming role of the guardian in the assimilation of a new protégé into the life of the orphanage. He describes the great anxiety that seized him when he was told that he was to be placed in an orphanage, the sensation of humiliation and pain when the barber shaved his head before entering the orphanage, and the first, harsh encounter with Stefa:

> I stood rooted to the spot, my eyes staring into the lady's face. My eyes filled with tears, and the black mole on her cheek began to grow . . . suddenly I saw two moles, and then three and four, and they began spinning and whirling, and my head spun and whirled with them . . . despite all of my efforts, my tears flowed like water, wetting my entire face. I pressed against my mother, and in order to stop the flow of tears, I lifted my head very high, to the sky. A flock of black ravens, their wings spread, whirled hither and thither above me, coming and going in a cross dance under a grey sky.[22]

The shock of his encounter with the orphanage began to dissipate when Beinem, his guardian, arrived. Despite his limp, Beinem made a good and soothing impression on him; Beinem then slowly introduced him to the secrets of the institution that had seemed so threatening and intimidating from the outside.

The guardian's role was very important in the case of children who were sentenced to expulsion from the institution by the court of the orphanage because of severe transgressions. The only possibility of postponing the expulsion was if the guardian agreed to guarantee the protégé's behavior and be responsible for him before the court. Israel Zingman tells of a series of trials in which he was accused before the court of the protégés, and how the judges increased the severity of his sentence from one trial to another until at last they sentenced him under section "900," which meant expulsion from the orphanage, unless a guardian was found who would be willing to devote himself to assisting his rehabilitation and improving his ways. Luckily, a boy named Laufer was found, who took it upon himself to take him into his custody, thus preventing Zingman's expulsion.[23]

At the end of the novice's first year at the orphanage, the protégés would hold a referendum in which the novice was awarded one of the following titles: 1) burdensome, 2) indifferent, 3) inhabitant, and 4) required. The burdensome child could be expelled from the institution if his behavior did not improve, although the institution's reports and various testimonies indicate that such an expulsion occurred very rarely. Nevertheless these titles determined an orphan's degree of citizenship at the the institution, beginning from full member (required) through temporary citizen (inhabitant) or just (indifferent), and down to a child whose membership was in doubt (burdensome). The temporary inhabitant who was destined to become a full citizen received the following letter:

If you have enough good will, wisdom and proper virtues—you will have full rights in our community, but you must win these rights. Without labor there can be no fruit; no sunlit playground, no summer in the village, fairy tales, hot buns, milk semolina, there are no days without duty—if you do not truly and faithfully prove that you wish to enjoy these terms. The wages are in proportion to the deed.[24]

The level of citizenship was not permanent, and the participants of the general referendum had the right to change it. It is important to stress that those who had a low level of citizenship were not entitled to be elected to a committee. Korczak's brand of democracy and self-rule, which he introduced into his institutions, did not uphold the idea of unconstrained equality.

A protégé who wished to rectify his status as a citizen and proceed to a higher level could do so, but he had to find a guardian who would help him in the processes of correction and rehabilitation. Only after a certain period, usually one year, could he ask for a vote in order to rectify his status. Ada Poznansky-Hagery tells the story of a protégé she had interviewed:

After a year my status was very bad. I received more minus signs than plus signs. It seemed that the children did not like me. Then they gave me a guardian who would help me improve my status. She took care of me, and I tried my best. My status so improved, that one year I was "Queen of the Children."[25]

Though Korczak's motives in instituting these referendums are understandable and his wish to derive educational conclusions from their results is commendable, it seems to me that this method might be very dangerous, as it is not a sociometric referendum which is given to the perusal and use of the teacher and educator alone, but rather it is more in the nature of a verdict, and for the lower levels of the indifferent and burdensome—a condemnation, denunciation, and negation. Zvi Kurtzweil noticed this weakness, but sought reasons to justify it. He wrote:

The feelings which are evoked in the child following his rejection or negation by his peers, might, indeed, badly damage the development of his personality in future. There can only be one reason which would vindicate such a procedure, and it is the fact that this method worked as an enormous challenge and a factor motivating for desirable and acceptable social behavior. This was especially required because the children came from an inferior cultural and educational background, an uneven mob which had to be crystallized into an orderly and organized society. Moreover, Korczak believed in the rightness of the children's "public opinion," and was convinced that their judgment in the matter of ranking was right and unbiased.[26]

Perhaps in the case of Korczak, who had a wonderful pedagogical intuition and a deep personal involvement in educational situations, Kurtzweil is right. But there is great danger in adopting such methods in any other educational area or framework. Moreover it seems that Korczak himself was greatly exaggerated in his belief in the justice of "public opinion" and the judgment of children. Educational literature is full of examples of harsh bias on the part of "public opinion," and the unconsidered, cruel, and agrressive judgments of children.

Yet it is not only the results of these judgments that concern us, but their analysis and the conclusions which can be drawn from them. An interesting example of this can be found in an article by Ada Poznansky- Hagery that analyzes liking and disliking tests conducted by Janusz Korczak at the two other children's institutions,[27] that is, Vered, a Jewish institution for abandoned children, and Beitenu, an institution for children who had been raised by their families until the age of between three to four years. Korczak called each child separately and asked him about his attitude toward the children in the group, including himself. Once the child had given his opinion of the other children, he was asked to explain each response. Ada Poznansky-Hagery rightly noted that this referendum was very similar to the sociometric test commonly used today, except that in modern sociometric tests children are not asked to explain their likes or dislikes. She wrote:

> The inclusion of these explanations by Korczak permits the drawing of conclusions which go beyond the framework of formal problems arising from the structure of the children's group, and are applicable to more general psychological problems.[28]

Indeed, a number of interesting facts arise from the summary of Ada Poznansky-Hagery. The deserted children at Vered were far more parsimonious in their exhibitions of liking and more frequently exhibited dislike than their peers at the Beitenu institution. More than half of the reasons given by the Vered children in explanation of their liking appear under the classification of "Lack of aggression," while in Beitenu this class of explanation is very small. The author noted that among the children of Vered it was very clear that there were "few requirements." In order to be liked, one had only to be quiet, evoke no fear, and not be a dangerous opponent. Sometimes these requirements were truly minimal: One child liked a certain friend because he "rarely" hits, and another because he did not hit "today." There were even occasions in which a child's reason for liking a friend was that "He cannot hit now because he is ill."[29] In her analysis of his matter, she noted:

> This surprising proliferation of 'negative reasons', and the great difference between the children of the two institutions in this respect, (54% in "Vered" as compared with 4% in "Beitenu"!) faithfully testify to an emotional degradation and an inability to establish positive emotional ties—the fate of children deprived of maternal care during their early formative years. Such were the deserted children at "Vered" who were raised in institutions from birth. Lack of affection caused a child to give up all expectations of love, cooperation or good will, so that he was content when others did not attack him.[30]

These findings, which predated Bowlby's research on separation from the mother, point to many of the conclusions at which Bowlby arrived in his later methodical researches.[31] Bowlby showed that maternal deprivation during infancy adversely affected the development of personality and impaired social and other skills. Through his observations and by means of these tests of liking, Korczak, too, became aware of these phenomena. Like Bowlby, he, too, analyzed the various aspects of the family's contribution to the growing child, and understood that its role boiled down to three central issues:

1) Ensuring the fulfilment of immediate biological needs, such as food, warmth, a roof, and protection from dangers.
2) Ensuring an environment in which the child will be able to develop his physical, spiritual, and social talents in full, so that he will be able, when he grows up, to cope efficiently with his physical and social environment. For this purpose he requires an atmosphere of love and security.
3) The function of the father and the mother as figures that are internalized in the process of building and shaping the personality of the child.

Korczak attempted to provide these three essentials in his institutions by creating a protected and secure atmosphere, providing food and meeting the biological needs, attempting to create an initimate family atmosphere—and mostly by establishing an environment of love and security.

The summaries of these like–dislike questionnaires indicate that children easily form and express their emotional attitude toward their peers, and that they do so without hesitation and with great honesty. Hence one can ascribe a great measure of reliability to their responses and the results of the questionnaire thus reflect the actual social structure of the group or the institution.

An interesting phenomenon revealed in the questionnaires was that the group's opinion of the child and the child's opinion of the group are two unrelated phenomena. The children found it very hard to evaluate themselves and were almost incapable of self-judgment. Even more important was the fact that the group was capable of sensing any changes in the character of the child and of expressing them clearly. Korczak took great care of the organization of his institutions, and even in the most difficult hours of the Second World War with all its horrors, his institutions were always in perfect order. The lives of the children and their work were determined by a written constitution that could not be appealed. Precise and meticulous records were kept of all duty shifts, of the work units, and of the cleaning arrangements. Detailed protocols were kept of all activities, and everything was recorded and registered.

The institution's Annual was published every year from the date of the institution's founding throughout the years of its existence. This Annual included the reports of the guardianship-committee; the institution's budget; reports of important events; the doctor's notes; the fiscal report; transcriptions of lectures, conversations, and cultural activities; reports of members' trials; and copies of the pedagogical diaries of teachers who visited the institution. Korczak took great care to keep up his records and viewed the dozens of well-ordered files, marked with consecutive numbers and dates, as first-class pedagogical raw material, awaiting the processing of the scientist who may use it to establish the principles of an appropriate educational method, and to derive general conclusions of great importance for the theory of education.

Korczak reserved a special place for the role and function of the child-duty-officer at the orphanage. The choice of a duty-officer was to be made with great care. In any group of children there are clever, energetic, impudent, and egotistic boys, who wish to control their friends. These children repeatedly offer the instructor their services. An educator without conscience, who does not properly appreciate the "little" things and the needs of the children, is liable to give such a child-duty-officer a great deal of authority, and such a child might then become the terrible sergeant of the dormitory-barracks. Such a duty officer "manages" the children more easily than an adult. They are more afraid of him than of the educator for he is one of them and knows everything. He usually nominates a few helpers and stand-ins, and he commands, betrays his opponents, and appears as a responsible person before the educator.

Korczak warned of the phenomenon of the tiny tyrant and his gang and claimed that the violence of negative forces might become entrenched in the orphanage and poison the atmosphere, ruining the children's relationships—both among themselves and between them and their educators—thus destroying the life of the institution and leading to a dense atmosphere of deceit, coercion, evasion, pressure, violence, covert retributions, false betrayals, fear, and suppression, eventually even giving rise to epidemics of criminal acts. This warning, however, was not intended to detract from the importance of the child-duty-officer, but only to emphasize that the choice of a duty-officer was a matter of considerable gravity which must consider the merits of the child, his character, and his motives.

Korczak also ascribed great importance to the private property, money, and other personal effects of the children. The children were paid wages for certain jobs, and Korczak stressed that they must be educated from an early age to know the meaning of money and to recognize its necessity, but not to view it as an end in itself. Their attitude toward money and private property must be realistic, and the child must be taught to know the value of money in the world beyond the orphanage.

As to the child's private property, it must not be viewed according to some objective criterion of value, but rather according to the child's own subjective estimation of it. Korczak fought the contempt which educators have for objects that the child collects, his "treasures," which they deem to be without value because they have no material worth. He castigates those who know the "price" of everything but do not know the "value" of anything. Korczak stressed that:

> It is the educator's role to demand that every child shall have something which is not the anonymous property of the institution, but private and uniquely personal and that it will be possible to safely hide the object. We must also ensure that once a child has placed something in his locker he will be certain that no one will touch it. . . . I fear that a cruel educator, who is lacking in understanding or is foolish, will in certain moments . . . collect all the "treasures" into one heap and throw them away, or into the burning furnace, and this is an inestimable wrong, a barbaric and criminal act. How dare you, illiterate ignoramus, feel free with the property of another? How dare you demand after such an act that the children love anything? You are not burning paper, but beloved traditions and lofty aspirations to a wonderful life.[32]

Lack of respect toward the property of the child teaches him to disrespect the property of others, fosters a wrong and imbalanced perception of material achievements, and might even occasionally give rise to a destructive-aggressive attitude.

Korczak took pains to provide every child of the institution with a personal drawer in the communal cupboard, to which none had access and all but the child himself were forbidden to take what was in it. In this drawer the child was allowed to place whatever he wished, whatever he valued, whether of great material value (an extremely rare prospect at the institution) or of great emotional value. The child was entitled to do whatever he wished with his possession. If he wished to swap it, give it away, or sell it, he was entitled to do so. In order to educate the child not to treat his possessions lightly and to prevent him from rash and ill-considered transactions, Korczak instituted the registration of transactions in a special "Notarization Book." The very process of registration was a delaying factor, which allowed the child time to deliberate. The child knew that he would not be able to change his mind once the transaction had been validated through registration.

Korczak placed special emphasis on punctuality, which he viewed as the first sign of human culture, believing that there were very few, and very exceptional children, able to develop positively without order and without punctuality, and that most children would fare ill without them. Thus, for example, if the serving of dinner was delayed by a few minutes, Korczak would call the workers to a trial.

With great humor, he wrote a letter emphasizing the importance of punctuality to the children of Israel:

> I have heard that many children are late to school, and that it cannot be helped. I propose that a rooster be placed in the yard and that he will wake the children up. And should the children fail to awaken to the call of the rooster, I hereby suggest that a cannon be placed in the yard, so as to awaken the children by firing. And if the children are late because they make their way to school very slowly, I suggest that planes be sent out to pour water onto their heads from above, ensuring that they run. And should all these measures fail, there is nothing better than to publish the names of the tardy children in the newspapers. And a last measure: let the adults set up a notice stating that they shall never be late and that they request the children to act in the same way.[33]

Special importance was attached to the activity of the children's court, which was comprised of five judges, three of whom would actively preside in court, that is, an educator and two children. The court based its judgments on a detailed constitution that included dozens of sections and subsections. It was convened once a week, and every month the verdicts given for every individual were summarized and publicly posted. The verdicts were registered in a book and read to all of the children. A child who wished to appeal a verdict was entitled to demand that his case be rediscussed, but not before one month had passed from the date the verdict was given. By adding up the points of each verdict (a high number indicated a greater misdemeanor), the behavior of each child could be graphically emphasized, illustrating improvement, decline, or stability.

When Korczak wrote the institution's book of laws and formulated its purpose, he wrote:

> If someone has done something bad, there is nothing better than to forgive him. If he did this bad thing because he did not know, then he now knows as the court has explained it to him. If he has done wrong accidentally, he will be more careful in future. If he has sinned because it is very hard for him not to sin, he will try harder. If he has sinned because his friends put him up to it, he will not heed them again. The court must protect the quiet ones, so that the strong and aggressive shall not harm them . . . it must take care of order, for the first victims of disorder are the good, the quiet and the honest . . . the trial is not the embodiment of justice, but it must aspire to justice. The court is not the embodiment of truth, but it must seek truth. The judges might be mistaken, they might punish for deeds in which they themselves have failed. They are allowed to judge their own acts as well, but it is a disgrace to knowingly pass false sentence.[34]

A special board was placed in a prominent place at the orphanage on which any child could write the matter that he wished to present before the court. Besides the subject he wished to raise, he had to write his name and the name of the defendant. In the evening, the court secretary would copy the requests into a special book and would gather testimonies on the next day.

These are the sections of the book of laws:

> 1–99—These ninety-nine sections state that the court does not pass judgment. Once the debate is ended, it is as if nothing has happened. But the traces of guilt obligate the accused to do his best not to repeat the deed.

> 100—The court does not pass judgment and does not rebuke or castigate the defendant, but the defendant's matter is added to the curve in the diagram of court punishments.

> 200—The accused did not act properly, and this is a shame. Although this could happen to anyone, the accused is requested not to do so again.

300—The accused had acted badly. The court finds him guilty and firmly demands that this act not be repeated.

400—Great guilt. This is the last attempt to save the accused from disgrace. Last warning.

500—The court finds the accused guilty and denounces him, for not respecting himself and his friends in the orphanage. The verdict, noting the full name of the accused, is published on the first page of the institution's newsletter.

600—The court finds the accused guilty, denounces him, and places the verdict on the court's board for one week, as well as publishing it in the paper.

700—In addition to everything stated in section 600, the contents of the verdict are also brought to the attention of the family as a warning that the accused stands in danger of being expelled from the institution.

800—In addition to the statements of the above section 700, it is also stated: The trial was of no use. Perhaps the punishments that were used in the past in other institutions will be of use, but these are not practiced at our institution. The accused is allowed one week for contemplation and for mending his ways. The verdict is published in the newsletter, is posted on the board, and the family is given notice.

900—Expresses despair from ever correcting the behavior of the accused. It is decided to banish him from the institution. He can stay only if he can find a guardian who is willing to vouch for him. The court shall then hold the guardian responsible for all of the child's transgressions.

1,000—Expulsion from the institution. The accused is permitted to request readmittance after three months.[35]

Of special interest are the formulations of the court's verdicts. These were mostly acquittals. Here are a few examples of such verdicts according to their types:

(a) The court does not pass judgment: 1) The court thanks Reuben for describing his transgression; 2) The court recognizes that Reuben could not have acted otherwise; 3) The court places the blame on necessity—on the conditions—on chance—on other factors.

(b) The court asks to forgive: 1) The court considers that Simon should not be angry with Reuben; 2) The court asks that Simon forgive Reuben; 3) The court asks to forget.

(c) The court forgives for it sees no malice: 1) The court forgives Reuben who did not completely understand what he was doing (saying); 2) The court hopes that Reuben shall not act similarly in future; 3) The court forgives Reuben because he did not foresee the outcome, because he did what he did unintentionally, because of carelessness, by mistake, through forgetfulness.

(d) The court forgives, taking the following extenuating circumstances into consideration: 1) The court forgives Reuben because though he acted out of false ambition and arrogance, he now wishes to improve his ways; 2) The court forgives Reuben because though he did what he did not out of fear of responsibility, he will now make an effort to be braver.

(e) The court forgives because the accused has already been punished and repents: 1) The court forgives Reuben because Reuben repents his act; 2) The court forgives Reuben because it considers that only goodness can set him right.

(f) An extraordinary verdict: 1) The court forgives, considering that Reuben tried hard but did not have the strength to resist temptation any longer. 2) The court forgives because Reuben has been with us for only a short time, and cannot yet understand order without punishment; 3) The court forgives because Reuben does not wish to say what caused him to act as he did, and had he wished to speak he could have justified his actions.

(g) Convicting verdicts: 1) The court determines that Reuben has behaved very badly, the verdict shall be published in the newsletter and posted on the board; 2) The court abolishes Reuben's rights for one week, calls the family to reason with him, and publishes the verdict in the newsletter; 3) The court expels Reuben from the institution.

It can be seen that the court does not punish, and that its main role is very often to explain, to advise, to warn, and even to thank the accused when conditions other than himself are to blame. The court not only wished to help the child recognize the objective social law, but also to help him search within himself for the motivations of his transgression, what brought him to sin, what caused him to behave in a certain way.

Korczak assessed the value of the court after a trial-run of one year. Summarizing the activity of the first year, thirty-five hundred trials were conducted. The least number of trials during one week was fifty, the greatest number—one hundred and thirty. During the course of that year, twenty-five notebooks were filled and published in the form of "The Court Newsletter."

Korczak emphasized that during the first weeks of his work at the orphanage he came to recognize that numerous little matters which bothered the children and that destroyed order never came to the attention of the educator. He recognized that there was a whole heirarchy at the institution in which anyone bigger or older was allowed to look down on anyone younger and to hurt him. The existence of the court solved these injustices as the court gave everyone an equal right to demand trial and justice.

There were, of course, various problems and difficulties. Thus, for example, the affairs of the court were seriously encumbered by the young children's "love of court" as they demanded that every little thing be debated. There was an obvious need to decrease the number of trials and clarifications in a plausible and nonabusive way, but this was difficult as it was not possible to decide that "nonsense" suits were not allowed, since there is no plausible definition of "nonsense." Thus, although at first the judges tended to belittle the complaints of the little ones, they quickly came to recognize that the measure of a complaint's importance is by the sorrow that was caused, and the child's sense of having been wronged.

The trials were very valuable in learning to know the children. Korczak stressed that he had frequently learned more about a child in one trial or clarification than he had during a period of months. Occasionally a clarification served to indicate necessary changes. Korczak wrote:

Thanks to "small" clarifications, I was forced to re-examine all the complex problems of the general communal life. The unsocial, antisocial type, the individual who refuses to adjust his customs and his tastes, would stick out, and forcibly demand an answer to the firm question: What to do?[36]

It was not always easy. A small, but bothersome, group of children exploited the court to their own ends, respecting it when it suited them and mocking it when it limited them.

Another problem was the great liberalism of the verdicts. No group of judges dared give out initial verdicts higher than four hundred. Moreover, the daily ties between the "judges" and the rest of the children caused considerable difficulties in the very process of judging and in the fabric of interpersonal relationships following the judgment.

At a certain point Korczak decided to temporarily abolish the court in order to effect changes and reorganize. A month later he instituted an appeal system; he removed a number of issues from the responsibility of the court of three judges and transferred them to a court committee numbering five judges; and he gave the children the right to call the adults, the educators, and the rest of the staff to trial.

He even made it possible for a child to put himself on trial. Thus, for example, Korczak brought himself to trial five times within a six-month period. Once because he had pulled the ears of a boy, once because he had expelled a boy from the dormitory, once because he placed a child in a corner, once because he had insulted a judge, and once because he suspected a girl of theft. In his trials, Korczak presented a written declaration of his actions, his motives, etc. When summarizing his evaluation of the court, he noted:

> I firmly contend that these clarifications were the cornerstone of my education for the role of the new "Constitutional" educator, who does not wrong the children, not because he likes or loves them, but because there is an institution to protect them against lawlessness, and the arbitrariness and tyranny of the educator.[37]

It should be noted that the judicial process was always accompanied by the encouragement and reinforcement of good deeds. Tokens of appreciation and esteem for good deeds were given to the children in the form of commemoration cards which they received for good work, for taking care of a new child, for helping a child in difficulty, for surmounting their own difficulties, etc. Special commendation was given for work at the institution. For every half hour's work the child would receive a commemorative card. Five hundred such cards provided the child with a flower card. A child who acquired twelve such flower cards was crowned with the honorary title of "Worker." The bearer of this title had certain privileges and was even awarded a monetary prize!

Besides the court, the following institutions were also active in Korczak's orphanage: the parliament, which went some way to realize Korczak's dream of the children's self-rule; a children's council, which supervised the institutions of self-rule; and an internal newsletter, which played a most important educational role.

The parliament numbered twenty-two elected delegates, and its sessions were held in the large hall of the orphanage and presided over by Korczak. These sessions were in the nature of public ceremonies. The delegates would sit by a long table covered with a green cloth, and the crowd of protégés would observe them and closely listen to their discussions. While the council was more in the nature of an administrative, supervisory, and executive arm, the parliament concerned itself with general, educational, and ethical issues. The members of the parliament discussed the general problems of the institution and authorized proposals for laws or for corrections to laws. The council was comprised of ten elected children and one educator who served as chairman and secretary and mediated between it and the pedagogical council. In certain cases, members of the children's council were invited to meetings of the pedagogical council. The council was elected for one year, and was responsible for determining the students' status, for supervising order and hygiene, for monitoring the children's institutions of self-government, for formulating new laws, and for rectifying the institution's existing laws and regulations.

It should be stressed that by this adherence to order, regulations, and the protégés' rights of self-rule, court procedures and the like created a democratic but very orderly way of life. Everything was clear; it was not subject to ambiguous interpretations and was known to all. A new child arriving at the institution immediately encountered the stable framework of the regulations and customs that ordered and defined every possible development. The bewilderment, the confusion, and the floundering of the new child were ameliorated by the very existence of such a precisely ordered procedure so that both the weak and shy and the strong and aggressive found their place. The weak, the passive, and those lacking in initiative found protection in this framework, an aid in organizing their personality, an impetus to overcome their weakness, and a fertile ground for social integration, which would have been extremely difficult for them without this stabilizing infrastructure. The aggressive child, who easily lost his temper and believed in the power of his fists, soon realized that in the new framework and under the newly defined conditions, there was no need and no use for his violence and tantrums.

The orphanage newsletter reflected the weekly affairs of the institution and included verdicts, plans for the future, descriptions of the events of the passing week, issues to be clarified, articles written by Korczak and the other educators, articles and notes written by children, and so on.

An important part of the material included in the institution's newsletter was prepared by the children themselves. Every day, at an appointed hour, one of the instructors would sit in the large dining hall, where the children spent their time before supper, and write what they told him about the events of the institution or the school as well as their wishes or feelings, plans or thoughts. Much of this material was later transferred to the institution's newsletter. The newsletter was an important factor in the life of the orphanage. The excitement of writing and the ritual of publicly reading the paper at the ceremonial party that was held once a week provided children with potent experiences and supplied observational material for the educators. Korczak wrote:

An educational institution without a newspaper is no more than the plodding and grumbling of the staff, without purpose and without hope, walking around in a circle, without direction and without criticism in all that pertains to the children. Something passing and circumstantial, without tradition, without memories, without a future line of development. The paper is the strong link, which joins one week with another, which unites the children, the educators and the workers into a single unit.[38]

In his conversations with educators, Korczak frequently spoke of the importance of the children's self-rule, and stressed that this self-rule fortified their feeling of responsibility, made them active participants in the care of the institution's property, its development and existence, and bound them to it. It also provided them with a knowledge of democracy and democratic habits, taught them how to chair their meetings independently, developed their social sensitivity and responsibility, endowed them with the technique of democratic institutionalization, and encouraged social justice. In Korczak's opinion, true democratic education cannot be brought about through preaching and lecturing on the importance of democracy, but only through the actual experience of democracy in the life of the institution.

It was Korczak's habit to involve both the children and the teachers in all the chores of the orphanage. In this, Korczak served as a living example for the teachers. He would bathe the children, cut their hair, trim their nails, and weigh them every week. It was his wont to join groups of children who were busy peeling potatoes, washing vegetables, and preparing fruit for marmalade, and he would both work and converse with them. The life of the orphanage, with all its variety, was his life, and he participated in every one of the many and varied activities.

Throughout his career, Korczak always strove to involve the educators in all the work of the institution. He noted in his diary:

> I am fighting to bring the orphanage to a state in which no difference shall exist between light or heavy work, between wise or foolish work, between clean or dirty—between work for dainty maidens and for simple folk. There shall be no wholly menial laborers nor wholly mental workers at the orphanage . . . he who says: "Work is dirty because it is physical," is lying. It is even worse when the hypocrite says: "No work shames its doers," while he himself chooses only the clean, white work and avoids all work termed menial, deeming that he must shun all physical labor.[39]

This involvement in the various chores was also very valuable in getting to know the protégés on a more direct and intimate basis. The educators would often join the protégés in various regular chores such as cleaning, shining shoes, peeling potatoes, and the like. In the course of mutual work, joking, singing, and friendly conversation, it was possible to learn much about the children, who on such occasions viewed the educator as one of them, felt friendly toward him, and were therefore more open to converse candidly with him.

Korczak opened his children's institutions to students of the teacher's seminary and to university students who received bed and board at the institution in exchange for part-time work. Once a week the educators held a pedagogical meeting in which Korczak also participated and in which they would mutually explore educational problems, report the results of their observations on the lives of the children, and raise questions for mutual clarification.

In the procurement of young educators, Korczak was helped by the Burse—the boarding school he had set up for youngsters who intended to continue their studies at colleges. These youngsters were among the main helpers in the chores of the institution and often infected all the other workers with their youthful freshness and great vigor.

In exchange for his bed and board, each Burseant was obliged to work four hours a day in his area of specialization. One contributed to the physical education of the children, another helped them with their homework, a third taught them Hebrew, a fourth organized games, etc. The working hours of the Burseants were flexibly tailored according to their study hours at the various educational institutions. Korczak met with the Burseants and the workers once a week. These meetings were devoted to various educational problems pertaining to the life of the institution. Korczak would analyze the problems, remark on them, and share his thoughts and views on the subject with the listeners.

In the life of the institution, the Burse substituted for paid staff and thus aided the educational work. It served as an excellent training and testing ground for the talents of the Burseants as educational workers, and those who stood out were encouraged to specialize in education and be accepted as educators at the orphanage.

Jacob Zuk was among the protégés of the Burse during a three-year period (1929–31) and for one year was also a novitiate educator intended, in time, for the role of educator at the orphanage. He related Korczak's attitude to the protégés of the Burse:

The doctor and Stefa viewed the orphanage as their life's work and the proteges of the Burse as their successors. They were always ready to instruct them, converse with them, introduce them into the secrets of the institution's organization and explain the phenomena and mysteries of child development. Besides the Saturday night talks which were devoted to clarifying events and problems in the life of the orphanage, the Doctor held individual conversations with the workers, and especially

with the Burseants he liked. During one of these talks he revealed to
us, that in his youth he had dreamt of founding a secular order of men
and women who would devote themselves to the service of the child.
The members of the order would abstain from family life, from lust after gain, etc. and their lives shall be devoted to the care of the child
and to saving him from starvation and from exploitation by parents and
relatives; and all this—so as to permit the child a few years of happy
childhood. The members of the order will live a humble life and wear
working-smocks, the color of which would be as green as the wild grass
which is refreshing to the eye and is satisfied with no more than a
little.[40]

The candidates for the role of educational instructor at the orphanage
were accepted after a strict screening procedure that assessed their personality, their motivation, and their willingness to devote themselves to
their role. During the final stages of candidacy they would report for conversations with Korczak and Stefa Wileczinska. All candidates, except for
the few who won Korczak's and Stefa's hearts with their educational personality, were asked to provide proof of pedagogical training at a university or teachers' seminary.

When it was decided to accept a candidate, he was first put on a
month's trial. During this month he was stationed at one of the fifteen
tables in the dining room. He dined with the eight protégés eating at that
table, and was responsible for them during the meals. Apart from this, he
was also employed four hours a day like all other educators, working in
the playground, the reading and homework room, the bathroom or the
dormitory. During the month, Korczak, Stefa, and the other educators
kept track of the candidate, observed his character, estimated his devotion to the work, and weighed the extent to which the protégés accepted
him. At the end of the month, a "general poll" was held in which all the
children cast a secret ballot deciding whether the instructor would per-
manently remain in his role or be forced to resign.

David Zilber described the experiences of such an instructor during his
probation month when he was subject to the "blackmail" of the protégés
on whom he depended. There was a child who sat by the table for which
he was responsible, who would thus wring his cocoa from him—that
sweet and aromatic brew for which he yearned so avidly, it being the only
delicacy in the dull and paltry breakfast. He wrote:

Life under the dictates of the youngsters was thus not always pleasant,
when one had to bribe them . . . and if someone were to ask what
association the word "poll" can evoke in me, I will immediately think
of a beverage which smells like cocoa but tastes like the poison which

Socrates was given to drink during the hiatus of the Athenian democracy, when in the year 399 B.C. his fate was decided in a general poll by 281 votes to 219, thus endowing him with eternal life.[41]

In his lectures to the students of the Burse and in his lessons at the two teacher seminaries in Warsaw, Korczak repeatedly stressed the great importance of learning by experience and of the constant educational action that shapes the good teacher. This was the reason why he so adamantly objected to the practice whereby directly after finishing their theoretical studies, seminary graduates immediately began working as fully fledged teachers, without first having undergone a preparatory period intended to gain experience or to seriously specialize.

He objected to frozen knowledge, the possessors of which are walking educational encyclopedias, pregnant with knowledge but barren of action, lacking that living knowledge which is mostly practice, good hearted diligence, and the willingness to constantly give. Hence his injunction that no educational work should be given to anyone who loves the book but not the child. He believed theory was not all. Moreover, the teacher must recognize that his knowledge, great as it may be, is tentative and open to change. The educator who clings to a system of knowledge without constant feedback from practice is dangerous. And indeed, Korczak frequently told the students of the Burse that there is no shame in not knowing, and that the great disgrace is in the convering up of ignorance, in evading and in cheating.

Korczak also stressed his strong objections to physical punishment. Thus, in his *Humorous Pedagogy* he wrote:

I am a total and uncompromising opponent of physical punishment. Beatings, even for adults, are no more than a means to dull and dim the senses, but are never of educational value. Anyone who hurts a child is no more than a skinner of carcases and an oaf. One should never hurt a child without warning, and then only for the most necessary self defence—once!—with the hand. Only once and without anger (if one really cannot do without it).[42]

When Korczak came to summarize his ideas about education at the institution, he stressed that there was no room for iron-discipline, petrified seriousness, forced coercion, or fanatic belief. On the contrary what was required was an atmosphere of tolerance to pranks and tricks. Korczak was also aware of the great danger of raising the children in a greenhouse, lest as a result, protected and cloistered from the lying ways of the world, their world should crumble when they eventually came into contact with the harsh existence outside. He therefore stated:

Shall we only equip him with the blush of shame and the silent sigh when life demands claws? It is our role to educate people rather than sheep, workers rather that moral preachers. What they require is physical and moral health, and health is neither sentimental nor generous.[43]

Korczak warned the educator against fostering excessive morality in the child as it was apt to turn him into a tyrant. He provided many examples of educators who were overly suspicious of their children without basis and who thus damaged both the children and their own status as educators. He stressed: "Educator, if you single-mindedly watch over the morality of the children, then I fear that you yourself are in the wrong."[44] At the same time, he instructed the educator in how to deal with those negative behaviors that are common in the life of the institution. He directed his attention to the phenomenon of informing on friends and pointed out ways to deal with it. He wrote:

Do not preach to him—one can instruct him in a more generous attitude; and if not, a number of heavy questions, and a decided lack of interest in the information he brings are punishment enough.[45]

He proposed a number of ways to deal with lies, theft, cheating, and other negative behaviors in firm cooperation with the children themselves. He was well aware of the limitations, and he wrote:

I can foresee the necessity of struggling for the creation of a constitution which will provide security for both the unscrupulous and the honest. I will call all of the positive values of the public into play and pit them against the powers of evil. Only then shall I begin programmatic educational work, acknowledging the limits of educational influence in this area. I can create a tradition of truth, order, diligence, honesty, directness, but I shall not change the nature of any of the children. The oak remains an oak, the willow shall remain a willow, the pine, a pine. I can perhaps awaken what has been lying dormant in their souls, but I cannot create something out of nothing.[46]

The permission to fight was an interesting educational-psychological act intended to put a stop to violence in Korczak's institutions. The protégés were given the right to solve small and isolated conflicts among themselves by fighting, on the condition that the children interested in such a solution register their challenge on the notice board. Joseph Arnon wrote:

The provision of this right stemmed from Korczak's assessment of the reality in each children's group, and especially groups of frustrated children . . . since the license to fight was known to all, most such challenged fights took place in public and the children took care to keep it fair: Equal forces, non-use of dangerous implements, etc. The official approval given to these fights minimized and almost completely abolished all mutual underground-vengeful activities on the part of the children. Cruelty and violence were prevented, and the witnesses assumed the role of inhibitors. The registration of the challenge provided the child with time for serious reconsideration: Is this way to "settle accounts" the most appropriate? The child could thus evaluate his motives before the act.[47]

Thus Korczak sought ways to dissipate tensions by providing possibilities for the direct discharge of moderate aggression, controlled by both the child and his peers. Moreover, Korczak acted directly in order to help the children overcome their difficulties, their aggressive tendencies, and their personal problems. On a certain day of the week, he set a period of admission during which his door was open to the children who could visit and converse with him. Many of the children availed themselves of this right to meet him, and these meetings would often turn into hours of confession during which the children told of their difficulties, raised their problems, and described those weaknesses that they found hard to overcome, such as lying, a tendency to fight, small thefts, and the like. Korczak was an excellent listener, and he knew how to talk to a child.

Orna Friedman-Diller told of wagers he would make with the children:

A child who participated in fights two-three times a day—would now do so only once daily. They wagered two sweets a week (if within a week the child should fight more than seven times—he had to give Korczak two sweets), and the bet was on for a period of four months. At first they only wagered over fighting inside the institution, but later also over fighting at school. The number of fights allowed was further minimized from time to time, until there was no longer any fighting. . . . It was very difficult for a child to drop the habit of lying. The "bet" on this matter began at 14 lies a week. During the weekly meeting, Korczak would ask the child if he had withstood the test he had taken on himself. The child answered yes or no, and no one checked whether he was telling the truth or not. Korczak would then add a few words of encouragement (spiritual food) and a number of sweets (physical food). And in this way—conversation, encouragement, love, patience and slow liberation—he would help the child free himself of his problems and instill him with a love for difficult challenges.[48]

This open-door pedagogy, the willingness to cooperate with the child, the assistance given to him in his internal dialogue, the psychological support intended to fortify his "ego," have made Korczak's contribution to the liberation and improvement of his protégés a very sound and serious one.

Although it is difficult to transport Korczak's solutions to problems in one educational sphere to another sphere, the very existence of his enterprise and the example set by his educational work serve to fertilize educational thought and urge creative educational acts. We must remember Korczak's words:

I agree, it is hard, one can even say, very hard—Everyone encounters difficulties, and there are different ways to solve problems. The solution shall always only be comparatively correct, for life is not a collection of arithmetical problems, all requiring one solution achieved by, at most, two methods.[49]

5

The Child is Father to the Man:
The Concept of the Child as the Focus of
the Educational Process

Children and young people are a third of humanity. Childhood is a third of life. It is not that children will become men in time—*They already are men.*

They have a right to one third of the fruit and treasures of the earth. They deserve one third of the victories of human thought.[1]

During his conversations with instructors at the orphanage, Korczak attempted to provide them with a set of educational rules, the basic point of which was the view of the child as a person worthy of respect who should be accorded full human rights. Should one lose sight of this basic point, the whole educational process is voided.[2]

Though it is doubtful if Korczak can be viewed as a paedocentric educator like A. S. Neill and his followers, his concept of education certainly has a great deal in common with individualistic approaches to education such as those of Jean-Jacques Rousseau, Alan Kay, John Dewey, A. S. Neill, and others, with whom Korczak shares the basic assumption that the child himself is an educational authority and that the essential aim of education is to fully develop his personality and mental faculties.

Like some of these thinkers, Korczak viewed the experience of the child qua child as the focus of education. He rejected the assumptions of traditional education that adult values should guide the education of the child and that school is a place where the child must prepare himself for his future life as an adult, rather than simply exist. Korczak rejected the discipline which had become such a basic concept in traditional pedagogical thought that it was sometimes perceived as an end in itself, rather than a means to academic and educational objectives. Korczak abhorred generalizations and dealt with each child individually, recognizing his specific talents, interests, and needs. It is for this reason that he rejected any attempt to impose accepted, predetermined forms of living and society on

121

the child. He feared the kind of conformity that breeds uniformity, blur-ring the individual worth of each child. He strove to discover the optimal conditions for a child's development and growth.

The essential requirements of Korczak's educational theory, stipulated that one must get to fully know the child, understand his spirit and unique world, and acknowledge his right to respect and love. Korczak railed against those adults who, belittling childhood, do not understand or know the child's world. Such adults, believing they know children well, may un-intentionally cause children unhappiness. Thus, as a consequence of this attitude of scorn toward the child, adults assume the role of sole judge of the child's behavior, movements, thoughts, and dreams while, in truth, they are incapable of perceiving his great sensitivity, his compassion for the pain of a slaughtered chicken, his love for a dog or a bird, his feeling for the butterfly and the flower. Children's doubts, hesitations, and tears seem inconsequential and unimportant to adults. Wishing to shape the child in their own stern image, they burden him with their concepts, de-manding that he comprehend and submit to them, and above all that he be grateful. Angrily, Korczak wrote:

> We hide our faults and punishable acts . . . pretend to perfection. By force of threats and severe humiliations we preserve the secrets of the ruling sect. The caste of secrecy is sanctified by the most sublime posi-tions. The child alone can be shamelessly exposed in all his nakedness and put to the pillory. We play a crooked game of cards with the chil-dren. We trump the weaknesses of childhood with the lucky cards of adult advantages. Gambler-like we fix the card pack so as to pit their worst cards against our best.[3]

Korczak fought against adult domination of children, and adult abuse of power and authority used to "lord it over" children. In Korczak's mind the tyrannization of the child, the enforcement of authority in every mat-ter of consequence, the adult command that brooks no argument, and the oppression of the child were all examples of bad education. Moreover, the child's feelings of helplessness in confrontations with adults teach him to respect power, and, as a direct result, to look down on anyone weaker than himself.

The child is totally dependent on adults, and commanded to obey in all things. He has no private property, and nothing that is truly his own. Even the gifts that he receives from the adult are supervised, lest he break, tear, soil, discard, or give them to another. "It is perhaps because of this that the child appreciates little things, so pitiful. . . . "

Stressing that adults evaluate and perceive the world differently from the child, Korczak demanded respect for the child, for this lack of knowledge and his great efforts to know, for his defeats and his tears, his tiny and humble possessions—his toys, his working tools, the pebbles and butterflies that populate his world. Korczak wished to make childhood a secure and joyous period in the life of man. How can the child be expected to grow into a socially responsible adult if he is denied a full life during the fleeting hour of his childhood. "Clumsily, we think of the years as of greater or lesser maturity; (yet, in truth), no day is immature. There is no hierarchy of age and pain and happiness, hopes and dissappointments cannot be graded."[4]

Korczak differed from Rousseau in that he recognized that the adage "man is good by nature" is not always right, and that among children one can find the entire range of humanity: the good and the bad, the talented and the useless, the gay and the somber, the sociable and the reclusive, the kindhearted and the depraved. In order to recognize the unique quality of any child, one must first get to know and respect him.

Each child carries his own particular world within him, his own needs and wishes, hopes, and dreams. The educator is obliged to respect this unique world, while helping each child to discover the beautiful and the sublime that he carries within him. Korczak was well aware of the difficulty of getting to know the child, of penetrating the secret of his maneuvers and changing moods, of understanding the essence of his joy and the meaning of his sorrow. He wrote:

The child is like spring, or the sun. The weather is wonderful, and all is joy and beauty, or suddenly, a storm, lightning, a rolling, then thunder cracks . . . and the tower seems to be in fog, immersed in a great darkness. No great joys, no great sorrows. Dullness and somberness . . . our joys and sorrows ride like a storm, while their joys and sorrows, plod along.[5]

Korczak wrote of the child's great sensitivity, of how easily he was impressed and how quick to anger, to love, to hate, to cry, to admire. The child's heart is open to the world. He attends its sounds and views its sights, creating his own personal world from these impressions. In this the child is akin to the poet, who is open and strongly emotionally aware and whose only wish is to shape the primal matter of his emotions. Korczak wrote:

A poet is a man who is very happy and very sad, who angers easily and loves deeply—a person who feels strongly, is easily excited and quick to empathize; and such are children. A philosopher is a man who contemplates and deliberates, who wishes to know how everything really is; and again—such are children. Children find it hard to say what they feel and what they are thinking, because speech requires words. And it is even more difficult for them to write it down. But in truth, children are poets and philosophers.[6]

These children, whose feelings are strong and whose sensations are intense, have no one to whom they can express their experiences, their doubts, their childish concepts. Adults always seem to be occupied in far more important matters than those which concern children. The child wishes to tell the adult of an Eskimo and a dog, of a victor and an innocent victim, of a bird and a flower, and the adult, from his great height, offhandedly delivers the verdict to the little creature at his side: "Nonsense." And as Korczak so nicely put it:

You (the adults) say: We are bored by children. You are right. You say: Because we must lower ourselves to their concepts . . . in this you are mistaken. It is not this which tires us, but rather the fact that we must climb and rise to their concepts. Climb, stretch out our hands, stand on tiptoe, reach out, so as not to hurt.[7]

These words of Korczak testify to his clear awareness of the fact that childhood is not a period preparatory to life, but an essential and integral part of life itself, which cannot be measured by its usefulness for adulthood, but is absolutely valued for itself, like any other period in the life of man. Throughout his educational enterprise, Korczak strove to realize this concept which he expressed in his book *Humorous Pedagogy*: "When shall that happy hour come when the lives of adults and children run along two parallel lines?"[8] Based on this concept, Korczak demanded that children be awarded the "Great Bill of Rights" (Magna Carta Libertatis). This is a child's bill of rights, and it includes the following three basic rights from which all other rights can be derived: "1. The child's right to die. 2. The child's right to the present. 3. The child's right to be what he is."[9]

Although Korczak knew that the first right entailed great pain, he claimed that true human dignity and freedom demand that man be master of both his death and his life. Deprive a man of the right to die and you have deprived him of control over his own life. Thus, Korczak wrote that:

A mother's burning love, which is both wise and balanced, must allow the child the right to die young, to complete life's cycle not in sixty orbits of the earth about the sun, but in one spring or three. . . . "God hath given and God hath taken away," says the son of nature who knows that not every grain gives rise to a stalk of wheat, not every chick hatched of an egg is fit to live, and not every bush is father to a tree.[10]

This right, however, is very problematic, and the debate as to the right of any man, not only a child, to take his own life, still goes on and will probably never be settled. Yet Korczak had no intention of legitimizing suicide. It seems that he intended more of a potential right, a realization of liberty as a theoretical option rather than as an actual practice.

The option of death was always alive in Korczak's world. In his personal life, he was frequently given to thoughts of suicide, and on a more philosophical level, he believed that eugenics could be a solution to some of the suffering, woes, and agonies of human beings in our world.[11]

Beyond the basic rights of self-actualization, deciding one's own life and fate, and living in the present, Korczak posited another central right of great importance: the right to express oneself and one's thoughts and to participate in all decisions pertaining to one's life. Although to a certain extent this latter right can be derived from the three basic rights, Korczak gave it particular stress because of his belief that "When we (the adults) grow to dignity and trust, and when the child himself shall believe and say what his right is—then shall there be fewer riddles and mistakes."[12]

Korczak appreciatively mentioned a long list of prominent educators whose common virtues are their struggles to free the child, the importance they ascribe to him, and their attempts to radically change the binding and oppressive traditional education, which presented goals external to the child's world, and was limited to a certain lump of lifeless knowledge and formal achievements, unable to discern that "a well patched sock is equal to a well written page, and an imperfectly peeled potato is equal to a lesson wrongly done."[13] Despite Korczak's disagreements with the educational methods of Rousseau, Pestalozzi, Froebel, and Tolstoy, he appreciated their important contributions to the liberation of education. He wrote:

Rousseau will not allow children younger than 14 to be taught; Pestalozzi wished to simplify learning to such an extent that every mother could become a teacher; Froebel transferred teaching to the kindergarten; and Tolstoy uses a number of examples to prove that it is not children who must learn from us but we who must learn from them. The Dalton method is the right one—the traditional school must abdicate in favour of self-learning, self-criticism, movies, radio, concerts, lectures by different lecturers, outings, theatre—let each take what and as much as he wishes. Otherwise, there is only coercion and boredom and rebellion. A war between the world of the little ones and the world of the big ones.[14]

Korczak's educational concepts are often similar to those of John Dewey. Like Dewey, he, too, believed that education means the growth of a person out of his own world of experiences and memories. He is often pragmatic in his approach to education. Rather than deal with an abstract model of the child, he dealt with the individual child whose personality he valued for itself. The educational method he espoused was that of experiment, direct action, and experience in the belief that actual learning comes about mainly through a set of tangible, planned, and meaningful actions. Repeatedly Korczak stressed the uniqueness of the individual and upheld individuality as a supreme value.

Though Korczak's and A. S. Neill's educational theories have much in common, there is a basic difference between them, which has been described by Joseph Arnon in his analysis of innovations in English education. Arnon wrote:

> Theoretically, Korczak fought for the rights of the child in society, under any form of social rule, while in practice he fought for the rights of the child under a capitalist regime. Neill, however dreams of the liberation of the child and his emotional, sensual and instinctive world. He rebels against the bonds of morality which enslave minds and hearts. He places himself above society and the social order—he is an anarchist without being aware of it.[15]

Moreover, while paedocentric individualism is central to Korczak's educational ideal, he aspired to go far beyond it, envisioning his protégés as free and active persons, who live full individual lives in the midst of society, and whose very existence and image realize a faithful moral and human vision.

In some respects Korczak's educational concepts are similar to Buber's dialogical educational philosophy. Korczak's attitude to the child can be characterized as a Buberian "I-Thou" relationship. Like Buber, for whom the Thou is revealed to the I in all its individuality and uniqueness, so Korczak viewed the child as a person of equal value who fully confronts the educator and is not inferior to him, who is not in need of completion nor is given to the educator's manipulation. There are no barriers of purpose or of level or of quality between the I and the Thou. Only when barriers dissolve and dissipiate can any true meeting take place,[16] that is, a meeting in which two subjects act and are acted-on by each other. Indeed, Korczak's vision of the meeting between teacher and student is just such a meeting of mutual influence.

However, even Buber himself had already sensed the existence of certain situations and areas where this mutual affiliation is curtailed. He wrote: "There are certain 'I-Thou' relations which by their very nature are not allowed to fully mature, for should they do so they shall forsake the uniqueness of their nature."[17] Such situations are the educational and medical situations. The relationships between doctor and patient or between teacher and student (both characteristic of Korczak, who was both physician and educator) are subject to the limitation that exists in those practical areas, where the affinity is the "product of purposeful action intended and directed from one to the other"[18] The educational affinity, and the doctor-patient affinity, are destined to remain forever unfulfilled in all that concerns the mutuality of the relationship. Total mutuality would destroy the educational relationship. The educator, who wishes to aid the student in realizing the positive potentials inherent within him, must always direct his student's heart, both as it actually is and as it will potentially be. Buber defined the educational situation as bipolar, one with the student at one pole end and the teacher at the other. This means that the teacher is aware of his influence both at the student's pole and at his own pole; an educational attitude that Buber termed "encompassing."[19]

When "encompassing," the teacher alone knows and feels the opposite pole. The educator is aware of his student's learning, while the student cannot become aware of the educator's teaching. The educator stands at both poles of their mutual experience, while the student remains only at one pole.

Although Korczak did not aspire to such philosophical-theoretical formulations of teacher-student relationships as 'encompassing" and he remained bent on a more concrete description of the texture of relationships, an examination of his attitude to theoretical generalizations indicates that this is indeed his educational conception. He, too, thought that in the educational situation, both educator and student regard each other as unique, real, and tangible beings. While this honest mutuality is the basis of educational affinity, for it opens a window to the student's heart, at the same time, it is also a one-sided "encompassing," preserving the "distance" on which the ability of the educator to assist in giving birth is predicated. It is within this relationship that the educator discovers his student, learns what special measures are required in order to develop the student's powers, and becomes aware of his own limitations.

Thus, Korczak embraced the way of dialogue when he rejected all non-dialogical methods such as coercion, indoctrination, punishment, and the like, which are contrary to dialogue and prevent dialogue. Korczak recognized that the dialogical approach fosters trust in the protégé. The educator is no longer perceived as an external agent who wishes to shape the student to social, political, or personal ends, but as someone who shares the student's life, shows an interest, and accepts him as he is, wishing only to help him realize his inherent potential and introduce him to the world and to knowledge.

In contrast to the "I-Thou" type education which is based on dialogue, the traditional education that Korczak criticized is of the "I-It" type, characterized by relationships of utility, oppression, and external coercion. Korczak wrote about such relationships bitterly:

> None but us. We alone are everything. It is we who know the ways to success, we who provide instructions and give advice. We who develop the advantages and block the failings, we who direct, embetter and improve. He is nothing, we are everything.[20]

Korczak's own dialogical stance can be seen in his words: "When I talk or play with a child—two moments, of my life and his, equally matured, are woven together."[21] Because of this dialogical approach, and out of respect and appreciation for the child, Korczak shied away from any attempt to beautify reality, to provide the child with illusions, to hide the truth, and weave tall tales in the futile hope of avoiding the sorrow that knowledge may bring. Korczak wrote:

> We are tempted by the illusion that the child will be content with the view-point of an angel for long—that perception wherein all is simple and good and wise—that we shall succeed in hiding ignorance, weakness, contradictions and our own failures and mistakes—as well as the fact that a formula for happiness does not exist.[22]

Such an approach, though seemingly for the good of the child in his wish to avoid anything that might darken his joy and rend his dreams, actually disrupts dialogue, diminishes trust and respect, and introduces an element of untruth, which shatters the immediacy of the relationship and weaves the educational attitude into the "world of objects." The child's trust in the educator is broken and is replaced by suspicion and evasiveness.

> They know something. They are hiding something. They are not what they say, and they demand that he too not be what he in fact is. They who praise truth are themselves liars who uphold lies. They speak to children with one voice, and among themselves with another, and they become very angry when the child wishes to understand this life. They want the child to remain gullible and they are happy when by an innocent question he reveals his ignorance. Death, life, money, truth, God,

woman, wisdom, all carry the taint of falsehood. It is a kind of ugly riddle, an evil secret. Why do they refuse to say how it all really is?[23]

The essence of the dialogical encounter is the true affinity realized in the meeting of I and Thou. Should a lie be introduced into this "between," the I-Thou affinity will evaporate, and the false attempt to protect the child will be self-defeating.

Do you wish the realization to come suddenly, that with a brutish fist the world should also crush all the ideals? Is it possible that once he discerns your first lie, he will not stop believing all of your truths?[24]

Korczak did not formulate any particular educational philosophy, both because he had no inclination to do so and because he viewed the formulation of such a theory as a potential danger to education in that it might freeze living processes and dynamic relations into fixed theoretical schemes. It may also lead educators to forsake the constant and immediate contact with the educational act itself by becoming a mere reference. Korczak stressed that:

One can learn the theory of education by rote, but an understanding knowledge of its secrets is not thus attained, rather it is a way of life based on individual personal experience.[25]

6

The Growth of Spring: *Rules of Living*

I have weighed and measured a hundred children every week—and always with happy excitement. The two hundred grams and quarter centimeter of growth per week—these are the growth of spring and the future of life reborn.[1]

One morning Korczak awoke from his slumber at the orphanage. A sharp cold prickled his bones. He sat up in bed and saw that the windows were open. It was raining heavily outside, and the protégés of the orphanage stood in the dormitory, their satchels on their backs, all ready for an outing. He tried to prevent them from going out in such violent weather, but they insisted, pleading and attempting to convince him until at last he granted them permission. On their return Korczak reported:

Well—it was wonderful. One of them sank in mud up to his hips. A soldier allowed them to shoot with a gun. The rice was burnt, but it was even tastier. Those gentlemen in the village did not think they would come and were very surprised . . . gave them some tea. They played ball with a racket. On their way home they were chased by drunks. They did not bathe in the river, kept their promise. It was very nice.
—But you got wet.
How much darkness and sunlight must rule the soul, so that the cold rain shall have no dominion. And what do we have—what program—for children and youth, not for rainy days particularly, but for smiling, sunny ones, for the great springs?
We have school examinations in store for them.[2]

Korczak understood to what extent we do not understand, to what extent we have no youthful program for youth, to what extent we attempt to force our tired, conflicting, sober, and pragmatic adulthood on children. Adults are busy with their many worries and have no time to instruct the child, who taking his first steps in the walks of life, is full of anxiety, wonder, and curiosity. It is only rarely that an adult finds the time to answer the child's many questions and to explain things camly and

130

attentively; usually they dismiss the child with some offhand evasive remark. Sometimes they might even become angry.

Thus, Korczak decided to write a children's book entitled, *Rules of Living*. This book is neither an adventure story nor a description of a journey over the high seas, but it is nevertheless an adventure. It is a journey into man, a trip into the very essence of life. The way stations in this journey are home and the family, the street and the school, fun and the talents, games and the thoughts.

> Youngsters have matters of their own, cares of their own, tears and laughter of their own, young opinions and young poetry. Frequently, they hide things from the adults because they are shy, do not trust the adults or are afraid of being ridiculed. They love to listen while adults talk among themselves—and avidly wish to know. They want to know the rules of life.[3]

Korczak ascribed central importance to the influence of the family on the child and his future development. He knew that the first years of life have a crucial bearing on the formation of the child's personality, though his recognition of this important fact was not based on any scientific research, but rather on his pedagogical intuition. Today, thanks to modern psychological and pedagogical research, we are all aware of the crucial importance of the family's influence on the child. Not only does the child accept what his parents tell him, but he also introjects their figures when forming his own personality. The family provides the child with a framework in which he is able to develop and establish contacts with the world and other human beings.

Korczak understood the natural, primal and extremely deep ties of the child with his mother. He stressed:

> Even a very small baby is already capable of recognizing his mother. He cannot speak or walk yet, but he stretches out his arms to his mother. He recognizes her even in the garden when she approaches— and laughs to see her from afar. Even at night, he recognizes her voice, her breathing. Even blind children who have no eye-sight recognize her and say: Mother!, when they touch her face with their hands.[4]

Korczak recognized the great damage done to the personality of a child raised in a broken family, or outside the family—among relatives or in an orphanage. Indeed, modern research has now shown that the separation of a child from his mother at an early age has severe consequences for the development of his personality. The child is apt to be disturbed in more than one psychological area: a lower intelligence quotient, withdrawal from his environment, inability to establish deep ties with another person, attention deficits, lack of concentration, damage to his ability for abstract thinking, and the like.[5] Although Korczak did not scientifically examine the consequences of a child's separation from his home, he sensed the great damage done to him and wished to relieve his suffering both within the family and outside it.

When Korczak discussed the totality of relationships between parents and their children, he stressed that education must be based on the right measure of attention and supervision on the one hand and a great measure of freedom and independence on the other hand. He encouraged the child to share his worries with his parents and always ask for their advice.

> A rule of life is never to hide anything from the parents. Sometimes the youngster believes himself to be helpless and without advice, and the advice could have easily been given if only the parents had known.

In his *Rules of Living*, Korczak reserved an important place for the discussion of the street, with its many temptations and many dangers. He counseled the child to withstand these temptations and find strength in the test of the streets. "I know many who have not been spoiled by the street at all, but rather only hardened and strengthened in their will to be an honest, moderate and sensible person."[6]

The school occupies an important place in the life of every child. He spends many hours within its walls, thinks of it often and finds many joys and sorrows within it. Not everyone is capable of equal scholarship. Some learn easily and some have a harder time. But the difficulties and worries are also interesting and can stimulate thought. Thus, for example, the untalented boy who invented learning games, so as not to be bored:

> When I do my arithmetic, the numbers are soldiers and I—the general, the solution—a fortress which I must take. If the result is wrong, I collect my defeated army and make a new plan of attack—and lead the charge once more. A poem which I must learn by heart is an airplane, every verse I have memorized is one hundred meters, I will learn until I know it without error; and I fly the whole three kilometers of poem without faltering, it is so pleasant not to make a mistake.[7]

Through his careful examination of children's games and his excellent analytic ability, Korczak described a number of psychological explanations for play, which had been developed by other philosophers and psychologists before him by way of research. Although he never formulated his conclusions in the form of definitions and rules, nevertheless, it seems he identified with some of the theories that explain the psychological nature of play, such as the opinion of Friedrich Shuller the eighteenth-century German poet and historian, that play serves as a vent for man's surplus energy. Korczak was also enchanted by the formulations of Karl Gross, the German psychologist of the turn of the century, of play as a preparation for life. Gross claimed that through his play activities, the child develops his abilities and practices the knowledge he has acquired during the day. Korczak was also taken by the view of the Jewish-Austrian psychologist, Alfred Adler, that play is an activity which compensates the child for his feelings of inferiority. In the world of adults, the child is inferior, for he cannot, nor is he allowed, to act as he wishes. In his games, however, he creates a world of his own, in which he is the master and can act as he wishes.

Although avoiding scientific formulations, Korczak managed to intuitively arrive at the same results that other researchers had attained after long periods of research. He perceived the diagnostic function of play, and tried to analyze the child's nature on the basis of his play. He placed a great deal of emphasis on the importance of play as a means of both release and recreation, as well as stressing its educational values. Moreover, he viewed play as the realization of childhood dreams:

> I have observed and seen, that the little ones do not always willingly tell of their games, when an adult listens—they are afraid lest they be ridiculed, because they do not know how to defend their young dreams.[8]

Korczak recognized that:

> Play is not just the child's instinct, but especially the only area in which we allow him initiative to a lesser or greater measure. In play, the child sees himself as somewhat independent. All the rest is but a passing mercy, a momentary allowance, while play is awarded by right.[9]

Korczak discussed the function of play as a release for energy, and as a means of escaping from the dullness of real life. He saw play as an arena for imagination and creativity, and as a satisfying substitute for reality. In his characteristic humor, he noted: "Yes, the child prefers to play, even over learning grammar rules or the multiplication table by heart."[10]

Occasionally, Korczak became carried away, and it seems that his literary talent and his need for expression led him to extravagant theorizing. Thus, for example, he wrote:

> The child turns to play out of a driving need, escapes into it for fear of boredom, seeks a haven from the terrible emptiness, hides from cold

duty . . . the soul of a child becomes attached to a doll, a bird, a flower, for he has yet no more in his world, and the prisoner and the old man are also thus captivated for they no longer have anthing more. The child plays with anything which comes to hand, in order to kill time, for he does not know what to do, and has nothing else to do.[11]

Although there is an element of escaping from boredom in play, of passing away the time and of avoiding unpleasant duties, Korczak himself was well aware of the fact that these are no more than isolated aspects of the motivation to play and that play is not just the fruit of "emptiness," but also a vacation from rich and intensive action—not only an "escape from boredom," but also a channel for creativity. And play is not only a "time-killer," but also an excellent utilization of time in its richest and most enjoyable moments. "Not only because there is nothing more in his world" or because "he no longer has anything more," but also because this is the "more" in life, the borrowed experience, the borrowed dramatic expression of life that is sometimes the best and most enjoyable in it.

It seems that Korczak hits the mark in another description of play in which he portrayed games as:

A conversation, an exchange of thoughts, the weaving of dreams about a chosen theme, a dramatization of the dream of power. During play, the children express actual views, in the same way that the writer develops his basic idea in the plot of the novel or the play. One can often observe an unconscious satire of the adults . . . when the children visit, entertain their guests, feed their dolls, buy and sell, hire servants and fire them. The passive children seriously play at school, wishing for praise, while the active ones take on the role of the unruly and ill-behaved whose pranks often evoke group protests. Do they not thus unknowingly reveal their real attitude toward school?[12]

Play endows the child with a sense of achievement, of self-worth, of ability and capability in the adult world of limitations and prohibitions. It enables him to command troops and lead war parties when he leaves his home where he is insignificant and inferior. It enables him to sail great oceans and explore unknown countries, when all he really has are the rain puddles in the streets and the swamp at the edge of the neighborhood. It enables him to experience, to examine, and to see. For example, the child can learn the quality of flint-stones which, when rubbed together, give out a spark and light a fire; the quality of the magnifying glass which concentrates the rays of the sun; or of sound waves as he listens to the whisper of seashells.

According to Korczak, it is particularly because of the learning and experiential quality of play that adults sin when they demand of their children that the playroom gleam with cleanliness, serve as a showcase for toys, and be in perfect order at any given moment. It seems that even today Korczak's words have not been understood or realized when he said:

> Despite our prohibitions, the children's room is often a workshop and a junk yard, i.e. raw material for the execution of planned projects . . . perhaps it is not carpeting that the floor of a child's room requires but a barrow-full of yellow sand, a large bundle of sticks and another barrow-full of stones? Perhaps a wooden board, a cardboard sheet, a kilogram of nails, a saw, a hammer, a lathe, are a more pleasant gift than any toy. . . . It is imperative that the stillness of the hospital be banished from the playroom, as well as cleanliness and the anxiety for the scratched finger.[13]

Korczak formulated additional rules for living. In the chapter titled "Rich-Poor," he discussed children who grow up surrounded by material riches, and children who grow up in poverty. He discussed the role of money in the world of the child:

> The child is ashamed for his drunken father. As if the poor boy was responsible. And he is ashamed because he is hungry and because his home is very poor—I do not know why this is so. I cannot understand why, sometimes, spitefully, they mock their own torn shoes and faded dress, but at heart they hide their sadness and misery.[14]

Korczak taught his students to recognize a man through his being and not to judge by external appearances. He considered it a real sin to make generalizations, and he believed that wealth is not synonymous with good and poverty with evil. One has to get to know each person individually, and this acquaintance must not be a shallow one, but deep and thorough. One must examine a person's character, his words, his thoughts, his feelings, and his behavior before passing judgment.

As early as 1908 Korczak wrote:

> So long as we do not provide all citizens with food and shelter, so long as we do not enable them to develop spiritually, we are not entitled to the illusion that we merit the title of *human society*.[15]

In his *Rules of Life*, Korczak supplied viable tools for the humanization of society, for converting it from an egoistic, oppressive society based on coercion into a *human society*.

Korczak was well aware of the fact that death frequently disquieted the imagination and thoughts of children, and his conversations with educators, and a number of his notes, dealt with preparing the mortally sick child for death. He saw it as one of the duties of the faithful physician, who recognizes that he cannot save the life of the child, to lead him to his death with a loving hand, a soothing story, and a smile of illusion. The physician must not tell the child that death approaches if the child does not know nor understand what death is. It is better that he does not understand; let him leave the world in innocence and dreams.

In his conversations with Yerachmiel Weingarten about the death of children, he said:

> It sometimes happened that children sensed the approach of death and talked about it with a stupefying calmness. Possibly, this strange calm stems from the fact that childhood is so close to the time of birth, that the child does not lose many experiences at his death. It is possible that the life experiences of the child are limited and the phenomenon of death is less incomprehensible to him than it is to adults. Perhaps the belief in God, which seems natural among many thoughtful and imaginative children, has an effect on this. Possibly, there are mysterious reasons which keep many children from crying out or fearing death.[16]

Engraved in Korczak's memory and heart were the nights when he remained the single physician on duty at the hospital, by the bedside of mortally sick children, many of whom died in his arms.

This consciousness of death is, of necessity, another rule in the *Rules of Life*. Korczak believed that every child frequently struggles with the question of death and that we must be prepared to answer him, whether by explaining something of the unceasing rhythmic cycle of life and death, or by means of a story or fable that lightens the struggle inherent in this bitter knowledge, through identification with imaginary heroes and borrowed reality.

Korczak taught children a way of life in which they could overcome their own limitations and realize the good that is within them.

> I love difficulties. I want to conquer. I want to be the victor. I know myself. I know when to keep silent and when to command. I am a forgiving hero. I am lenient with others and severe with myself, and joyous: I am never embittered and never complain. I am as old as I am. I am not ashamed of my youth, nor of my thoughts or feelings. I will force others to respect me and the goal which I serve.[17]

Korczak was aware that the state, the church, society, and the employers all wish to subjugate the individual: "The state demands that one love one's country, the church requires an unshakable faith, the employer—undying loyality, and all expect mediocrity and submission." In the midst of these demands the child stands exposed to social manipulations. He is ordered about by the various authorities, threatened by them, and subject to their decrees. The *Rules of Life* that Korczak wished to give the child do not guarantee survival, but they do offer a chance for a better life.

7

Between a Pulse and a Heart: Korczak's Conception of Medicine and Education

> How wonderful it is that doctors and policemen are barred from dictating the number of times per minute one is allowed to breathe and the number of times my heart is allowed to beat.[1]

Korczak ascribed great importance to his experience as a physician and to his medical studies in Paris and Berlin. These studies provided him with the "tools" and the methods which he later employed and applied as an educator. They taught him to think of the achievements he had attained and accustomed him to a working day full of care and tiny efforts, yet simultaneously laden with strong hopes and big successes. They developed his will power and instilled him with the pain of ignorance and the joy of investigation and research, as well as providing him with the technique of parsimony, of discovering the little things and the order of details.

Medicine taught him the extremely important rule which the educator must heed: One must observe the child daily, in the golden period of his health, and not only circumstantially when he is ill. Only thus can illness be prevented and made harmless. His medical studies had also provided him with research methods and with the discipline of scientific thought. The educator, like the physician, must also be able to discern the changes that take place in the child, in both their external and internal manifestations. For both the physician and the educator, no detail is insignificant; they must carefully keep track of even the most seemingly random and unimportant detail. Sometimes a slight observation, which seems unworthy of note, can lead to the discovery of an important rule, and some trivial and seemingly inconsequential discovery might be linked to an important problem. Moreover, a slight complex can sometimes ruin the whole of the personality and destroy a great educational work in one fell swoop.

His medical training contributed greatly to his educational work. It taught him to link diverse details and contradictory phenomena into one plausible diagnosis. It gave him the objectivity necessary to observe phenomena without agitation, and the knowledge that treatment is not always successful and that a new one must be tried. One must never lose one's temper, but only continue to examine and persevere. There is a similarity between the roles of education and the roles of medicine. Both struggle for health, for the immunization of the child against disease, and for healing him of the illnesses he has contracted. One cannot apply the same treatment and the same medication to every individual, nor can one apply the same educational method to every person indiscriminately.

> The angry glance of the educator, words of praise, a warning, a joke, advice, a kiss, a fable told in reward, verbal encouragement—all these are medical means which must be used in greater or smaller doses, and frequently or infrequently—all according to the case and the individual qualities of the child.[2]

Korczak believed that an educator who had not experienced clinical or hospital work lacked several important qualities. He wrote:

> My role as a physician is to relieve when I cannot help. To stall the advance of the disease when I cannot cure. To battle all of the symptoms, some of them, and if there is no other choice—a few of them. This is the first rule, but it is not enough. I do not ask how my patient will use the health which I give him—for good or for evil.[3]

Drawing a parallel, Korczak was of the opinion that the educator has no responsibility for the distant future, but every responsibility for the present day. Despite the fact that he recognized that this conception may evoke disagreement, Korczak stood firm in his belief that although "the educator is indirectly answerable to society for the future as well, directly he is first and foremost answerable to his protégé."[4] Thus, even though the educator might find it very easy to belittle the child's passing day in the name of noble slogans for tomorrow, his main task is to foster the good that is in every child, despite weaknesses and failings, faults and difficulties.

As a physician, Korczak advised parents on all subjects pertaining to the development of the child, including growth, nutrition, illness, and even psychological problems. Thus, for example, he discussed diet and the changes which have taken place in the feeding of babies.

> When we served proteins and fats, we wished to force the organism to develop according to a diet we had especially prepared. Today we serve

everything: Let the living organism choose what it requires and what it needs, let it rule its realm by itself, the health it has inherited, and the potential energy of development.[5]

Regarding the issues of nursing he was truly revolutionary for his age in that he recommended that the mother order her nursing according to her and the baby's needs rather than by any schedule dictated by various doctors.

> How many times a day must the child suckle?
> Between four and fifteen times.
> How long can he be given the breast?
> Between four and forty-five minutes, and more.
> Some breasts provide milk easily, some with difficulty. Some are plentiful, some are sparse, some have a good nipple, some a bad one, some a vulnerable one. Some babies suckle gustily, some capriciously or lazily. For this reason there is no general instruction.[6]

In this area, as in many others, he was far ahead of the man who was to become the idol of mothers and their advisor in the West, Dr. Benjamin Spock, who in many of his suggestions and explanations came very close to the conceptions of Korczak.

Korczak devoted many chapters to instructing parents about children's diseases and various developmental problems. Besides his various suggestions concerning the constant observation of the child, he provided advice as to the recognition of various symptoms and the early detection of illness through an understanding of how to analyze the various changes in the behavior of a baby who is unable to express himself. Of great importance was his admonition to parents not to fuss over every little illness or cold, for a small infection immunizes the child against more severe infections and protects his immune system. No one would imagine isolating the child from the air he breathes even though it contains thousands of bacteria per every square centimeter.

He stressed that both parents and physicians were frequently concerned for the baby's physical well being, for signs of illness and wounds, for questions of nutrition and the like, yet far less attentive to his mental life. He wrote:

> Besides his vegetative life, we must clearly distinguish the personality of the baby before he is a year old, his mental life and his development . . . we are confronted with an infinite number of psychological problems, as well as problems which are in the intermediate region between the soma and psyche of the baby.[7]

Korczak attributed great importance to parental observation of children claiming that there is nothing better than these observations which can easily reveal phenomena that a physician's cursory examination will be unable to uncover. He told of a mother who brought her baby, who was no more than a few weeks old, to the hospital to be examined. She complained that it would not suckle. The moment its lips took hold of the nipple it let go of it with a cry. On the other hand, it willingly drank with a teaspoon. Korczak examined the mouth and throat of the baby and did not see anything. He asked the mother to suckle her baby. The baby took hold of the nipple with its lips, tried to suck then spat out the nipple with a cry. Korczak did not understand the phenomenon. The mother drew his attention to a strange inflamation in one of the gums. Korczak discovered a slight swelling and on closer examination located the husk of a seed. It turned out that a canary's cage had been placed above the baby's cradle. The bird had thrown out the husk and it had fallen onto the baby's lips, slipped into its mouth and become lodged in its gums. Were it not for the mother's perspicacity, the baby's suffering might have continued and the inflammation become more severe.[8]

Korczak spent a great deal of his time observing children, keeping track of their physical and mental development with the eyes of a physician and an educator. He observed the changes taking place in their bodies and noted any indications of tiredness or instability, changes in their posture, and the like. He noted down all of his observations, conducted statistical analyses, and drew a developmental graph for every child. In his diary, he noted:

Statistical texts have deepened our understanding of medicine. Statistics has given us the art of thinking logically and of objectively assessing the facts. After having weighed and measured the children every week for a period of twenty-five years, I have an incomparable collection of diagrams—profiles of children at the learning age and at adolescence.[9]

Korczak stressed that in education, as in medicine, one must observe the child daily in health and in sickness, in his joys and sorrows. Korczak applied this theory in practice. Observing adolescent children, he noted that many of them did not lift their legs while walking but rather shuffled along the floor. When he first noted this phenomenon, he became angry and wrote:

This elderly walk of a young girl seemed to me unnatural, ridiculous, ugly and may I add—contemptuous. Later, however, I noticed that this walk was not only natural, but also characteristic of children when they reach an age of accelerated development. They are simply walking so because they are tired.[10]

He closely followed the unstable posture of children at certain ages and their straightening up at another age, the paling and reddening of faces, the periods of calm followed by periods of irritation, stubbornness and lack of discipline followed by periods of peace. He stressed that:

> Much of the corruption surrounding the use of arsenic-based medications and orthopaedic chicanery would vanish from medicine, if we were only aware of the springs and autumns of the child's development. Where can one discover these if not in a dormitory?[11]

Korczak regretfully noted that instead of studying the child, it was common practice to rely on two or three articles which have been written about him and view them as authoritative texts. The smallest medical detail has had more volumes written about it than entire areas in the life of the boarding house. The prevailing method at the boarding school was one of preaching morality to the child rather than conducting a thorough investigation.

Korczak attempted to clarify various issues connected with the development of the child during adolescence and noted with regret that education and medicine have not cooperated in order to understand this period properly, and to explain the extreme situations revealed at this stage.

Korczak was aware of the importance of his many measurements of the children, of the graphs of average growth, and of the medical observations of physical problems, but he complained that:

> We do not know the meaning of preconsciousness, retardation and deviations in growth . . . we have honestly examined the sick child, but we have only just begun observing the healthy child. For one hundred years our clinic has been the hospital while the educational institute has not yet begun to serve as a clinic.[12]

Korczak's greatness can be seen is in his ability to combine medicine and education. He viewed the educational institution as a clinic not only for the ills of the body but for the whole of a child's problems—physical, mental, social, and behavioral.

Korczak stressed the importance of recognizing individual differences in development and shying away from any rules provided by popular instruction books or from generalized solutions which gave rise to false patterns of behavior. When parents anxiously asked, "When should the child walk and talk?" Korczak's answer was "When he walks and talks."

"When should his teeth emerge?" "Exactly when they emerge. The great fontanelle in the baby's cranium should close exactly when it closes. And the baby should sleep as much as it wants, in order to rest well."[13]

As a physician, Korczak provided parents with an explanation of the differential and individual development of children. He warned them against adhering to parental instruction manuals and various popular articles published in the newspapers. As an educator of parents whose main concern was the growing child, he wrote:

> Carriage numbers, seat numbers at the theater, the date at which the rent must be paid, and everything which has been invented by people for the sake of order, can be strictly adhered to. But for anyone who wishes to rely on a nature-book, and who lives with the aid of a mind schooled by the regulations of the police, it is only fit that all the great weight of anxieties, disappointments and surprises should fall on his head.[14]

His words were not only directed at parents and educators but at physicians as well. The central question that few have considered is: "What is a living organism and what does it require—this is a great truth, but it is still under investigation."[15]

Korczak devoted a great deal of thought to the question of heredity. He knew that heredity set a strict biological limit beyond which it is difficult for education to pass but refused to believe in congenital moral degeneracy. Rather, he ascribed many developmental deficiencies to a retarding childhood environment, an inhibiting family background, and a disadvantaged social environment. He believed that it is possible to create a therapeutic environment inside the educational institution, which would compensate for the child's cultural deprivation. He stressed that:

> A boarding school for orphans is similar to a clinic in that one can encounter all the illnesses of the body and mind. Where faulty heredity disturbs and delays recuperation, there is a risk that it might become a source of disease, if the boarding house does not serve as a moral convalescent home.[16]

On the other hand, because he recognized the central role of heredity in the development of man and because he was haunted by the constant fear of going mad because of the mental illness of his father, he adopted an extreme viewpoint as to the right of a person to bear children. He believed that care must be taken not to give birth to sickly, crippled, retarded, or demented children. Society must intervene and have the right to allow healthy couples to reproduce or prohibit those couples whose heredity is suspect from doing so. In his article "This and That about Children" he wrote: "Sterilization, in the German way but without the abuse of the Germans and without their exaggeration—is imperative."[17] Out of his concern for the future and a sense of responsibility for the whole of humanity, he stressed that the whole of society must ask itself who has the right to father or give birth and that it should adhere to its decision on this issue.

In discussing extremely defective children with Yerachmiel Weingarten, Korczak stated his position that children whose retardation is hereditary are doomed to a difficult and dark childhood and adolescence, to a life of degeneration and suffering and that in those cases where there are firm grounds to suspect that parents might give birth to retarded children, they should be prevented from doing so. Korczak's utterances on this subject were radical and amazing in their extremity. Weingarten quoted Korczak as saying: "I see only one way out of this scandal. It is recommended that such a defective-hereditary child throw a ball into a deep well, and ask his father to jump in and retrieve it."[18]

Korczak believed in selective breeding as humanity's hope for preventing the pain, sorrow, suffering, and agony of those people who are defective on account of their physical or mental heredity. He used the term eugenics (improvement of the human race through selective breeding) in many of his writings. Although it was always in the context of care for the child, one can occasionally discern further intentions of birth control, not only for preventing defective heredity, but also aimed at certain social-economic aspects. He wrote that:

> At the same time as we give birth to children we should also give birth to schools, workshops, hospitals, and a cultural ambience. I view fertility without check as a wrong and irresponsible act. It is possible that we are living on the eve of new laws which will be dictated by the rules of eugenics and the policies of population control.[19]

His great love for the child, and his desire to prevent his suffering and humiliation, sometimes transported him to the point where he advocated population policies, agreed with social laws intended to invade the private lives of individuals and families, and upheld the right of the authorities to determine the right of the individual to live.

In light of his position on this issue, his enthusiasm for the plan of his close friend, Dr. Zigmond Bichovsky, is understandable if frightening and abhorrent. Dr. Bichovsky also believed that eugenics could save humanity from barbarism and degeneracy and had devised a monstrous plan to save the Jewish people in Palestine by means of selective breeding. Korczak eagerly told Yerachmiel Weingarten of this plan and emphasized the nobility of Dr. Bichovsky, his fervent Zionism and his talent as a physician-psychologist. Dr. Bichovsky advocated a national-Zionist effort to bring the best European Jewish youths to Palestine. The Zionist Federation would supply these new immigrants with lands and employment and ensure their livelihood as productive workers.

> He has a precondition: all candidates are to be examined by teams of expert physicians and psychologists, in order to assure their physical and mental health. It is also important to conduct a detailed medical investigation of their origins and mental heredity over the last three generations. Such a strict screening procedure will enable the selection of only the best people for immigration. Persons of exemplary character, idealists who uphold the good of their nation and the good of the world. They shall give birth to a Jewish generation which will be healthy in both body and mind. The schools and the families which they shall establish in the promised land, will educate for a life of morality and culture and shall be a shining example to the Jewish people in the Diaspora, and to other nations.[20]

Dr. Bichovsky even went so far as to send a memorandum to the Zionist Federation in which he outlined his plan for Palestine to become the center of Jewish eugenics and for premium Jewish sperm. The Federation did not respond to his racist ideas.

In this respect Korczak is revealed as someone whose good intentions, which only sought the welfare and well being of the child, paved the way to a racist hell.

Korczak stressed that in order to prevent warped development, one must implement preventive education in the same way as one would apply preventive medicine. Medicine has taught us the great importance which sunlight, fresh air and open spaces have for the development of the child. Baden-Powell, the father of scouting, has taught us the importance of movement, social cohesion, scouting activity, and group conversation by the campfire under an open sky. Education must recognize this and instill these concepts into the life of the child. "The physician has saved the child from the grip of death; it is now the educator's duty to let him live and win his right to be a child."

8

To Touch without Burdening: On the Educator's Image

When school begins providing children with knowledge rather than advantages, we shall give the children Spring, rather than examine them[1]

The art of education is a very complex one indeed. It is the art of touching the student lightly rather than burdening him, enabling him to soar rather than putting him in chains, conversing with him rather than forcing him to accept preconceived opinions, offering him a choice rather than one set response, encouraging his questions without dampening his curiosity, and fostering him as an individual rather than shaping him in our own image.

For many years, Korczak followed the progress of teachers and instructors in training and attempted to understand their personality as educators. He observed one of them and sadly thought: "The poor man won't hold out, such a pity"; looked at another and sighed: "He'll manage, unfortunately, and will rage among children for many years, like some chronic epidemic of influenza, with dripping catarrah and an ache in bones and souls."[2]

In order to demonstrate his observations of educator-types, we shall examine a number of his diagnoses:

Different shades; types; personalities. Subject for a thick volume. One is full of doubts, a stickler who alternatively blames himself (rarely), the children (often), and the working conditions (always). A second knows, understands and is capable—enjoys his actions and accomplishments and does not care one whit that his achievements have been attained at the price of ruining gifted hearts and minds, and destroying the will to work, to read a book, to live. To bend or to break, to uproot—to stifle and train and force his own order as he has understood it or has been commanded to understand it. The cleanliness, the good manners, the duty of progressing, and even of developing physically.[3]

146

Korczak carefully chooses the *verbs* he uses in order to describe the activities of this type of educator: "to bend, to break, to uproot, to stifle and train." This is not accidental, and, in fact, enfolds his entire educational philosophy—"to work, to read, to live."[4]

In his attempts to uncover future educators, Korczak observed various classes at school, wishing to find out what type of child was more frequently nominated by teachers to social duties. He wrote:

> With great disquiet I saw how they force these social duties on ambitious youngsters with a jailer mentality, on obvious misanthropes, on active and sycophantic careerists, and finally, on loners, ascetics and intellectuals.[5]

The nomination of these types of children to social duties indicates the teachers' preferences and their social conceptions. Korczak contrasted these educators with persons of intuition and empathy, who have the ability to sympathize with another person's sorrows and conflicts. Often it was not among the professional educators that he found such persons, but among the general public, that is, craftsmen, laborers, and others. Thus he told of a waitress who was revealed as a great-hearted educator and a whore who became a nurse and subsequently worked for many years with great devotion and genuine educational involvement at a children's hospital.[6] In summarizing the essential test of a good educator, he poetically defined him as someone whose "thinking is like spring".

Korczak was deeply appreciative of the image of the devoted educator, whose whole personality is given to his work, and whose constant attention is given to the child and his well being. The educator, wrote Korczak, must know how to sacrifice all of his time, comfort and personal ambitions for the child. Korczak himself behaved exactly thus, always involved in the life of his protégés and giving them his entire being.

> I give of my thoughts, I provide advice, warnings and feelings, giving generously. At every moment, a child approaches with a different demand, request or question and takes up your time, disturbs your thoughts and upsets you. Sometimes you feel that while you are serving this bunch, you yourself are petrifying and losing your light-rays one after the other.[7]

Thus, the educator is obliged to know the secret of giving, the secret of surrender, the secret of devotion.

Yet, even if he were to devote all of his life to education, even if he were to give up his youth, even if he were to have no family and material cares and were to devote every single hour of his life to the educational ideal (as Korczak did), still one cannot but especially like one particular child and naturally prefer him over another. Yet we demand that the educator be objective, unbiased, and fair toward all children, though such egalitarianism goes against man's very nature.

> When he [the educator] comes home, which must be his private home, and cannot sincerely greet all of the children, has he not the right to smile at one? When he leaves the dormitory at night, and cannot bless all of them warmly, has he no right to sometimes bless one or two with a special word of affection—sleep, chum, sleep, little spark?[8]

There is no educator who loves all children equally, and any demand that he behave so is apt to only stifle the natural emotions of love and affection which are found in any man.

Every educator has certain types of children that he especially likes and feels warm toward. Each has his own "soul's Sunday-children," whom he loves because they are beautiful, pleasant, easy-going, happy, smiling, serious, miserable, grumpy, clumsy, orderly, obedient, or rebellious—all according to the set of the educator's mind and his ideals. And among all these, there is sometimes one child who is especially close to the teacher, someone for whom the teacher cares, whose tears cause him a special pain, and whom he loves more than others. In Korczak's opinion, a teacher should not hide his special liking for a certain child. The other children will understand and not begrudge it for they, too, have soul mates.

The choice of "teacher's pet" is not always a happy one. The teacher's favorite frequently seems completely worthless to the other children, and, when the teacher's choice is a very bad one, they may sometimes retaliate. Korczak described certain types of children who might worm their way into the teacher's affections, and wrongly evoke his enthusiasm.

> The poet, if you but knew, that the poetic child carries only one secret behind those large eyes and long, graceful lashes—the secret of tubercular heredity—possibly, instead of expecting some great poetic effusion, you would expect a cough, and instead of kisses you would award him with castor-oil as medicine. You would thus save him, yourself and the other children from many unpleasant moments.[9]

The educator's attitude toward the child should be that of a grown-up and knowledgeable friend to a younger companion. He must respect his efforts and his work, involve himself in his fate, and help him in planning his future. He advises the child, listens attentively to all he tells him, comforts and consoles him, and prepares him for life. But under no circumstances should this relationship entail any false tolerance, gentleness, or flattery. Quite the contrary, the educator must be firm and demanding in his relationship with the child, so as to raise him to be a brave man rather than a capricious damsel. He must prepare him for a hard life and must not provide him with any false illusions which shall never be realized.

Moreover, Korczak claimed that this pedagogical love is a genuine gift and no empty sentiment. In his opinion, the romantic-sentimental love of an educator for a child is doomed to be an educational failure, for the roots of such sentimental affection are to be found in the educator's psychological need for compensation and self-assurance and, being essentially egoistic, carries the stigma of weakness. Educational reality, however—and especially the educational work at an orphanage—demands a position of authority, requires balance, self-awareness and that the educator keep a watchful eye on himself and his students.

Before getting to know the children, the educator must first understand his own character, and recognize his abilities and limitations before making his own educational way. In his relationships with the children, he must act naturally, observe them closely during their more revealing moments, and become acquainted with the personality of every child.

> And you yourself? If you are not blessed with an attractive bearing and an iron heart, your attempt to shout down the children's noise will be in vain. A pleasant smile and a forgiving look—do not say anything at all; and they might calm down by themselves. Find your own way.[10]

The sooner an educator forsakes all sentimental notions regarding the child, the better. He must be careful not to develop overly optimistic theories about the effect of education, nor be too enthusiastic as to the responsiveness of the student to his educational efforts. Korczak did not believe in the omnipotence of education. He recognized its biological and social limitations and stated that the same range of characters that is to be found in the adult world is also to be found in the world of children. There are definite and inherent limits on children's ability to be shaped both intellectually and by way of character, and it is only proper that we should be realistic when planning educational action.

Korczak stressed that the educator should help his protégés adjust to the narrow and convoluted patterns of real social life, so full of hypocrisy, tyranny, and coercion, rather than prepare them for life in some sort of would-be heaven in which only peace and mutual cooperation have dominion. The students often resist the teacher's work even when it is intended for their benefit. They are defensive and sometimes even bear him a grudge. Moreover, it is a far cry between educational ideals and reality, between the desired and the extant, and hence the constant and severe internal tension and the great conflict that characterize the educational process. You wish them to be "honest and well-educated, while worldly life is often deceitful, and honesty is considered an impudence,"[11] laments Korczak.

Korczak was well aware of the severe attrition of the educator, who, in time, is apt to lose his enthusiasm and become a creature of habit.

> In the past, he was happy when an idea for a new game came into his mind, a surprise for the children. He aspired to inject life into the dull and monotonous routine of the boarding house, a new spirit, joy of life. And now he is pleased when he can hopelessly write: everything is as it was.[12]

The educator must uphold his authority and take care lest it be diminished, but he must not seek it nor force it on his children-protégés. He should not expect false respect nor make do with lip service from the students, and it is better that he refrain from emulating veteran educators.

> Do not require yourself to be a serious and elderly educator, who has let psychological book-keeping replace his heart and a pedagogical standard, his head. You have an ally in the magic of youth, yet you want to use grumbling and experience instead.[13]

Korczak disapproved of the educator who fears surprises, who makes use of an abundance of prohibitions and orders, and who approaches the child with suspicion out of an excessive concern for his morality. Such an educator tyrannizes his protégés and causes more harm than good.

One of the gravest faults which Korczak found in an educator was that of suspicion. Instead of remaining open and attentive to the child's experience and lovingly accepting his mistakes as he looks for his own way in the world, the suspicious teacher views all of the child's actions with distrust, does not encourage him when he fails, punishes him for the slightest mistake, and is quick to shout and scold, punish and castigate. Instead of being a faithful friend and guide, such an educator becomes a judge and policeman. Korczak severely criticized this type of educator:

> This is the way in which an educator degenerates: he belittles, he has no faith, he suspects, he spies, he catches in the act, he castigates, he blames, he punishes. He seeks easy ways to ward off this evil, he prohibits more frequently, his coercion becomes increasingly absolute, he does not perceive the efforts of a child as he carefully attempts to write a page or an hour of life, but only passes the verdict: bad. Scarce is the

light blue of forgiveness and common the deep purple of anger and chastisement.[14]

Although the plethora of prohibitions and commandments that such an educator issues to his protégés are seemingly dictated by his care for the welfare of the child, they are in fact generated by his excessive care for his own personal comfort and peace. Such an educator wishes to avoid unexpected and unpleasant surprises, and therefore tyrannizes the children.

The best educators differ from the worst ones only in the number of mistakes which they have made, the number of wrongs they have perpetrated. There are mistakes which a good educator makes only once, and analyzing himself critically does not often repeat . . . a bad educator blames the children for his mistakes.[15]

Korczak warned the educator against the wish to shape the character of all of his students according to a single template, or the desire that everyone should behave in accordance with one example. He should not attempt to instill everyone with uniform character traits, or direct everyone to ideals that he holds as especially worthy. Some of the children will masquerade as he wishes and mislead him. Others will be affected by him and follow the example he provides, but not for long. When their true character is revealed, it is not only the educator who will feel defeated, but the child, too.

The greater the effort invested in masquerading or submitting to the influence—so shall the eventual reaction be more violent; the child, once the truth of his aims has been exposed, has nothing more to lose.[16]

Honesty and the quest for truth are two central and indispensable traits for every educator. He must have the ability to admit his mistakes, confess to ignorance, and shy away from pretense and hypocrisy. He must teach his protégés to speak the truth and take care not to cause them to lie. He must not force them to divulge their secrets, lest they lie, or pressure them to express their emotions, for they may put on an act. He must never reproach them for having spoken the truth, so as not to teach them how to lie. He must respect the silence of children, for sometimes the silence of a child enfolds the greatest measure of truth. Frequently a child will not respond because he does not wish to lie and for reasons of his own cannot tell the truth either. One finds that, in its rebellion against lies, silence is occasionally an expression of true honesty.

According to Korczak, the educator's attitude toward his protégé must be based on respect for his work and efforts, on sympathy for his fate, and a sincere interest in his future. The educator must always perceive his student not only as of this present moment, but in expectation of the future as well; and it is toward this future that he must direct his education. The educator is enjoined to sympathize with his student's fate.

As a direct consequence of this perception and out of a deep recognition of each student's unique character, Korczak stressed that it is simply impossible to treat all childen in a like manner. Many children adjust to conditions only with great difficulty, submitting only when forced, and the educator must treat them firmly. Others find it hard to control themselves or their ambition is so great that they do not wish to work hard in order to adjust to the conditions of communal life. The educator must treat these latter children with care and encourage them to behave like everyone else rather than according to momentary whims. The proper approach to each child is a very complex thing, depending on the child's unique personality and his life expectations, on the openness of the educator, on the child's ability to adapt to society, and on his willingness to do so.

Korczak claimed that the educator's heart, his intuition, and his emotion, are more important than "intellect" and cold consistency. Korczak's biographer, Hana Mordetkovitz Olatchkova, related how Korczak gave his first lecture at the institute of special pedagogy in 1919. The students were amazed when the lecturer arrived leading a small child by the hand, and they were even more surprised when he notified them that the lecture was to take place in a dark x-ray room. The young child was frightened by the people and the dark. He shivered all over when he was asked to undress and stand in the dark before the strange apparatus. Korczak operated the machine and the students saw the child's quaking heart. Korczak then told them:

> Look well and remember, when you are tired and angry, when the children are intolerable and drive you out of your minds, when you are irritated and angry, when you wish to punish in a rage—remember that this is what the heart of a child looks like and this is the way he reacts.[17]

Of his own educational experience, Korczak wrote:

> When I see the eternal fire in the child, a light taken from the original fire stolen from the Gods, the spark of critical intelligence . . . a spurt of enthusiasm, autumn sadness, the sweetness of sacrifice, the energetic, joyous, trusting and challenging search for reasons and aims

... then do I kneel before him ... what am I to you if not a burden encumbering your free flight, cobwebs on your variegated wings, murderous scissors snipping at the growing buds?[18]

Though Korczak loved children and stressed this love as the basic principle of child education, he was opposed to any emotional excess and any overindulgence expressed in hugs and kisses. Korczak held his feelings of love for the child in check and expressed them by his many acts of devotion to his protégés.

Korczak relegated a central position to experience, to physical sensation, and to learning through doing. He instructed his students never to accept anything at face value, to experience everything for themselves, to deliberate, struggle, and discover. Olatchkova quoted his views on this issue:

No opinion should be absolute, or eternal. Let the present day forever be a passage from the sum of today's experiences to tomorrow's greater sum of experiences ... my experience, that is my past, my life, the sum of my subjective existence, memories of failure, disappointments, defeats, accomplishments and victories, positive and negative emotions.[19]

And, indeed, throughout his life, Korczak never rested, but continued to develop, continued to learn, continued to create his own image through constant contact with ever-changing reality. Throughout his life he was a man becoming, and he never tired of learning from life, from his students, and from his friends.

Korczak attempted to influence the development of the educator by personal example and by describing his own educational experiences. He knew that educational work was full of difficulties and that each teacher encounters his own unique problems and solutions. Any pre-prepared scheme of solutions is false, for every solution is right only under particular circumstances, and even then, only relatively.

Korczak stressed that, in education, everything was a matter of experiment, and that no fixed rules should be formulated for the educational act. One must neither set any permanent or definite patterns nor attempt to avoid mistakes and failures. The experiment should be carefully and cautiously set up so as not to endanger the protégé, but it must not be foregone. One should not force any ready-made patterns and educational methods on the educator.

Only one-sided, dumb and arrogant self-assurance conducts its experiments by way of a despotic coercion of its will and opinion. Yes, it, too, conducts experiments, but without knowledge or criticism. It attempts to force and constrain.[20]

This method of experimentation and personal experience were so important to Korczak that in the introduction to his book *How to Love Children*, he wrote:

> I fear that the reader will be content with believing me—if so—the book will only be detrimental to him. I therefore, precede and say: The way which I have chosen, though it is not the shortest and most comfortable, is the best for me, because it is mine, my own. I have found it with much effort and no little suffering, only when I understood that all the books I had read and all the experiences and knowledge of others, were false.[21]

Korczak was averse to anything which could petrify the dynamic process of education into a static reality capable of presentation in a book, an instruction manual, or a textbook. He felt the same aversion toward schools dealing in the art of books rather than the art of life. The students in such schools are required to learn history, geography, and natural science by rote. Anyone who fails to do well is considered a failure. And so as not to fail, they copy, evade, cheat, and pretend. Thus are corrupt character traits added to ignorance through the very ritual of learning.

Korczak compared actual science books with textbooks. While everything in the textbook is clear, simple, and sure, the science book is full of questions and reservations such as: "The matter requires further research for little is known yet." One finds many confessions of ignorance, of continued searching, thinking, and experimenting.

Korczak realized that there are millions of books and no one can possibly read them all, or know all that is written within them, yet he considered that an important precept of teaching is to provide the knowledge of where to look for a solution to questions. He viewed cooperative learning, mutual discussions, and learning from each other as no less important. He quoted the Jewish proverb: "I have learned much from my teacher, but from my friends and students more than all," and he added:

> The golden seeds of science are scattered everywhere. We gather together in order to seek them. One famous scholar once said: "I know that I do not know"—so let us not pretend that we are wise and all-knowing. Let us be frank and unashamed in frequently repeating that we do not know.[22]

Although Korczak recognized the educator's right to create his own educational method based on his views on education, he conditioned this right on the educator's ability to prove that his educational method or his views are grounded in his actual working experience and in his educational work. He must prove the rightness of his position, provide examples, and verify his conclusions. The motto of the educator should be a creative "I don't know" because he is not content with his ignorance but uses it as only a springboard to investigation, unconventional thought, the posing of questions, and the search for truthful answers.

One should stress that in all of his writings, Korczak's method always led from practice to theory, and that he was never content with theoretical assumptions without actual application, verification, and experiment. Addressing the various educational theories expounded by educational philosophers, he noted that theory doubtless enriches the intellect but that this is not enough. Out of the various theoretical assumptions, he chose only those which suited him and integrated them into a theory of his own, developed through actually coping with reality and based on experience. He wrote of this experience:

Experience—that is my past, my life, the sum of my personal experiences, the memory of failure and disappointment, victories and successes, both positive and negative emotions. Experience is the suspicious and critical assessment which attempts to find the imprecision and fault of the theory.[23]

Korczak attributed great importance to evaluating facts without illusions, to an open and direct struggle with these facts, and to drawing honest conclusions. As to failures, he stressed that:

I appreciate failure not as a sum of unfulfilled ambitions, but because of the goals attained. In its own way, each failure serves as an impetus to mental effort. Today's truth is but a station. I can never know the last station in advance, and I am content to recognize my first working station.[24]

He summed up his opinion on theory and practice in education by saying:

It is by virtue of theory that I know, it is by virtue of practice that I feel. Theory is but an extension of the mind, while pratice diversifies the emotions and exercises will power. I know—does not mean that I act according to what I know. The alien view-points of foreign people must take root in the individual self.[25]

Korczak warned against educational routine, claiming that:

> Routine permits one to become emotionally detached from the work, and alleviate the suffering. It is calming—you fulfill a function, you are an agile clerk . . . the ideal of routine—lack of excitement and a self-styled authority based on ad-hoc speculation.[26]

Yet, having cautioned his readers of the possible pitfalls of educational theory, Korczak nevertheless attempted to outline a number of guiding rules for education and the educator:

1) Work among children should be open to any person who loves children, is willing to devote his entire efforts to educational work, and whose purpose is to benefit the child.
2) One should never give the child a teacher who loves the book but does not love man.
3) The teacher must know that his knowledge is small, temporary, and tentative. There is no shame in not knowing, there is disgrace in trying to cover up ignorance, evade and falsify. The child is a consumer capable of demanding and a critic capable of being severe.
4) The teacher is but a sympathetic friend who is stronger and more experienced, but is not an authority.
5) The teacher must recognize that "practice is the soul of theory," and that one must not enslave life to a book.
6) The teacher should expose the child to limitless knowledge, rather than stay tied to any limiting and segmented curriculum which presents small pieces of knowledge and views them as all-important. The curriculum is the distorter and murderer of knowledge—it sets limits while knowledge has no limits. All that is dear and true takes place outside the curriculum and in spite of it.
7) In contrast to Rousseau who believed that the wisdom of education is to waste time, Korczak was of the opinion that one must never postpone or waste time, and that everything should be done immediately.
8) Knowledge is important to a teacher, as is memory, but this is not enough. His eye must be open and his ear attentive, but this is not enough. His heart must be understanding and his attention keen, but this is not enough. He must know that he does not and at the same time be capable of deep emotions and sensations. Only all of these taken together can properly characterize the educator.

In order to aid in the training of educators, Korczak proposed an educational seminary to replace the form of teaching seminary that still exists to this day. The proposed seminary will not focus on the instruction of various subjects but on the child's knowledge and perceptive powers from the moment of his birth throughout the various periods of his life. This seminary was to remind educators once more that besides the intelligence of the brain there is also what Korczak termed an "intellignce of the heart," and there is an "intelligence of character"—certain individual talents worthy of fostering and realizing, and there is "the mind of emotion," which is the essential joining of the head and the heart, a link that must never be separated in education.[27]

In this Korczak is close in spirit to A. S. Neill, one of whose central claims for school and education is that insufficient attention is given to emotional life, and that the "heart" is sacrificed for the "head."[28] Korczak, like Neil, believed that true learning was not to be gained from books or the lectures of a teacher, but through active involvement in life and work, experiment and research. Academic learning is to concern oneself with reality substitutes, and bookish learning is to deal with a castrated, artificial, and false reality. The textbooks do not provide a true picture of life, but a synthetic one shaped in accordance with the goals of the writers, the society, the religion, or the state that they represent. Even when the picture is as full and balanced as possible, one cannot equate literary reality with actual participation and involvement in life itself. This is even more so when textbooks deal with specified subjects that are at most segments of reality, when the approach is intellectual, and when there is almost no attention given to the needs of the soul. Neil laments this in a similar vein:

> Their textbooks do not deal with man's character or with love or with freedom or self definition. And thus is the system perpetuated whose goal is the standard of bookish learning—and the separation of the heart from the head continues.[29]

Accordingly, it is not the various certificates and titles that define the good educator. Korczak expressed himself radically, as was his wont, and wrote:

> It is possible that you do not know how to read yet are a good nurse. It is possible that you have an academic degree on the subject of infant care, yet give children opium on the sly so as to put them to sleep and give yourself some rest. The things which you know and which you can do are of no value, but the things which you know how to give and wish to give are of value . . . wisdom has not been given to us so that we should make it into a laurel to rest on, but so that we distribute it. There is a dead capital of petrified wisdom and there is wisdom of the

living kind which is like a full and open hand, like air, like water, like the sweetness of a fruit, to all who approach and desire it.[30]

Korczak viewed the professionalization of education and teaching as one of the main causes of the exaggerated emphasis placed on certificates and titles. He considered this focus on certificates, the stress on grades, on formal achievements, and on learning this or that segment of lifeless material as a sign of social degeneration and an inhuman technocratic vision. He wrote scathingly:

Examinations and bookish learning have completely degenerated and spoiled the students. They have satisfied the lust for honour and opened many avenues to easy achievement. They have blocked the way of honest, humble workers and have flooded the market with the filth of their diplomas.[31]

Korczak delineated a number of guidelines for the curriculum and work of his proposed seminary of education. Candidates would be accepted from the age of fourteen. Each candidate will be asked to report on his previous life, tell about himself, and attempt to compose a self-portrait. One of the requirements would be a good command of reading and writing, but the impression made by the candidate's personality, by the encounter with him and the intuitive perception of his character, were of great importance.

The first year of study would mainly concentrate on guided self-learning, independent work, learning from books, and working in the laboratory. Keeping a detailed work and progress diary, receiving instruction from teachers of the seminar, and written guidance from professors at various universities would also be included.

The second year of study would concentrate on work among children and with children. At this stage, there would be only a few children. The student must observe the child, report his progress, keep track of school activities, and participate in teachers' meetings, work consultations, and the like. He must keep a detailed diary of his observations, of the school work, and of his work with the child. He must critically assess the educational work, the local culture, and the life-style of his particular settlement and provide suggestions for improving the aesthetics of the settlement, the living arrangements, and the educational and cultural activities. The seminary student will live in the settlement and involve himself with its life.

The third and fourth years would be devoted to theoretical studies. Out of a variety of about thirty subjects the student must choose five to be thoroughly studied. Of this five, one or two should be foreign languages and one or two should be arts. Studies would be conducted in groups and through individual work, in large classes and in small workshops. Collective work is greatly stressed. During the third year there would be little actual school practice, and it would not be obligatory, while during the fourth year there would be much kindergarten and school pratice, both through observation and through direct involvement in educational work. During these two latter years the students would reside in rooms of their own at the seminary's boarding house. These communal dwellings would not only be for their convenience, but also directed at developing educational affiliations, joint study, teamwork, and mutual ties.

During the fifth year, studies would be held in the city and combined with visits to museums, libraries, the theater, the conservatorium, laboratories, and meetings with specialists and the like.

During the sixth year, the students would be fully employed as auxiliary staff in schools, clubs, institutions of special education, and as stand-in teachers. Their work would be accompanied by constant guidance, consultations with the seminary's teachers, and reports, and they would be assisted by the seminary in all areas of experience.

Korczak viewed this program as no more than a tentative and unripe first draft, a demonstration of the way in which theory and practice are to be combined. He wrote: "I am well aware of the drawbacks of my program,"[32] and reasserted his claim that beyond all curricula one must adhere to the principle that "The child must not be given a teacher who loves the book and does not love man."[33]

Following his recommendations for the training of the educator, Korczak examined the educational conclusions of his thirty years of thinking about the child. In a concise and condensed article entitled "6 × 5,"[34] he divided thirty years of educational experience and thought into 6 five-year stretches, six developmental stages in the life of an educator. These five-year periods overlap and complete each other, intersecting, mutually interpenetrating and interweaving, thus creating the developing and diverse picture of the educator's world. The first five-year period is noted by its freshness, the magic of first efforts, the enthusiasm of youth. The educator feels his power, believes in the children, wishes to explain, to educate, to invent new programs, to make up games, to encourage the children, and to arouse their curiosity. He still believes in bookish theories, in his ability to convince, and in the great educational chance.

During the second five-year phase, the feeling of magic is replaced by the beginning of continuous, thorough, and intensive work. Besides the victories, the defeats are also beginning to accumulate. Besides the enlightenments, there are many conflicts and doubts. Feelings of anger and humiliation begin to seep in. There are first signs of frustration and helplessness. A reserved tiredness begins to arrest the urge. There is a certain measure of withdrawal into oneself. The anger becomes intensified and increased rancor is directed at the books which have disappointed, at the theories which have been found to be untrue and inapplicable.

The third five-year period is characterized by factual curiosity, an increase of the analytic powers, the desire to learn the truth, to analyze the methods of education, and to reach conclusions. There is still a belief, perhaps illusory, that it is possible to foresee educational developments, that one can prevent certain events, that it is possible to plan far ahead. This five-year period is characterized by an increased tendency to place prohibitions and issue orders. The books that have disappointed are completely rejected, and the educator seeks his own independent way.

The fourth five-year period is characterized by the first signs of anxiety and increased worry. There is a feeling that life is stronger than the educator and that the ability to change is limited. The educator copes with serious problems, complex situations, and difficult children. He stands on guard, is constantly on watch, seeking ways to make amends with the protégé so as to make his life a little easier. As a result of these difficulties, there is a renewed tendency to seek help in books, firm theories, and utilize instructional manuals and the experience of others.

The fifth five-year period is characterized by greater comprehension, which, of necessity, also leads to a measure of reconciliation. The educator recognizes the power of time. He knows how to wait patiently. He is aware of limitations and is capable of setting limits.

The sixth five-year period is characterized by a sense of security that is partially grounded in the surrender and wisdom gained by experience. The educator surrenders to life. He is forgiving and absolving. He sees education in the perspective of many years of activity. He does not rebel against the book that does not know the answer, nor is he angry at himself for not knowing. He finds it easy to admit his ignorance. He begins to look for someone who will carry on the work after him.

These thirty years of constant educational work are summarized in Korczak's statement:

Satisfying work. Hard, interesting work full of anxiety, under wary supervision, despite changing moods, with confidence and faith in the future. How did someone put it? Our generation, is only on the brink of civilization.[35]

9

To Be a Light: On Educational Teaching

And I saw that only fools insist that all men be like one another. And the wise man is happy that there is night and day in the world, summer and winter, young and old, birds in the trees and birds on the wing and that the colors of flowers and the eyes of human beings are different. And God who created man—created them male and female. Only he who dislikes thought will be disappointed by differences and angered by variety, for they cause man to think, to see and to understand.[1]

At the beginning of the thirties, Alfred North Whitehead[2] stressed that we must train a person to be able to cope with changing conditions that we must liberate him from the burden of "lifeless concepts" and of information compressed into memory without ever being actually used, without being examined or placed in new contexts. Whitehead emphasized:

Throughout history, every intellectual revolution which has brought man glory, has also brought an excited protest against lifeless concepts. Unfortunately, these very movements themselves have not refrained, with a surprising ignorance of human psychology, from imprisoning the spirit of humanity once more within lifeless concepts of their own by means of their own educational methods.[3]

Without any knowledge of Whitehead or his theories, and unable or unwilling to make such theoretical formulations, Korczak viewed the essence of teaching as *education* in the many senses of the concept of education. Like Whitehead's proposals, the educational methods suggested by Korczak focus on experiencing the joy of discovery, on active learning, scientific training, the development of thought, constant experimentation, and learning from life while teaching the art of making use of knowledge.

In many respects he shares, again unknowingly, with certain reservations, and obviously without direct affinity, Dewey's attitude and concepts of progressive education. Dewey had objected to those conceptions of traditional education which viewed the child as an immature creature that

161

must be matured, or as a shallow being that must be given depth. This type of education claimed that it is the child's sole duty "to absorb and acquiesce" and that his role is finished once he is agreeable to authority and pliable enough to accept the shape given to him.[4] Progressive education, of which Dewey is one of the major architects, stands in sharp contrast to this type of traditional education and is characterized by:

1) Fostering the individual's personality rather than handing down orders from above.
2) Free activity rather than external discipline.
3) Learning from experience.
4) Fully taking advantage of life's opportunities in the present, rather than preparing for some future time at which life shall begin.
5) Becoming acquainted with a changing world rather than becoming dependent on static goals and materials.[5]

It seems that Korczak would have accepted these five articles, for when he wrote of educational teaching he formulated these precepts in his own characteristic style.

In his evaluation of teaching and didactic methods, Korczak emphasized the education of the child's entire personality. Teaching has an important role in the education of character, thus affecting the lives and conflicts of people, the course of their struggle to uncover their identity and endow their life with meaning. The child, who is in the process of shaping his personality, tends to identify with heroes and is liable to absorb many of their life values, hence, the important role of literature and history, and the special position of the historical and biographical tale. This form of literature is in fact a method of teaching, as it is full of historical information, yet, as a literary creation, it also arouses the child to perceive the meaning that lies beyond what is explicitly said, and creates a new understanding of reality and man. A historical tale worth its salt is capable of motivating the child and illuminating meanings which exceed specific events and situations. It endows the child with a new, clearer vision of man and of himself. Goethe's statement to the effect that he hates anything that only increases his knowledge, without augmenting his actions or instilling them with greater vigor, is congruent with this approach. Teaching is not intended just to increase knowledge, but must expand vision, establish the proper mental attitude, and involve the reader in the experience of the ages in a mutual, uniquely human, emotional, and intellectual fashion.

The lessons of history and of historical literature usually present the reader with great figures, famous commanders, and persons of renown.

Yet it is worthwhile remembering Richard Livingstone's important distinction between greatness and virtue. There are such figures as Napoleon, Friedrich the Great, Bismarck, and others, who changed the face of Europe and the course of history, but who must not be allowed to blind us with their genius and achievements to the point of ignoring the warped and dangerous power of their influence. According to Livingstone:

> Greatness does not atone for sins or crimes, but only intensifies their effect . . . and if indeed the mark of civilization is the progress of justice, mercy and truth, cooperation in place of struggle, and an increasingly growing sense of the meaning of a man's obligations to his fellow man—then it would have been better if these three great personages had never been born; for Europe paid, and still pays, for their lives with rivers of blood.[6]

And, indeed, many have challenged the accepted method of teaching history, contending that it is a history of slaughter and the biographies of great criminals, while little attention has been given to the development of culture, the discoveries, the inventions, the systems of working conditions, and society. Korczak stressed the importance of learning social-cultural history, but noted, at the same time, that one might also make educational use of the history of victories and battles, so long as the events and their development are illuminated in a proper light. In a passage titled "Small Victories" he wrote:

> The victories and defeats are described as if they depended on the genius and the will of kings and other unique commanders—little consideration is given to the fact that the final determinant of a victory is the last moment of the battle, a single soldier and his final shot. When we examine a victory for its constituent components, it disintegrates into thousands and tens of thousands of tiny fragments—small individual victories. Were history to be taught thus, youths would possibly dream less of great acts of heroism and brilliant and surprising victories and instead respect the many small successes which together coalesce into the outburst of victory.[7]

Throughout his educational career, Korczak aspired to teach children to win at every moment of their lives, to pay attention to small details, to pass the tiny tests they encounter daily, and to bear the burden of life with full seriousness and devotion. He wished to instill his protégés with respect for effort and an appreciation of the man who wishes to make his own way in life. He often told his protégés:

You are wanderers. Are not the water-bottle and the slice of bread seemingly redundant objects. Yet, will not some item of attire determine at a certain point whether the wanderer shall reach his goal or die on the way?[8]

Korczak recognized the importance of learning and did not view the informational aspect of learning lightly. He noted that every man must be knowledgeable about what goes on in the world, become acquainted with new countries and other nations, learn the life-styles of other people, and study other cultures. Hence, he vindicated obligatory studies for everyone and did not accept the complaints of students that some subject or other was too difficult. He explained to them that this subject might seem difficult and dull at the outset, but that the student will recognize its importance later on and find it both interesting and enlightening. Despite the importance of knowledge and learning, it was the understanding, the deeper study, the perception, and the personal involvement in learning that he considered truly essential and important. He wrote:

It does not matter that a man know a lot, but it is essential that he know well. It is not important that he know anything by heart, but it is essential that he understand it, it is not important that he concern himself a little with everything, but it is essential that he have one special interest.[9]

He regretted the fact that schools had given knowledge the first priority and stressed memory rather than understanding. He emphasized: "Respect the hand and its working tools, and respect science which encourages you to think your own thoughts. The book's role is to help and to demonstrate, not to replace you."[10]

Korczak stressed that the accumulation of experience, the constant discoveries of various scientists, the unceasing scientific research—all change the world of knowledge and our conceptions of the world. Hence the written word sometimes conveys many outmoded or false theories. It is for this reason that every child must develop tools of criticism, methods of analyzing texts, critical judgment, and the ability to examine what is written in books and compare it with the state of knowledge in the present and the new scientific developments.

New beliefs have many enemies: those who do not wish to think; those who refuse to admit the mistakes of the past; those who hold on to petrified doctrines; those who base their authority and rule on well-entrenched lies; and all other fanatics and narrow-minded people. Therefore, one of the educator's most important functions is to teach his students to doubt the commonly accepted and the sacred, to critically examine the knowledge contained in books, and to remain open to change and innovation.

Korczak scathingly criticized the school system he himself had known. In a thrilling work titled *The School of Life*, which he began publishing in 1907 as installments over a long period, in two radical periodicals, he described the existing school as: "A School of Death" that causes children immeasureable damage. He claimed that all who pass this valley of death become frustrated and dishonest persons, well versed in various manipulations and dishonest methods. They are semi-literates whose literacy serves to screen their evil ways. Their souls have been stolen so that they are but frightened little copies of all the evils of school and its injurious ways in educating the children to "get along" at any cost, to beat the system or the method, to pretend, to be cynical pragmatists, to be forever on the lookout for an advantage, etc.

Korczak's description of the old school system preceded those of the radical educators of the fifties and sixties such as Neil Postman and Charles Weingartner,[11] Paul Goodman,[12] Paulo Friere,[13] Jonathan Kozol,[14] John Holt,[15] Herbert Kohl,[16] and many others. Like them, he too complained that school cuts the child off from real life, stifles his creativity, and distorts him into uniform shapes in artificial environments. The school does not allow the children to encounter life, and rather than open up a future:

> The past mockingly rattles its chains as it dogs their steps. And is it any wonder? Have they not embarked on their life equipped with the multiplication table, dead historical dates, a few tales and the rules of grammar. They have survived without the ability to thoroughly and comprehensively deal with any serious matter, any problem which arises in a person they encounter. They are quick to despair, for they have lost life's most important treasure: interest, involvement, contemplation, dilligence and an open joy over innocent discoveries.[17]

Nearly fifty years after Korczak wrote this serious criticism of school, we find its like in a document issued by students in the Montgomery region of the United States titled "Human Education Wanted," in which they complain that school is based on fear, that it compels students to be dishonest, that it destroys the natural joy of learning, and that it encourages obedience to authority.[18]

In contrast with the old school, which survives in many respects to this very day, Korczak depicted a future school in which children would not learn from the dead letters of books but from life itself. It would be a school of life in which one would first learn about man and his environment, cope with man's customs, ask questions about the meaning of life, and the possibility of influencing it, and about the chances for happiness, love, and humanity. It would be a school in which the emphasis would be on questions rather than answers, in which the educator would approve of his protégé as a whole person equal to himself, and assist him in formulating his questions and searching for solutions. It would also be a school in which the educator would foster the student's thinking and acquaint him with the sources of knowledge and culture, not as normative authorities but as reference points that can be utilized to verify and examine the way he has chosen.

When we read Korczak's criticisms of school, it seems as if we are understanding the words of Paul Goodman who stressed that some of the reasons for the failure of the school are to be found in the philosophy that guides it, in its organization, in its binding curricula, and especially in the coercive authoritarian relationships between adults and children. Other faults can be attributed to the unique instrumental status of the school in the community and in society. School teaches the multitudes of future citizens that life is but a continuous routine, lacking in any personal imprint, and that there is no room for spontaneity or a free spirit. They are trained and broken at school and then go out to assume the same types of roles in life and in society. This is the education, or more precisely the mis-education, which schools provide, the single aim of which is to socialize children to accepted norms and create the corps of national servants according to the needs of the state, the church, the party, the industry, and so on.[19]

Is there any great difference between such words, spoken by the radical educators of the fifties and Korczak's words when he fervently wrote in the first decade of the century:

> The students of the schools of death [the school existing in his time] have received an answer even before they have posed the question—a shallow, cynical answer, full of assured arrogance. For this reason they do not know how to ask and are afraid of any new truth which has not received the benediction of the great magician. In their innocence they believe in every relative truth with which this great sage has agreed with no more than a slight nod of his head.[20]

Korczak's future school, by contrast, the school of life and dialogue, is a human gospel of education, a gospel of freedom, respect for the child, and future hope for society.

Korczak was not solely concerned with visions of the future, but also with the daily practice of school and of teaching, with didactic questions and the handling of students. Thus, for example, as a sharp-eyed educator, Korczak noticed that talented children often did sloppy work. Since the study material in class is uniform, and the tasks set to the students are also uniform, the brighter children are quick to grasp the material, and as a result, they waste their time and become used to sloppiness and effortlessness. Even worse, some of them acquire negative character traits, such as: pride, disrespect for others, and lack of seriousness in work. Some differentiation of the tasks given in class might contribute to the interest of the more talented students in class and to the forging of their character. Otherwise:

> Because [the talented student] he holds himself to be wise, he thinks that he should have everything. He looks down on quiet effort and slow and constant aspiration, which forges toward the goal by slow inches. He admits no talent but his own kind and makes light of others.[21]

Korczak reserved an important place for creative learning and creative work at school. He encouraged educators to provide children with possibilities of expressing themselves dramatically, and poetically, through creative writing and in movement. He stressed that a student should be given as little direction as possible in dramatic expression, that no set patterns of expression should be forced on him, and that his original ways of expressing himself be considered a true expression of his experience.

Korczak attributed great importance to free reading and understood its important formative role in the life of the child. He objected to the censorship of books and emphasized the need to allow children to read what they will. Any prohibition or confiscation of books leads to secret reading, any coercion of reading leads to opposition and aversion, which are both negative. It seems that his words on free reading should still be heard today for there are still many mistakes made which are liable to alienate the child from books. According to Korczak:

> Adults view some books as important and others as harmful, some as wise and some—as foolish. I, on the other hand, permit all books, because I do not wish anyone to read in secret and I have discovered, on observation, that some books arouse the desire to read, while others weaken this desire—and this has nothing to do with the value of the book. A good respectable boy will seek out respectable books—in the same way as he chooses friends. It is better to let him search, make mistakes and wander off-course until he finds good company among books, because difficult books are unattractive and only irritate. It is imperative that an educator be patient. It is better that he wait until the talents have matured and the desire and understanding for better books has ripened.[22]

Korczak viewed the essence of education as "the knowledge and observation of the child from the moment of his birth, and the good intention of serving him at every period of his life." Hence he criticized the distorted role of schools as institutions for the provision of certificates and diplomas, as places concerned with external goals and bookish learning rather than with the child. He demanded that the school direct its attention to the child's character, personality, traits, and life rather than to information and academic knowledge alone:

> For encyclopedias can be printed and referred to when needed. The brilliant injuriousness of the school is the poison of a crumbling world, a world of knowledge peddlers and knowledge forgers, parasites and profiteers. To mock, to degrade, to lie evasively, to win the teacher's heart, to cunningly hide ignorance, to step on a friend's opinion—that is the comedy. The bad comedy of the old school—one must learn to know the child's character and take care that the school not distort it, not do as it will, not instill the child's emotions with the feelings of inferiority.[23]

When he examined the positive activities of school, he found these to be distorted and inflexible, too. Thus, for example, he discussed the outing and its educational value at some length. He viewed outings as an important activity for both adults and children but claimed that were we to examine these outings as they are usually conducted in school, we would find a guiding concept that totally deprives them of their importance. "The outings are organized according to a fixed form: to visit, to see, and then to boast that I have been and seen."[24]

According to Korczak, outings should be an active ingredient in the strengthening of character and the quenching of the soul's thirst. The aims of such outings can be diverse and include such themes as escaping from the ugly and suffocating city into nature ("So long as we do not desert the dead cities, which will one day be visited by tourists who will be amazed that people could have lived in them, and wonder how it happened that people did not chew each other to death in these warrens, so long as we live in cities, we shall send the children out of them in spring"), or the search of man for himself and his god; the enjoyment of beauty as of a single sunset or an oak tree; or a tour of release and sensual delight; or of reminiscence; or of pilgrimage; or for the purpose of honoring an old teacher, a poet; or for swimming in the river or the lake—outings in which one reads the world, nature, and the environment and in discovering man also finds oneself richer and fuller.

Korczak devoted a not inconsiderable part of his discussion of school to the issue of discipline. He was well acquainted with the tiresome educational reality of the class, the many tensions, and the disciplinary problems that might lead the educator to nervousness, impatience, and even an outburst directed at the child. Sympathizing with the teacher's plight, he wrote: "He too is a living person and has nerves and aches of his own as well as family worries and kidney stones. Have you ever seen a man talk until he is hoarse only for the pleasure of croaking?"[25]

Korczak understood the teacher who orders a child to leave the class, but he reminds us that while banishing a child from class can only help the teacher to proceed with the lesson, it does nothing whatsoever for the banished child. Proper educational measures must be taken after the lesson has ended. The teacher must then converse with the child, examine the reasons that led to the disturbance, and in cooperation with the child, attempt to find a way to prevent such an occurrence from happening again. Korczak offered five rules for weaning a child of his weaknesses:

1) If he finds it difficult, let him mend his ways gradually rather than all at once.
2) One should choose only one failing, the lightest, at the outset and cope with it first.
3) One should not lose patience if there is no improvement over a long time, or if at first the behavior of the child becomes even worse.
4) One should not condition too little, but enough so as to win.
5) One should not be overly happy if the child is weaned immediately, for it is easy to get rid of acquired failings, and very hard to be free of congenital ones.[26]

The educator's goal should be to help the child know himself, thus providing him with a means of improving himself.

Just as one must consider the unruly children at school, so one must also pay attention to those boys and girls who wish to win the heart of the teacher by flattery. Korczak warned the educator of the class "witch":

Remember, she is always at odds with her own environment, and attempts to sneak in under the wings of an adult. Do not reject her, treat her factually and keep the required distance, take care!—They have claws, these little vultures![27]

On the issue of dicipline Korczak was a steadfast opponent of the great mainstay of authoritarian dicipline—punishment. To punish a child who is late to school, while a late teacher is not punished, seemed nefarious to Korczak. He considered all punishments, starting from oppressive and humiliating physical punishment and ending in other punishments bent on subjugating the child, as anti-educational.[28] Korczak stressed: "A fist, a threat, ridicule, taunting, lies, a broken promise, disrespect, sycophancy, hollow platitudes—a filthy stage—have we not then corrupted the child's spirit?"[29]

10

A Hundred Rebellious Ideas:
On Punishment in Education

Sometimes, when you scold a child, you can read a hundred rebellious ideas in his stare.[1]

Korczak was strongly opposed to corporal punishment and viewed it as a totally unacceptable educational means. He considered that only when there was no other recourse should one make use of corporal punishment, and always with great care and without rancor. He wrote: "I am totally and uncompromisingly opposed to corporal punishment. Beatings, even for adults, are nothing but a dulling and stupefying means of correction, they are never educational."[2]

Many of his articles and books addressed the question of corporal punishment. He saw the main fault of education as the heritage of the Prussian school which had been very strict in adhering to an inflexible external discipline and had ordered the teacher to strike without anger, to strike like a machine. Cold and emotionless beatings served as a disciplinary tool, as if the social machine were protecting itself. This bitter concept served as the justification for beatings to the point that they became an obligatory procedure. The cane became a "solution" for educational problems, despite the fact that, in truth, it magnified such problems a thousandfold.

In his wonderfully poetic article, "The Spring and the Child," Korczak wrote:

It seemed that after this war [The First World War] no adult would ever dare to strike a child again for having broken a window, or for having disturbed the somber atmosphere of a class lesson. It seemed that we would pass by these children with our heads bent in shame, for it is we who are responsible for this raging madness—the one touch of which has caused more destruction and devastation than all the misdirected balls and pranks of children, who were the first and foremost victims of this war. It is a disgrace that the pedagogues have allowed the bamboo cane to remain in the schools of Poland—and perhaps this is but the last icy gust of cold and bloody enslavement. Perhaps the spring is really already on its way? And perhaps these are truly the last tears? Perhaps it is already possible to really start healing the bruises and the wounds?[3]

All forms of corporal punishment were forbidden at the orphanages directed by Korczak, including isolation, curtailment of liberty, withdrawal of food and the like. Though it was permitted to order a child to sit somewhere to cool off, this, too, was only for a short time and not intended as punishment. It was considered a most serious infraction if an instructor or teacher happened to lose his temper and strike a child, and he was required to register his act on the board. The stricken child was permitted to sue the striking teacher at the orphanage court, but the striker was required to precede the child in this and place himself on trial so as to explain his failing to the court and the circumstances that caused him to beat a child.

Korczak viewed all forms of punishment with equal disdain. Threats, isolation, curtailment of liberty, placement in a corner, seating the child at a separate desk, confiscation of private property, limitations on play, and even a cool and indifferent attitude were considered severe punishments. He wrote: "One can torture the child's self-love and feelings, in the same way as the body was tortured before."[4] Although it is possible to hold the children in strict discipline by means of threats and be firmly convinced by the shallow belief that this is a comfortable modus operandi, even an unrealized threat constitutes severe punishment, while doing nothing in the way of educating the child.

Korczak rejected the unfounded opinion that a child is quick to forget his anger and sorrow. He contended that children foster their pain a long time and remember their punishment. Among the various punishments, Korczak found ridicule and the belittling of the child totally unacceptable. Ridicule and abusive words damage the child's personality and haunt him for many days, while the vociferous shout and reproach are both useless and ridiculous. The first commandment of the educator, who wishes to control a group of children, is to keep his emotions in check. Hysterical shouting will only make him the subject of ridicule.

Yet it is only natural that the educator lose his temper occasionally, and Korczak wrote of this in a letter:

To Sabina Damme.
When I shout at one of you, look to see if I am merely shouting with my mouth, my tongue and my throat, if I am only angry in words— or—at heart. Should I reproach one of you, take care to see if I am

really angry or only pretending to be angry . . . though I am not really so. For I love you, but must scold in order to keep the kindergarten in order and prevent disturbances; I want everyone to be happy and none of the children to cry, for I am sad when children cry; because I love you—yes. Perhaps I shall sometimes scold you without your having done anything wrong, because I am sad, or something upsets me. If I were alone at home, I would cry, but I cannot cry in class for it is shameful for an adult to cry in pain. So I shout.[5]

As to the child who promised the educator to better his ways but who failed and resumed his infractions, Korczak emphasized that the educator must be patient. Were he to attack the child with shouts, insult him for not having kept to his promises, and threaten him, he would destroy instead of correcting. It is only natural for a child to find it difficult to wean himself all at once from bad behavior, and anyone who is not capable of helping the child wean himself gradually and punishes him instead is only pushing him into sin. According to Korczak:

In response to his anger you approach him with your own temper—shouting. The child is not listening, but he feels your rejection of him. You are depriving him of your generosity. He feels alienated and lonely, surrounded by emptiness. And in your anger you make use of all forms of punishment: Threats, ostracism, ridicule and direct oppression. Look how his friends commiserate, with what gentleness they attempt to console him.[6]

Korczak was particularly opposed to collective punishments and collective blame. He saw them as a wrong perpetrated on the majority and as basically anti-educational acts. Indeed, why should everyone suffer for one or for a few guilty ones? The truly guilty parties—if they are corrupt and cynical—will be glad that the anger is directed at everyone instead of just at them; and if they are honest, they shall be hurt by the fact that many innocents suffer because of them. Korczak emphasized:

Every time I made use of general blame, I saddened the honest, irritated everyone, and made myself look ridiculous in the eyes of the critics: No matter, let him rage awhile—it is very healthy.[7]

Korczak believed that the educator should be a virtuoso in the use of different reactions, commencing from slight grumbling and scolding, which are entirely sufficient for sensitive children, through careful rebuke and ending in severe reproach. But in the same way as one must know if, when, and how to punish so must one be careful of forgiveness. Forgiveness can be an educational act if it is well timed, but it might also become a serious hindrance if children who expect to be punished do not understand its meaning or reason. He wrote:

> If you intend to forgive, the children must know why you have chosen to do so, and the child whom you have forgiven must know that he is no better than the others, otherwise it might go to his head, and he will be victimized by the society whose rights he has infringed. You will have made a mistake and the children will punish you.[8]

The problem of punishment is a very serious one, and one must not suggest one-sided and uniform solutions to the questions that arise. The behavior of the teacher is conditioned on the particular nature of the specific pedagogical situation, on the child who has erred, on the circumstances, on the status of the educator and the group, and on many other elements. There is no doubt that a group of children accustomed to an atmosphere of freedom, trust, and respect will have to be treated very differently from a group of children raised at a boarding school where the discipline is coercive and the educator is a novice. Korczak described this situation:

> How difficult it is for a new educator in a class or at a boarding school where the children have been subjected to strict discipline, and have bunched together, impudent and touchy, on the violent basis of the street gang. How aggressive and threatening they are when they storm your will collectively, seeking to uproot the obstacle—not children, but a mighty force.[9]

Korczak proclaimed that problems of discipline and order are usually not solved by punishment but through cooperation with the children and by establishing their self-rule. And, indeed, two important principles are capable of preventing many future disciplinary problems and helping to solve existing ones: the first is a genuine understanding of the child, his world, his wishes, and his interests, and the second is genuine cooperation with the child. Korczak stated that:

> Only the bad educator is of the opinion that children really shouldn't make noise or dirty their clothes, and that they should instead diligently learn the rules of grammar. A wise educator will not lose his temper when he does not understand the child, but will think, examine and ask the children's opinion. They will teach him how he must behave so as not to insult them overmuch, if only he is willing to learn.[10]

11
Youth—That is Madness:
On Sexual Education

The excess of energy overflows like waves over a river bank, and in its rolling madness sweeps everything in its path and flows away frothing madly in great noise and commotion! Youth—that is madness.[1]

In his work at the boarding house and orphanage and in his writings, Korczak reserved a special place for sexual education. He stressed that sexual feelings are already evident in the small child. Sexual emotions do not suddenly appear out of the blue, but are constantly developing in the child. The educator must therefore pay attention to manifestations of sexuality at the boarding school, as these are expressed in movements, hugs, kisses, and sensual childhood games, both in secret and in public. Sensual or "depraved" children sometimes seek special gratification. They like to caress the hand of the educator, kiss his ear or neck, and such exhibitions are not an expression of innocent affection but, in truth, of lustful delights. The educator is obliged to examine himself and his behavior as well. Since he, too, has erotic feelings, which might be revealed in his attitude to the child, he must be aware of his tendencies, especially where it concerns an educator who is erotic by nature. A sexual element is also to be found in the emotions of parents. An innocent caress of the child's face or hair, tucking him into bed, a loving kiss—are all considered normal manifestations of healthy erotic feelings. But there are mothers who find such emotions too moderate and are not content with them: they shower kisses on the child's feet, shoulders, and abdomen. In order to experience the emotion that a healthy mother feels with a light touch, they must lust hungrily. The educator should be aware of these phenomena and be well acquainted with them, so as to be able to overcome them in the course of his educational work.

When educating the child, the educator should not deny the area of sexual education. When he encounters manifestations of sexual behavior among children, he should not ignore them or reject them in disgust.

Rather, he should give the life of the child a boost, relieve him of his boredom, allow him to run and make a noise and sleep as much as he wants. In this way the child's sexual feelings will be able to develop quietly and remain uncontaminated and harmless. At the same time the educator must not treat the child as suspect and must free himself of those irrational suspicions that are founded on ignorance of the child. Korczak provided an example of such unfounded suspicion in his book, *How to Love Children*. He wrote how one day he noticed two youths who led some younger boys into the lavatories amid much secret whisperings, and after a short while, the younger boys would return to the play hall, with a somewhat puzzled expression on their faces. It was only by dint of a great effort of will that Korczak managed to remain sitting and continue writing quietly without interfering. It eventually turned out that the whole thing was no more than a most innocent game.

> One of the youths (who worked with a photographer) would cover a box of cigarettes with an apron. He would place those wishing to be photographed beneath a faucet which was fixed in the wall of the lavatories, and when the children froze a pleasant expression on their faces in order to have their photograph taken, a cold stream of water was let loose on their heads to the count of "three."[2]

Too much prying into the sexual lives of children, excessive suspiciousness about their behavior, and the use of threats and severe punishments for manifestations of masturbation—all these create an unpleasant atmosphere in the institution, and rather than indicating any immorality on the part of the children, point to defects in the personality of the educator.

Korczak emphasized that one must provide honest and serious answers to the questions of children concerning sex, that one must not silence them and certainly not evade answering. When a woman educator asked him how she should answer provocative questions, he answered that there were no stupid or provocative questions if the answer is given sincerely and with some knowledge and if we ourselves know the answer.

Korczak claimed that the usual attitude toward adolescence was distorted and not based on genuine research and observation. In his opinion there was no place for the air of mystery that seemed to shroud his age, or for adults to avoid their responsibility for educating adolescents. He believed parents and teachers did not understand how one should help adolescents and guide them. They do not consider the fact that the physical transformations of this age are also accompanied by deep mental changes. Adults attempt to solve the problem of adolescence by means of such empty phrases as: "life is awakening," "the spring of life," "the age of storm and passion"; yet in certain circumstances, severe crises might emerge at adolescence that are liable to rock the life of the adolescent. It is, therefore, necessary to faithfully and honestly prepare every boy and girl for their approaching adulthood, including the preparation of the girl for menstruation and the preparation of the boy for the appearance of semen. One should not place these phenomena under a wrap of secrecy. At the same time Korczak objected to the excessive emphasis placed on this age in comparison with other ages. Although he considered it to be "the age of great inequality," he viewed it as part of the general development of the child, and he did not place any particular emphasis on its sexual content or the dangers of perversion that threaten the adolescent child.

Korczak was well acquainted with adolescents and their physical passions, their restlessness, and their many doubts. In his book *The Drawing Room Kid*, he provided an excellent portrait of the life of an adolescent, and wrote of youth:

> Youth-Oh-youth! What power, what force in that short expression, which holds such great content? Oh, you proud ones, have you managed to penetrate the heart of an adolescent boy? Do you know what raging youth is like? Have you observed the hell in the soul of the seventh grade student, where a great and mighty storm rages?[3]

He recognized the rebellion of adolescents against the authority of adults, their wish to cast off the external authority forced on them by parents or teachers. He knew how withdrawn children became at this age and how unwilling to divulge their intimate secrets to the educator. When asked by a young woman to try and influence one of the boys, he answered:

> Children of the same age can influence one another, adults are too strict and quick to anger; although they teach and influence, they do so from the top down, laying down the law from Mount Sinai. There are matters in which the wise, experienced and mellow advice of the adult can be of help, but the good warm advice of one's peer is very much needed and required.[4]

Korczak observed his adolescent protégés closely and saw their physical development, the awakening of their passions, their first loves and strong emotions. He told of one of the girls who fell in love with one of the boys and kept thinking about him constantly. When Korczak began discussing this love with her, she became confused and wondered how he knew. He answered her:

Once, you hear me, I saw you methodically pluck the leaves off a sprig, and then you were sad because the outcome was: "He loves me not," but I assure you that he too likes you, but he does not want to show it openly for fear that you will then be the subject of jokes and ridicule.—And he—he has a very strong sense of honor.—You remember that incident with the cakes? He only took one for himself, and then moved the plate in a kind of off-hand way to place it beside you; but you did not take it, and the other girl ate the remaining cake; and he was angry and irritated that she took it instead of you. And out of anger he then said that she has a red nose, which is not true. And you did not eat because you were ashamed that everyone will see you and then understand that he gave up the second cake, for you—such a sacrifice. And you did not accept it or heed him.— And he too, then sought an answer among the leaves of the acacia, and when he finished plucking he began whistling merrily, for his result was good: "She loves me." How well I know boys; but I have never been a girl in my life, and therefore only know what I read and what they themselves tell me from time to time.[5]

This passage reflects Korczak's penetrative powers of observation, his deep understanding of the behavior of adolescents, their conflicts of love, their shame, the intensity of their emotions, their frequently changing moods, and the unique character of this turbulent period of their lives.

It is especially because of this knowledge that he recognized the importance of educating for sexual responsibility, family life, and parenthood. Many times he emphasized:

I know one thing: to give birth to a child is a great responsibility toward him, and much is required if one wishes to be a father or mother . . . it is hard to raise a child. There is much duty, and responsibility toward the nation, the world, God, and one's own conscience.—This I know.[6]

12

Free Will and Coercion: Janusz Korczak's Literary Creation

"I am your rejected prophet—and your brother!"[1]

In the diary that he kept during the last months of his life, Korczak wrote, "If I were to say that I have never written a line which I did not want to write, it would be the truth. But it will also be true if I were to say that I wrote everything under compulsion."[2] And indeed, his great literary oeuvre as an author, playwright, writer, and children's author was written in response to a deep spiritual need. It expresses his suffering and conflicts, and represents a compulsion stemming from his explosive inner world, his humanistic vision, his total devotion to his educational-social mission, and his struggle for the child.

In his oeuvre, one cannot separate his inner world from his unceasing practical work. He believed that literature should attempt to express social and human existence, deal with human problems, and describe humanity. When he was told that the writing of Marcel Proust is long-drawn and boring, he replied:

Proust is long-drawn-boring and goes into minute details? Oh, no. Every hour—is a thick volume. An hour's reading. You would probably have to read a day in order to somewhat understand my day, a week for a week, a year for a year. And yet, we wish to experience the whole of a long and busy life, within a few hours. This is without basis. A loose synopsis, a clumsy sketch can teach you but one episode out of a thousand, a hundred thousand.[3]

Korczak read a great deal and was deeply immersed in the writings of Polish authors and poets as well as internationaly known writers. The writings of Maria Konupnicka (1842–1910), a socially minded poetess, whose creations expressed the sufferings of the Jewish multitudes, and the writing of the Polish author, Joseph Ignaci Krashavsky (1792–1887), who advocated the complete assimilation of Jews in Polish society, deeply influenced the young Korczak, torn as he was between the wish to become assimilated in Polish society and the memories of his Jewish world. He was a Jew whose roots had been severed, yet continued to bear the pain of the amputation. He was also deeply affected by the writings of Stephan Zeromasky (1864–1925), one of the leading authors of the new Poland, who described the poverty and sorrow in the life of the individual and of the Polish public.

When he grew older, Korczak was captivated by the works of the French-born Jewish writer Marcel Proust (1871–1922), whose writings deeply moved him with their great psychological depth and reminiscent-symbolic tone.

Korczak read Nietzsche's writing many times, always with aversion and disagreement. He rejected Nietzsche's concept of man as no more than a collection of instincts and drives that clash with each other and attempt to defeat each other. He refused to accept Nietzsche's claim that relationships between people are also determined by the instincts, which are the ruling force both in nature and in the life of man. Korczak objected to Nietzsche's notion that life is full of constant violence and is based on the destruction of others, so that the strong must overcome, enslave, or liquidate the weak, and freedom is no more than the ability of the strong and talented to act with initiative and power. Korczak was shocked by Nietzsche's claim that God is dead and that the strong person should rebel against the rule of the crowd, deride morality, and thus go beyond good and evil. Zarathustra frightened Korczak who felt no sympathy for, and was angered by the idea of a superman who wishes to experience everything and recoils from nothing. As he did not have the theoretical tools which would have enabled him to contend with Nietzsche's theories, he never entered into philosophical debate with Nietzsche. However, his very being and way of life stood in stark contrast to Nietzsche's theories, as can be seen from some of the literary notes in his diary:

> I wish to answer the illusory book of a false-prophet. This book has caused great damage . . . I too have conversed, have won the honor of conversing with Zarathustra. His secret sermons, so heavy, hard and sharp, have put you, poor philosopher, behind the somber walls and massed bars of the insane institution. For it was so. Black on white it was written: "In his battle with life Nietzsche died—a madman." In my book I want to prove that Nietzsche died in a regrettable battle with the truth. This very Zarathustra has taught me a different lesson. Perhaps my hearing was better, perhaps I was more attentive . . . for when I complete the reckoning, I do not find myself in the saddest cell of the saddest hospital; but—butterflies and grasshoppers and fireflies,

and the concerts of the crickets, and a soloist in the high blue—the lark. My God! Thank you my good God, for the lawns and the multi-hued sunsets, for the cool evening breeze after a day of heat and toil.[4]

Korczak's entire literary creation is antithetical to that of Nietzsche. Even his *Senate of Madmen*, in which the voice of Nietzsche can be heard to echo behind the scenes, strives to affirm life, to instill values with a new sanctity, and to enliven God in the heart of the child.

Besides his great involvement in reading, he felt a need to write. He was constantly taking notes, accumulating observations, writing the beginnings of works, composing stories for children, and plays for presentation at the orphanage and adult creations. And he was always making rich plans for future writing. Once, when he visited Palestine, he was seized with the idea of writing a grand epic of the third return of the people of Israel to their country, to be composed through the mutual cooperation of poets, musicians, the young, and the old. He wrote:

> It would be very strange, were the new Hebrew language to relinquish its right and ability to create a new epic—not a continuation of the present, as of now—but as the third sequel in a trilogy, following the holy scriptures and the New Testament.[5]

This epic was to be created in a unique fashion:

> The way of the river is to gather its waters from many streams. Each group, each settlement, can instill the common poem with its own flavour. A small event, the short note of one poem might grow and develop into a great and independent poem, which does not attract but a small part of one sector.[6]

Some of his literary creations, like the *Drawing Room Kid* and others, clearly reflect Korczak's own image and express his conception of life and his attitude toward society and man. The flavor of his writing is often that of an intimate confession so intense that a distance is established between the writer and his creation only when it is complete. Referring to his own diary, Korczak wrote:

> I read, and barely understood. And the reader? It is no wonder that the diary is incomprehensible to the reader. Can one understand the memories of a stranger, an alien life? It seems that I should be easily able to understand what I wrote. Aye, there's the rub! Can a man comprehend his own memories?[7]

The "Artist's Prayer," which is included in the prayerbook for people who do not pray, *With God I Shall Converse*, may reflect Korczak's self-perception of the creative artist as a blend of contrasts: "I am a protest, fickle, arrogant, there is none like me in all that obedient herd, I am a clown, silly, incorrigible".[8]

Korczak stressed the otherness of the creative artist, his nonconformism, his internal conflicts and tensions, his protest against evil, his frontier stance, his contempt toward all the various institutionalized vessels of holiness, his sensitivity to inner truths, his addiction to the world and the exprience of the senses, his empathy and personal loneliness, his joy and love of life. He teaches tired humanity to love and breathe deeply:

My prayer today, my Creator, is not as it was, not like that of others,— and I too am different today—and at this very moment—this special moment which shall never return. Understand: I am your rejected prophet—and your brother!—I—do I know, what I am? I do not even know myself, am I miserably glorious or gloriously miserable: proud, submissive, sensitive, threatening, arrogant and flattering as a cat, withdrawn and endlessly talkative. I sell tears, easily lose sticks and pocket-knives, am sensitive to the shadow of enslavement which is revealed to me. I cast away my fetters and burn them in the flame—and experience You, Creator, only in total silence.[9]

The artist's strength lies in his great sensitivity, in that vision of his which constantly exposes new things, and daily finds something fresh in things that have always been before him. His uniqueness is to be found in his eyes that are ever-open to the world, in his merging with his environment, his ability to read the book of nature without keeping a constant accounting of profit and loss, his capacity to accept things and introject them, his ability to see the world and all that is within it as God's hand-writing that he deciphers.

Blessed art Thou, Creator, for having created the pig and the long-nosed elephant, for having given us the tongue of leaves and hearts, for having given black faces to negroes and sweetness to sugar-beets. Thank you for the nightingale and the flea, for giving a girl breasts and making fish unable to breathe out of water; Thank you for the existence of lightning and cherries, for having commanded us to be born in a most wonderful fashion, and for having made man so stupid that he cannot even conceive that all could have been otherwise. Thank you for giving thought to stones, to the sea, to people. A thought which whispers tall tales in the ears of the listeners and weaves a great legend for itself—it is the sky—the blazing sunrises and sunsets—it is an eagle, a merrymaker, a liar—how I love it.[10]

The poet and artist seems to have been born five hundred years before and after his time. In many respects the artist is like God for they are co-creators. The artist's ability to create stems from an innocence, that is virginal and pure, primal and fresh, yet at the same time is born of the rift in his soul, a rift of question and doubt, disappointment and frustration—a blend of opposites that provides the creator with his enigmatic, intangible, and elusive character which defies definition. Yet, it also allows the artist to pose real, major questions that are central to the meaning of life. It is not for nothing that the poet has said: "A hundred thick-witted professors spend their entire lives trying to answer a single question of mine."[11]

It is particularly because of this cryptic quality of the artist that some people esteem him beyond reason while some find him contemptible. With wry humor Korczak wrote: "And it seems to me that you created us together and cast the world on its axis as a prank. You must have been a little inebriated at the time: Art is not to be created when wholly sober."[12] Yet he concluded on a sharp note, as if to crystallize the manifold aspects of the artist:

> There are strange creatures among Your sons—we are snow in summer, we are the red poppies growing on icebergs, we are—billowed sails. I play with the cat and grandma's cotton ball, no matter—we are the destroyers of the crowns of tyrant kings, we erect isolated towers. Out of our demented souls sane acts are born. We obey the sounds of the Waltz issuing from the jukebox and split the present with the logic of a future anthem, we die and are resurrected at our own behest. On the gravestones of failures we erect a monument to our common helplessness. And for this do I bless you, Creator, and tremblingly cast all of life's wonderful pleasures on that one card. Going for the jackpot: A life in exchange for creation![13]

This trembling valor characterizes large sections of Korczak's writing.

It would be a grave mistake to claim that Korczak celebrated literature above all other interests or upheld writing as all-important. He recognized the value of writing both for the creator himself and for his reading audience, but did not exaggerate its importance. In his conversations with Yerachmiel Weingarten he talked of the responsibility that lay on an author's shoulders, so that rather than serve some personal catharsis or express the detached observations of one who stands outside life and society, Korczak's writing was involved from the very first. Korczak dealt with man's existential problems directly. He visited the impoverished Soltz area, lived there, and cared for the poor, and then described their suffering and poverty in his books. He challenged the social charade and futilely struggled against those foci of power which literature is power-less to change.

His participation in the First World War on the Japanese front and his close view of the Russian revolution of 1905, shattered his faith in the power of various ideologies, including the power of literature. He stres-sed that as his knowledge of man increased, so he came to realize that even the noblest ideologies held no hope for man. He recognized that no revolutionary ideology could ever be realized without struggle and vio-lence, thus igniting the great chain of terror that passes through war, vengeance, and reprisal and back again. All philosophy, all satire, and all dramatic protest fall on deaf ears, or more rightly, ears that have been deafened by the noise of the great wars and the small. The philosophers and creators speak truly and justly to an audience of people whose entire life-style from birth to death is based on war—the struggle for survival, the battle of the classes, the reactive wars, the fight for democracy, the revolutionary war, the wars of reprisal, the wars of ambition. Wars are based on a policy of cheating, on the interests of the arms industry, and the capitalists, and they are founded on the love of power and the lust for domination. Korczak wrote:

No literature can possibly change the essence of things. True—there is such a thing as harmful literature—which incites to wars—but there is also useless literature—that which exposes the cruelty of wars. The achievements of good literature amount to no more than a diagnosis. Yet, the diagnosis is worthless if there is no one to cure the disease or innoculate against it.[14]

In order to demonstrate the various facets of Korczak's writing, we shall discuss a number of his works for adults, each of which reveals a different aspect of his creative world, beginning with his unique style and his interesting achievements in literary form through his expressionistic passages and stylistic concentration, and then ending in the intimate-confessional writing of his "diary." His writings are marked by his penetrative perception of human beings, his sincere wish to get to know them, and his great love for them. He wrote in his diary: "How many jewels can a man lose, for the sole reason that he has lost his patience for talking with people with no other motive or purpose than to get to know them."[15]

In the collective human portrait that Korczak presented to us, we recurrently encounter his own personal portrait as he looks at humanity and discovers himself. He wrote: "Sometimes we meet a man who we have not seen in many years. In his changed visage we see how we too have changed from what we were."[16]

13

The Drawing Room Kid

The Drawing Room Kid is Korczak's first important book, although it is the third he wrote, following *The Street Kids* and *Straw and Stubble*, both of which preshadowed the particular style and special thematic character of his writing—his penetrating satire of the Polish bourgeoisie and his deep spiritual affinity for the abused child. *The Drawing Room Kid*, a superb satire, exposes the decadence of the Polish bourgeoisie and the narrowness of its attitudes through shockingly realistic descriptions of the poverty of the proletariat.

Though Korczak wrote with pathos, his writing is always contained and never hysterical. The scream is mutely expressed through starkly exposed and painful descriptions. He wrote: "I want to cry out loud, but I cannot, I choke on the words, for they are hard and their edges are brittle."

The first installment of *The Drawing Room Kid* was published in 1904 in the weekly *Gloss*. The *Gloss*, edited by Yan Vladislav David, was a democratic-radical weekly concerned with philosophy, literature, society, and science, and some of the best creators and social philosophers in Poland contributed to it. The authors were members of liberal circles and were affected by the social and spiritual unrest of Poland at that time.

In a long line of pointed portraits Korczak revealed the face of higher society and the spiritually destitute bourgeoisie. His book describes the dreariness and misery of the "bosom of the family":

After I had spent a few days in the bosom of the family, I felt as if I had spent these days sleeping in dust and heavy heat; the eyes burn, the throat is dry, your whole being becomes engulphed in sticky dirt. . . . Every time a boring novel falls into my hands, I do not finish it, but rather cast it onto or into the oven without compunction. Yet, such a boring book, I have never encountered in my entire life. What utter poverty of content! Nauseating. The breath becomes heavy—and the soul yawns.[1]

Korczak found contemporary Jewish life distorted and poor in both spirit and action. During a conversation with Yerachmiel Weingarten, he said:

I am especially repelled by the assimilationist Jews, who are the only Jews I know. I see the great tragedy in the lives of the best of them, and they are the minority. Most of them are deeply buried in fear, in charade, in cheating and vacuity, and do not have the courage to take one valiant step in this or that direction. Most of my book *The Drawing Room Kid* is based on the hypocritical and false Jewish bourgeois class, which dares not mention its origins. You must learn what it does not have, in order to understand what it has, but I cannot identify with the great masses of ignorant Jews, the rabble. They too have been contaminated with repulsive customs and vices—the noise, the dirt, the cunning, the fear . . . perhaps I am wrong, but it is hard for me to adjust to their ways. When I write of them it is with an anger and scorn which are a sincere expression of my feelings—Yet I often regret it after the act . . .[2]

Yank, the hero of the book, the son of such a bourgeois family, introduces us into the very midst of the bored bourgeois house. From the moment we enter, we sense its misery, its lack of spirit, both in the shallowness of the relationships and in their emptiness. Yank observes this house, his glance first clinging to its external appearance, to the exhibitionism of its "modern" furniture, then continues to penetrate it more and more deeply, right into the empty core. He stressed that in this house there is not one piece of furniture in traditional style, not one object carrying memories of the past, signs of heritage, indications of continuity. This apartment carried all the arrogance of the nouveau rich who have purchased everything in style, thrown out the memory-laden old furniture, and replaced it with new and "stylish" furniture, identical to that of all other bourgeoisie like them.

It is not only external appearances that are empty and exhibitionistic, but the relationships within the family are impoverished and depressing. The relationships between fathers and sons are shaky. The father wishes to educate his son, but has nothing to educate him for, no tradition on which to build, no values to uphold, no certainties to believe in. During his conversation with Yank, the father tells him that he wishes him to be a human being, but he is incapable of defining the meaning of being human, and when asked about it, he stops by the window and taps the pane in perplexity. Yank interrupts and says:

If being human means to earn a certain number of thousands a year, to marry a woman, to beget children, to educate them to be parasites, and in time, when these children ask what it means to be a human being— to tap on the glass in place of an answer—then such humanity does not attract me even for a moment.[3]

It seems that this house lacks for nothing. Money is abundant, there is great affluence, all the funiture in the drawing room is fashionable, and there are even a few books that no one has read, which are placed on display in their decorated covers—yet, in fact, the home lacks in everything. Beyond the external relationships, the polite kisses, the empty conversations about art and literature, the arguments over taxes, markets, levies, the corruption of the workers and the dangers of socialism, the forced manners—one can see the terrible alienation. Yank calls out in pain:

> Why sir, my lord and father, are you such a stranger to me? When I look at you, sir, I see before me an industrialist, in whose manner and speech one can discern a large dose of dishonesty, I see an unsympathetic gentlemen, my usurer . . . and I his debtor, who has not paid my debt yet. I know that my lord will not send me to the executioner, I know that he will not send me to jail, that he will not abuse me, moreover—I appreciate his politeness and perhaps his generosity, yet despite this, please forgive me sir, I would prefer to owe anyone else but yourself sir.[4]

This alienation is slowly established as a result of faulty relationships, the false educational conception of the parents, and (mostly) because of their negative personal example. Yank relates how he sat in his father's office and read Anderson's tale about the mother who sought her dead child and sacrificed her beautiful hair, her teeth, and her eyes in order to find the way to death—and to her child. Still immersed in the deep and painful impressions of the legend, he saw a woman enter the office and kneel before his father. She kisses his hand and begs him to forgive her husband for having stolen two rubles' worth of merchandise. She beseeched his father and said that her husband was neither a thief nor a drunkard. Two of their children died last week, and the third is lying sick. The father remained as solid and cold as ice, replying that he cannot help her as he spares no pity for thieves. Yank ends the passage: "As she went out, the glance which she directed at me was one of impending doom. I shook with terror—clutching the Anderson tales in my hands. This was the first time my soul abhorred you out of fear."[5] Through this terrible combination of a legend of maternal devotion unto death, matched with the stony implacability of the father, Korczak is revealed in his full power not only as a portrayer of reality but as a forceful poet.

These descriptive passages show Korczak to be not only a master storyteller but also a sensitive educator whose sharp observational powers enable him to assess the distorted education of the Polish bourgeois family and to note how the parents destroy their son's world and damage his personality through a long line of acts and omissions. The parents do not notice how their offhand remarks, their words of caution, and their explanations shape the child's world, evoke his fears, and ruin his confidence. Yank said:

> You told me that one should not approach strange people, because they sell little children to beggars—that one should take nothing from strangers: neither sweets nor cherries, lest one's nose should fall off— that one must not lift anything off the ground, neither in the garden nor the street, lest one's body break out in ugly spots and boils. It seemed to me that beyond the four walls of the house there lurks a hidden force, a threatening foe, and that all strange people were enemies, seeking to destroy me.[6]

Korczak noted that the character of children is indeed destroyed by the fickle attitude of parents, their inconsistent allowances and prohibitions, their abusive pampering, their lack of attentiveness to the child and their incomprehension of his world. There are parents who imagine that by giving the child everything he desires, flooding him with presents, aiding him in everything, and preventing him from exerting himself or hurting himself, they are doing their best for him. They do not understand that they are thus destroying his independence, ruining his self-confidence, wounding his pride, and castrating him. Korczak portrays the relationships of parents and children with a great deal of irony:

> Here my son, have a muffin. Here dear, a clean handkerchief. Don't stick your head out of the window dear, you might fall! Don't run my angel. . . . Here you are son—education. Here, my darling, a diploma. Here, my treasure, a girl! Here swine, have some fun! Youth must have its fun. Darling, here, take it, favoritism, a job, status, a position in life. Do you see my love how good we are, we give you everything. We remember everything. Do you love us?—what? Give us a kiss . . . and now my son, here's a mate, you see—we have even thought of a woman for you. And now, take your wife's arm, take her to the bedroom—and now make some children yourself, you must do it yourself—there is no choice. But, can you do it?[7]

Korczak not only castigates the parents for their acts, but also for their omissions, for their inattentiveness to the child, for not providing the child with freedom, and for their inability to educate him to realize himself, to listen to his own heart, the secret of silence, the way of the soul. In Korczak's opinion we teach children a long list of external things: to find logarithms and to seek factors in a solution—anything rather than their own souls. Care is given to external things, to hygiene, to cleanliness, to manners and customs, but nothing is done to nurture the soul.

"You have bound my acts but my thoughts flew free. Because your care was always shallow, you did not manage to go deeper than my mouth: am I eating—and my earlobe: Is it clean."[8]

In contrast to the descriptions of the spoiled and hollow bourgeoisie, Korczak presents us with a great number of simple folk, the children of the tormented proletariat. Yank, the nervous and frustrated student, leaves the protective "bosom of the family" and wishes to take care of himself. He moves to live in the poor neighborhoods. From morning to night he is busy running from the private tuition which finances the lectures he attends and back again, encountering dozens of characters from among the poor and the miserable—victims of sickness, hunger, and constant worry. He follows the orphans and the homeless children who wander about the city. One never knows what they eat, where they live, and whom they befriend. He sits beside the bed of a sick child in a small hospital and tells him a beautiful legend. He meets the children of the poor, to whom life has been cruel, who remain full of imagination, clear of thought and full of longing for a story, some human kindness or an expression of love. He himself experiences the worries of earning a living, and of finding food and shelter.

> The thought wanders, veers off the narrow path of little cares. Little cares do not make rainbows in the skies, but entangle many creatures in their web. At the same time, there are the greater cares, for one must feed the children, one must feed oneself, and bread is hard to come by, though the land is so bountiful with grain; and one must have some place to live in, even in partnership—and that costs at least four rubles a month.[9]

Korczak compared the life of the bourgeoisie, ruled as they are by hypocrisy, cheating, corruption, and conventional lies, with that of the poor who live in destitution and distress, and who often succumb to despair, from which it is but a short step to crime and social degeneracy. He wrote:

> Now I understand how one can support a family with daily wages of four, three or two guildens, out of which one must pay for rent, food, clothing, laundry, oil, a doctor, medicine and a priest for the funeral. . . . I understand why the color of the children's faces is like that of a prison, like the color of the earth, why their eyes are stuffed in rotten frames, why their legs are bent as bows, and why only four out of ten remain alive.[10]

Yank also encounters a rich gallery of adult types. He has a long discourse with a whore, whom he encourages to talk in the hope of discovering the spirit that lies behind the vulgar facade. He wishes to expose that which takes place within her when she walks back and forth across the street and people pass her indifferently, as if walking by a lamppost. He does not wish to be sentimental but cannot hold back the question that leaps from his mouth: "Listen, little one, does not the sadness sometimes stick in your throat like a bone? Yes, like a bone, which seems to choke you until you feel terrible?"[11] He listens to the story of a mother who describes the death of Franusz, her little girl. He listens to the tone of her voice, reads her expressions, feels the pride that hides within the words of this miserable and destitute mother, with her many children and cares, as she involves the listeners in the story of the death, and says: "The graves of babies, strewn so thickly throughout the land, are the poetic element in the grey reality of tomorrow's workers."[12]

Faced with the intensity of the pain and the depth of the tragedy, the author loses confidence. All of the moral certainties in which he believed seem to collapse. Doubt gnaws at his heart. He is no longer sure if there is any truth worth living for, no longer certain that there is any hope or sense in the struggle. He bitterly demands—Does altruism really exist, or is it just modern literature on altruism? Can one still trust the leaders or has corruption destroyed them completely? Is a responsible leadership at all possible? Do all those scholars and persons with diplomas perceive the distress of society or do they only care for their own selves? He castigates the doctors who do their work mechanically and heartlessly, without any human feeling or empathy for the patient. He explains to these doctors that 80 percent of their patients are the victims of social ills, exploitation, and oppression.

> Tell them of the correlation between a damp apartment and a cardiac disability, between a heart problem and coughing—do something so they will believe in you, and stop treating the boy with cupping glasses . . . tell them, that a day will come when a landlord who lets out a damp attic, or an industrialist who lets out a suffocating workshop, will be tried for their sins in court just as a knife-man is tried for plotting against another's life.[13]

Korczak's descriptions are very intense. He does not use external literary effects to evoke shallow emotionalism, nor does he become entangled in his own emotions. His portraits are very sober, somewhat tough and painfully honest. Gdalia Alkoshi was right when he indicated that:

> A trend can be discerned in this story, which in time came to characterize Korczak's educational method: A deep internal resistance to the emotion of pity; that mental state of hypocrisy, which is fostered in bourgeois philantropic circles and termed altruism.[14]

Yet, the restraint of Korczak's expression, the parsimoniousness of his statements, and the moderate pathos of his words do not make his writing alienated or uninvolved. On the contrary, one finds evidence of a deep involvement in the fate of the characters; a true spiritual identification that does not allow for any fraud or rhetoric. At the same time, especially because of its precision, his writing often soars to the level of poetry. Korczak can perhaps be likened to that wonderful grandfather from the lyric chapter "Grandfather," who:

> walks from one apartment to another and sees tiny dust specks of eternity, a hive of people scattered over life's highway, which extends to infinite distances. I see human beings hanging on the long cobwebs of existence, as I see the dew, thick as tears, which drenches the air. I see tiny droplets of a huge wave of people. I see lonely willows. I see isolated grains of desolation, and each grain carries a thought and a feeling.[15]

Ytzchak Perlis rightly notes that Korczak was influenced by Chekhov in his analysis of the problems of social life and their artistic representation. Korczak respected Chekhov as a "social diagnostician and clinician of genius."[16] And, indeed, the heroes of *The Drawing Room Kid* remind one of Chekhov's short story figures: failures, unfortunates, and the wretched poor, whose lives he artfully portrayed.

The Drawing Room Kid was published in 1906, and it evoked a strong reaction from the reading public. The literary critics praised the book and stressed Korczak's literary achievements, acclaiming him as one of the leading authors of the period.

It is important to note that Korczak did not limit himself to writing literature with a social message. Simultaneously with the publication of *The Drawing Room Kid*, he continued publishing articles, sketches, and notes in his column "Horizon" in the periodical *Gloss*. In these articles he continued his battle for the improverished classes, spoke of the distress of the workers, presented proposals for social change, demanded reforms in the medical and welfare systems, and was revealed as a fearless social agitator.

A comparison between these articles and *The Drawing Room Kid*, highlights Korczak's artistic power and his ability to carry out a thrilling literary metamorphosis of his social struggle, thus endowing us with a literary creation in which the social pathos does not impair the artistic fabric.

In this book of Korczak's, with its many autobiographical elements, we can perceive the roots of his soul as a creator and the spiritual wellsprings of his educational enterprise.

14

When I Shall Be Little Again

Korczak's book *When I Shall Be Little Again*, published in 1925, is an interesting blend of his pedagogical writing and his literary-fictional writing. He tells the story of an adult who returns to childhood yet who has not forgotten his life experiences, his knowledge and his learning as an adult. In this way Korczak managed to create a double perspective: the perception of life and the analysis of events both through the eyes of a child and through the eyes of an adult. This double vision enables Korczak to conduct a thorough, intensive, and genuine examination of the world of children and the attitude of adults toward children. It also helps him analyze the educational system, illuminate the relationships between teachers and students, describe the school system, and deeply penetrate the kingdom of the child.

Zvi Kurtzweill was probably right in viewing this story as an illustrated example of how Martin Buber's idea of "encompassing" or "enveloping" might be realized in practice.[1] This concept describes the educator as simultaneously co-existing at the two poles of the educational situation: his own pole as the influencing party and the student's pole as the influenced party. The educator must sense what his opposite pole feels, he must know the limits of otherness and the grace to be found in establishing contact with the other.

The educator is aware of the student's experience, while the student cannot know the educator's education. Thus, while the educator exists simultaneously at both poles of the mutual experience, the student exists only at one pole. In Korczak's book the educator who becomes a child again can project himself to the other pole and create, in Buber's words: "A third figure in the dialogical affinity, based on the acutal and mutual encompassing, the mutual embracement of human souls."[2]

By availing himself of the help of a benign dwarf who converts the teacher into a child, Korczak is able to present the educational process both from very close up and from afar, both through the child's vision and the reflection of adult experience, from inside and outside at the same time. And, indeed, he successfully illuminates the problematic relationships between adults and children. He describes the child's conversation with adults as a dialogue of the deaf, in which the adults talk without speaking, and say their piece without listening. They say what they want to say without paying any attention to the words of the child, without any respect for his questions, and without any real communication:

Once I even asked:—Mother is a red ribbon prettier for a dog or for a cat? and mother said:—You've ripped your trousers again. I asked father:—Does every old man need a footrest when he sits? and father said: Every student must have good grades or he'll be sent to the corner.[3]

This incomprehension not only exists between parents and their children but also between teachers and their students. Korczak described the school of his youth as a prison in which children were beaten and given severe corporal punishment. Yet the new school, too, from which physical punishment has been excluded, is nevertheless oppressive to the child. Sometimes the teachers' mistakes are seemingly small and inconsequential such as when a child writes or paints something with dedication, with inspiration, as if driven by some inner creative enthusiasm, and the teacher suddenly interrupts him in order to rectify a small error or ask him for some trifle, and in a moment all is lost. The enthusiasm is gone and there is no wish to continue. Teachers do not understand that children often find it hard to answer even those questions for which they know the answer. "They are afraid lest they say something wrong and be embarassed. School demands that one speak as written, for the grade, whether good or bad, and not from the heart."[4]

When Korczak's temporally displaced hero thinks of the day in which he will return to adulthood and be a teacher again, he makes plans for reaching an understanding with his students, plans for breaking up the two enemy camps: the class on the one hand, and the teacher and a few apple polishers on the other hand. He tries to show the children that the life of the teacher is linked with the school and that there is no doubt that he strives within him to improve the place where he is destined to spend most of his life. "You shall complete your school studies and go your way, while we shall continue to frequent the school throughout our lives."[5]

Korczak devoted special attention to the relationships between the children themselves. With attention to minute details and a great deal of understanding, he presents dramas of jealousy and competition, spite and taunting, malice and vindictiveness, coexisting with true friendship, fraternity and close relationships. He describes how weak and sensitive children can sometimes become the victims of abuse by their peers. He shows how children can be tough and cruel yet at the same time loving, and weaves wonderful chapters of friendship between his hero and a boy called Mundak, or portraits of pure and sensitive love between his hero and a girl called Marichanka.

In many chapters he would enlighten adults and make them realize the extent to which their relationships with their offspring are based on misunderstandings, and the extent to which their good intentions often lead to misconceptions and injustice. The older child is often blamed for things that were perpetrated by the younger, thus creating a sediment of bitterness in his heart. Worse—such misdirected blame warps and distorts the relationships between brothers, branding these relationships with artificiality. Thus, for example, older children are told that they should surrender to their younger brothers whether they are right or wrong. They are forced to serve as a model and required to play with the younger siblings when they bother them. "We are often chastised on account of our younger brothers and sisters. Our suffering is thus doubled: because of ourselves, and because of the young ones."[6]

Adults refuse to act in equal fairness toward themselves and toward children. They do not think that a child may be offended, nor do they comprehend that when he is shaking with rage, he cannot concentrate on his lessons; that when dreams of love bloom in his heart, he finds it hard to pay attention; that when he worries about his hungry dog, his thoughts wander, and he is incapable of listening to the teacher's words.

By means of a story, a description, and a portrait, Korczak wished to open adult eyes, to awaken adults to a better understanding of their children, to cause them to perceive that children are more than just future people who have no existence in the present and must only wait and prepare for the future. His hero says:

> Our language is limited and hesitant (so it seems to you), for it is not completely grammatical. Because of this it seems to you that our thinking is confused and our feelings shallow. Our beliefs are naive for they are not based on bookish learning and the world is so wide. Tradition serves us in lieu of written laws. You do not understand our customs nor comprehend our affairs. We live as a nation of dwarves vanquished by giants, by priests who derive their coercive power from the occult. We are an abused class, which you would keep alive in exchange for tiny concessions and very little effort. We are very very complex creatures—taciturn, suspicious and close-lipped—and the scholar's glass and eye, will tell you nothing if you do not believe in us and sympathize with us.[7]

By means of a detailed portrait of the mental life of the child, Korczak would teach the adult the extent to which a child's day is full of experiences. In the space of a few hours, he is an Eskimo and a dog, chasing and fleeing from pursuit, a victor and an innocent victim of circumstance, a loving friend and a frustrated mate, a philosopher and painter, a sportsman and dreamer. The adult does not understand all of this because he looks at the child through the barrier wall of adolescence, and it is this barrier that Korczak wishes to break down.

On the other hand, because his hero is endowed with double vision, he is also well aware of the world of adults with all the cares, troubles, sorrows, fears, and lack of solace in their lives. The child is given a narrow window through which to look into this world:

> If I knew it then, I would never have wanted to grow up. It is better a hundred-fold to be a child. Adults are so miserable. It is absolutely not true that adults can do as they wish. We are allowed even less than the little ones. Our duties are greater. We have more troubles, our thoughts are more seldom happy. True, we no longer cry, but only because there is no use in it. We sigh deeply.[8]

The book's hero tells the children of the many moments in which the adult longs for a father and a mother, for it seems to him that only they would be able to listen, understand, advise and help, forgive and pity. He, too, yearns for the warmth and security of his parents' home and feels himself orphaned and alone in the world. Korczak's hero is overcome with a great joy when he becomes a child again and hears his mother say "my little son."

> The windows are transparent again. The carpet has regained its vivid colors. And my hands are young again, my feet are young, my bones are young, my soul is young, my tears and my happiness are young. Young joy-tears-and-prayer, a childhood prayer. I fell asleep. As if tired from a long walk?[9]

This book of Korczak's is especially worthy of note not only because of its educational ideas, its clear assessment of the world of childhood, and its wealth of observations, but also because of its literary quality, its rich illustrations, and its ability to give life to characters who are full of internal dialogue and spirit. Because of the clear vision of life that it presents, and by virtue of Korczak's great descriptive talent, this book is perhaps more poetic than his other books. He frequently makes use of imagery and allegory, of comparisons and portraits, of natural descriptions combined with philosophical notes, of spiritual passages colored with the hues of spring and sun or autumn and clouds.

The child is like spring, or the sun. The weather is wonderful and we have joy and beauty, or suddenly a storm, a flash, a rumbling—and thunder rolls—and the grown-ups—they dwell in a fog, surrounded by a sad darkness. No big joys and no big sorrows. Grayness and seriousness—I remember. Our joys and sorrows are a storm, while their joys and sorrows drag along—I remember.[10]

15

Bobo

Bobo[1] is one of Korczak's most perfect lyrical-philosophical creations. He called it a "story-sketch," which seeks, amid philosophical thoughts, to trace the growth of a baby's consciousness and feelings. Yet, rather than a mere story-sketch, this book is pure poetical-philosophical-prose: its philosophy is poetry; its associations enfold the entire cosmos; and its rhythm is the rhythm of poetry and song.

In the introduction to this work, Korczak describes the baby when it is already "old," has two lower teeth and four upper ones, and its mother thinks it is the wisest baby in the world. There is seemingly nothing new in the fact that a mother views her baby as unique and special, for it has been the way of mothers since time immemorial. Yet Korczak, who describes the excitement of the mother, cannot but insinuate a doubtful knowing tone:

> The mother is so proud, as if it were her own invention unknown to anyone before her, an invention which should be copyrighted, *which must be given a number, and handed over for continued exploitation to a capitalistic consortium in America*.[2] (Emphasis added.)

From this point on the work becomes totally absorbed in the wonder of the creation of life, and the secret of Bobo's formation, who in his first year is already "old" and full of experience and who came into the world bearing the story of the whole of life.

Korczak wove a new creation myth out of the chaos of alienation, non-communication, and lack of cooperation. In those days before creation, before life—"Each speck which met a similar or different speck, or which passed indifferently by it, lived alone, for itself."[3]

Although the future was already inherent in this chaos, this nonlife, it was not actualized and could not be realized for the question had not yet been asked, and no heart had yet predicted it.

It is here that we find one of Korczak's most basic views on creation and perhaps on life in general. There is no creation and no life without

197

questioning, without intending, without wishing. In the beginning there was the question, and the answer to that question is life, creation. Hence, when coming to educate a man, to teach him, to prepare him for life, it is not answers that you must give him, but the questions that you must encourage, you must foster wonder, promote the dream.

In contrast to the world of chaos, which is a universe of rift and dissociation, Korczak's created world is one of affinity, sympathy, and cooperation. "A strong voice shall be heard to command the scattered atoms to unite *and mutually build, out of self-surrender.*"[4] This force that disrupts alienation and indifference and creates cooperation is the power which creates the coalescence of atoms into the microconstellations of worlds, in which only the penetrating thought of man can reside.

Bobo, the human baby, exists millions of years before he is born to his father and mother and is registered in any communal register. He carries within him the very inception of life and has been present at all human events throughout history, from the spectacle at Mount Sinai to the destruction of the Bastille, from Sophocles' staging of Antigone in Ancient Greece to the building of the Egyptian pyramids, from the discovery of America to Space Travel, and his life shall continue to pass on from one generation to the next:

> Bobo has always existed, even in the most ancient of times. He has lived in the plasma of a lazy amoeba, has existed in that primordial chaos from which God created the stars, hung them in the firmament, fortified them with hidden strings of interdependence, and grouped them in star clusters.[5]

Korczak describes the moment of Bobo's birth as a moment of pain. The first great pain. It is not the aware and experienced pain of the adult, for such pain comes with greater wisdom. Bobo's birth pain precedes knowledge, is devoid of pictures, and empty of content or visions. Yet it exists and ushers in the knowledge of life. It is not by chance that Korczak, whose life was etched with pain, stresses that "The priest-pain has betrothed the tiny human creature to life?"[6]

Korczak recognized that the way before Bobo is fraught with difficulty and fear. Although the posing of questions may be the key to a meaningful life, Korczak is also painfully aware that "If you cast one doubt, a thick forest of questions shall arise—without answer, problematical. Bobo is cold. Bobo is afraid—bad."[7]

Using rich and original metaphors, Korczak described the development of thought—"Beneath Bobo's skull, in his brain, there are strange butterflies, woven of a mysterious fabric, in which colorful pictures move from one station to another, slowly forming into families and nations of picture-thoughts."[8]

Korczak recognized that knowledge, in the sense of information and realization, is impossible without knowledge in the sense of direct contact. Bobo's meeting with the world is one of knowledge in both senses. At the first stage, the essence of his knowledge is in the physical contact, in the direct relationship with the mother. It is with a distinct purpose that Korczak anchored the metaphors he used to describe those first relationships, in the act of *suckling*. Bobo seeks his mother's breast and wishes to suckle. On hearing his mother's voice, he wants to suckle her love with his lips. When the sun's rays warm his pillow, he moves his lips as if to suckle the sun. When his mother sings him a lullaby, he tries to nurse at the song.

Very gradually Bobo's eyes begin to perceive the pictures of the world about him. He touches the world with his vision and is thrilled with the sight. Yet night suddenly comes, vision dissolves, the contact is broken, and he cries. The parents rush to feed him or change his diaper, but he is not crying because of hunger or uncomfortable dampness but because he has lost the world he had touched. Then, he begins to suckle avidly and learns to make do with substitutes to drown his pain in food, in drink, in the readily available, rather than the longed-for and unattainable.

The adults are ignorant of Bobo's thinking. His aunt states that his brain is still asleep. She does not understand that the human brain is awake during every period of human life, and that Bobo's brain is fully aware. In their blind misunderstanding, the adults seek to feed Bobo's brain with nonsense, banter, and silly rhymes, when all the while it is acting and creating with tremendous force.

> Bobo looks and thinks. He thinks in a secret language which is the living basis of all languages, thinks without sentences in the pictures and picture fragments which serve every Bobo and every living creature in the world. He accumulates and sorts these pictures, populating the spiritual telegraph stations, gathering the material for building that wonderful edifice of symbolic human language in which every picture has a sound and spirit of its own, either good or bad, loved or hated.[9]

In the midst of this ode to human creation, to the powers of thought and creativity and to the great life potential inherent in Bobo, there suddenly comes an interval of pain, a sigh of sorrow. Korczak's lauding of Bobo is cut short. Although he is deeply moved by the natural powers of creation, he cannot cast off the burden of adult knowledge, of life experience, which is frequently a great load of disappointments. He foresees a future conversation with Bobo and speaks to him in the stuttering tongue of experience:

> My poor one, how I sorrow for you!
> For there is no greater tragedy than to be born a man.
> Since you were obliged to awaken to life, why not as a flower?
> Why were you not born a butterfly?
> Why not the tiny chick of one of the forest singers?
> As you grow taller so will you grow sadder . . .
> People thirst for knowledge.
> Bobo, how great the pain of seeking causes, purposes, ways and paths.
> How great the pain. . . .
>
> .   .   .   .
>
> Do not cry, Bobo! Little wrongs are not worth crying for, the great wrongs will come, and you will have forgotten how to cry.
> And the generations flow—flow. . . .[10]

In its poetic form, this conversation provides a sense of the special rhythm with which Korczak encapsulates the wisdom of the aged as it is brought before Bobo. Yet Korczak checks himself and says: "You laugh Bobo, you do not believe? You are right. This path a man must walk alone, and no one is to be believed."[11]

Following this contemplative, deflated intermezzo, which confuses the Canticum Canticorum with Ecclesiastes, Korczak resumed his description of Bobo's life's creation. As a great believer in direct contact, in doing and experiencing rather than passively accepting the opinions of others, Korczak stressed Bobo's hands as his most important means of communication with the world, of touching, doing, and creating. He warned against tying Bobo's hands, against limiting his reach and grasp, his touch and creativity, for it is with his hands that Bobo creates his hands and kneads his realizations.

At first, Bobo is busy accumulating, absorbing, and collecting. He builds himself a small hut of thought and fills it with everything he painstakingly accumulates and purchases as he diligently connects one pebble to another, one grain of sand to another, one marble rock to the next. It is only much later that he will begin to chip the marble and shape the pebbles into a statue of his own thought.

The magic wand that helps Bobo in this fantastic effort of self-creation, which provides him with the tremendous power required for the intensive activity, is the mother's smile, the feeling of love that she projects to him, the sense of continuity. In his poetic way, Korczak wrote:

> It seems that every bird smiles at its fledglings, that the affection toward the next generations surrounds every creature which blesses

tomorrow with its tiny movement, like some light blue nebula, full of heart stirrings. . . .

Even the old provider-sun reserves a smile for the forest mayflower, and the mayflower returns the gesture with a shake of its white petals, its pure fragrance.

Bobo returns a smile for a smile, not because he understands it. No, he does not yet know the happy language of the smile—but because it has been so for hundreds of thousands of years, because this day blesses the morrow with a tingle of exitement and the morrow answers in kind, for this smile flows through thousands of generations and makes one brotherhood of the white bones of heathens which lie in graveyards and the flesh of Bobo who ranges out into the far reaches of space, because this smile is the most fascinating of the links which bind the chains of the generations.[12]

Toward the end of the work, it seems that Korczak's strength fails him and his descriptions become shorter, faltering, and somewhat trivial. His poetic force seems to ebb, and one frequently encounters bland statements. One cannot decide whether this trend stems from impatience, a weakening of the creative power, or the disillusion that accompanies the first anniversary of Bobo: the grey secularity of life that increasingly impinges on the holiday of creation, shattering dreams, and dulling the excitement—casting a great fear on Bobo's first steps in life, until the writer cries: "Bobo, Bobo, with what frightening trust you march toward life!"[13]

In *Bobo*, perhaps more than in all his other works, Korczak has given birth to a work of art that excels in its lyricism and its poetic style, until at moments it becomes an ode to creation. Yet, as always, Korczak is wary of "art for art's sake," and between the lines, deep within the metaphors, he embeds a philosophy of life and an educational message as to the raising of a child who comes into the world with all senses open, who is often progressively dulled by harsh and insensitive educators.

Korczak perceives the great creation of nature, which no man-made artifact can equal. It seems that the Korczakian pantheism finds its ultimate expression in this work, with its great respect for creation and the acknowledgment of the necessity of providing the forces of creation with a human outlet for their realization:

In its creative inspiration, nature has wonderfully shaped the tiny man. Nature's inspiration has the conscience of a saint and the force of a giant. Nature casts great mountain blocks in anxious disorder, uses dew-drops to carve out every crevasse, crowning it with moss, and even the moss-buds are alive and happy and full of faith.

The work of art, that fruit of man's weary labour, misleads the eye and betrays nature. Hit the statue with a hammer and you are left with ruins, shells, a broken pot. But nip a tiny crumb off Bobo's shining pink fingernail and you will discover in it a new and beautiful series of pictures under the microscope.

Even if the blood had not flown in Bobo's fine, tiny veins, coursing in rivulets and rivers to the sea of the heart, even if sensations had not streamed through the rivers of his nerves to the sea of the brain, even if Bobo had lacked his great and wonderful power, still he would be a million times more prefect than all the creations of dead art, hanging in the somber halls of important museums.

Yet people come from all over the world to see these creations— torn, faded and soaked with sweat after many hours of repairs and improvements, registration in catalogues, adoration and tagging with market prices.

"You, Bobo, are priceless."[14]

16

The Senate of Madmen

About twenty years after he had won commendation for his first play *Where To?* in a literary competition where he signed the name Janusz Korczak for the first time, Korczak wrote his play *The Senate of Madmen*. This play, which he called a "somber comedy," was based on a fable he had written titled "How God Escaped from the Holy Church." And, indeed, somberness tinges the entire play, though it does contain some elements of humor, and perhaps could be best described with the term "somber grotesque" for it is a stark combination of satiric and grotesque elements that together create a nightmarish picture of the world.

Korczak used a triple dose of dark satire and black humor in this play in order to present his audience with a view of our modern world, warped and lacking in values as it is. The play was presented at the Atheneum Theater in Warsaw under the direction of Stephan Waracz, who adapted the play for the stage. The main forte of the play is in its social and moral message, for its theatrical and artistic drawbacks are many.

The play evoked considerable and mixed reactions from the critics, who were unanimous in pointing out Korczak's attempt to present a satirical-sarcastic picture of our modern world, but were divided in their opinion as to the success of this attempt. One critic, Anthon Slonimsky, claimed that "Korczak wished to solve all of the world's problems in two hours of empty talk."[1] While another critic, Karol Irjkovsky, lauded the play as a real contribution to humanity and noted that:

> The madmen in the play give the impression of being mad, but what are they really like inside? Behind the mask of madness they are men like all other men, differing only in that the problems of the world have reached the boiling point in their souls. They radically represent social, philosophical and cosmic problems. Hence they are philosopher madmen, people who have gone out of their minds instead of millions of others and for their benefit.[2]

In a conversation that took place with Korczak following the opening night of his play and after he had read the various reviews, he stated that he saw the play as the late draft of a play that is yet to be written. It was the actual staging of the play that taught him its weaknesses, its structural drawbacks, and dramatic failings.

When asked why he chose to express himself in a play, he stressed that he was not attracted by any ideational innovations or dramatic insights, but rather preoccupied by his wish to present well-known but neglected truths in the most effective way. It was not the philosophical revelation that he found important, but the emotional experience of things, and he considered that there was no better way to make such an emotional impact than by means of a play.[3]

The play is set in a hospital for the insane. The stage background included a giant globe made up of broken wood and pieces of colorful paper. A large clock was placed beside the globe, its single arm shaped into a giant sword. Amidst this symbolic scenery the madmen convened their senate. There are a few sane persons in this world of madness—the doctor, the child, and the woman Barbara, whose attempted murderer is incarcerated at the institution.

This attempted murder is strange, for though the man is right handed, he shoots Barbara Schultz with his left hand as if he were intentionally intending to miss. He shoots her for vulgarity and for what he calls a lack of education and a slight to culture. He believes that the extraordinary crime he has committed will provoke a debate, arouse a wide response, and cause the language of our faulty laws to be re-examined. He laments the fact that our courts seek out the big, extraordinary crimes and disregard the tiny, constantly recurring daily crimes that destroy the quality of life and make life ugly and disgusting. He complains that an infinite number of aggravating, small, and daily slights against *culture* are disregarded, and claims that this must be destroyed at the root, for there is no room for coarse people in a civilized culture. Such a man never relents, never gives the right of way, shoves everyone, pushes in everywhere. He is as scalding as the touch of poison ivy, and poisons the entire environment. Thus, the would-be murderer states: "It was not an uncontrollable urge, nor a spontaneous reaction nor a taking of the law into one's own hands—it was a *social act*. I wanted to shock public opinion."[4]

The logic of the speaker is a mad logic, and when he becomes carried away by this reasoning and proclaims that every civilized citizen must be given the right to annually kill one such bitch, one can easily hear the voice of madness that attempts to define his insanity as a humanitarian act, based on his generalization: "Killing in self-defence is permissible. And I have tried to defend humanity."[5] Yet, if we were to peel away this external mask of madness, we shall discover that the words of this madman and the words of the other madmen in the instituion contain bitter truths. There are ideas which go directly to the heart of the problem though they are presented in the form of demented ravings and great excesses that fall beyond the pale of what is defined as "sanity." In a world whose sane inhabitants are deeply mired in wars and enmity, oppression and blood, it is somehow hard to truly define "sanity" and decide what is sane and insane. The doctor in the play treats his patients with respect, permits them free expression, and allows them to live as they will, to convene and to act according to their own conceptions. The doctor is not understood by his colleagues who are strict and learned psychiatrists, who constantly see things from the outside; they are arrogant and aloof, safe and certain in the external norm which they represent. In contrast, the doctor emphasizes:

> I do not conduct doctor's inspections, but live with my patients. Rather than commiserate, I share their sorrows. I never belittle illusions. I can reject or accept the opinion of others, but I have no need for humiliation and feelings of superiority.[6]

It is especially because he is so involved and embroiled in the life of the psychiatric department that he is able to declare: "The percentage of stupid people is no different here than anywhere else." Although he recognizes the strangeness and uniqueness of the psychiatric hospital's world, he does not despise it or belittle it, and therefore states: "I insist that this place be a health clinic, rather than a place for the exploitation of helplessness. It is not a matter of knowledge, but a question of conscience."

The doctor's greatest success is a patient who has recovered but continues to visit the institution with his son on Saturdays and holidays. Rather than view the mental institution as a place that alienates people, casts them out of society, and locks them up by force, the doctor sees it as a station on the way to light, a place where stray thoughts might focus, and where one may have time to regroup oneself. He stresses that "Were our hospitals open to all (like churches) we would have far fewer cases of insanity and suicide. The proximity to a hospital could keep people from prisons."

A wonderful definition of the world of dementia as contrasted with the world of sanity, a definition which is both mad and sober at the same time, is provided by the worker who stands beneath the clock, stares at it and talks of life as dictated by the dictatorship of the clock. He describes our world as "A struggle between those whose clocks are slow and those whose clocks are fast, as well as those who forget to wind the clock when it stops. I thought it would be different here." He wished to believe that the realm of madness is free of the dictatorship of time, that it is another planet where the advancing hands of the clock do not scratch into the hearts of the citizens, and where the tempo of breathing is not that of the passing seconds. Thus the "madmen" seek to rest on another planet, free of the tyranny of time. And the worker says: "The doctor is right: When I tire of it, I shall arrange my thoughts, pack my belongings and change lodgings."[7]

The officer, too, does not view the time he spends at the mental hospital as squandered time. He reads and thinks a great deal and sees things in a different light than he had seen them when he was on the outside. He says: "Here, one sees life as if from the inside of a convex mirror."[8]

The decorator, another madman, believes that every man has a grain of madness within him, and in a blend of humor and sarcasm he asks the professor:

Do you know, my learned friend, this children's toy: A large egg made of wood—its colour red—and inside it, a smaller one, blue, and within that an even smaller yellow one, and at the very center, a tiny ball? Every man has such a ball within him. (Here, another character, the reveler, cannot hold back any longer and bursts out): If you were to thoroughly examine your balls, professor, I swear that you too would find your little ball of madness.[9]

Another member of the senate, Bison, is even more radical and claims that madness is the only possible reality, the salvation of a gradually cooling world and a degenerating, crumbling life of misery, in which the only law is the law of the jungle, in which people build sycophantic careers, in which the great peaks are slowly being leveled, in which everything becomes bowed and debased, in which prayer psalms are but empty tokens in the hands of avaricious priests, and poets and authors are lackeys of the establishment and the wealthy. In part madness, part clear sanity, he calls:

We are the last. We who carry the flag of madness. Only here. No longer do we do battle, but stubbornly fight for a humiliating existence . . . and what next? The pain seeps in like a rain of blood on barren sands. We are the last reserves, the last of the philosophers, the last who are still ready for sacrifice, for a life of truth and modesty.[10]

The truths of the play are placed in the mouths of the madmen. They are the honest speakers who do not know how to hide their thoughts, wear disguises, pretend, bury the truth that is within them or present an empty mask. They say their piece without fear and without discrimination. They speak the full and bitter truth, and hence there is great power in their words. Bison rejects an offer to put aside the mask of madness, for it is in madness and nowhere else, that he sees the last refuge in a world of bankrupt values, of sullied flags, of trampled ideologies. Angrily, he says: "You, sir, you wish to shed the disguises of madness? Where shall we wear them if not here? This is the only refuge, the last position. Freedom-equality-flags are in the gutter."[11]

Among the members of the *Senate of Madmen* we also find a royalist-nobleman who lives in the past and wears a tattered crimson coat. He carries ancient memories of kingly conduct and court manners and fights for the rights of the conservative nobility. Another member is a profiteer who knows all about lies and theft, and is constantly thinking of cheating, of making profits, of speculations and the utilization of connections for making money. He sarcastically notes that "The trick today is to turn decent hardworking people into thieves . . . our time will go down in history not as the time of wars but as the time of thieves, beginning with diplomats and ending in pickpockets."[12]

It is interesting that Korczak chose to present a Jew as the figure of the profiteer, and that even in the madhouse the stereotype of the Jew as an avaricious and greedy money grabber does not dissipate. Nevertheless, this profiteer is neither the Shylock nor the Fagin we know. Although he knows the ugly world of trade and theft, he is not involved in it, and when Jews are slighted he makes a stand and strikes back with a pointed barb, declaring: "The Jew has invented socialism, the promissory note, God and tolerance, and left you with the troubles."[13]

Also included in the Senate is a homosexual who sees life and the whole world through the reflection of his sexual abberation. The homosexual speaks in the language of smells. He dreams of a harmony of the senses and in a world full of stink and soot, grease and burnt concrete, he cries: "More flowers—give us fragrances!"

With a compass that always points at the poles, we could classify the words of the homosexual under the madness column of the table of sanity and conventional boredom. Yet there is poetry in this madness, and if we know how to look beyond the superficial meaning of the words and seek their deeper connotations, the madness will soon disappear. He says: "Perhaps we shall have smell concerts. A small hall, carpets, chairs, perfumes, body odors, hair, stockings, handkerchiefs."[14]

Just as the homosexual is obsessed with smells, so the innovator is involved with taste, and bases his entire philosophy on the pleasures of eating. Like Bernard Shaw, who once cynically stated that there is no deeper love than the love of food, the innovator claims that "Without an excellent cuisine and good wines, neither politics nor diplomacy would exist . . . the ideological battles are nothing but the rivalry between a glass of wine, a tankard of beer and a tumbler of vodka."[15]

It is interesting to note that Korczak picked the homosexual as the figure most suitable to express the most radical eugenic opinions. The homosexual proposes that couples who wish to have children should undergo a thorough examination, and that special matriculation tests be instituted, so that only those passing will be licensed to have babies. He considers it collective suicide that parents of crippled and demented children go unpunished.

The somber atmosphere engendered by his words, which darkly prophesy the Nazi vision of selective breeding, is dissipated by the jokes of the renovator, who proposes an amusing and enjoyable curriculum intended to prepare the examinees for their matriculation examinations in improved breeding. The argument ends with the cry of the reveler: "Long live uncle condom and aunt sulpha!"[16]

Additional members of the Senate are a worker who dreams of a day of liberation, a day without oppression or coercion; a reveler, already mentioned, who sees the world reflected through the bottle and the cuisine; an old man bent on seeking God who has been lost; a "sad brother" who carries the pain of lost ideals. The Senate is chaired by a uniformed colonel with crooked thoughts and a warped soul. This character drips venom and aggression and bodes destruction for the human race. He is a misanthrope who mocks education and is full of irrational hate for Jews. He is the arch-enemy of all socially progressive regimes, and he dreams and preaches of a dictatorship that will execute all artists and philosophers, stifle the supporters of progress, and liquidate the Jews. He makes a speech in favor of barbarism, which he sees as the natural state, and upholds war and killing. He demands that garrotes be built in the town squares and that all innovators and philosophers be hanged there. He dreams of cities that go up in fire, their whole populations burned to death. He proposes that the bodies of Gutenberg and Edison be exhumed, violated and burned, and that bloody madness should rule the world.

Is it any wonder that this colonel who harks back to the days of the Inquisition has a burning hate for democrats whom he proposes to sew up in bags and drown in the river. His fascism complements his male chauvinism and his great derision for women whom he proposes to drive to the marketplace at the point of a whip, there to be beaten. He hates the simple folk and technological progress. He laments the advances of life-saving medicine and despises the masses whom he views as repulsive and vulgar rabble.

He reserves particular hate for education which he blames for the dissolution of the family, for the loss of paternal authority, and for the provision of rights to women and their appointment as educators. He attacks women with a burning wrath and in doing so bares his Achilles's heel, his miserable sexual experience with a woman:

She even had something to say: that I am weird, a failure. And how they pretend to be weak, fragile—everything in order to put one off guard. They look down on us, and soon they will also be filled with revulsion.[17]

As with women, his venom is also directed at the Jews:

Behind everyone's back there is a Jew and a woman. Listen to what I tell you now: Judaism is not a religion, nor a race, but a *sex*. Something between a man and a woman. Less than a man, more than a woman.[18]

Like all tyrants, fascists, and various fanatics, the center of the colonel's life is war, and he rebels when anyone wishes to deprive him of it. He rejects the humanitarianism and culture that the reformers wish to foster, and cries in a bloody ecstasy: ". . . to destroy, to burn, then build again. To give birth then bury in mass graves. Oh, oh, the city is in flames, the inhabitants flee to the river. To persecute, to rob, to murder, to rape, blood!"[19]

Opposed to these terrible words, the worker bursts out in anger and warns of the pleasures of war enjoyed by the various officers, who drink until senseless, play cards, and fornicate while the soldiers rot in mud and in trenches, are shot and die so that their officers can receive citations of honor and climb through the ranks. He calls for the fostering of life and the replacement of the ritual of death initiated by the officers and leaders, the rulers and various governors. "Let each polish his own life himself, so that it shine with all the colours of the rainbow. The religion of freedom does not recognize the sin of happiness."[20]

Another who stands in sharp contrast to the monster who wishes to strangle the world is the demented old man who seeks God, whom he claims has escaped from the real world once He no longer felt wanted. The old man pulls Yank, the carpenter's son, to the front of the stage and asks him to tell of the search for the lost God. It seems that Yank, the child, is an improved image of Korczak himself, and that in the story of Yank, whose father was cured of his madness, Korczak therapeutically reworks his own experience with madness. Ada Hagery (Poznansky) phrased this well when she wrote:

The child Yank (a shortened and affectionate version of the name Janusz), is the son of a cured madman. The father is incarcerated at Yank's birth. His mother died in childbirth, but Yank was fortunate in that his father got well and was able to raise him. Throughout the week, his father works as a carpenter and Yank studies at school, but

what should they do on Saturdays and holidays? It is boring at home
and they therefore return to the same place where salvation was
attained—the madhouse. Yank's father serves the patients by doing various maintenance jobs, and Yank spends his time listening to them.
Thus, there are no dangerous madmen. Rather, one can learn from
these people, pass the time with them. This is Korczak's attempt to
work through the severe trauma he himself had experienced.[21]

The old man tells Yank that the true God has left humanity because human beings have become mired in materialism and technical achievements.
They distorted the human form, forgot to dream, and lost their feelings
until their heart turned to stone. They erected magnificent churches for
the absent God, but God rejected them and their glory and chose instead
to visit shelter-houses, hospitals, garrotes, and orphanages, and participate
in the meetings of criminals and prostitutes. One day He was discovered
by the little girl Marczisza in the nest of a lark and was returned
with great pomp and extravagance to the magnificent temple. Once He
smelled the incense, saw the empty rituals, so rich in external grandeur
and so poor in spirit and inner experience, he ran away again and
deserted humanity, soaring to the skies. On his way to heaven he cast a
shower of shining pearl-beads down to earth, and these entered the hearts
of children and were fixed there.

A very interesting figure is that of the "Sad Brother," whose heart
weeps over a world that is ruled by "poverty, suffering, revolutions, wars,
explosions, poisonous gasses, swords, shards and wreckages, and the ravings of Typhoid fever." It is he who opens the play by introducing us into
the atmosphere of a nightmare world. In a jumble of associatively flowing
words, he portrays the torn, rent, and warring image of this earthly globe:

> The mad globe of a crazed world. A sea of blood. Deserted continents
> of somber men (He climbs the podium and winds the clock), this
> crazed clock of an era gone mad. . . . I feed and douse fires [one
> should note that feeding and dousing a fire are the kind of opposites
> which cannot be reconciled, an intersection of opposites which create
> the rift], revolutions and wars. He lights a fuse. The explosion of poison-
> ous gasses. Ruins, avalanches. Smoking embers. Feverish ravings.
> Loss of consciousness. Long live the heroes![22]

The sad brother opens the meeting of the *Senate of Madmen* by praying
to a God whom he calls "The Artist of Artists." Not a vengeful and
jealous God, nor a merciful God whose created beings are dependent on
Him, but a God noted for his act of creation. When the monk says his
prayer, he does not ask any of the conventional requests of the accepted

litany, but only that God give those convened some of this power of creation so that they be able to build man and the world anew. And these are his words:

> Artist of Artists, weave our thoughts in light blue, endow our emotions with calm and peace, glorify our hearts, give us the power to hold out. May it be that a whit of your inspiration shall reach our minds and stir our blood through the bars and high walls. Lend us your ear, allow us to build anew, to rebuild man, life, the world, time, You.[23]

In a later part of the play, he has a touching monologue about the disappointments of life and the loss of religion. He laments the man who exchanges his life for a bag of rags, who puts his life on sale for a stale slice of miserable existence. The whole of life seems to him to be symbolized in the collecting of rags into a sack.

He is swept away in his own ecstasy and wrestles with life as if it stood before him, striking and ducking, yelling and cursing, bobbing and weaving, until he is completely spent and feeling himself alone, mumbles: "Alone, yes, madness, submerged like a deep sea diver."[24] Korczak placed some of the deepest and most beautiful poetry in the mouth of the sad brother. He is the hidden philosopher of the play, or perhaps the hidden poet. It is he who asks the questions which have no answer, but cannot be left unasked. It is he who says unconventional, sometimes controversial things, which though they might evoke objection, never permit us to remain indifferent. He challenges us with such statements as:

> Perhaps the sinner is the one who strangles sin within him? Perhaps the act of crime is the very act which awakens conscience? And perhaps conscience has gone mad? Perhaps to kneel over the grave of shattered dreams is the greatest agony of all.[25]

In his final monologue, which is very long, too long, the sad brother's philosophy seems to crystallize, and his figure grows until it dwarfs the madhouse and embraces the whole of the world to which he directs his song, ending in the words: "Your son and progenitor, your brother, my child!"

His moral-human tone of sadness supplements the madmen's sickening prescriptions for a world cure. One madman bears the message of Marxism and historical materialism, another calls for a dictatorship to save the world, a third believes in atheism, and each of them expresses his own opinion of life, saying his piece in total disregard of the words of his fellows. There is no contact or negotiation between the members of the Senate, no understanding between them—a blatant lack of communication, a garble of empty slogans and platitudes. Mirroring the larger outside world, a tragic chaos is created in the madhouse, in which madness and sanity become so intertwined that they are inseparable.

We find a later echo of Korczak's aversion to all forms of empty slogans, of his suspicion toward all bloody social experiments, and of his great disappointment in society, in a letter which he wrote while making his way to Poland from his second visit to Palestine:

> There are plans and prescriptions for revolutions, which are without fault or blemish, and which are boringly proper. It is for this reason that I have no curiosity about Russia, that tragic and bloody attempt to change and renew humanity. There was cruelty, there was madness, there was forced violence and valor under the whip. The same thing happened in Germany. With what arrogance and dishonor was the humanitarian flag sold out. For the measly price of inverted slogans. I have no curiosity as to lying Austria, nor frantic, tragic, France.[26]

The only ray of light and optimism in this play, whose atmosphere is so somber and destructive, is in the ending of the legend, wherein God has entered the heart of children, to be preserved there. Here, as in all of his works, his great faith in the child is once more restated. His belief is in the redemption of humankind. Moshe Zartal relates:

> In order to endow his work with authority and base it on precise knowledge, the doctor-author took counsel with a renowned psychiatric specialist; while the actors spent many hours and days at various mental institutions in order to absorb the atmosphere and the expressions of this world.[27]

Korczak viewed this work as more than a literary creation. Rather, its face was the bitter visage of the destruction of our world, which he evoked by dint of his own searching intuitions and fierce moral drive. He used strong colors, grotesque etchings, and horror-laden symbols to portray our self-strangling modern world, a world threatened by a terrible social and moral tyranny. And indeed, this terrible vision of Korczak's was to eventually come to pass, for the blood-thirsty colonel has been horrifyingly incarnated in Adolph Hitler and his murdering minions. And how mortifying to know, that even now, though that particular sea of blood is past, the *Senate of Madmen* is once more to be convened.

17

From the Ghetto

During his last year, in the months of May through August 1942 (until August 4th, the eve of his dispatch to the death camp), Korczak kept a diary that included notes, remembrances, deliberations, musings, plans for the future, dreams, and observations of life.[1] This diary passed to Korczak's friend and close helper of many years, the Polish author, Igor Neverly, and was published in Poland in 1958 after having passed through many hands.

The diary contains hints of Korczak's life in the ghetto and of his educational enterprise, and is a refined literary expression of Korczak's emotional personal confession. During those terrible days when he felt that the "Earth is trembling," that everything he had believed in throughout his life, and all he had striven to attain, was crumbling before him, he grasped at memories, at his lost childhood, at the landmarks of his stormy life. He recognized the fact that he would soon reach his last resting place, that the final accounting was at hand, and looking back on his life, he knew that though the defeats were more frequent than the victories and the suffering greater than the joy—yet his life had not been in vain. He was filled with a deep optimistic faith in the eventual victory of man, and despite the crises and the terrible obstacles, despite the sense of failure, he preserved that great positive sense and inner assurance that man will be ultimately victorious, that out of the monster's hide, a real man shall be born—for the monster is nothing other than man petrified. Because of this positive sense which Korczak carried within himself, he could never agree with Friedrich Nietzsche, who was the bearer of negativism, and whose harsh and pessimistic philosophy finally drove him behind the somber walls and bars of a mental insitution, where he died, at war with life.[2]

The notes in the diary are mainly a kind of inner journey. Korczak's descriptions and portrayals are not merely external sketches, they are paintings of his soul's impressions and his inner musings. The writing is not uniform. There are no guidelines or external order. The contents of the diary seems to have assailed the author during those nights of disappointment, pain, and insomnia when he sought to escape the nightmare reality of the ghetto by writing. The words burst forth from him in waves of memories mixed with daily events, snatches of dreams and excerpts of prayers, realistic descriptions and poetic hyperbole. It is a mixture of passing thoughts, unfinished philosophic fragments, grotesque and sometimes macabre sketches of the life of the ghetto, musings phrased as stanzas, wild imaginings, descriptions of meetings with both loved and hated characters, bits of conversation, headlines for future works, and even dry reports about daily life. In the introduction to the Hebrew translation of the diary, Ytzchak Perlis rightly noted:

> He attempts to analyze the reality of the present in which he lives; yet the present itself is not a normal concept to be expressed, as is usual, in the time-units of the day, the month, the years. In the ghetto there is only one form of present—Now. This moment. A man does not know if he will live another hour, let alone a day or two. Hence Korczak's attempt to flee the present in two directions: toward the past, the retrospective course, or toward the far future in which he seeks to find solutions to human, social and world problems; and when he does not find logical answers, even here, he goes "beyond man."[3]

It was especially in the face of death that Korczak devised rich and comprehensive plans for the future. He wished to write a book on night at the orphanage and the sleep of children; to write a two-volume novel about two pioneers at the foot of the Gilboa mountains in Palestine; to create a series of biographical stories as a sequel to the story of Pasteur, including books on Pestalozzi, Leonardo Da Vinci, Kropotkin, Pilsudsky, Ruskin, Georg Mendel, and others. He also wanted to write a book about the child-king, King David; to prepare a comprehensive study (based on five hundred diagrams of the heights and weights of the children which he had accumulated over the years) of the development of man; and to publish an autobiography.

Because of the central weight that he left to personal example, Korczak attributed a great deal of importance to the writing of his autobiography. Akiva Ernest Simon, who wrote of this matter, was right when he noted:

> One of the most effective means which Korczak used to influence his pupils was, it seems, his own direct and personal words. In his autobiographical urge he was no different than the other master pedagogues—Rousseau, Pestalozzi and Tolstoy. This is not surprising: Anyone whose attitude to the private life of his fellow man is one of deep respect, naturally holds his own inner history, his own personal spiritual drama, as both important and valuable.[4]

In writing of his intended autobiography, Korczak stressed: "Yes, about myself, about my own small and important personality."[5] He also noted the great effect that such a work might have in its presentation of a man, unadorned, in his moments of weakness and moments of strength, in his lassitude and valor, his saddest hours and most beautiful moments. He wrote:

Someone once maliciously wrote that the world is a drop of mud, hung in space, and that man is an animal with a career. Possibly, this might be so. But we must add: This drop of mud knows suffering, knows love and tears and is full of longing, while the career of man, should we honestly examine it, is doubtful, very doubtful.[6]

Korczak clarified that autobiographical writing might be full of repetitions and that the telling of facts and experiences might entail, in fact must entail, some contradictions. This is no defect, but proof of the fact that an autobiography is not a scientific and factual report of life events. It is a focus on the most important of past moments, those events which were deeply engraved in the soul of the writer. Moreover, memories depend on the writer's experience at the time of writing. It is these current experiences that stimulate him to encounter the past and bring it magically to life through the spiritual coercion of daily experience.

When he reviewed his past and the various life plans he had devised, Korczak quoted Dostoyevsky, who said: "All of our dreams come true over the years, but their shape is so altered that we no longer recognize them," Korczak added—"I recognize my dream from the years before the war."[7]

In one of the most interesting chapters of his memoirs, Korczak divided his life into seven-year periods and sketched a short portrait of each such period in his life. One can learn a great deal about his personality from these terse sketches, each of which is marked by one dominant life experience. The first seven-year period is marked by his early family experiences, and the second period by his many unrequited loves, by his introspection of the world, and by the birth of his sense of having a mission in life. He wrote:

The fascinating world is no longer external to me. It is within me. I do not exist in order to be loved and admired, but in order to act and love myself. The environment is not obliged to help me, but I must care for the world, for man.[8]

The third seven-year period is marked by religious maturation and his service in the army. If it was school that trapped him and depressed his spirit during the first two seven-year periods, it was the army and society that imprisoned him during the third period. He felt a great urge to conquer, to fight for space. "One must conquer and do much, so one will have something to lose."[9] The fourth period is marked by the need to act proficiently in his own limited workshop. He wished to become his own model, to be a good doctor. He did not wish to emulate known figures of authority. The fifth seven-year period was marked by a sense of frustration, the loss of the chance to take first prize, and a deep loneliness. Indeed, despite Korczak's endless addiction to children, to his work, and to his educator friends, he nevertheless remained, throughout his life, a very lonely man. He wrote:

> Loneliness is not painful. I cherish my memories. A schoolmate on which I chanced on the way—a pleasant conversation over a cup of black coffee in his cafe. None will disturb us here. I do not wish for a friend, for I know that I shall not find one. I do not seek to know more than is possible. I have reached an agreement with life: We shall not disturb each other. A man should not leap higher than he can jump. It is fruitless, besides. It seems to me that in politics one terms it thus: "We have delineated the areas of influence and set them here and no further. Not beyond. Not above. You and I."[10]

The sixth seven-year period is marked by the first glimmerings of the sense of death, and though he does not yet feel death to be within him, he nevertheless thinks of it often. The seventh period is marked by expansion and the will to go on living. He wrote: "A wide course, I would say, like the grandly flowing Wisla."[11] The eighth seven-year period is marked by a diminishment of power, health, and energy, while the ninth is marked by the direct encounter with death, by the sensation that the circle is about to close and the dream of childhood is about to meet the awakening of death.

> A dream again. Inside a train I am transported into a small cabin, one meter by one meter, in which other Jews are already present. More dead tonight. The bodies of children. A dead child in a tub. Another body, flayed of its skin, is lying on the morgue bench, clearly breathing. A new dream: I have climbed high on a double ladder and father feeds me with slices of yeast cake. A large chunk, covered with melted sugar and full of raisins, and everything that cannot fit into my full mouth, he crumbles and puts into his pocket. Drenched in sweat I awake at the most terrible moment. Is not death just such an awakening at the moment when you deemed that there was no way out?[12]

Doubtless the qualities that Korczak ascribed to his life did not fully characterize his various life periods, but there is much in his attitude toward his own life to illuminate not only his past but also his mental reality at the time of writing. On the other hand, these fragments, which echo the horrifying experiences of the ghetto under Nazi rule, faithfully describe Korczak's inner world. In hints, in telegraphic language, he described the changes that took place in the Jewish quarter as it became a mixture of prison, plague arena, madhouse, and bordello—a gambling casino where life is the stake. Faith, the family, motherhood—all were trampled. All spiritual values were traded in the market place—a terrible moral wilting. In the context of this deterioration, Korczak wrote a parable in which he is the moral:

> A blind old Jew was left in Meishineitz. He was walking, leaning on his stick, between the wagons, the horses, the cossaks, the cannons. Such cruelty to leave a blind old man like this. They wanted to take him— says Nastke—, he insisted on remaining, because someone must guard the synagogue. I met Nastke when I helped her search for her little pail, which the soldier had taken, and said he would give back but didn't. I am the blind Jew and Nastke at the same time.[13]

Korczak's diary is a reliable literary witness of the world of a man involved in the creation of a man, the liberation of a human form from the cruel slab of stone in which it is trapped.

Of special interest are the testimonies of Korczak's helpers and friends that his diary was written in the exact style he used in his conversations with the educators, instructors, and the Burse protégés at the orphanage. Many chapters do not seem to have any central issue. There is a sense of improvisation, of associative leaps from one matter to another, and an almost stenographic brevity that transmits a wealth of emotional and mental material in a few verbal units. Yona Buchan describes such conversations at the orphanage and tells of Korczak's style:

> In a few words it tells of his new research in the area of nutrition; which with a light sketch—tells of the new story he is writing; notes a letter he has received; hints of some child, who was at the center of the institution's events this week; and then—associations and dreams of the future. Suddenly, you realize that all these strings are somehow tied and that all lead to one purpose, which was his intended purpose for today. Sentences which are sometimes bereft of verbs. One word. Another word. A parenthetical clause. And again, a hyphen (i.e.: a hidden, yet tangible, purpose), colon: conclusion. Almost without pre-

positions, yet nevertheless, behold: A language clear and transparent not only to professionals and those in the know![14]

These style-traits can be found in most of his books. They can be discerned in those of his radio talks which have been preserved in writing, in the chapters of his *Humorous Pedagogy*, and in his various scattered articles. This special style also attracted the attention of the many linguists who considered Korczak's works to be innovative Polish literature.

18

The Miracle Worker: Janusz Korczak's Books for Children

The child, like the spring, understands and works miracles.[1]

In the introduction to his poetic work *The Spring and the Child*, Korczak wrote:

> Perhaps the child can feel the approach of spring, but cannot understand. He feels it, as he feels the truths of life, the tragedies which we take such great care to hide from him. Perhaps, because of this premonition, he is the only one who is right in laughing while crying.
>
> He senses the approach of spring beforehand. Senses that moment at which man will reach an understanding not only with his fellow man, not only the black with the white, the rich with the poor, the man with the woman, the adult with the child—but an understanding with the sun and the moon, the water and the air, the white birch and the forest mayflower, the dog and the sparrow. His heart tells him that it is not through passion and struggle, but by means of play and voluntary effort that we will attain all that lonely, tragic, godforsaken humanity has striven and longed for through crosses and pyres, blood and sweat.[2]

These lines aptly express Korczak's perception of the child, his great faith in and his vision of the child as a sensitive reader capable of apprehending what is said between the lines. In his books for children Korczak did not hide the darker and sadder aspects of life, neither did he sweeten or distort the facts. Nevertheless many of his children's books and stories are characterized by a great deal of optimism, arising from his belief that the child is the herald of spring and that the child shall bring the wished-for reconciliation between races, nations, classes, sexes, and ages, as well as the acceptance and embracing of nature.

Korczak did not present children with an idyll. He did not provide them with illusions of a beautified and joyous reality, but with the bitter truth of an embattled and squabbling world, and a perplexed and violent society, whose members are suffering and conflicting humans. His portrayals, his descriptions, and his plots all carried the message of the ability to attain; the power of passionate struggle, devotion, and sacrifice; the tenacious struggle to create a new world order; the establishment of a new understanding between adults and children; and the application of imagination and initiative. The message was one of a new, better, and more beautiful life.

Korczak is revealed as a children's author of great stature, great love, endless warmth, and one who had a deep knowledge of the child's world. His books provide reliable educational instruction, deep observations of the child's soul, and a strong desire to give the child something of an adult's life experience. Korczak's writing combined a simplicity of style with ideational depth, and he battled against the mistaken and anti-educational concept that writing for children is easier and less of a responsibility than writing for adults. To the contrary he was of the opinion that anyone who wished to write for children was burdened with a double or even triple responsibility, for there is no one so open as the child to influence and impressions. Above all, the children's author must know the child, understand his pure world, and be careful not to mar this purity. The imagination of children is active and blooming; a small cloud or passing butterfly can become worlds of magic. The young child has a world of his own, a world created entirely for his benefit. The skies come down and entertain him with their myriads of shining stars and wonderful clouds. The author must be able to penetrate this world and soar with the child to the skies of his dreams and imaginings. Korczak was especially adept at penetrating this, and he was revealed as a master storyteller for children. With a great ache in his heart he voiced his complaint against children's authors:

> Is it by chance that everything done for children is done badly? An excellent painter for the adults, and a less outstanding painter for children. The stories written for them, which seem to have been written out of charity, composed by any fool who has a way with words, and the same holds true for the poems and rhymes written for them. All that the adults refuse to hear, is given to the child.[3]

Janusz Korczak's children's books are full of his childhood dreams, wishes, and aspirations. In his books he realized his wishes for children's self-rule, for world justice and equality, and for the victory of honesty and goodness. Korczak knew that imagination is the child's omnipotent force, which compensates him for his helplessness. "When the child cannot go out onto the street, he conducts tours to desert islands and far away oceans. When he has no dog—he willingly commands a platoon."

Korczak allowed his imagination free rein in his works and created wonderful worlds for the young child, worlds rich with the color of dreams, brimming with creative ideas, and captivating to the heart of the child. Moreover, every book is full to overflowing with educational ideas, intended to prepare the child for a better, more beautiful world. Despite this legitimate wish to educate, Korczak's stories never degenerate into sermons, and didactic content is never their main focus. The educational ideas are blended into the rich tapestry of the story, in the form of situations from the life of the individual and society, which are woven into the interesting texture of the plot and the riveting descriptions of characters. Even when he would provide children with practical advice, moral counsel, and rules of conduct, these were never appended to the story extraneously, but were always a direct consequence of its inner texture, its literary essence.

Because of this deep faith in the child, most of Korczak's works for children go deeper than what is directly evident on the surface; they constitute a multilayered structure whose upper layer exposes hints of a deep and rich inner world, of social views and radical social criticism. Korczak's books are also full of humor, with its ambivalent attitude—both intimate and detached at one and the same time; of lashing satire, of grotesque portraits, and sometimes even of a tiny hint of sarcasm. This is the reason why Korczak's children's books are also read with great pleasure by adults. The dramatic structure of the various scenes, the shaping of the dialogues and monologues, the author's many remarks, and his involvement in the plot itself—all serve to open gates to the many layers of the works.

Korczak believed that children are very close to poets, that they are similar to the poet in their characteristics, and that this spiritual kinship is the source of their great impressionability as well as their capacity to enter into a story, totally identify with it, and introject the characters and the behaviors described. Yet, in his books, Korczak was careful of any manipulation of emotions, and he avoided melodrama and emotional blackmail. He knew that though they are quick to feel and to identify, children are capable of intellectual criticism, and are able to differentiate between the true and honest and the false and deceitful. He wrote:

A poet is a person who is capable of great happiness and great sorrow, easy to anger and deeply loving,—a person who feels strongly, who is easily excited and who sympathises with the feelings of his fellows. And such are children. The philosopher is a person who deeply contemplates and weighs and who wishes to know how everything, in truth, is. And again, such are children. Children find it difficult to say what they feel and what they are thinking about, for speech requires words. And it is even harder for them to write. But, in truth, children are poets and philosophers.[4]

Korczak noted the ways in which children expressed themselves. He was very attentive to the style of their narrative, their mode of description, and the emotions that they expressed, and was deeply impressed by the parsimony, restraint, simplicity, and directness of their style, in which expression is intimately tied with the experience itself. All redundancy and embellishment are removed, and the expression is crystalline and strong. He excitedly quoted the story of six-year-old Stefa, which he viewed as a poetic gem:

When we came home, there, behind the fence, lay a little bird. Then Ruma wanted to take it and I saw it too. I wanted to take, and I took it from that fence.—When we took it, all the girls began to gather and look. Then we brought it here. It had such white and grey feathers, the beak was with blood and its eyes were still open.—We brought it here and the girls buried it.—They made this little hole in the yard and wrapped the bird in paper and covered it with earth. Perhaps a boy, who killed on purpose. Its beak was wounded and its head moved.— Rotkovskit almost cried.—That one. When she sees something she moves her hand like that and already wants to cry, but she didn't cry. Only sort of choked on her tears.[5]

Korczak strove to write precisely such a naked story, without pathos or platitude, preserving the direct expression and the tone of the child's voice in many of his short stories. He was not always successful, and in a number of stories, such as *"Human Beings Are Good,"* the writing seems forced, and the adult tone, concepts, and worldview, as seen through the eyes and expressed through the mouth of a little girl, are blatantly phony. Other of his stories excel in their clarity of expression and in the direct and honest appeal to the child's world.

Korczak was aware of the subjects that are of interest to the child, which attract him and evoke his curiosity and imagination. He wanted to fulfill the child's wishes, meet his spiritual needs which demand satisfaction through reading, and enrich his world. Although he undoubtedly wished to promote the child, shape his character, and open his eyes, he always did so with full respect for the child's world, the problems that bother him, and his ability to grasp what he reads. Thus, Korczak related how before he wrote the book *Yotam the Magical*, he talked with children about sorcery and necromancy, read them various chapters, and corrected, changed, and reworked the story a number of times because he wanted it to be an interesthing book, suitable for the development and intellectual grasp of children.

Korczak was well aware of the capacity of children to read, the extent of their attention span, and their interest in the written story or the orally told fable. Though he did not set any rules for the writing of children's books, or formulate his ideas on the subject in any abstract form, his great understanding of the essence of children's literature is clearly evident in his stories. For example, he recognized the importance of reiteration both in the written and spoken children's story. Repetition helps lighten the reading load of the child who has not yet completely mastered the art. It establishes the new concepts he has learned, entertains him in its evocation of what is already known to him, increases his confidence, and amuses him with the rhythmic movements to which his ear has become accustomed.

Reiteration contributes to the feeling of the child that he has mastered a story. When there are no repetitions, the child might lose both the idea and the background. The child must be returned to the events and the ideas by means of reiteration.[6] Korczak planned to write a book intended for two year olds, which was to be based on a series of repetitive, very simple sentences that are on the borderline between alliterative mumbling and a lullaby. Although this particular book was never written, Korczak fostered his element of reiteration in his stories for children, taking care to introduce both contextual and colorful linguistic reiterations. Many excellent examples of this can be found in his legends for children, such as *A Tale for the Youngest*.[7] He also implemented this reiterative technique in his longer stories such as *King Matia the First* or *The Stubborn Boy*.

Let us examine the opening of *King Matia the First*:

> *And* so it was. . . .
> *The doctor said* it will be very bad *if the king does not get well within three days, so the doctor said*.
> "The king is mortally ill, *and if he does not get well within three days*, it will not be good."
> Everyone was very sorry, and the eldest minister put on his spectacles and asked:
> "Well, what will happen *if the king does not get well?*"
> The doctor did not give a clear answer, but everyone understood that the king will die.[8]

The exact repetition of sentences does not indicate a loss for words on the part of the author, but a conscious desire to help the child, to introduce him to events through things he already knows, so as to enable him to easily grasp the tale being told.

Another example of this style of writing, and perhaps a more strictly structured one in the repetition not only of words but also of the form of the musical verse, can be seen in the opening of Korczak's book *The Stubborn Boy*:

> *This is no legend, this is the truth*
> *This is no legend. This is the truth* about one stubborn boy.
> I begin so.
> *There was a poor house.*
> A small village and *a small and poor house.*
> Louis was born here.
> His mother was the daughter of a gardener.
> Louis does not play with the boys, and his mother calls him to come home.
> Louis *reads, writes, draws, goes to school.*
> *Plays, reads, writes, draws and goes to school. He is a boy with all the other boys.*
> *He is a boy like all other boys*, but he will be *great.*
> Not *great* in stature, not high, but a *great* scholar. *Books will be written about him*, they will *write about him* in newspapers, *books will be written about him.*[9]

Korczak also considered the intonations of voice, the narrative tone, and other effects involved in telling a story or fable aloud. Sometimes, he would leave a story incomplete, content with having evoked the children's reaction, with having left room for thought, and with having worked his arousing action on the soul of the child. He wrote:

> When you begin to tell a tale, do not try to end it. A tale can serve as an introduction to conversation, or can be woven into the conversation. A sequel is to be supplied only on demand.—One tale can be retold many times.[10]

Korczak recognized that the legendary tale for children must take account of the differences between children because the capacity of different children to absorb a story is conditioned on a complex array of factors stemming from their personality, the situation they find themselves in, their emotions, their expectations, and the like. In discussing the legend for the child, he wrote:

> Children are different, their life experiences are different, their psychic structure is different, their day is different, their present moment, their feeling of self, their desire to listen. The self-same legend which was

desirable yesterday, is not so today, and might even become a nuisance. Possibly if that self-same legend was told in the evening, at dusk, or in a forest, under the shade of a pine, or on stairs or by an attic, or perhaps when a peer relates it, or grandmother, and possibly if just a small group is listening, then the legend might have been different, totally different.[11]

Korczak claimed that it is best to tell a story to individuals—to no more than a few children gathered about the educator. They look into his face; they follow his movements, his expressions, his smiles, and the look in his eyes. The attention of each child is different and is expressed differently. One child sits immobile, stares into the eyes of the storyteller, and hangs onto every word he utters. A second is restless, moves around but never stops listening. A third, mumbles, telling it to himself in his own words. A fourth shares his impressions with his friends, and each absorbs his impressions in his own way.

Although a legend may be told many times, no telling is like another. Each time the understanding of the storyteller deepens; he tells it with a special intonation, he tailors it to the particular audience before him, and so on. Korczak related that he once asked a great actor if it were not boring to repeat the same role on stage night after night, and the actor had said:

Memory serves the lines mechanically and the actor instills the role with warmth, color, tone, and new inflection, every time. Above all, the actor always senses and tests the reaction of the listening audience.[12]

This must also be the way of the storyteller. Only if he were to act so, look at his listeners himself, examine himself anew every time, and remain open to his environment, only then will his tale become an act of creation rather than mere work. Korczak related that he had no more than ten legends at his disposal in the course of his practical work at the institutions, for he always felt that one must get to thoroughly know the legend, that one must rework it and polish it with great skill, and tailor it to the hour and place. During his thirty years of work, he told "Puss in Boots" hundreds of times, and it was never exactly the same story. He wrote that he knew at precisely which point in his story the listener would laugh, when he would draw closer, and when he would touch his hand.

Because he recognized the importance of children's literature, Korczak suggested that a special chair should be provided for this important subject in the framework of one of the pedagogical departments of the universities. In his humorous style he added that if such a chair should be established, he would be able to write a two hundred and fifty page monograph on the subject of *Puss in Boots*.

Korczak frequently thought about his writing for children. He recognized that the subjects of children's literature should be taken from the child's world. The child must feel a special bond with these subjects, identify with them, be curious about them. When reading or listening to a work of literature, the child fully enters the literary world of action and actively participates in it. He sees the heroes of the work as a reflection of his fears and wishes, his reality and dreams, and it is utterly irrelevant whether the hero is an adult, a child, an animal, or an object, for all these are alive and active in the child's world. The child is therefore especially fond of those subjects which allow him to identify with the heroes and participate in the events of the story. Hence, the child's special liking for works whose characters are children. And, indeed, most of the heroes in Korczak's writings for children, are children. Children's literature reveals the child to himself, shows him his own hidden emotions, provides him with an opening to knowledge of the world and knowledge of himself in that world, and to a better understanding of both his immediate and distant environment. Korczak wished to adapt his writing to this world of the child and to his desires. He wrote:

I have spent many years with the youngsters. I see what they do, converse with them, hear their questions and complaints. I know what bothers them, what disturbs them, I understand the difficulties—and I happily sit down to write, but the moment I take my pen in hand and begin, everything is immediately very different than it was in thought. Everything becomes so difficult and heavy. It is only after the chapter is finished that you remember that there is still something missing, and another thing, and another, and discover that you have written too briefly on one thing and it is therefore incomprehensible, while another less important thing was discussed overmuch and at length. You begin to correct and rewrite, but that does not help, as if someone else wants to do the job and someone else is writing. Things are one matter in thought, in the imagining mind, and another matter on paper—in letters and words. And even the desire is gone: why write? are there not enough interesting, beautiful and useful books? And besides, are things really as I think they are? Perhaps, wishing to clarify, I am only complicating things and making the understanding more difficult? It is very easy for an old man to err when he writes about youngsters for youngsters. And if there is a mistake, instead of winning trust one can lose it entirely.[13]

The conflicts that beset Korczak in connection with his writing only go to prove his serious, responsible attitude and the great responsibility with which he approached the task of writing for the child, and particularly the writing of children's literature.

Korczak's books for children are wonderful in their capacity to instill values. They are not didactic books, and he does not teach or preach, but they educate by presenting life itself, by weaving thrilling action stories, and by presenting characters who seek, struggle with their fate, and shape their own lives. The young reader's knowledge of life is deepened, his critical thinking is sharpened, and his empathy with his fellow men is increased.

Because of the deep respect Korczak felt for the child he treated the child with full seriousness and appreciation. He never allowed his writing to become childish, was never vain, and never attempted to hide anything, but, on the contrary, he wished to involve the child in everything, to cause him to recognize the different and sometimes distorting faces of society, to think about life, and to consider its essence. He fought the belittling, forced, childish attitude that dons a mask of consideration and care for the child in a vain attempt to conceal the basic distrust of the child which is displayed by so many adults. He wrote:

We see children in their stormy exhibitions of happiness and sadness, and deeming them different from us, we fail to notice their quiet moods, their silent thoughts, their deep emotions, their painful doubts, their gnawing suspicions and their humiliating uncertainties, in which they are very much like us. "Real" is not only the child who jumps about on one foot, but also the child who unravels the secret of the wonderful tale of life. We are obliged, however, to disregard the truly "artificial" children, who unknowingly repeat the phrases they have snatched from the mouths of adults. A child does not know how to think like an adult, but he knows how to childishly weigh the serious adult questions. Lack of knowledge and experience force him to formulate his thoughts in another way.[14]

In his children's stories Korczak attempted to rectify this lack of experience and adapt his writing to childish thinking. He established a running dialogue with his readers. He told them a thrilling story, yet occasionally interrupted the narrative, broke into the story and discussed it with the readers, voicing his opinion and sometimes even providing a moral. There are moments when the voice of the teacher and educator got the upper hand, and, unable to contain himself, Korczak ended his story with educational instructions. Thus, for example, he ended the story "Listening Son" with the following lines:

If you have such a boy at your school [an innocent and clumsy boy who becomes the butt of much ridicule and reproach], do not laugh at him and do not taunt him. He might not be very bright, but he can be pleasant and good, and will not disturb anyone. Yet if you ridicule him, he will begin to act up in order to please you. If you anger him he will become bad and malicious. He will then become an enemy both to you and the teacher, and remember! He too has a mother who loves him and wants him to grow up and be a man.—And who knows? A good, if not very wise man, might do much for mankind, while a wise but evil man might, in his life, cause much evil to humanity.[15]

Occasionally, the pathos increases and the ending becomes overly bombastic, perhaps even detracting from the force of the description and marring the quality of the story. This can be seen in a number of his creations for children such as *The Glory*, whose closing lines are both didactic and blaring: "Children! Your goals must be lofty, your ideas sublime. Soar always toward the light of glory! The desire for good is not in vain—the fruits shall be attained."[16]

Such rhetoric-pathetic-didactic endings can be found in a few more of his creations such as *The Stubborn Boy* and others. Usually, however, Korczak holds such superficial educational pathos in check and allows the children to cope with the reality of his books.

Korczak believed that "life makes dreams come true. Out of a hundred young dreams it forges one statue of reality."[17] In his children's books, he wove a number of these dreams and cast them into the hearts of children, believing that they will help them to shape their world so that it will be a richer and better place.

19

King Matia

And the whole city already knows that Matia is dead.
And the whole country.
And the whole world.
Matia was buried on a tall mountain on a desert island.
Everyone has decorated his grave with flowers.
And canaries sing above the tomb.[1]

And, indeed, the whole world already knows that King Matia is dead, that his children's revolution has failed, that many of his dreams came to nothing. But the world is a slightly better place for Matia's having been in it, and children love him and continue to be captivated by his adventures and experiences. With him, they rock the world and are exiled to the desert island; and when they part from him, they understand the world a bit better and a bit more. Their concept of life is slightly wider. Another wrinkle of wisdom appears on their forehead and a happy and sad smile lights their visages.

Among Korczak's children's books the most well known are *King Matia the First* and *King Matia on the Desert Island*, in which Korczak wove his educational Utopia—transferring the government into the hands of the child. In them, he related the story of little prince Matia, whose father died and who was anointed king in his father's stead when he was a small boy. The little king does not find it easy to rule, when all the great ministers want to continue to run the country as if it were their own personal property. Matia decides to get to know his people better and to fight among the ranks of the soldiers against the armies of three kings who declare war on his country. He volunteers into his own army as a simple and anonymous soldier, participates in the war, and learns a great deal about human nature, about life, about commanders and soldiers, about the leadership of the army, and about the government of the country. He meets a wonderful king who widens his horizons, teaches him a great deal about kingship and rule, and befriends him. The friendly king tells him that the lives of kings are hard and sad and explains to him that the king's only mission in life is to make his citizens happy.

Listen Matia, my grandfather gave his people their freedom but it did not help. They murdered him and the people were no happier afterwards. My father erected a huge memorial to freedom. You shall see it tomorrow, it is a beautiful memorial, but of what use is it, if wars continue to rage, if there are poor and miserable people. I ordered that this large building of parliament be erected, and nothing has changed. Everything is as it was. . . . You know Matia, we always made things worse when we tried to make amendments for the grown-ups, why don't you try and make amendments for children: You might succeed.[2]

Matia recognizes the complexity and difficulty of the affairs of state. He understands that he cannot actually lead the country, and, therefore, he relinquishes his position and asks to be the king of children alone. The grown-ups do not understand or recognize his greatness and his wish to make changes for the good of the citizens. They foil his innocent intentions and cheat him. As a result of their treason, Matia is dispossesed of his kingship and is sentenced to death. At the last moment, the verdict is commuted to life imprisonment on a desert island. The days of his confinement on the desert island, his attempts to escape, the help of his good and faithful friends, his many battles and difficult struggles are described in the book, *King Matia on the Desert Island*. At the end of his adventures, Matia abdicates his throne in favor of a democratic government. He ends his life as a workman in a factory, where he is killed in a work accident.

These two books were very popular among children. Korczak masterfully wove many of his educational ideas and his views about life and society into the fascinating plot. The books were based on his ideas about the child's right to respect and about the absolute equality of the child, not as a future person, but in the immediate present. For many years, Korczak dreamed and thought about the utopia of fully realizing the rights of the child in a children's state, and he attempted to manifest this utopia on a literary level. Gdalia Alkoshi was right when he asserts that the King Matia books are a "poetical transposition of Korczak's personal aspirations and the social experiments which he conducted in the orphanages which he managed, into the realm of utopian fiction."[3]

The Matia books are highly and pointedly critical of the administration of states, of ministers and generals, of bureaucrats and men of authority, and of the ways of government that are rotten with treason, treachery, theft, injustice, empty arrogance, lust for power, abuse of authority for personal gain, betrayal of democracy, etc. We see all this through the eyes of a young and innocent child who does not yet know the deceitful and unjust ways of government and who believes in the possibility of improvement. We are witness to the process wherein little Matia is disillusioned and becomes fully aware of life's harshness and ugliness. He learns the nature of true rulership and stares into the terrible face of war. Thinking that the central issue of war is the speech he will give to the people and his riding on a white horse at the head of a brave army, he does not understand why his ministers constantly talk of trains, money, rations, boots for the soldiers, hay, oats, oxen, hospitals, and the like, instead of his glorious ride. Only when he is baptized in fire, as a soldier among soldiers, does he begin to understand the meaning of rations and boots and the connection between these and the war. At first he only grasps the external and optimistic meaning of concepts and definitions, and does not yet comprehend their hidden practical content. Korczak stresses: "Matia is still a very young king and does not know the nature of diplomacy. And diplomacy means that one must lie in everything, so as to keep the enemy from knowing anything."[4]

Korczak's stark satire of the ways of government is in evidence from the opening pages of the book. For example, he castigates the manners of government by describing the royal outing:

For every royal outing, the police received three thousand shekels, and the Department of Health received a barrel of eau de cologne and a thousand shekels in gold. All this because for every outing of king Matia two hundred workmen and one hundred workwomen thoroughly cleaned the garden. They swept the paths, painted the benches, sprayed the avenues with eau de cologne and even wiped the dust off trees and leaves. Doctors supervised the work to make sure that everything was clean and that no dust remained anywhere, for dirt and dust are harmful to health, and the police made sure to keep the garden free of the kind of wild children who cast stones, push and hit each other or scream overmuch.[5]

No subject is spared the lash of the satire. For example, he wrote a dialogue on the subject of war in which one of the soldiers says, "Kings no longer ride to war these days." And the argument becomes heated:

"All kings are the same. Perhaps it was different once."

"How can we know how it was once? Perhaps they hid under their quilts, and because there is no one to remember this, they can lie today."

"What is there to lie about?"

"Well, answer your own question. How many kings have been killed in wars, and how many soldiers?"

"Big deal. There is only one king and many soldiers."

"Do you wish for more than one. We have enough trouble as it is with this one we have."

Matia could hardly believe his ears. He has heard so much about the love of the people for the king, and especially about the love of the army. It was only yesterday that he thought he must conceal his identity, lest they hurt him because of their great love, and now he finds that had his identity become known it would not have evoked much enthusiasm.[6]

Korczak's satire of royalty was sharp and bitter, as can be seen in the following passage, in which he relates how King Matia, were he only allowed to do so, would have preferred never to go into the royal garden.

But that is impossible, because the manners and ceremonies of the court obligated the king to pass directly from the throne-hall into the garden, and twenty servants were waiting to open the doors leading from the throne-hall into the garden. Had Matia decided not to go into the garden, these valets would have had no work and would have grown very bored. Perhaps some consider that the opening of a door is no work at all, but this is an ignorant opinion which does not understand court manners. I must therefore explain that these kings were busy for long hours. Each of them would bathe in cold water in the morning, after which the barber took care of his haircut and shaved his face. Their uniforms had to be spotlessly clean because once, three hundred years ago, Henry the Irritable was the regent and a flea had jumped from one of the valets onto the king's sceptre. The hangman then decapitated the head of that bungler, and the minister of court almost paid with his life as well. Since that day the minister of court supervised the cleanliness of the attending valets. As early as seven minutes past eleven they stood dressed, washed and clean in the corridor, waiting for the clock to strike seventeen minutes past eleven, for the inspection of the master of ceremonies himself. They had to be doubly careful, for they were liable to six years of imprisonment for an unbuttoned button, to four years of hard labour for a sloppy haircut, and for a sluggish bow—two months imprisonment on a diet of bread and water.[7]

It seems that this passage is perfect in its evocation of the folly of royal traditions, the emptiness and ugliness of the ceremonies, the silence and degradation of the low in rank and the servants of authority, the extravagance of the mighty, the stupidity of their arrogance, and our own foolishness in kneeling down to allow others to ride on our shoulders. Yet, is it only with royalty that we are concerned here? In what manner does it radically differ from other forms of government? Is this folly not the heritage of all the various kinds of rulers? Does a democracy not uphold its chosen representatives and celebrate their greatness?

Should we continue to leaf through the pages of *King Matia on the Desert Island*, we shall discover dozens of examples of ways of government and the customs of kings and regimes. For a moment it almost seems that it is not a meeting of kings that we are witnessing, but the meetings of the present "Security Board" or the discussions of the United Nations in that glass building which exposes the lying deceit of the multinational Tower of Babel on the banks of the East River in New York.

Let us examine the suppression of the children's rebellion against the regime: the factories that manufacture King Matia pens are shut down, shops which display postcards bearing Matia's visage are heavily fined. The editor of the *Green Flag* is thrown into jail. A famous poet who wrote songs praising Matia is put on trial. The army is sent to surround the schools. Even the green cloth from which the flags are made is forbidden. Children who play a "green" game are strictly punished by teachers, and the epitome of it all is the declaraion of the Emperor Papoccino demanding that all the garden plants, the trees, and the city parks change their color within one month.[8]

Do we know nothing of universities surrounded by armies, gentle poets castigated as traitors, the closing down of newspapers, the arrest of newspaper editors, attacks on the media, boycotting of products, prohibitions, censorship and the like, in this day and age? Does Korczak not strike home with his satire? Are its details not right to the point? Is his force diminished in any way in this day and age?

And the picture becomes even more extreme, more blatant when the young king wishes to defeat Matia, his competitor, whose social amendments have caused him great damage. And what is the best way to do this?—"The young king's plot was to present Matia as a madman."[9] Is this picture so very different from what can be seen in the present? Do we not know the use of such a claim of madness in order to discredit political rivals. Are we totally innocent of the use of mental hospitals as prisons and brainwashing institutions for the "opponents of the regime," "objectors," and their like?

Penetrating insights into the horror of war, which is caused by the insensitivity of rulers, the darkness of superstition, and the stupidity of certain customs, are provided by the description of the fifteen-year war among the African kings as it is told to Matia by Bahem-Drum. The war broke out:

for the sole reason that some gave greeting by putting the fingers of their right hand into the left nostril, while others gave greeting by putting the fingers of their left hand into the right nostril. The conflict engulfed the whole of the nation. Priests and other kings became involved. One side said thus, and the other side claimed thus, and they began battling over who was right. They burnt huts and entire villages, killed women and children, took hostages, cast slaves to the lions. Until a plague broke out and there was such a famine that they were unable to go on fighting and each kept to his own version of greeting.[10]

Korczak used this satire to wittily and pointedly expose the roots of conflicts between countries and nations. He criticized the prejudices of people and described the irrational hate that accompanies conflicts and wars.

Matia's experiences as a soldier in battle endow his conception of life with a new dimension of depth and experience. He begins to take an interest in the fate of weak children and patients, children who live in dark and damp hovels, who are often hungry and suffer a bitter fate. Korczak's deep and sincere care for suffering children is expressed in Matia's aspirations.

Matia has learned the taste of these dark and damp hovels and has learned the sensation of hunger. He remembers how he sometimes chose to sleep on the cold ground in the yard, giving up the farmer's hut. Matia remembers how bandy-legged and pale-faced children came to the camp and asked for a bit of soup from the soldier's pot, and with what avidity they then drank the soup. Matia had thought that hunger and distress were to be found only in times of war, but he learns that even in times of peace children are often besieged by hunger and cold.[11]

Matia's greatest dream is to found a kingdom of children. He delivers a speech in which he raises two issues—the rule of the whole nation and the rule of children. He stresses:

We have decided that the whole nation shall rule, that the whole nation shall be able to state its wishes. But you have forgotten, gentlemen, that the nation is not entirely made up of adults but of children too. We have a few million children—and they too should therefore rule. Let there be two houses of parliament, one for adults—where the representatives and the ministers of the adults shall convene, and one for the children—which shall house the children's representatives and ministers. I am king of both adults and children, but if the adults consider me too young, let them elect an adult king, and I shall be the king of children.[12]

As one event leads to another, the government is eventually left entirely in the hands of the children. They fill all the positions that were heretofore in the hands of the adults, while the adults are returned to school. This act leads to the collapse of internal government, destruction of industry and the economy, blocking of transportation and communications, and has generally destructive results. Matia understands that no children's government can exist without adults. The war is not one of generations, for adults and children do not compete with each other for rulership; rather, the struggle is for the liberation of children, for the provision of equal rights, for the actualization of the child's independence and his right to respect and self-expression. It is not the wish of the inexperienced to dominate the experienced which guides Matia. In fact, this is no other than Korczak's most basic wish, which is expressed in all his pedagogical writings and which guides his way in education:

We have grown used to this: Either the life of the adults at the fringes of the children's life, or the life of the children at the fringes of the adults' life.—When will that happy hour come in which the lives of children and adults shall be as two parallel rows?[13]

Matia's early conceptions of his role as king of the children are extremely naive. He requires a long period of study before he begins to understand the true arrangements of society, the power struggles within it, the plots of government, and the problems of ruling. At first, he is completely captivated by the concepts of childhood and he dictates to his advisors:

And now please write down what I wish to do for the children. I now have money and I can free myself for making my amendments. I want every child to receive two balls in summer and skis in winter. Everyday, after school, each child shall receive one sweet and one sweet cookie coated with sugar. The girls shall receive one doll per year, and the boys shall have penknives. Every school must include swings and merry-go-rounds. In addition to this, every book and notebook sold in the shops shall include colourful pictures. This is only the beginning, for I am thinking of making many further amendments. I want an estimate of the cost of all this and the time required for execution.[14]

His later attempts and many disappointments slowly open his eyes so that his social understanding deepens and his critical powers of observation are sharpened. At first Matia dreams of a true democracy, and he even has a vision of an international children's parliament which will discuss the unique problems of children. He addresses the delegates of the children's parliament:

> You are delegates. Until now I was alone. I wished to administer the state for the good of everyone. But it is very hard for one man to guess what others require. It will be easier for you. Some know what is needed in the city, others know what is required in the country. The youngsters know what the smaller children need, others what older boys and girls require. I think that now all the children in the world shall convene as did kings not long ago, and white, black and yellow children shall discuss their needs together.[15]

The awakening comes later on, when the idea of a children's parliament fails. The same burden of aggression, jealousy, envy, and violence that weighs down the world of adults can also be found in the world of children. Klu-Klu the African girl attempts to speak to the children of the parliament about the equality of the sexes, equal treatment of boys and girls, equality of rights, and so on, and the children, who have already deeply assimilated the sexual stereotypes of their elders, run wild and break up the parliamentary meeting with cries of ridicule and contempt:

> Look at her, coming to teach us!
> Off to your cage with the monkeys!
> The king's bride!
> Wishy washy Matia!
> Bride and groom!
> And if anyone disbelieves, let him come in years!
> And see them married!![16]

In *King Matia*, Korczak was more sharply aware of the limitations of education than in all his other literary and educational writings. He limited his great optimism as to childhood's potential for good and moderated his romantic conception of the child. For example, a sharp debate takes place between the kings about the provision of rights to children. Almost all of the kings reject the idea with distaste. They are afraid of the disquiet that will spread in the world—chaos in schools, rebellion, and the like. King Papanucci declares that if his son had dared join the rebellion of the children, he would have taken his pants down and spanked him forcefully. He rates the various beatings—with the hand, with the cane, with the tawse. King Orestes rejects the idea of corporal punishment and suggests imprisonment in a dark cellar and starvation. The friend of the yellow kings rejects beatings and starvation and suggests propaganda and persuasion. Only the sad king supports the rights of children and stresses:

> Everything you now say of children, was once said of farmers, laborers, women, Jews and blacks, these are so and these are thus, and can be given no rights. But they were given rights. Things are not much better but better than they were.[17]

He supports the provision of rights for children, but is aware of the failure of Matia's first revolution and stresses that amendments must be made slowly and gradually. Children must be accustomed to self-rule, and one should examine how one can extend their rights.

It is not only the kings and rulers whose perception of the world of childhood is distorted, but the official educators, teachers, and headmasters as well. In his satirical-sarcastic manner, Korczak artfully formulates the speech of an orphanage director. One has only to listen to his oration to immediately grasp the depth of his stupidity, pompousness, and empty arrogance, his trivial conception of education, his vision of the institute rather than the child, his external-economic concept of education, and his lack of minimal educational understanding and dearth of any real-human sympathy for the child. He begins his speech by saying:

> I, gentlemen, am an educated educator. I am the author of important books on children. I have written a book entitled *365 Ways to Silence a Child*. I have written another book entitled: *Which is Better, Tin Buttons or Horn Buttons*. My third educational book was published under the title of: *Raising Herds of Swine in Boarding Schools*. For you must know, gentlemen, that where there were many children, there are a great deal of left-overs which it is a shame to waste. In my boarding school even the thinnest of piglets grows to be a fat healthy pig. I have received two silver medals. I have only to glance at a child, to instantly judge his worth.[18]

Do we not know such educators who write books on how to silence children? Are not many renowned researchers of education caught in the grip of that key question: Which is better, tin buttons or horn buttons? Do they not distribute questionnaires, make tabulations, sketch out curves and draw far reaching "educational" conclusions as to the superiority or inferiority of tin buttons? And where are the economists of education, the knights of thrift and parsimony? Would they not be happy to applaud the revolutionary suggestion of growing swine on the left-overs of the institution's children? And do we not know the managers and headmasters of education, its speakers and experts, sporting medals and educational prizes and knowledgeable as to the worth of every child? And is the child himself not lost in all of this?

Was Korczak exaggerating when he described the director of the orphanage as he firmly commands the employees to change the children's underwear, to wash their ears, and to wipe their noses because important guests are about to arrive at the institution?

> I hope it is clear: Not even one dirty nose! And the girls must give the Minister of Police a bouquet of flowers. Perhaps that little one with the calm face. And I demand that the cleaning team immediately set to work![19]

And does the director of the orphanage not go right to the heart of the matter when he defines the role of the educator as it is perceived in a strict bureaucratic system, lacking in any real affinity to the child—"I am a great educator and learned author. It is my duty to see to it that none of the children lose their handkerchiefs, that they not make any noise and not rip their buttons."[20] Does the director not succinctly describe the conception of education as training, as behavioral shaping, as the enforcement of law and order, as the prevention of noise and disturbance and as the preservation of property?

The criticism of the world of adults and their attitude to children is not only presented in direct statements but also hinted at in the description of characters and events. When Korczak described Raphael's father, the regimental commander, who beat his son at every opportunity, his portrayal evokes a sharp protest against this common perversity in the behavior of adults. This protest of Korczak's figures prominently in his essay, "The Child's Right to Respect," where he stressed:

> Who and when, and under what extraordinary circumstances, shall dare push a grown man, hit him, beat him? And how common and surprising is the blow which descends upon the child, the strong pull on his arm, the painful hug of affection. The feeling of helplessness educates the child to respect force: Everyone, not only the adult, who is older in years and stronger, can cruelly express his displeasure, enforce his demands with coercion and administer discipline: Oppress with impunity. By the very example we set, we teach the child to look down on anyone weaker than himself. A bad school, a dark foreboding future.[21]

At the same time it is only right to point out that in a number of chapters of *King Matia on the Desert Island*, Korczak awoke from his dream of childish justice, from his belief that "man is born good," and from his assurance in the final victory of the forces of good if only children were to be allowed their freedom. He did not, however, equal the bitter disillusionment of William Golding in *Lord of the Flies*, who upheld the view that "Man is born evil" and that if one should provide him with a full measure of freedom to build a new world, that world shall be as evil and cruel, violent and steeped in the lust for power as is the world of the adults. Yet, Korczak, too, speaking through the mouth of Matia, is disillusioned. He stated:

> I thought that children are good, but miserable. Yet it turns out that they are evil. I did not know the children, but now I know them. They are evil. Very evil. And I too am evil. Evil and lacking in gratitude. So long as I was afraid of the ministers, of the master of ceremonies, of the educator and all the others—I listened to them and sat quietly. But when I became a true king, I made mistakes for which I now suffer, and it is not only I who suffers, but many innocent people as well. . . .
>
> The children are evil, lying, easily abusive. If a child stutters or squints a little, or is red-haired, or limps, or is hunchbacked—they are quick to ridicule. A ten year old makes fun of an eight year old. A twelve year old refuses to play with ten year olds. When they see something of value in the hands of another, they take it from him by treachery or flattery, or bend him to their will and force him to give it to them. When they see that one child is better than others, they are envious and take their revenge. When a boy is strong and knows how to fight, he is allowed everything. When he is good and quiet, he is completely disregarded.[22]

The list of faults and sins is long indeed—the divulging of secrets, the calling of invectives, fighting, theft, blows, cheating, attacks on younger children, and more. Matia slowly begins to understand why his rebellion failed and says,

> Now I know why the children's parliament failed. How could it have succeeded? You understand, just a moment ago they held me in regard just because I still had sausages, and a moment later they wanted to betray me.[23]

These accusations are not spoken shallowly, but constitute the sum of disappointments and frustrations as he returns to school and is tortured, humiliated, hounded, and tormented by the children. This disillusionment does not cause him to reject his former views, his belief in the right of the child to respect, to appreciation, and to a greater measure of rights, but his educational optimism is now tinged by shades of doubt, which rather than discourage him, only deepen his keen awareness of the importance of education and the intensive care of the child.

Should someone claim that Matia, being a fictional character, does not necessarily represent the whole of Korczak's educational conceptions, he would be only partially right, for Korczak deeply identified with his characters, and even shaped historical ones, such as Louis Pasteur, in his own spiritual image.

The importance of this book is not in the educational ideas, the social critique, the perception of life, and the comprehension of government with which it provides the child, but first and foremost in its literary worth. As a literary creation, the book excels in its clear and flowing plot, and is written so as to increase suspense. It is full of imagination, inventions, wisdom, surprizes, humor, and satire. Korczak did an excellent job of weaving a thrilling plot, brightly sketching the character of Matia, describing the image of society, weaving reality with fantasy, and blending his educational ideas into a colorful and attractive literary fabric. Rather than forced naivity, false childishness, or the masquerade of an adult in the guise of a child, the book is completely faithful to the world of the child. Its language is clear and simple, true to spoken language, rich with humor, and capable of being directly apprehended by the child. An important role is reserved for Korczak's special brand of humor, which colors the various situations, enlivens them, and makes the reading a joyful experience. One feels that every description was written with an "impish" grin, half in seriousness, half in jest. This quality of the book dissipates the tensions, deflates pretentions, and staves off melodrama. Thus, for example, did Korczak describe the troubles that the teachers encounter in coping with the adults who have been returned to school:

> There were many wildcats among those who had not yet turned thirty: They taunted, laughed and made a lot of noise in class; The older ones complained that their seats were uncomfortable, their heads ached and the air was stuffy—that the ink was no good; And the elderly slept and learned nothing. And if the teacher scolded them, they did not heed her, for many among them were deaf. The younger adults tormented the older ones with all kinds of pranks, and the elderly complained that they disturbed their rest.[24]

This humorous approach provides the description with the right proportions, both in its realistic and fictional aspects.

Even when coming to describe the debates of the king's committee, a kind of exhausting report on governmental discussions, where the threat of boredom looms large, Korczak skillfully wove amusingly sarcastic barbs into the negotiations:

"When the King's Committee gathered, King Matia asked:

"Have you mended the railways?"

"We have," replied the minister.

"That's good, otherwise I would have commanded that you be boiled, dear sir, in crocodile juice. And have the factories been built yet?"

"Yes, they have," replied the Minister of Industry.

"That's good, otherwise I would have commanded that my lord be baked with banana stuffing—"

The minsters where so shaken with fright, that Matia burst out laughing.[25]

A number of the book's chapters are dedicated to thought and contemplation and to pleasant philosophy. With great humor, Korczak describes Matia who has become a philosopher, and at the same time attempts to humorously define the nature of a philosopher:

A philosopher is a person who thinks of everything and does nothing. A philosopher is not a lazy person, for thinking, too, is work. Even hard work. An ordinary person sees a frog, and couldn't care less, while the philosopher thinks: Why did God create frogs? For they do not enjoy it.[26]

Using this light definition as a springboard, Korczak goes on to weave a poetic-educational chapter on the importance and essence of thought:

Every man has tiny men in his head, and each such tiny man probably knows and says something different. Sometimes they fight each other or one corrects something which another has said, or advises another. For example, something suddenly reminds Matia of something which he has long ago forgotten. It seems as if one tiny man in his head was asleep and is now suddenly awake and talking. . . . Matia thinks differently on each occasion—and tries to fit everything together. Actually, he does not know, just like a real philosopher, who also thinks much, but does not really know.[27]

Korczak's portrayals are long and educational and carry a message, the message of the pleasure of thought, the catharsis, and the joy of discovery. Matia enjoys himself in a way that he has never known in the past. In the past he brought every quesion that he encountered to the teacher, the adult, and the expert, and they explained it to him. Their teaching was external, alien, distant, and now he asks himself the questions and provides his own answers. He talks with himself as if he were talking to many people, and thus he never feels lonely, is never alone and bored and unsatisfied. There is no greater pleasure than the ability to think and discover and no greater joy than the joy of discovery. He learns from the "tiny men" in his mind. Sometimes they are wise and sometimes rebellious and wild, and sometimes he sits by the sea, casts pebbles, and thinks. A wonderful coversation goes on in his head and he finds himself learning from thousands of teachers at one and the same time. And sometimes his thought is a prayer, a longing for God:

> What, for example, is prayer? How can God know what people are thinking? There is a tiny man in every person—perhaps he is called the soul or the conscience. This tiny man knows well, for he resides within the person—he has wings—and when the person is asleep, he comes out, for example, from the ear, exactly like a bee flying out of the hive—and flies, and tells God everything. . . . And when a person prays, he then sends this tiny man—this conscience—of his own free will, and the tiny man can then fly to God even in the full light of day.[28]

Now, looking back, we know how well children received the books of King Matia. They evoked their keenest interest and provided answers to many of their most secret questions. Even today, these books are popular among children. In describing them, one may perhaps quote Korczak's own words:

> A book—that is a wonderful thing. Everything. Everything that was invented by the wisest of people—is written in books. Sometimes a man spent his entire life in thought, a hundred years, and then wrote a book. And Matia can read for no more than an hour, and he already knows. Someone has died long ago but his thoughts are set in the book. The book seems to speak, to advise.[29]

Bookish wisdom and advice are not enough. A person must assimilate the books, must struggle with them, must order their teaching in his own head: "There are many things in books, but not everything, and only after reading should one arrange everything in one's head."[30]

And, indeed, Korczak's thoughts and dreams are set in books, and all we have do to is to open ourselves to them and then arrange everything in our heads. . . .

20

The Stubborn Boy

This is not a fable. This is the Truth. This is no legend. This is the true story of one stubborn boy.[1]

The book before us is no legend. It is a true story. And who was it who said that a legend cannot be true. And perhaps it is especially the legend which is true? Some consider *The Stubborn Boy* a realistic story while others classify it as a biography. Both are right for we have here a realistic-biographical story that is a legend which is true.

In discussing this book with Zrubavel Gilad, Korczak said:

People are different and wills are different, but we must help the children expose the beautiful and the sublime which they carry within their hearts. I intentionally wrote the book about Louis Pasteur's life now—in this period when tyranny and spiritual enslavement rule the world, when this madness called Hitler conquers everything—so that the children growing up now shall see that there are other people in the world, people who have devoted and continue to devote their lives not to the destruction of people, but to their salvation and liberation, to the enrichment and beautification of the human world. For these are the greatest dreams of Louis Pasteur![2]

This book was written in years when the image of man was diminished, times when the face of human society was warped and a satanic tyranny threatened to drown humanity in a flood of blood. And in the midst of these terrible days, Korczak's book appeared, proving the existence of a human chance and presenting Louis Pasteur's life as a model of the conquest and victory of man. In *The Stubborn Boy*, Korczak artfully described the life of one of France's greatest scholars, his conflicts and doubts, his stubborn perseverance in his search for truth, his great struggle to have his truth accepted and his victory. Through his perseverance and stubbornness, he saved the world from terrible diseases and made his dream of a better and more beautiful world come true.

Korczak did not wish merely to present the achievements of Pasteur, but rather, mainly, to portray his way of life and his unceasing struggle to discover, innovate, and redeem humanity. He stressed:

> The life of Pasteur teaches us how hard it is to find a new truth. But finding this new truth is only a small beginning. People must be brought to see this new truth and believe in it. Everyone must know that matters stand thus, so that none dare to say otherwise. When one announces a new truth one uproots ingrained mistakes. When one announces new truths one destroys old prejudices. A new truth breeds enemies.[3]

Pasteur battled in all of these arenas: he strove to discover new truths, he devoted his entire life to his research—his battle against germs; he was forced to expend a great deal of his resources in order to support his research, to overcome the lack of proper working conditions, paucity of means, lack of experience and prejudices. He was obliged to fight ignorance and lack of minimal hygiene and to personally supervise cleanliness, disinfection, vaccination, and the preservation of food products, as well as to contend with the enmity of rival researchers, of narrow-minded men of science, of "learned doctors," charlatans, and forgers, who attempted to discredit him and ridicule his attainments.

Korczak strove to present the life of Louis Pasteur as an educational model for his young readers. He believed that the lives of great men should serve as a guide for everyone; and hence the great importance of the biography that can make a meaningful contribution to education and to the shaping of character through its presentation of a personal example. Korczak's views on the educational value of the biography are very close to the views of Richard Livingstone and many other educators of the neo-humanistic school in education. Livingstone stressed the necessity of educating youngsters in the light of visions of greatness in the lives and figures of renowned persons in literature and history. He wrote:

> The figures of persons in history represent the best means we have of explaining the nature of courage and endurance, of thirst for knowledge and devotion to good—those great positive forces which brought mankind from the caves into fresher air.[4]

He believed that the reader might identify with the heroes of the biography and make them into personal role models or into criteria by which to examine values and actions. The fact that the child is in the process of shaping his personality causes him to tend to identify with heroes, and he might thus assimilate a great deal of their life values. In his close observations of children, Korczak noted an increased interest in biographies among children aged 11–15. The attention of young adolescents is directed at life and at the future. Various plans and aspirations begin to germinate within them and they seek "true" stories—stories of people who struggled with reality, overcame, and made their own way in life. At this age, they require sources of inspiration in order to fortify their belief and confidence in man's ability to act and attain, in the victory of the human will and the rewards of effort and perseverance.

It is for this reason that Korczak did not choose to present his readers with Pasteur at the height of his struggles and achievements, but rather he began with Pasteur's earliest childhood. Korczak described Pasteur the child and adolescent at great length. He attempted to endear him to the young reader, presented his simple family background, and described his childhood experiences. He related how Pasteur's parents had devoted themselves to the education of their son, and enriched him with possessions that are far more valuable than material ones. Korczak stressed Pasteur's great adoration for his mother, who taught him to love learning and love his country, and extolled Pasteur's deep and faithful affection for his father, who by his hard work, set him an example of patience and effort, and instilled in him a wish for achievements and respect for men.[5]

In presenting the life of Pasteur the child as full of wonder and love of nature, and in relating his adolescence and devotion to science, Korczak wished to clarify that childhood should be respected for what it is, that the child must be allowed to mature and discover himself, to foster the potential within him—a potential that is sometimes dormant and undiscovered and sometimes already giving some signs of future achievements.

With obvious educational intention, Korczak stressed Pasteur's doubts and his stubborn forward striving. He counted the three main traits, a strong will, untiring work, and devotion to his goals, which brought Pasteur his great achievements. He told the young reader that Pasteur did not excel in his studies and often found them difficult, but did not give up and never stopped his unceasing efforts to make progress. In the tone of a teacher explaining something to his students, he wrote:

Louis does everything slowly, with patience. He listens because he wants to understand well. When he does not understand he asks that things be explained to him. He is stubborn, if he does not succeed—he does the same thing a second and third time. A fourth and fifth time. He does not brag that he understands or already knows how to do something.[6]

Throughout the book the reader observes the unceasing struggle of Pasteur the child, the boy, the husband, the father, and above all—the stubborn scientist who continues to try, fails and tries again, ignores the contempt of his environment, and tirelessly tries again and again. He works himself to the point of exhaustion, tires his eyes to the point of pain, climbs high mountains in order to obtain material for his experiments, and does not return home at a time of disaster when he is told of the death of his daughters, but instead devotes his entire life to his discoveries in his sincere wish to help humanity. Using the example of Pasteur's life, Korczak conveyed the message that a great man knows no rest, that the researcher feels himself responsible not only to his family and immediate environment but to the whole world. He does not set his goals in accordance with his powers, but rather exerts his powers according to the greatness of the objective. Korczak noted: "There is a field of battle. There is a field of work. A soldier falls wounded or dead, the gun in his hand. Pasteur's battle field was the laboratory, his weapon the microscope."[7]

In contrast to those who claimed that Pasteur was cruel to his wife and children, that he was hot-tempered, quickly angered, and generally of a foul disposition, Korczak clarified that this portrait was far from the truth and that Pasteur greatly loved his family but in his devotion to his greatest love—that of the entire human race—he did not allow himself to stop his work which brought salvation to so many suffering people.

Korczak substituted the positive term "stubborn" for the negative one of "bad-tempered," and stressed:

> Pasteur was only stubborn, he was neither a quarrelsome nor bad-tempered man. He told people the truth to their faces, and people do not enjoy such honesty. He grew angry when he was disturbed. He fought for the truth, and mercilessly exterminated prejudices and mistakes wherever he found them.[8]

Korczak provided the young reader with a description of Pasteur's working method. Pasteur thought nothing insignificant and was meticulously careful of even the smallest of details. He considered everything important and looked down on nothing. He took nothing for granted, and always investigated and asked for reasons. He hated all unfounded opinions and rejected any generally accepted truth which was invalidated by his laboratory experiments. It was his sincere, serious approach, based on unceasing effort, which enabled him to become the discoverer of the carbunculus germs and the way to cure the disease, to uncover the secrets of fermentation and the way to battle it, to discover the diseases that beset silk worms, to cure rabies, and to become the founder of the theory of hygiene, disinfection, pasteurization and vaccination.

Korczak particularly emphasized the fact that Pasteur, though his scientific enterprise was intended for the whole of humanity, nevertheless remained a loyal son of his people and country, and an enthusiastic French patriot. He rejected the medal of excellence given to him by the Berlin Academy, and told the Germans: "Science has no motherland, but scientists have a motherland."[9] He dedicated a great deal of the money that he received for his discoveries to France, which was then burdened with heavy debts, imposed upon it by victorious Germany.

In the books about King Matia, the educational ideas were directly ingrained in the meaning of the events, the choice of situations, and the fabric of the plot; while in the *Stubborn Boy*, the didactic tone is very much in evidence. The explaining voice—preaching a moral and pointing out desirable traits—is heard throughout the work, and hence the book's not inconsiderable literary weakness. One constantly hears Korczak's voice as he explains the examples, appends a moral to events, and provides his readers with such generally instructive rules as: "He who wishes to learn, he who wants truth, will find a book and a teacher everywhere,"[10] or "The kind of company which a boy keeps is important, very important, and the company his father keeps, no less," and the like. This preaching voice, which closely accompanies the story and constantly badgers the reader with its summaries and golden rules, is off-putting, annoying, and turns the experience of reading the book into a disappointing one. It seems that Korczak's educational will has, in this case, overcome his literary-artistic powers.

At the same time, it is only right that we emphasize the stylistic innovations of this book. Korczak chose a very parsimonious, concentrated, almost telegraphic style. The sentences are extremely short, sometimes no more than a word or two. The tempo is fast, the sentences bare and exposed. There are a great many repetitions intended to help the child grasp the ideas more easily and enable him to absorb matters more slowly and selectively. The sentences repeat themselves with light variations, and one sentence is intended to clarify another. Thus, for example, in coming to describe the war between France and Germany Korczak wrote:

> Those were very troubled times, those were times of war, the French and the Germans fought. Russia, Italy and Spain also fought. There were fires, there was hunger, there were plagues. The nations fought in the high mountains and in the forests.[11]

By means of this reiteration, Korczak not only wished to clarify, but also to create an illusion of time and space. This stylistic element is very interesting, but it is more appropriate for folk tales, legends, and poetry for children, as well as stories intended for the very young, than for a biographical tale intended for the older child. Although by means of this style

Korczak attempted to make it possible for children younger than those who usually read a biography to enjoy the book, he missed his audience, for the younger child is rarely interested in biographies and many of the events described are incomprehensible to him, while the adolescent child shrinks from the endless reiterations, the unceasing commentary, and the heavy-handed style.

The entire story is written like a long speech delivered by a teacher to his students, and in order to instill this long-winded monologue with a taste of dialogue, it is very frequently interspersed with rhetorical questions that create the illusion of dialogue and attempt to draw the reader's attention and arouse his curiosity. Thus for example, Korczak wrote:

We have all seen soured milk, but none of us think to ask why should milk sour. We eat bread. Why is yeast required? Why do bread and cakes sometimes rise and bake wonderfully, and sometimes not go well at all? We drink ale, wine and spirits. How are they made? Why does meat spoil and rot? Why can a healthy person catch a disease from a sick one?[12]

This literary means adds an interesting stylistic variation, but is tiresome in its verbosity.

The book, the *Stubborn Boy* has an important human and educational mission. It opens eyes, educates, and provides the child with an excellent portrayal of the figure of the researcher and scientist. "The thought of the learned scientist is like a bird, when it begins to fly—who knows where its flight shall take it? Columbus, too, when he sailed out to sea, did not know where he will make land."[13] However, the book's artistic force falls far short of its educational vision. This lack of artistic-literary power is doubly saddening as it might have given wings to Korczak's mission when it speaks to us with such words as:

Happy is the man whose soul carries God within it, the vision of beauty and the love of science and country. For these shall enternally be the joysprings of great ideas and great deeds, all of which shine in the glow of infinity and eternity.[14]

21

Little Jack

I often hear people say:

—They are all like that.

For example:

—All boys are mischievous and dirty.

Or:

All girls are cry-babies and quick to complain.

This is not true. One has to know each one *separately* and appreciate each one separately, and one has to know them deeply rather than superficially. Not only what a person says is important, but also what he thinks and feels, why he is like himself and not like another.

Only a lazy person who does not like to think, says: "They are all like that."[1]

In his book, *Little Jack*,[2] Korczak wished to present the unique individual, his character and thoughts, his aspirations and dreams. *Little Jack* is the story of a child who is a leader, who is the living spirit among a group of children, who encourages them to important deeds. Contrary to the King Matia books which were purely fictional, the story of Jack is anchored in reality, and might take place anywhere. Korczak called this story of his a "Financial Tale," for Jack, the hero of the story, who is a third-grade student in an American school, founds, administers, and heads a cooperative in his class. He is a boy with great organizational skills, who loves his peers, takes care of their needs and does a great deal for the common enterprise. Jack is serious, consistent, and honest, has a strong will and an expansive imagination, and all these make him the leader of the children's group. The story is full of love for children and describes the life of a primary school class with a great deal of humor and liveliness, presenting the children's problems both large and small, their daily affairs, and their common enterprises.

The book reflects Korczak's thorough observation of the life of the school, his knowledge of class life, his ability to create characters of students and teachers, and above all, his educational approach which finds expression in all of his writings. He describes and criticizes the distorted pedagogical approach of teachers who are quick to jump to conclusions and in their impatience pass sentence without prior inquiry, tending to insult a child in public and even physically harm him. Little Jack takes great care of his books and their cleanliness. He knows the difficult financial situation of his parents, and recognizes that his father saves every penny so that his son shall not lack in anything he requires for his studies. Because of his wish to take good care of the books that his parents bought out of their savings, he refuses to lend his book to Wilson, whose parents are rich and who neglects to bring his books to class. Jack remembers that last time, when he lent his book to Betty, she smudged the cover with ink stains and crumpled the pages. The teacher does not bother to find out why Jack refuses to lend his book, and when he breaks into tears as Wilson attempts to forcibly take the book from his hand, she shouts at Jack, calling him:

> A miser and a bad friend. She explained that the rich must help those poorer than them. While in fact Wilson's father was richer than Jack's father. And afterwards the teacher said something more, but Jack did not hear her, because if one is very angry at someone, one never knows what is said. Finally, the teacher said that when Jack grows up no one will love him.[3]

In such a situation the teacher makes countless educational mistakes, she judges without prior clarification, breaks out in anger without basis, publicly insults, says totally unfounded things, and criticizes not only the issue at hand, which seems to her to be unjust, but directly attacks the personality of the child, passing judgment on his future fate. Is it any wonder that Jack is hurt and humiliated, and withdraws into himself. The teacher continues to exhibit a negative pedagogical approach in not letting bygones be bygones and in being quick to suspect a student, frequently and stupidly referring to past errors. When a theft occurs in class, she does not examine the situation but immediately suspects Jack, without explicitly stating his name, thus depriving him of any chance to defend himself. She says: "If someone does not even lend his friend the nib of a pen, it is only inevitable that theft should occur. He who does not help his friends in their time of need, will easily take from others."[4]

Korczak also remarked on educational phenomena, which are seemingly less serious, but the effect of which is actually very far-reaching and severe. Thus, for example, he stressed the lack of deliberation and the gross error, in the procedure, which yet exists today, wherein teachers meddle with the seating arrangements of the students in class, sometimes even forcing children to change seats.

The student knows better than the teacher where and with whom he wishes to sit. . . . The teacher will seat you in another place and forget all about it, and you—you will suffer for four whole quarters a year.[5]

As an educator who always placed the child at the focus of the educational process, Korczak criticized the assignment of uniform duties to an entire class and the lack of attention given to individual differences. He was always attentive to the needs of the individual child, and when he described Little Jack, who is obliged to copy out a poem about a swallow that trains its chicklings to fly, he stressed:

Though it is true that he must think of the swallow, at school the teachers do not allow one to think of anything else during class, and they are right . . . for even Jack himself has already erred twice. But sometimes it is very difficult to think of the lesson when other things come up in one's mind. You want to force yourself to think of the swallow. You have even begun thinking of it—and suddenly:—Happy swallow, which needs no shoes and no coat. It needs nothing, and then:– What a pity, that man needs so much. And so on, and so forth, and you suddenly remember Mrs. Sanders who hits Robin with all her strength, and you do not feel that in the meantime—you have made two mistakes and the teacher says:—You are not listening. And you also feel uncomfortable, because the copybook is not clean. But what can you do, when you want something and cannot get it?[6]

The teacher who hurt little Jack, insulted him, and passed a rash judgment on him did not really wish to hurt him. She was a devoted teacher, who invested a great deal of effort in her work and wanted to advance the class, but her mistake was a very serious one indeed in that she did not examine the details of the event, and saw the class as a whole instead of the children in it. The concept of "class" is an artificial, unnecessary, and deleterious one, if one accepts it at face value as an anonymous conglomeration, as the sum of the character traits of individual children. Only when he sees individuals and their needs, possibilities, unique characteristics, particular interests, initiative, and specific likings can a teacher progress in his educational work, finally enriching the class as a whole. Every child has his own particular inclinations, and if a teacher is attentive and notices these inclinations, he can foster them and enrich the world of the child for the benefit of the whole class.

Jack's teacher wishes to encourage the class to read, to foster the children's interest in books, and to encourage lively social interactions focused on books and reading. She wishes to institute a class library, but when coming to put her idea into effect, she fails because she is not sensitive to the interests of the children and does not discern those students who might take to the idea and thus help actualize it. She nominates children who are not suitable to this role, and the whole idea fails. Only when Jack volunteers to administer the library because he has an inner inclination for this role is the idea successfully applied. And indeed, Jack, views this enterprise as the realization of his dream of commercial endeavor or "financial dealings" in the words of Korczak. When he is allowed to do so, he invests his entire energies and time in this work, expands the enterprise, and turns it into a cooperative. He always buys things in which the children are interested and which suit their tastes. He invests the little personal money he has for the benefit of the cooperative and is willing to suffer humiliations and suspicions, to fall behind in his studies, and to stand up to other children in order to foster his enterprise.

Korczak wove many important human and social values into the fabric of the plot, and the description of the development and success of the cooperative. Jack is revealed in his kindness, his consideration and his care for others. He brings a present to little Nellie, who is orphaned of her father, and adds the expenditure of buying morning rolls for a hungry old man who refuses to be reduced to begging to the list of the cooperative's expenditures.

Korczak used this book to educate, not by means of explicit statements as in *The Stubborn Boy*, but through description, the shaping of character and the weaving of lives. Rather than preach the excellence of a stable family life and good educators, he lets us read of the life of Jack's family, providing us with an example of a poor family, living off its own honest toil. The parents' relationship is one of understanding, mutual affection, and love. The father is a proud and devoted man who serves as a focus for the identification and adoration of his son. The parents do not spoil their son. They allow him to experience life himself. They do not protect him from the consequences of his actions, but know how to assist him when required, to explain things to him, to foster the appropriate attitudes in his heart, and to instruct him faithfully. Jack's father has a habit of saying: "Try to be an honest boy, and if you fail in something, do not try to find crooked ways, instead, come and tell me about it." And his mother is wont to say: "One should not scold children, one should only explain things to them. Because the child is learning to live in the world, just as in school he learns to read, write and calculate."[7]

Korczak believed in the importance of constant experimentation, of learning through experience. Though little Jack falls somewhat behind in his formal education, he learns a great deal about life through his work and experience in the administration of the cooperative. He learns to deal with life's difficulties and acquires the art of coping with various situations. He learns to recognize various types of persons and to differentiate between true friendship and sham, and realizes that only effort and perseverance can bring results.

A child reading this book can learn many things. Through the development of the plot, Korczak provides him with information about the world of business and all that is involved in it. He elucidates the problems involved in the administration of a cooperative, registration in stock records, writing of reports, keeping of books, pricing, discounts, buying and selling, and the like.

The book's style is simple and coherent, its expression clear and its language appropriate for the perception of children. Korczak penetrates a little into the inner world of the characters and presents something of their motivations, dreams, and aspirations, and though he does so only superficially and does not succeed in redeeming the figures of their two-dimensionality or in providing them with any meaningful depth, he nevertheless points to their inner lives, thoughts, and character traits.

This book, too, like most of Korczak's books, is rich with his prolific wit and his ability to create humorous situations. It was well received by children, won thousands of readers, and still continues to evoke an interest in young readers.

22

Yotam the Magical

This is a difficult book. I dedicate this difficult book to restless boys, those who find it difficult to change. One requires a strong and consistent will. One has to strengthen the will power. One has to be useful. Life is puzzling and seems like some strange apparition. He who has a strong will and a burning desire to serve others will make his life into a wonderful dream, even if the way is complex and full of contradictions.[1]

The book before us is a book of wondrous changes. It is the story of the power of will and the power of magic, and at the same time it is also the story of a complex journey, of difficulties, of dreams, and of the struggles to toughen the will and turn life into a wonderful dream. This book is in no way didactic, does not contain any sermons, and is a riveting piece of fiction whose message does not detract from its artistic merit.

Yotam the Magical is a book of particular charm. In our discussion I will use the nickname *Yotam*, which has been given to the hero by Joseph Liechtenbaum, the translator of the book into Hebrew.[2] In the original Polish, the hero's name is Antek, and the children in the playground and the school dub him with the name of Kaitoch.

This is a work of fiction that describes the deeds and imaginings of little Yotam, the mischievous son of poor parents, who loves adventures and who sometimes sails on the wings of his imagination to a world of dreams and hallucinations. Yotam is given a secret power, the power of wizardry and magic, and he uses this power to entertain his friends and himself and to enjoy many adventures. Yotam is kindhearted, loves knowledge, and strives to discover hidden worlds. He wishes to create a world more beautiful than our own, a world of joy and fun. The book is written with charming simplicity, in a light and flowing style, and successfully draws the reader into the child's world of dreams and imaginings.

As in many of Korczak's books, this book, too, is a monument to Korczak's wry sense of humor, his ability to create comic situations, and his tendency to joke and jest. For example, following a well-known tradition-

254

al joke, Korczak tells of the porter who accuses Yotam of throwing a herring through the window and hitting the landlord on his head.

> Throw? Not true. First: It wasn't a herring at all, only the tail of a herring. Second: Not on the head, but on the hat. Third: Not through the window, but through the staircase railing. Moreover, he missed, the clumsy fool.[3]

From the very first chapter the whole book is rich with comic situations, jesting descriptions, and funny witticisms. At the grocer's Yotam asks for "One hundred grams of pickled whale," at the hairdresser's he asks for "A majestic-bread growing cream," and when the hairdresser offers him some perfume, he cries out "No. The boys will laugh at me and say I want to get married." At a kiosk he orders a glass of soda, and when the vending girl pours him a glass and serves him, he says, "I don't want the water miss, only the soda." At a photography shop he inquires after "The cost of a half dozen pigeons?" and at a laundrette he asks: "Excuse me, can one iron a cat?"

More than all of Korczak's other books, this book is a celebration of the imagination.

Yotam is disappointed in the world as it is. It seems to him that the world was more interesting in the past.

> Where there are now houses and cities, there were once forests and bears. Bandits hid in the forests. There were knights and crowned kings. Six white horses pulled the king's golden carriage, it was a sight to behold.[4]

The daily, tiresome reality is lacking in magic, devoid of imagination, and incomprehensible, but perhaps this is just its external grey and uninviting cover, while on the inside daily reality is also magical. And indeed:

> strange and wonderful is the world. For look—father was once a small boy, grandmother played with dolls and even mother once had a grandmother. Is it not strange that when Yotam grows up he too shall be a father? It is hard to grasp. One thing did indeed happen, but a long time ago, another thing will only come to pass in future. A third thing exists, but far far away.[5]

By dint of his imagination, Yotam wishes to unite the past, the present, and the future, to create one single time in which the existing, and the destined to be, the far and the near, will all co-exist at one and the same

time. This is a time in which wishful thinking and imaginings, stark reality
and dreams are intermixed, in which things are not written from an objective external viewpoint, but from a subjective internal one. This wish
gives rise to the unmistakably surrealistic style that Korczak adopts in
this book.

Yotam undergoes many adventures. He raises such havoc as the world
has never seen. He causes a world war between cats and dogs, magically
raises an island on the river, and creates a castle on that island. He travels
to distant Paris, where he wrestles with a huge Negro in a cruel wrestling
competition, stars in movies, participates in a swimming demonstration,
avails himself of seven-league-boots, is twice imprisoned, narrowly
escapes death three times, wears a cap of invisibility and is carried to
Africa, China, the bottom of the sea, and the arctic pole on a typhoon
while clinging to his idea:

> I want to know the world, I want to know the entire world. I want to
> know what lies above ground, below water and in the lands of ice and
> eternal winter. The lives of the negroes, the cowboys and the Chinese
> . . . I want to know.[6]

Yet, in all of his adventures he does not find happiness. His use of his
magical powers usually brings harm, sorrow, and calamity to others, and
Yotam is often beset by severe pangs of conscience. His morality and
conscience undergo serious trials in which his entire personality is tested,
and his real self is revealed. And, indeed, the final trial is the trial of
man. Yotam passes through the whole world in order to rediscover man,
and he recognizes that: "Man investigates the sea-bottom and its
mysteries—the hero can go anywhere—in thought, in word and in action.
He encompasses the stars, the past and the future."[7] Even in the distant
icy wastes of the pole, he discovers the shattered sleigh of a man and a
lonely mound of stones. Between two of the stones he finds a faded flag:
"The miracle and the grave of an indomitable man."[8] It is on this grave
that Yotam vows to be honest and brave.

Reality and fiction mingle freely in *Yotam the Magical*, and in fact, the
fiction serves to intensify reality and emphasize a number of its facets to
the point of caricature. Korczak expands and enlarges reality, changes its
tempo and abstracts its processes and ways. This very quality of enlarge-
ment and expansion of reality enables the reader to seriously contend
with a number of its aspects. Moreover, Korczak anchored his flights of
imagination in Yotam's concrete reality, thus providing us with a constant
reference point in tangible reality, with criticism of adults and their attitude to children, with a description of the methods used in school and an
indication of their faults. Thus, for example, Korczak made use of times

of crisis to magnify human characteristics. When Yotam causes great havoc in the town, a mass fight breaks out, and Korczak notes: "They fight, for that is the way of the world. People are bitter and instead of helping each other, they begin to bicker. They fight and in the empty castor-oil jar a parrot swings and calls: Fools! Fools!"[9]

Korczak's satire directs sharp and penetrating barbs at sensational journalism, which invents information in order to enflame its readers and will have nothing to do with the truth or with social amendments, with true cooperation or the creation of a bridge between people, but is solely concerned with its own self-worth, with attracting additional readers, and increasing profits. Thus, when a journalist reports of the boxing match between Yotam, who appeared as "The Red Mask" and the Negro boxer, he writes:

The Red Mask, who vanquished the black boxer, is the son of a drunkard. He was sold to gypsies by his father and appeared in wandering circuses. This is his first appearance in Paris.

In his second report, the information is already different:

The anonymous boy is the son of a lord. When he was six years old he was already amazingly strong; he killed his brother in a quarrel, was driven out of his home by his father and hid in a fisherman's shanty. He participated in a whale hunt.

In his third report he exaggerates even more:

He was lost in a forest when no more than a year old. A brown she-bear raised him in the mountains, and hence his great strength. It was not long ago when he heard a human voice for the first time, the first word. His grandfather uprooted mountains and his grandmother tore up rocks. Besides, write what you will, I'm hungry and I've finished.[10]

No less penetrating is Korczak's parody of the League of Nations, "their impotent discussions, ridiculous actions and tasteless prattle."[11]

Korczak avails himself of every opportunity to reiterate his basic view that adults do not understand children.

He criticizes the belittling attitude of the adults toward the child's property, as Yotam bitterly complains: "The grown-ups think that anything which does not concern them is foolish, and that anything which cannot be bought or sold is garbage."[12]

Yotam is rankled by the way in which academic achievements are evaluated in conjunction with the behavior of the child, and he says:

What connection is there between behaviour and learning? If he knows, he should get a good grade. The mischievous boy can be a good student and the quiet boy might be lazy or untalented—why learn, if learning is not appreciated?[13]

Korczak described the strict and stony-hearted teacher who does not understand his students and enjoys displaying his arrogance and mocking the students. Thus, he latches onto Yotam:

"Ah, you're Robinson Crusoe? And when will you run away from home again? I hope your father showed you a thing or two?" And as if this were not torture enough for Yotam who stands by his desk and is not allowed to answer while his comrades laugh at him, the teacher continues to torment him by calling him to the board and attempting to confuse him with a problem.—"Well, Robinson, come to the board, let's see what you have learned on that desert island of yours."[14]

School recognizes nothing but blame, castigation, and punishment and makes very little use of praise, the noting of good works, and encouragement.

They scream and threaten only when something is lost, or when there is a fight, or when glass is broken, or ink is spilt. When there is a quiet day, nobody talks about it at all. It is always when something bad happens that there is a great scandal. As if laziness and neglect are all that exists and there are no such things as diligence and good-will.[15]

One of the things that Yotam finds most oppressive is the lack of faith in the child—the supercilious attitude and especially the suspicion. Yotam follows the janitor who attacks an innocent boy, screams at him, and threatens him, and sees the spark of rebellion light up in the boy's eyes. Yotam remembers how, through no fault of his own, he himself was blamed and suspected countless times and was deeply offended, and he thinks: "What can one do so that a man shall trust and believe other men? False accusations breed rancour and thoughts of vengeance, and suspicion deadens the truth in man."[16]

Educational distortion begins at the moment the teacher ceases to see the individual and only regards the anonymous whole, which is nothing but a conglomeration of individuals. It begins as early as first grade—"Sit straight: Don't turn around! Don't talk! Don't play with the pencil! Listen!" The rigid sitting position, the petrified procedures, the oppression are suffocating and rankling. Yotam complains:

At home one is allowed to lean on the table when father tells a story, one is allowed to lie on the bed when mother relates a legend, or to put one's face on one's knees when grandmother reminisces of past times. At home one can bend and stretch, and ask for clarification when one does not understand something. But in school, if you want to say something, you immediately have to raise two fingers in the air and wait. True, the class is full of children and the teacher cannot hold a private conversation with each of them, because the others will then start making a noise, but all the same, it spoils a great deal.[17]

In contrast to his harsh school experiences, Yotam adores Zusia's mother who establishes a real dialogue with her daughter and himself:

Totally different from school, totally different from how it was during the nature outing. She never said anything unimportant or silly, never wondered how "such a big boy does not know one thing or another and did not say that he should have already known it himself."[18]

He is enchanted to see how she asks for her daughter's advice and converses with her as one would with an adult, treating her with respect. Korczak's ideas about the right of the child to respect are reiterated when he writes: "And indeed, there are such people who respect children and rely on them—and Yotam loves these people especially."[19]

From a literary point of view, *Yotam the Magical* is Korczak's most cohesive and structured book. There are few didactic digressions, and Korczak suppressed his tendency to preach and allowed his imagination to soar unfettered, permitting the story to flow in a dazzling and satisfying artistic demonstration.

23

At the Summer Camp

> So long as we do not desert the dead cities, which one day tour-
> ists will come to visit and wonder at how people could have
> lived in them, how it could have happened that they did not
> gnaw each other to death in these warrens—so long as we live
> in cities, we shall send the children outside them in spring.
> —Korczak, *The Spring and The Child*

Korczak's book *At the Summer Camp*[1] is a children's story directly based
on Korczak's experience working with Jewish and Polish children in summer camps. In a very short introduction to the book, he notified his
young readers in advance that:

> This time I shall tell you of the deeds of Jewish boys at the summer
> camp in Michaelovak. I was their instructor and I have forgotten
> nothing. I will tell you only of what I myself have seen and heard.[2]

This tale is true to life; it reliably describes the work and play at the
summer camps where Korczak instructed. At the same time, this conformity of the story to actual events does not turn it into a dry and factual
report. Rather it is an attractive and deeply interesting literary portrait,
written with great talent, psychological understanding, and observational
skill in a lyrical spirit and with true understanding of the world of children.

Serious perusal of this book can shed light on various aspects of Korczak's educational enterprise and reaffirm important qualities in his personality as an educator. His faithful vision of the child and his educational
understanding are obvious right from the first lines of the story. As a
talented educator, he knows those moments of mutual inspection in
which students assess their teachers, and teachers assess their students.
He knows that from the moment of the first meeting: "The instructor is
under minute observation: What is he like, is he good or bad? Will he
allow or forbid tree climbing, throwing stones at squirrels and noise in the
dormitory at night?"[3] This inspection is mutual, and the good educator,
who has some pedagogical intuition, learns a great deal from this first

meeting. Thus did Korczak stand and observe the children as they exposed themselves in that moment of separation from the parents. One is afraid and clings to his father, a second is impudent and mischievous, a third shy, a fourth aggressive, and so on. It is in these first moments that Korczak makes the first rough sketches of his protégés' personality traits.

The whole book is full of observations, educational notes, and thoughts about the importance of the summer camp for the children of the poor, as well as introspections and contemplations of life. Recognizing the educational value of the freedom of nature, Korczak stressed:

> Laughter bursts out loud at the summer camp—an enchanted laughter, a laughter whose curative properties certainly far exceed those of the most expensive medicaments, and whose educational powers are far superior to those of the wisest teacher.[4]

He knew his protégés well, knew their background, the poverty of their families, and their harsh educational conditions.

He deeply empathized with these children and wished to introduce a ray of sunshine into the darkness of their days, to paint a smile on their lips, and to envigorate them with a dose of sunshine, freedom, and joy. He observed each of them and wished to devote his full attention to every single one. He wrote of the depressions and conflicts of Anshel, who was very pale and very ugly and whom the children did not like. He sympathized with Aharon Nimister, the orphan, who could not play catch or run long distances for he immediately began coughing. Nimister, thus liked to listen to legends and tales. Aharon was an excellent storyteller himself, and when he told a story all of the children were enthralled. Thus little Aharon compensated for his disability and found his place in society.

As was his wont, Korczak directed some criticism at the adults, claiming that they did not understand the child, that they disrupted his play, and that they misconstrued his world. Adults do not understand that the child is different from them in many respects, that his experiences and impressions are different. "When an adult person grows sad, he knows that the sadness shall pass and he shall be happy again. When a child cries it seems to him that he will always cry and always be miserable."[5]

Many of Korczak's educational ideas found expression in this book. He described the games of the children at great length and devoted much thought to analyzing their importance in the life of the summer camp. He artfully portrayed those games, which he considered a rehearsal for the game of life, such as the game of firemen, of war, etc. Korczak described the children's war games with great talent, in faithful detail, and at great length. The cunning plots and subterfuge in battle, the heroic charges, the initiative of the brave warriors, the conquest of goals, the tactics of battle, the retreat, the cease-fire, the upholding of military conventions, the treatment of prisoners, the respect for the flag, the signing of a peace treaty were all presented in great detail and with a high degree of reliability. He also devoted an important chapter to the children's court. As was later also the custom in Korczak's institutions, Korczak established a protégés' court at the summer camp.

Korczak presented a thrilling example of the action of this court in describing the trial of Grozovsky, the children's favorite. The judges, who loved Grozovsky, pronounced him not guilty. Grozovsky himself rebelled against the acquittal and demanded a retrial. When his case was brought up anew, the prosecutor said:

> Gentlemen, judges, you have a hard task set before you. You must pass sentence on a boy whom you like. Perhaps you wish to acquit him again? Remember then, that a biased verdict destroys all faith in the court. Think then, what others will say, when they have to be judged by an unfair court . . . you have made a mistake. It is now your duty to rectify that error.[6]

This time Grozovsky was sentenced to ten minutes in prison. Korczak stressed:

> In order to prove that he is not angry, Grozovsky promised to play his fiddle a long time that evening; but the sweetest concert he gave in the summer camp was the fact that he sat in prison for ten minutes, without rancor or anger, because he felt that he had really sinned.[7]

A special place in the life of the summer camp was reserved for parties, dramatic activities, plays, and celebrations. Special emphasis was placed on the playing of musical instruments. Each evening Grozovsky would play his fiddle for the children as they lay in their beds. Two or three children would join their voices to the music:

> The singing flows low, like a swallow, close to the ground, as if it is only trying out the power of its wings, and suddenly in a daring leap, it rises to the heavens, and the song sails its way among the clouds for a long time, after which it returns, tired, to the ground, to the people and falls asleep in silence.[8]

Of special interest is the Jewish issue, which is raised in a number of the book's chapters, such as when Korczak addresses a Polish farmer who allows the Jewish camp children to play in his field:

Polish farmer! Look well at these children. For they are not children but Jewish "bastards," who are not allowed to step into any park in the city; whom the coachman drives off the street with his whip; whom every passerby pushes off the sidewalk and every porter drives into the yard with his broom. These are not children. They are Muszky; will you not then drive them away from their sitting place under the willow by the roadside, and shall you then invite them to play in your field?[9]

Korczak deeply empathized with the children of the Jewish poor, and knowing that they had difficulties in mastering the Polish language, he took care to use only easy and simple words in the summer camp newspaper.

Breakfast, tea and lunch—everything is called dinner. When the bell rings, they rush with shouts of joy: To dinner! How are they to know that every meal has a different name according to the hour in which it is eaten, if at home, when they are hungry, they always get a slice of bread and a glass of tea which has not been sufficiently sweetened.[10]

He identified and loved these children.

The book is full of descriptions written with great literary talent; its language is both clear and rich, sometimes tending to poetry. There are many picturesque lines of great linguistic and semantic content that testify to Korczak's literary and artistic prowess. For example, bathing in the river is not just bathing but, "One dip in the river—a thousand laughs and a thousand miracles—a hundred interesting sights and at least ten adventures."[11]

Young readers find the book very attractive. It rivets their interest in its descriptions of the life of children, and provides them with a truly educational and literary experience.

24

An Unlucky Week[1]

What am I if not an obstacle in your free flight,
A cobweb on your variegated wings, a pair of
scissors whose deadly function is to snip
at your flowering buds?[2]

Korczak's story *An Unlucky Week—From the Life of the School* holds the essence of his devastating criticism of school as it is spoken through the mouth of Stachio, one of the victims of school.

Yet, it would be a grave mistake to assume that we are dealing here with some critical commentary written for children. For "An Unlucky Week" is first and foremost a work of literature that excellently portrays a bitter week in the life of Stachio. Korczak is once again revealed as an author who knows how to express moods and emotions in brief sketches and who can very skillfully describe relationships within a family and between children.

What better testimony to Korczak's illustrative talent, his penetrating vision, and his skill at depicting relationships within the family than the opening passage of the story:

> The coalman did not come.
>
> Father was very angry at mother for putting everything off until the last moment. Mother said that father knows nothing and had better shut up, because she had already ordered the coal on Thursday. Father said that there was more than one coalman in the city, thank God. Mother said that she is as well aware of the fact as he is and that this particular one does not cheat in his weights. Father said that her thrift was like a bone in his throat. Mother was deeply offended. Let father run the house himself. Father is an inconsiderate man, mother too could have said many things. And father said: "Here we go again" and went out.[3]

Should we listen attentively to this passage which is written in the third person in the form of a report, we can hear the stormy family debates, the sharp dialogues, the sarcastic exchanges, the casting of accusations, and the deterioration of the debate from a specific problem, that is, the non-arrival of the coalman, to general accusations such as—"her thrift was like a bone in his throat," to personal insults such as "an inconsiderate man," to accusing and censuring insinuations hinting that the main accusations have not been stated yet, such as "mother too could have said many things," until the whole quarrel ends with the father's departure and the slamming of a door. And all of this is in one concentrated paragraph which encapsulates the drama and the aggressive rhetoric beneath the seeming calm of a detached narrator. This paragraph heralds the general atmosphere of the story.

A somber atmosphere hovers over the entire story. On the one hand, matters at home are very oppressive because of the family struggles and the repetitive and depressing squabbles, and, on the other hand, there is no enthusiasm and no joy of life, no daring deeds and no message.

Dark, somber and flaccid, like the lives of the multitudes which crawl around and around, between one Sunday and the next, in a slow and senseless search for a slice of bread and something to wear, with no smile to illuminate the darkness, no dull longings. A shallow breath in a flat chest. None of them can utter even one cry of joy to echo among the trees of the forest, to carry across green meadows.[4]

When I read this paragraph, it seemed to me for a moment that it was not Korczak's story that I was reading but the stories of the angry young people of England, who published their writings in the fifties and sixties of the present century.

For a moment, we are reminded of the words of Jimmy, the hero of John Osborne's play *Look Back in Anger*, who screams his rage at life for slipping by in such greyness, such monotony, without passion, without joy, without sudden storms, but in a slow and nerve-wracking dribble, dribbling away in rusty pipes.

Oh God—he cries—what would I give for some simple human enthusiasm, just enthusiasm—that's all. I want to hear a warm, vibrant voice calling: "Halleluja! I am alive! I exist!" But this cry is suffocated by the grey reality which surrounds us.[5]

Indeed, Korczak manages to portray the social oppression and the pointless lives of the affluent classes as successfully and well as he portrays the lives of the poor, the destitute, and the unfortunate. Yet we are not concerned here with a Chekhovian tale, and although some of its aspects predate the theme of anger in social and world literature, the story is not one of social anger. Its main character, or more precisely, the evil spirit, which hovers over it, is the school.

Within the boredom and flaccidity of the long and somber days, Stachio calls:

> You have put millions of children under the yoke of school, and now they go about, poor souls, around and around, from Sunday to Sunday, progressively dulled in the course of years of suffering and silent, helpless rebellion![6]

Stachio does not want to get out of bed in the morning because he is afraid of the teacher's bad grades, of the humiliating tests on the blackboard, and of the brutality of the teachers who find joy in his failure. When he sits in class, he prays to God to be merciful and ring the redeeming bell as quickly as possible. When the teacher returns the dictation or the examination, he dares not look. Finally, he stares at his negative grade and no longer thinks of anything. His nervous system is totally shaken, he sits with his mind empty and can no longer study. And when he is asked to correct the dictation, he is assailed by dozens of rules and hundreds of repetitions of the same rule until he is exhausted and bored and becomes dull and cranky.

Korczak's protest against the school's judgment, against the grades that imprison, castigate, torture, and punish, finds its expression in the pained paragraph:

> Such a failed grade as one gets on the first day of the week, is like a large bothersome fly or an ink stain on blotting paper, for it buzzes like a fly, sticks itself into every thought at every opportunity and spreads like an ink stain on absorbent paper, spreads outwards and grows, constantly grows throughout the week.[7]

The failed grade that Stachio has received causes him to despair, damages his belief in himself, depresses all desire to work, and oppresses his soul.

Sometimes, Stachio overcomes his aversion and fear, and tries to think for himself, to find short-cuts, to propose methods of his own, but his original thinking is received with rejection, for the teachers stick to the accepted answers and are afraid of veering to the left or right. Thus, when he suggests a simpler method of calculation to the math teacher,

> The teacher began screaming that mathematics were invented by people who were somewhat wiser than he and that Stachio is lazy and instead of thinking a little, he prefers to invent methods so that he will not have to think at all.[8]

And thus is the creativity of the student slowly oppressed. His curiosity is not encouraged. When he wishes to read books that do not deal with school subjects, these books are taken away from him, and his sense of suffocation constantly becomes stronger.

In this atmosphere, relationships between teachers and students are perceived as a form of war.

> The teacher only thinks of how to fix them, cheat them, catch them at it, make them fail. The students do not remain indebted and the class and the teacher are as two enemy camps fighting a battle to the death. If you know the lesson and wish to show it to the teacher, you must hide, glance constantly at your watch, pretend to be frightened; and if you do not know, pretend that you wish to answer, and you can be sure that he will never ask you.[9]

Korczak follows Stachio as he is slowly ground down over the week. Frightened of his failures and scared of the threatening examinations, Stachio also becomes entangled with his mother who views his success at school as the only thing of importance and his negative grades as a sign of his failure as a person and of the hopelessness of his future—to the point of threatening to send him to become a cobbler's apprentice.

Stachio imagines himself dying a hero's death in an attempt to save a little girl from the hooves of a runaway horse, then imagines how

> his corpse is brought into school. The newspapers all carry stories describing him and calling him "The Little Hero." The entire school escorts him to his final resting place: The headmaster, the superintendent and all the students, mother and father—and the girl whose life he had saved.[10]

These dreams of vengeance by means of his death and the recognition won posthumously turn into a nightmare.

> And in the dream, an evil spirit lurks at the school's entrance, a monster who hates the laughter of children, and when their merry laughter is heard, the monster's eyes become blood-shot and with a careless movement it turns its head into the entrance and growls and drives away the laughter.[11]

It seems that one cannot find a more terrible dream to express the depth of the despair that school engendered in those days, the child-hatred which was ingrained into it, and its total educational failure, than this dream that Korczak—the great critic of school, long before the crushing criticism of the radical educators—has woven in pain.

Korczak felt that school, which might have been the kingdom of children, a place where they can realize themselves, foster their imagination, and enrich their world, becomes a whip and a curtailer of flight, a college of grayness and oppression, of a life without joy or dreaming.

Stachio examines the lives of his father and mother and recognizes their misery.

> Poor mother, she too is miserable, for what does she have in life? She sits cooped up at home all day. Father treats her strictly and without consideration, and when mother finally bought herself a fine piece of cloth for a dress, the seamstress ruined it all. And father, is he happy? No. Works to the point of torture. It is hard earning a living now, and when he finally goes out to the theater or something like that, mother makes a scene and spoils his mood.[12]

Stachio sees himself as obligated to succeed in school if only to add one ray of sunshine to the darkness of his parent's lives, if only to reduce their pain over his failures, and stop everyone's crestfallen march of failure for a single moment. In his soul he promises to try and make an effort. He decides with great force, and at the moment of his decision, he feels a sense of elation such as he had never known before. But at that very moment the teacher's question descends upon him—"What is the capital of Persia?" and he is not ready and does not yet know, and the whip of "Failed" dissipates his dreams and drives him back into the rut of disappointments.

Perhaps some will consider that this story is overconcerned with criticism, with the shattering of illusions, and with the blackening of school, but have such people ever examined the color of Stachio's day when his dreams have been extinguished? Korczak has done so.

25
"Fame"

Teacher, hey teacher, they say that he went with all the children. He went. Yes, yes. Does he tell them stories? Will
another legend be told? Perhaps he knows, the old teacher.
—Moshe Basok, "The Old Teacher"

In his article "The Legend and the Child," Korczak noted the naive and
limited perception of adults where it concerns legends. He wrote:

> Is not the whole world one single legend for the child? A legend of
> the birth of man, of the cradle and the grave. A tale about hospitals,
> churches, large market days, airplanes, circuses, cinema-houses, rail, sea
> and air catastrophes, a horrible legend about war. And where are those
> tales of which no one talks, those secret legends which the adult
> attempts to hide and not discuss in front of the child. The grey legend
> of the convict led by the police, the old beggar-man, the stories about
> orphanhood, a drunken father, a squabble or a fight between mother
> and father, a horrible depressing legend. And in contrast there are the
> sun-swept legends of ball-games, play-grounds, forests and their ber-
> ries, fields and flowers, grass pastures, the sea shore, golden sands and
> pretty shells.[1]

In this story for children, "Fame,"[2] Korczak wished to tell a grey
legend of poverty and destitution, of the struggle for existence and the
death of little children, of friendships and separations, of a great wish for
fame and a hard and impoverished life. Many of the qualities of his writing find their expression in this story which excels in its psychological
perception, its concentrated observations on the life of children, and its
descriptive skills.

In contrast to many other works in the area of children's literature,
which shy away from any description of death, disease, or the hardships
of survival, Korczak allowed his readers to peer into this dark aspect of
reality. He did not wish to hide, mask, or wrap life in gay, colorful cover-
ings. Death darkens the air right from the opening lines of the story, as

Korczak notifies us that Weiczek and Pachalka, the two little heroes of the work, will soon grow ill and die. In the last chapter death stares at us with its ugly and horrifying visage, as we witness the last painful moments of little Pachalka, whom we have grown to love for her joy and her attempts to instill a tiny ray of light and hope into her grey and humble life. We see her in her dying agony when she begs her big brother Vladek to return her debt of two pennies to Helenka.

> I will die and you must repay her . . . and do not be angry with me. Pachalka spoke quietly, for there were black wounds all over her lips, which caused her great pain and suffering. One had to change the bandage often and dip the cotton-wool in cold water. Vladek, ask mother not to change my bandages any more, for they cause me great pain . . . it hurts so much! They changed Pachalka's bandage only once more after that, there was no need for a second bandage.[3]

Korczak attempts to moderate the starkness of this meeting with death by shifting the perspective of the story to the secret wishes of children and their will to believe in reincarnation and life after death. Korczak does this in the song of the girl Mania, which ends the chapter:

> Do not cry mama, and papa do not weep—
> Pachalka's wings are now pure white.
> She and her brother Weiczek.
> Like two angels in the sky above.
> So they shall fly there, as in a dream.
> To mama and papa they call: hello!
> Pure and bright they shall light high above.
> And receive spring in psalm and song.[4]

It should be noted here that Korczak himself used a similar way to defend himself when he was confronted with the certainty of approaching death in the ghetto. He, too, wished to cling to life after death, to the belief in the immortality of the soul and the other life that lies beyond the borders of death. In his diary he wrote:

> The spirit yearns in the narrow cage of the body. People sense approaching death and discuss it from the point of view of termination, while, in truth, death is but the continuation of life. A different life. Even if you do not believe in reincarnation you will be forced to admit, that your body shall indeed live as a blade of grass, a cloud. For you are water and dust.[5]

In this story, more than in any of his other stories, Korczak is revealed in his sensitive psychological perception and his deep comprehension of the world of the child with all its difficulties and conflicts, anxieties and joys. He masterfully describes various situations in the lives of the children.

It had always seemed to Vladek that he did not like his little sister, who was stubborn and a crybaby, who understood nothing and who ruined everything that fell into her hands. He would become very angry with his mother when she ordered him to play with Abu and demanded that he give in to her because she was small and silly. But when he hears that Abu is about to be taken from them forever, that the grocer wishes to adopt her, he rebels with his entire being.

> Abu then suddenly became so dear, that he would not part with her for all the wealth in the world. Mother, I will work, Olak will find me a job! . . . No, no, mother, don't give Abu away, she is so small. She will be sad without Pachalka and Weiczek. I will give her my potatoes. Vladek totally forgets that he is already grown-up and breaks out in tears. He cries and runs away to the roof of the ice-shed at the end of the yard, where he continues to cry. He cried and cried and could not stop.[6]

A similar self-revelation, a sudden realization of the intensity of the emotions hidden within him, can also be seen in the relationships of Vladek with his grandmother. It always seemed to him that he only loves her "as one is required to love one's grandmother," for she was often angry with him and complained about him to his father. Yet when it becomes obvious that she is leaving their home for good, he undergoes a process of self-revelation:

> But at that moment, when he looked into her face and saw that she was very old, and when he began to think that she had no one in the world—Vladek felt the same as he always did when he wanted to cry, but he did not cry and only said to himself: Sure, I do not cry, because I am big, and it was the first time in his life, that he was not so happy at having grown-up.[7]

Korczak did not use any adjectives to describe Vladek's feelings, rather he manifested them in rich expressive sentences which spoke louder than any attempt at more precise definitions: "Vladek felt the same as he always did when he wanted to cry. . . ."

This work is full of Korczak's faithful inside knowledge of the world of the child. His was a true acquaintance without the counterfeit romanticism of the adult that attempts to reconstruct the world of childhood through a nostalgic prism of memories.

Korczak managed to convey the events of the story through the eyes of the child. He described his wonder and perplexity, his inner rebellion against the injustices which exist in the world of adults, the injustice in human relationships, in oppressive economic competition, and the like. Korczak did not write much about the economic crisis that swooped down on Vladek's home, following the completion of the new Dragon's cafe, which destroyed his father's business and caused the family to become up-rooted. Everything is seen through the eyes of Vladek who "knew that they have to move, but did not understand why: his father was here first, so why must he give in?"[8] Vladek wishes to rebel. In his innocence he goes to Dragon's cafe and asks Mr. Dragon to move his cafe with its marble tables and luxurious appliances to another place. He does not understand why Dragon casts him out of his cafe and curses him. He is bitterly puzzled and begins to pose poignant questions for which he shall never find an answer:

> It is very painful, when one wants to do a good deed and is not properly understood. So painful and mortifying is the injustice. Why did the children abuse and humilate him so severely today? He did them no harm. Why did Dragon scorn him? Was he not right, in wanting to protect his father? Why are humans worse than wolves? A satiated wolf will share his meal with a hungry one.[9]

Vladek learns the harsh facts of life when he sees the suffering of his father, who tries to find a job in order to provide for his family. Korczak did not try to hide anything from his young readers, especially since many of them had already encountered many of the things of which Korczak wrote. Thus Vladek learns that:

> Without some special favor, you will never find work. Every loaf of bread has a hundred hands reaching for it and the bread hardly ever finds its way to an honest man. . . . The winter is hard. Vladek already knows that this is fate and that it will always be so . . . that all poor people are in a similar situation. The price of coal has gone up again, hunger and cold are here again—it seems that it cannot be otherwise.[10]

Korczak never forgot his role as an educator, and this work, too, is full of educational notes and remarks. Once more we find his basic assumption that wild and unruly children are so only because adults have not found time to care for them, to guide them, and to instruct them in the art of differentiating between good and evil.[11] He encourages children to mutual cooperation, to helping others as if it were you in trouble,[12] to aspire to escape from their miserable situation, to climb forward even if the day is hard,[13] and he ends his story with the call: "Children! Your goals must be noble, your ideas—sublime! Strive always toward the light of glory! The aspiration for good is not futile—it shall bear fruit!"[14]

Korczak's ideas about the children's group, about the self-rule of children, and the culture of youth also find their expression in this work. Vladek and his friends establish an association of children called "The Association of Knights of Honor" and their slogan is "Fame." The aims and regulations of the association embody a long list of educational and human ideals such as mutual help, assistance to little children, prevention of cruelty to animals, prohibition on lying, aid to the sick, prohibition on theft, encouragement of cleanliness, encouragement of reading and study, and devotion to a way of life that is the way of fame not in its external manifestation but in its true internal revelations.[15]

From a literary-artistic point of view, the story excels in its clear expression, its flowing style, and its realistic descriptions. It opens with a direct appeal to the readers, in which the narrator raises the possibilities and preferences of writing, and begins with his initial characterization of the heroes. Such an opening increases the intimacy, creates an illusion of directly listening to the voice of the narrator, and provides a dimesion of proximity to the events. Moreover, in this way, Korczak introduced the first interesting stimuli pertaining to the figures and the events:

> It is very difficult to begin a story, because one immediately wishes to tell a whole lot, and if one rushes to tell everything all at once, it might confuse things. This is a story about five children, their parents, an old grandmother, an uncle, a cat, an aunt and other people. In fact, one should talk only about adults, for what can be of interest in little Abu, who is always asleep, crying or grumbling: Abu, Abu, Abu? Weiczek and Pachalka are older than Abu, but they will soon become ill and die. For this reason we cannot say a lot about them either, and grandma will soon also go away, and the cat will remain in the old apartment.[16]

The curiosity of the children, who have experienced the beginning of the plot, is aroused.

26

"People Are Good":
Korczak's Short Stories for Children

> I do not sleep at night and I therefore think. Thus do I think, as if I were making up a story. Not a story, but a tale of adventure. Various adventures. In the light of day, I know that none of this happened, but at night I think that this is the truth. In the daytime I know that I am an ordinary boy among school pupils, but at night I feel it is true, that it might be true.
> —"Thus do I think"[1]

Like the hero of the story "Thus Do I Think" Korczak knew the power of the story to enthrall the child. For the story is at one and the same time a tangible reality in which the child is involved and a distant figment of the imagination with which, magically, he is also involved. Moreover, Korczak knew the child's ability to create stories of his own: daydreams that are legends, adventures that add to the possibilities of his day, imaginings that allow him to soar above his dull and depressing reality, and the capacity to identify so deeply with the creations of his imagination until it is sometimes difficult for him to differentiate between reality and fiction.

Korczak knew that the child is capable of living, almost with the same measure of intensity, in two worlds at one and the same time—in the concrete reality of his life and in his substitute reality, that fictional reality which he creates for himself or reads about in a book. Because of his deep acquaintance with the child, Korczak knew the wonderful educational possibilities inherent in the literary experience. The identification with literary figures, the introjection of their values, and the emotional empathy required in order to cope with their problems present possibilities of catharsis, emotional liberation, developing self-awareness, and insight, as well as value education.

In his stories for children, Korczak wished to develop the moral sensitivity of the readers, to open their eyes to the knowledge of man. He wished to introduce them to the harsh and "prejudiced" world of adults, and to show them the great extent of the damage that people daily, even hourly, cause each other because their eyes are too blind to see and their hearts are closed to others. In his story, "The Evil Man",[2] Korczak tells of a man whom the whole village thought to be cruel and evil, although they did not know what his evil deeds were. This man was ostracized by the entire village; everyone kept away from him and treated him with enmity and scorn, until he was obliged to move outside the village. His life was harsh and very bitter. He spent his days alone, hated by adults and children, whom he secretly loved. One day, when the "evil man" was brought to trial before the village elders for having hit the village leader who had insulted him, his identity was unexpectedly revealed. While the entire village population called for his blood and screamed as one: "Death to the murderer! Hang him! Stone him!"—one of the judges, an ancient man, rose to his feet, withdrew a silver box from his pocket, opened it, took out a golden straw, and began blowing bubbles. Each bubble was a vision, a picture, and each picture depicted an act of grace and generosity by the "evil man." In the first bubble, they saw him saving the village idiot from the teeth of the village leader's dogs, who ripped the rags off his body and sank their teeth into his flesh. The "evil man" had rushed to help, saved the man from the dogs' jaws, and took him home where he cared for his wounds, fed and watered him, then saw him on his way. In the second bubble, they saw the "evil man" save a little kitten, which had been cast into the river by the village boys, from drowning. In the third bubble, they saw him helping the village orphan who had been sent by the village leader to the forest to gather firewood in the pouring rain. The "evil man" took her into his home, sat her down by the fire, and fed her, then went out into the forest to gather the firewood himself. The old judge thus let many bubbles float up into the air, and in each bubble the "evil man" appeared as a good-hearted man who had succored the poor and the destitute, the unfortunate and the hounded. In this way Korczak wished to acquaint children with the great wrongs in the world and to educate them to look at humanity with a fresh, clear, and more reliable vision. In another of his pretty stories, Korczak described the immigration of a little girl to Palestine and her adjustment to life on a kibbutz. This story, "People Are Good",[3] exposes Korczak's sharp perception, his faithful acquaintance with the soul of the child, and his great love for the land of Israel. He describes the world of a little girl as she encounters many phenomena that are incomprehensible to her, thinks her innocent thoughts, and is deeply involved in her childish philosophy:

Love is in the heart, so people say. The rooms in the heart are small, a hundred times smaller than dolls' rooms, and the heart must contain so much: Mother, grandmother, even father, who is no longer alive, and even Henry! What does it mean, that father will always be alive in memory? Grandfather says that there is a God which one should also love. So much to love and man has only one small heart.[4]

Noting the deliberations of his little heroine, Korczak once more reiterated the basic idea that passes through his entire literary oeuvre:

> The child knows a great deal but does not know how to express his knowledge. He is afraid to speak, he is not afraid but ashamed, he is not ashamed but simply does not know how to say it so that an adult will understand, so that he will not think his words stupid or childish or funny.[5]

Of special interest is the description of the way in which the little girl is assimilated into the kibbutz children's society. She is faced with a world at complete odds with all that she had known in the diaspora; it is like a world full of joy and happiness, a world in which even the laughter of children is different than anywhere else in the world. The thoughts of the serious little girl begin to change here.

> Here, I always think easily, with joy. There are painful thoughts; and here they float like butterflies. Over there, it was always the one thought: What will happen tomorrow? While here: What have I done today?[6]

The little girl discovers the kibbutz, learns about the cooperative settlement, gets to know a new life, and becomes a part of it. She is open to nature and loves every flower and shrub, sensing the secret life within them. The grain and the flowers seem to her like the gentle song of the earth, and the little children that surround them grow like flowers, too. The trees and the birds speak to her in their own tongue, and she understands them. She smiles at the smiling flower, converses with the bush, and whistles at the chirping birds. She wishes to care for people and tells her mother:

> If only it were possible neither to eat nor sleep, but only to seek places for people. If everyone finds his own place—he will feel good. And to care for them—like plants both big and small—like trees.[7]

Korczak wished to enrich the world of children with his stories, to expand their minds, to widen their knowledge of life and of different people, and to entertain their spirits. He wrote a number of stories about the lives of poor children in the pre–World War II Polish city and Jewish village. These stories, such as "The Tale of Hershke," "Esterel's Secret," "Ten Matchboxes," "Why Does My Father Shout?" "An Attentive Son," "Thus Do I Think," "Two Candles." and "Fame," are full of love for the destitute child, full of belief in the grains of goodness and truth that exist in the heart of every child and which shall eventually sprout and bear fruit. Korczak believed that in aspiring to goodness and excellence, children shall rise out of their poverty and abjectness and pull the whole world up with them. Each of these stories provides the reader with a new perspective on life. In "The Tale of Hershke," Korczak describes Hershke's poor home, which is illuminated with hope—hope that warms the heart and provides the strength required for struggling with a bitter life. In his story "Thus Do I Think," he relates the adventures of a child who wishes to help the Jews and save them from their plight. In other stories, he describes the lives and dreams of Jewish and Polish children. Korczak knew how to weave a ray of light into the daily plight of these destitute children, and with a few verbal sketches he managed to create whole worlds and illuminate human qualities with great psychological insight.

In "The Tale of Hershke" the adults try to believe in the tale told by their son, and Hershke's father meaningfully says, "When I and mother know interesting things, we tell you about them too. Can children not tell adults some stories as well"?[8] It is doubtful if their dream will ever come true, if Hershke's father shall receive money from his uncle, if the children will drink milk, if Esterl will ever have shoes, if mother will sew herself a new apron, and if Hershke shall have a book and notebook; but a new quality is added to their lives—they hope. Korczak ended the story thus:

> Hershke told his little sister a tale—and rays of sunshine burst into the tailor's little house, and it became warmer and more joyful in the house. Such a tale can be called a dream, and perhaps—hope.[9]

Korczak sympathized with the difficulties of the adults, who grew impatient, grumpy, bitter, and quick to shout and curse at their children, as a result of hardship. Esterl, the heroine of "Esterl's Secret," suffers although she has not sinned, and the days of her childhood go by without her ever having tasted real childhood. Korczak wished to console these children, to weave a fictional reality for them, full of imaginary joys and the pleasures known only to the sons of the poor. In the Jewish school room, the poor teacher gives his students ten boxes of matches and magically creates a world of games, pastimes, and joys. Korczak stressed:

> Sometimes a rich child will have many toys but will nevertheless become bored, while the poor boy often makes his beautiful toys for him-

self and for his friends. For sticks, tiny pebbles, rags and sand are very plentiful in the world.[10]

We discover Korczak's fine sense of humour in many of his stories, but an especially large helping of his jocular spirit can be found in the story, "An Attentive Son," which is Korczak's rendition of a well-known folk tale. Yet, as was his wont, Korczak could not content himself with laughter just for the sheer joy of laughing, and he added a moral to the end of the story: "A good but not very wise man can do much for the good of humanity, while a wise but evil man might do much evil to people during his life."[11]

In a number of his short stories, Korczak let his readers into the secret of the "Literary Laboratory" of the author, revealing the stages of a story's creation and allowing them to participate in the various deliberations of the author when he sets out to invent and shape events and situations. Korczak ascribed a great deal of importance to this technique and believed that one of the goals of a good children's story is to allow the reader to be more than just a passive recipient and to become an active partner who creates through the process of reading. Indeed, in "Thus Do I Think" he involved the reader in the process of creating the adventure, while in the "Ten Matchboxes," he presented the reader with literary challenges and created situations. He left the reader to complete them, and suggested that the reader continue and develop things for himself. Thus, he interrupted his story from time to time with sentences such as: "Something surely happens after this, but I am in a hurry, and if you wish, think for yourself what little Ruth may have done with the box she received, and what happened afterwards."[12]

The background of the four stories "The Tale of Hershke," "Esterel's Secret," "Ten Matchboxes," and "Why Does My Father Shout?" is the poverty of Jewish families living in Poland before the Second World War. The anti-Semitism that increased in those days finds poignant expression in "Esterel's Secret." A Polish lad calls Esterl, "a dirty Jew" and threatens her. A drunken Pole calls her grandfather the shoemaker "a thieving Jew" and takes his boots, which he left to be mended, without paying for the repair. Grandfather restrains himself and swallows his humilation. He does not know how to fight for his honor, and he says, submissively, "Sometimes a man makes a profit and sometimes he loses, thus has it always been."[13] Korczak wished to soften matters rather than emphasize the anti-Semitic hate. When Esterl complains to her grandfather about the Polish boy who threatened her, he replies that there are many Polish children who would not dream of hurting her and that "There are wild boys among the Jews as well." Korczak's gentle, all-embracing humanism did not allow him to harbor hatred, enmity, or a lust for vengeance, hence, the conciliatory attitude, which so often found expression in his way of life. This conciliatory spirit also characterizes the ending of his story "Thus Do I Think," in which the hero of the story brings Hitler to Palestine. Rather than seek vengeance the hero converses with Hitler, shows him the wonders of its economy, and tells him:

> See here sir, how well we run the economy. We did not purchase more than a few cannons and airplanes and submarines, only so many as were required; but we take nothing of others. And he: "I know this. The Jews are permitted to return to Germany." I laughed. Well and good, but none wish to return, because no one believed him. . . . I did not give him money, but bought the German children milk, butter and all that they needed and did not have.[14]

How characteristic of Korczak, who never held a grudge, In any situation he was quick to see the child in need regardless of his nationality.

Gdalia Alkoshi noted of "Thus Do I Think" that it: "constitutes a rough Jewish-oriented sketch of the story of *Yotam The Magical*."[15] Alkushi also empahsized that this story:

> Enfolds the essential problems of Zionism on the eve of the Holocaust. Beginning from the prohibition on entering Palestine which was imposed by the British Mandate authorities and ending in the problematic relationships between the Jewish settlement and the Arabs, as these are reflected in the thoughts of the Jewish boy who, sitting in the diaspora, yearns for a distant homeland. The story is characterized by a proud Jewish-National spirit, which, full of assurance, seems to rise from between the lines and instill a religious-mystical certainty that despite the obstacles—This country shall be ours and in their heart of hearts even the Arabs are aware of this.[16]

It is worthwhile noting that the Jewish-Arab problem greatly preoccupied the humanistic Korczak, who feared that the Jewish immigration to Israel, the settlement of the land, the building of cities and settlements, and the opening of the Tel-Aviv harbor would damage the Arab settlement, its sources of livelihood, and its way of life. These misgivings frequently appeared in the letters he wrote to his friends in Palestine and in the notes of his diary. In the above story, the imaginary friend of the Jewish boy dreams a dream in which the Prophet Mohammed is revealed and commands him to hand the treasures buried in the land of Israel over to the Jews and to purchase African land for the Arabs. And, indeed, "We have established an African bank. Every Arab who had five acres in Israel will receive ten acres of African land from the bank."[17] This story in which Korczak invested many of his longings for Israel and his thoughts of the revival of the Jewish settlement in Israel is of great interest. We hear of the plight of the Jews in the diaspora and of their longings for a shelter, as the little hero dreams that he is standing before the king of England and telling him, "People are suffering great torture, and my father and mother among them, for the Jews in the diaspora fare very ill."[18] He dreams the dream of the Jewish state and emphasizes: "I do not yet know everything, but the end will be thus—the Jews will have a state of their own in Palestine."[19] In his mind's eye, he lives the life of this future state with its conflicts and its struggles against the Arab attackers.

Yet there is no hatred for the Arabs in his heart. To the contrary—his best friends are the Arab boy Solan and his sister Chasina. He finds an understanding with these destitute and unfortunate children who are exploited by the rich Arabs.

An engrossing story of great literary, educational, and therapeutic merit is "The Scar."[20] One can see it as a miniaturized reflection of the world of the Jewish child in the diaspora. It also reflects both the Jewish reality in Poland at the time of the Nazi rise to power and the memory of the Holocaust. From a literary point of view, one must note the air of mystery that shrouds the story, the suspense, the dialogue, the vivid portrayal, and the restrained descriptions which are doubly expressive for their very restraint. It is no accident that many teachers have chosen to instruct their classes with this very story, that many editors saw fit to include it in their anthologies,[21] and that psychologists and bibliotherapists make use of it as a means of therapeutic education.[22]

Dvora Kubovi, a practitioner of therapeutic teaching, raises a long list of issues to be investigated in a therapeutic interview following a reading of "The Scar." Among them are:

1) The phenomenon of the "scapegoat" and some of the mental processes which engender it:
   a) The human tendency to seek a "legitimate" channel, even though irrelevant, in order to discharge aggression which for various reasons cannot be directed toward its cause; a tendency which stands in direct relation to the measure of repressed and denied aggression.
   b) The emotional reactions toward the different and the strange, and some of their causes.
   c) Distortions of perception and mistaken impressions, which stem from prejudice, and some of their causes.

  d) Some of the causes for being swayed by the majority, as con-
     trasted with a state of mind which allows the individual to with-
     stand social pressure.
  2) Possible motives for "going" with the crowd despite one's reluc-
     tance.
  3) The human tendency to avoid the memory of painful experiences.[23]

The possibility of holding therapeutic discussions about these issues and many others on the basis of "The Scar" testifies to the psychological texture of the story and its multilayered structure which appeals to the various layers in the reader's soul and evokes reactions on different levels, commencing from the conscious level, through the world of associative experience and ending in the depth of the soul and the deeply buried scars in the reader's heart.

We shall end our discussion of Korczak's short stories for children with "Why Does My Father Shout?"[24]

This story was written in response to the title question: "Why Does My Father Shout?" The beginning of the answer is heard far and wide while its end is no more than a whisper—exactly like the shouts of the father. In any case there is no need to search deeply or far in order to discover various shades of meaning which, right at the very opening of the story, endow the figure of the father with a completely different image than can be gained from the overt description of the boy narrator. A contradiction between the threatening image with which the boy would endow him and the more gentle reality of his personality keeps coming up despite the boy's attempts at camouflage. A fine and interesting tension is created, and the various contradictions between the childish descriptions and the details of actual reality endow the entire story with a gentle humor. These elements allow the reader to perceive the figures as they were initially intended to be perceived—with identification, with a forgiving attitude toward their human weaknesses, with a loving smile.

Following an impressive and somewhat frightening beginning: "Oh, how he shouts, how terrible he is when he shouts. The whole town shakes with fear"—we find that the mountain is no more than a molehill or better still, a cat mound—for the first victim of this awesome figure is none other than the house cat that flees from its place behind the stove. Nor do the other victims of this rage vindicate the assumption that these observations should be received at face value: peeping kids, the butcher's dog, and random figures that cannot perceive the true nature of a man, and are therefore unable to indicate what his true qualities are: the letter-bearing house porter and the neighbor—a loud voiced fright in her own right.

If we fail to be convinced by the "audience" thus cringing away from the father's shouting, we become even more uncertain when some of the consequences of this terrible shouting are revealed: It stops an unwanted rain during "Tabernacles"; its stops the war; it causes America to back away in fright . . . these events—all of which have happened in "bygone days" and that are recounted by the child as stories which he had been told, shed more light on the figure of the boy narrator than on the father. This is a narrator with a childish point of view, unreliable, bent on impressing his listeners and easily impressionable himself—and these very qualities comprise the charm of the narrator—a child among children, authentic, intimate, and capable of sweeping the reader along with him and showing him things through his own eyes.

The order in which details are provided is one of the important factors in the art of storytelling for reading itself is diachronic, and our impressions are deeply influenced not only by what has been described but also by the order in which things have been received in our consciousness. The order of presentation in this story is such that minor, secondary details are related first.

For example, we hear about the father's profession, which is an important element in the presentation of his character, only after a lengthy introduction. It is only then that we first encounter the mother, whose figure is also important in the overall shaping of the family's character. The narrator directly refers to himself and to his emotions toward his father, only after having presented us with the would-be opinions of almost half of the city's population: "I too, was at first afraid of my father, but when I grew to be five years old . . . I immediately stopped being afraid of him." The affair of the uncle—which is the essential answer to the question that opens the story—is only described at the end. When, finally, the father directly answers the question, his words no longer constitute a world-shaking revelation, for many small details have already shown us that he is not as awesome as he seems and that there is in fact a great deal of irony in his words: "I must shout, if I did not shout everyone would be crawling all over my head." We have already learned that this tactic is not successful, for his shouting does not frighten the son who asks for two pennies—and receives them despite the threatening bluster. Even this only serves to introduce us to the affair of the uncle who regularly succeeds in blackmailing the father despite his outbursts on this issue. Long before the ending we have already come to realize that this tendency to shout is not only harmless, but, in fact, constitutes a source of the son's admiration and pride in his beloved father.

In fact, the whole family is described as warm, loving, and supportive, despite occasionally gruff external appearances. Although the mother "is wont to often push you, sometimes beat you or grab you by the scruff of the neck and throw you out of the house," the child nevertheless learns that she is kind-hearted: "And one can somehow learn to live with her," and her face is always smiling, even when father shouts. And she is not afraid to scold him or to instruct him in the proper way to treat people, or to pacify him or conciliate him and touch his gentle soul to convince him to help his poor brother—a fact that simultaneously illustrates the qualities of wisdom, good-heartedness, and mercy.

Not all of Korczak's stories for children have such literary value. In some of them Korczak, the educator, gets the better of Korczak, the author, and the whole story is based on an idea rather than on any artistic quality. Yet all of his stories point to Korczak as a faithful educator and a believer that the light of human love shall never go out; that even if there are moments of eclipse, this light will eventually return to shine from the heart of the child, and bring the world a new redemption. All of Korczak's stories for children are written in a clear and simple style and an easily comprehensible language. He frequently reiterates certain sentences that he finds important, in order to engrave them in the hearts of the readers. He always envisions the young reader while writing, and he is attentive to his reactions and impressions. He does not merely write for the child, but rather he seems to be telling him a story. Korczak loved his little heroes, struggled alongside them to fulfill their dreams and, always tried to prove that man is good by nature, and, even when he fails, it is always because of some mistake or through ignorance, so that good shall prevail in the end. In this respect, Ytzchak Yatziv, former editor of the children's paper *Davar Layladim*, was right when he said:

> The man had an artist's pen, and among children's authors he is probably one of those very few authors in the world's literature who simultaneously with his special approach to children, the approach of an educator whose entire soul is devoted to children, is also a talented author of some stature. And out of this wonderful blend of precious qualities, he became a children's author. Hence his adjustment to the child's mode of perception. His great simplicity when he describes events while constantly and deeply observing the soul of the child and wishing to provide him with some of the life-experiences of the adult.[25]

Perhaps there is no better way to characterize Korczak's stories for children than to quote his own lines:

> There are four small rooms in the heart, very small.
> One loves with the heart, so everyone says.
> The rooms of the heart are small
> and the heart contains so much:

> Mother, father, grandmother, grandfather,
> and the little canary.
> . . . to love so much—
> and man has only one small heart.[26]

Korczak's stories contain everything: mother and father and the home, the sights of the small village and the big city, poverty and pain, longings and dreams and acts of redemption, and above all—lots of love.

27

To Children, by Children, for Children: About the Children's Newspaper

> I want to get to know my readers as soon as possible, so that I can write to them as acquaintances.[1]

Korczak viewed the children's newspaper as a multi-educational tool and even wrote a special article about it, titled "The School Newspaper." The main importance of the newspaper is not be found in the fact that it is addressed to children and adolescents, but that it is owned by children and adolescents. The adult will only assist, guide, and influence, while the main job of planning, writing, and even the initial editing should be done by the adolescents themselves. In his orphanages, Korczak began putting his ideas about a children's newspaper into effect. Children and educators cooperated in producing the newspapers, and throughout the many years of their publication, Korczak never shirked his self-imposed duty of contributing weekly. The children would insert their manuscripts into a box, and the teachers would read the material aloud to the students at a weekly gathering. Korczak was not content with the institution newspaper alone; he wished to found a large newspaper intended for all the children, which would allow them to express themselves, answer all of their questions, and provide them with a sense of independence and importance. This idea was realized with the help and initiative of the editor of *Nash Pshgelund* (Our survey)—a Zionist newspaper in the Polish language, which came out in Warsaw. The editor suggested to Korczak that a children's newspaper be published every weekend under the title of *Mali Pshgelund* (The little survey). In autumn 1926, *Mali Pshgelund* began to appear on a weekly basis, under the editorship of Korczak.

As far back as 1921, five years before the founding of *Mali Pshgelund*, Korczak published his ideas about the children's newspaper in a pamphlet titled "The School Newspaper," in which he wrote:

> I deeply believe that there is a need for children's newspapers, but these must be periodicals written by themselves. Newspapers which

deal with subjects which they find important and interesting, rather than periodicals which contain nothing but stories and poems. And what are the things which children and adolescents find important— they must say this themselves in their newspapers.[2]

He wished to relieve children of their fear of self-expression, of their aversion to public statement, and of the thought that writing in a newspaper necessitates some special grasp of the problem, an excellent style, and an involvement in current affairs. As his model he adopted the English newspapers in which the "Reader's Letters" section occupies a respectable place, and covers a great variety of issues: an insulted merchant or conned buyer lodge their complaints; a mother asks how to deal with her child at a certain moment; an offended citizen publicly castigates the local authority; and the like. The editor responds to some of the letters, while the readers themselves respond to others.

In quite a few of the articles that he published in *Mali Pshgelund*, Korczak dealt with the specific problems of children. In one such article he criticized the poor quality of the instruments sold to children, and the teachers who show no consideration and demand order and tidiness, beautiful writing and aesthetic appearance despite the inferiority of the tools. He wrote:

> The student's instruments—are a pen, a pencil, paper, blotter, compass, chalk, crayon, and the like. And all of this, when manufactured for adults, for offices and bureaus, is well made, expensive and of quality, while when intended for schools, is made in a totally off-handed fashion.[3]

He described those pens whose nib slips at just the moment which requires speed and care, or the pen whose nib sinks to such a depth that it can only be withdrawn with the teeth; he laments the poor quality of notebook paper, in which the lightest rub of the eraser leaves a hole; the blotter that does not absorb; the crumbling pencils; the falling-apart covers of books; the erasers that do not erase; the quickly worn-out rulers. He wrote, "All these hinder and make the work more difficult, poisoning the working hours, which are often not happy ones in any case."[4] His words are, in great measure, still relevant today. Every teacher can quote dozens of examples of workbooks printed on paper of low quality, of rubrics in which the student must write answers but which leave no room to write them in, of ugly textbooks that easily come apart and of faulty equipment.

In another article Korczak instructed children in the art of defending themselves against scarlet fever. He wrote:

Scholars have shown, that a hungry man contracts the disease more easily and his illness is more severe; there are many hungry children in schools, and there is no one to demand that hungry children be given food in schools. Scholars have shown that man requires fresh air, while in many schools the distress is very great as there are few windows and nowhere to play even during the break. Even in nice weather, there are no trips and outings to be seen—and no one demands that more excursions and less lessons be provided, while the plague rages.[5]

When Korczak dealt with the issue of the school newspaper, he stressed that there is no sense in nominating three or four outstanding students as editors who will issue the paper for the rest of the students. Rather many students should be included in the editing board, and distribute the work. No one must be given more than a little work, so as to enable one student to easily fill the role of another who, for some reason or other, cannot do his duty. The class newspaper and the school newspaper have great educational merit. The newspaper teaches the student to faithfully perform the duty that he has enthusiastically taken upon himself, habituates him to planned efforts based on the mutual contribution of different people, teaches him to openly express what he believes to be right, instructs him in the presentation of a fair and well-founded argument, and shows him how to steer clear of empty verbiage. The newspaper:

> Gives courage to the shy and meek, "wipes" the noses of the over-cocky, regulates and shapes public opinion—the newspaper serves as society's conscience. Have you a complaint—write to the newspaper; you are angry—write; you accuse me of falsification and incomprehension—fine, let's begin an open debate, show your documents, and know that you cannot deny it later. The newspaper brings the class or the whole school together. It encourages friendships between those who would not even have known each other otherwise; It gives the floor to those who can only express themselves in writing and even in the hottest of arguments will never get the right to speak.[6]

Korczak stressed that the bulk of the material provided by the school newspaper should be current, and the information about the affairs of the class, the school and the students, etc., should receive a respectable place within it. During editorial meetings the members must discuss ways and means to provide the news with more variety and improve the various sections. Besides the current material, the newspaper must have a great store of material on stand-by. If half the newspaper is to be dedicated to current affairs, its second half must be ready in advance. Before issuing one newspaper, one must already have three or four newspapers prepared in advance (not including the material pertaining to current affairs). Care must be taken to include interesting and varied material in the newspaper, and to combine lengthy articles with short ones, serious articles with humorous ones, and difficult ones with easy ones. Korczak stressed that "the newspaper can be likened to a bouquet of different flowers. The beauty of the entire bouquet depends on the variety of the flowers of which it is comprised."

The newspaper editor is not obliged to write in it, but it is essential that he know how to encourage others to write and to behave courteously and without bias. He must know how to entice contributors and how to guide the writers. The editor must add variety to the paper by means of various innovations. The reader loves the steady columns that appear in the newspaper on a permanent basis, but he also likes to find innovation, surprise and variety. The school newspaper should reserve an important place for writing competitions on some specified subject—a poem, political article, economic article, or the like. The ideas that Korczak raised in connection with the school newspaper were before him when he founded the *Mali Pshgelund*. The editorial board of the newspaper was based on the participation of children. Editorial members, even young ones, were paid a fixed wage or authors' royalties. In this context, it is worthwhile to reread Korczak's words in his first letter to the readers of *Mali Pshgelund*, dated the 3rd of September, 1926. In this letter he presented the ground plan of the future newspaper, which was to devote itself to doing everything justly. With his characteristic humor, he proposed the composition of the editorial board:

> There shall be three editors. One old (bald and bespectacled) who will have a mess to deal with. The other a young editor for boys and one girl—and editor for the girls. So that no one will be ashamed to write, and all shall speak sincerely and loudly. What are your needs, how have you been wronged, what are your troubles and cares? In the future, anyone who wishes to do so, will be able to come to the editorial board and write his piece on the spot. News can be given verbally or by phone, sent by post, dictated or written.[7]

He reiterated that:

> There are many children who have inventions, remarks and interesting observations, and who do not write because they do not have the courage or the will. Our newspaper will encourage the young to write.[8]

The principles that Korczak proposed for his futuristic newspaper were also the principles of the newspaper he actually founded. Among the important principles he repeatedly emphasized was that this was to be a newspaper of children and adolescents: everything shall be interesting; the newspaper shall deal with all questions pertaining to students and school, and will be so organized as to protect the children; it will be bent on acting fairly; and it will encourage children to write. The newspaper shall retain experts on football, cinema, outings, jokes, crossword puzzles, and riddles, and similar things intended to endear it to its young readers' hearts.

Right from the first year of its issue, the newspaper already had two hundred regular reporters, and more than ten thousand letters descended on the editorial board. Korczak treated these letters with great respect, and was wont to answer them, give advice, encourage, supply information, and criticize any overly florid phrases in the compositions of the young authors. In this way he established a lively contact between the readers and the newspaper. Children slowly began coming to the editorial board at first singly, and then in droves, until the entire editorial board was buzzing with readers. Korczak instituted the dispatch of colored postcards as prizes for contribution to the newspaper, the solving of crossword-puzzles and riddles, and the like. These postcards evoked a great deal of enthusiasm, and the winners kept them religiously.

Korczak wrote about the special qualities of editorship:

When I write a book, it is about one subject, while in a newspaper one must write about everything. In a book I can make things up, while in a newspaper I must write the truth, otherwise everyone would immediately grow angry and accuse me of lying. A book must be interesting, but not to everyone. Anyone who does not wish to is not obliged to read. A newspaper, on the other hand, must be interesting to all— one reads about events, another—the advertisements, a third—the sports supplement. And I must pretend that I know everything and am well versed in everything. When I write a book, it is like writing a letter to a friend, while a newspaper is written for strangers.[9]

Korczak was not prepared to allow his writing to become alienated from his readers. From the very first stages of the newspaper, he took care to get to know his readers, and greatly encouraged responses and meetings with them. This enabled him to write to them as one writes to acquaintances.

Korczak availed himself of every opportunity to emphasize the respect that he had for the expression of every child. He believed that a single sentence can sometimes reveal an entire world. In a conversation about *Mali Pshgelund* with his friend and helper, Yerachmiel Weingarten, Korczak said:

> When we find suitable boys and girls, we shall give our reporters the task of wandering about the streets of the city, describing events from the lives of children, games, mischievous pranks and good deeds, thanks and complaints.[10]

Besides the articles and the letters of children, Korczak viewed the newspaper as having an important role in aiding the children in their wishes and their psychological problems, in clarifying the world for them, in providing practical advice about the "I," and the environment.

A great many articles were devoted to questions pertaining to school. For example, in one of his articles, Korczak stressed the need for mirrors in schools, and claimed that the "absence of mirrors in school is a lie. A mirror has never spoiled anyone."[11] Occasionally he allowed teachers the right to answer or respond to criticism published against the school, its procedures and orders.

Thus, for example, he published a letter written by a teacher, from which it is evident that the teacher cared for the child and his education because he complained that all of his efforts to institute a children's self-rule ended in failure because the children did not know how to accept the responsibility and created chaos throughout the school.

The teacher wrote in pain:

> I could not understand, and was therefore forced to explain this to myself as the result of too much intimacy between teacher and students, and that things were better two years ago in the fifth grade, with less intimacy and more respect. And perhaps the self-rule is to blame. The gatherings, the debates and the pouring from one empty vessel into another?
>
> This reminds me how, in the Russian gymnasium, we used to taunt an educated and noble teacher who treated us well and how we adored the maths teacher who was vulgar and a tyrant and did not have one shred of intelligence. We respected the latter, and who thought himself obligated toward the former in any way?
>
> Indeed, the self-administration, in which I invested so many efforts, was probably the cause for this surprising change in the mood of the class which brought tears to the eyes of teachers, wracks our nerves and shortens our work-weary days.[12]

This letter, which is a very strong indictment of the ability of children to receive self-rule, to bear responsibility, and to study in an atmosphere of freedom, did not elicit from Korczak any verbose theoretical response to the effect that children must be prepared for the freedom given them, or that freedom, too, is something that requires learning and acclimatization, or that the passage from an ambience of strict and oppressive discipline to an atmosphere of freedom and self-rule causes a relief of tensions and a breaking of rules, and the like. Rather Korczak presented the story of Neuta who wrote about self-rule in her own class, having herself failed in the first year of this attempt, but later, enriched by experience and the lessons learned about the institution of self-rule, was greatly successful during her second year.[13]

Korczak felt he had a special mission to show his young readers the world of the adults and to help them understand more. Thus, for example, he published a highly instructive article under the title of "Don't Talk Nonsense",[14] in which he contended with this mortifying and humiliating phrase that severs all communicational channels, belittles the child and alienates him. With great psychological perspicacity, Korczak described seven reasons why adults use this phrase, in the hope that these reasons should increase the child's understanding, and he who understands—forgives.

Korczak not only wished to explain and clarify, to expose and discuss, but also to directly act and help, to participate when the need arose, and to be as involved as possible in the effort to alleviate the personal quandary of any of the readers. An excellent example of this tendency of Korczak is the story of six-year-old Natush.[15] Natush already goes to school. He is a talented and diligent student, and the teachers praise him. He has many friends. Yet, he suffers bitterly for his mother forces him to wear an apron at home and in school. All his pleas and entreaties are to no avail. In his plight he wrote a letter to the *Mali Pshgelund* editorial board and asked for advice. When days passed and no response was published in the newspaper, the irritated Natush sent a second and third letter. As it turned out, Korczak was not indifferent to his plight. Indeed, he did not content himself with some response or advice, but he sent one of the reporters to Natush's home to talk to his mother. Korczak believed that in this case, the persuasive ability of a child reporter, who would present the issue to the mother from a child's point of view, would be greater than that of an adult. And he was right. Following a long conversation with the mother, she removed the apron from Natush and the voice of *Mali Pshgelund* triumphed.

We have already remarked on the fact that Korczak greatly encouraged children to contribute to the newspaper, but was never content to merely receive the material that was sent to him. When children sent literary creations of their own to the newspaper, he instructed them, remarked on the faults he found in their writing, and did not hesitate to be strict. Thus, for example, when a child sent him a poem titled "A Future in Israel," he seriously analyzed the poem and wrote harshly:

> The more I read of this poem, the worse it becomes. And it is no wonder: it is only very rarely that a student of the 4th grade has the patience to work out the whole of this subject. He is quick to tire, and then—finish it already—and be done with it.[16]

Korczak flatly refused to educate children to treat a literary creation lightly, or for that matter any other form of expression which by its very nature must be artistic and sincere. He distinguished between informative writing, which he was always ready to accept despite its many mistakes and stuttering, and literary writing that he demanded be treated with the utmost seriousness and with full responsibility for what one writes. He advised children not to put everything that goes on in their hearts and minds on the market. Better to keep these things as their own secret treasures, hidden in their hearts, or, at most, their desk drawers. If they truly feel the need to express themselves, they will not hesitate to do so. He wrote:

> He, who when writing something sad actually wept, or when writing something joyful was full of gladness at having succeeded in inventing something amusing; he, who when writing did not think of his own intelligence, who completely forgot himself and his relatives; he who did not write because he suddenly remembered something and wished to emulate it, but wrote directly out of his own mind, his own soul; he who has the patience to rewrite many times, let him pay no attention to my severe tone, let him send again that very same piece and ask: Is it good?[17]

Korczak was very sensitive to the expression of the child. He wished to check graphomanic tendencies, and to encourage real and sincere expression. For this reason he established a column under the name of verses. In this column, he was wont to publish one line or one verse from a child's letter or creation, in which he found some deep truth, beauty, sincerity, message, bitter question, or original response. For example, he extracted the following words from a letter written by one of the children:

> Will this world never change? Will the one who suffered yesterday as deprived child, today, when fully grown, take his turn at the role of the oppressor?

Happiness will befall those future generations who will not forget their own childhood.[18]

An instructive example of Korczak's treatment of the writing of children who sent their words to *Mali Pshgelund* can be found in the description of the case of the child Falak.[19] Falak sent Korczak a poem and appended a letter in which he described the birth of the poem. In his innocence, the child did not know that he had in fact described a great literary catharsis with elements of compensation, of finding satisfaction and a grip on life through reality substitutes, through venting doubts he had about the love of his father and creating a receptive fantasy world, which fortifies the ego. Korczak discerned the talent of the writer and sensed his great sensitivity. He sent a letter to the father, asking for details of the boy and warning the father that "Judging by his letter, he is a sensitive boy and should be treated with care."[20] He began an exchange of letters with Falak, asked him for details of himself, and encouraged him to write back.

He explained to Falak that:

I do not print any poems at all in the "Mali Pshgelund." I do not print even the best of poems because:
1) The child thinks he has become famous once his poem is published. And this is not true for there are many poems which get published in the paper every day and aren't even worth the paper they are written on.
2) The children deem that a poet is something extraordinary, while in truth *all children are poets*. For a poet is a person with strong feelings, deep love and great anger, someone who greatly desires and strongly believes. *And every child is such.*
3) Merit, or as they say, talent is the gift of God, but it is a fragile gift, easily spoilt, broken and shattered. One must handle it with utmost care. One must work hard, one must learn to do one's work even when it is not liked, even when it seems unprofitable, unnecessary.[21] (Emphasis added.)

These words show us the emptiness of Korczak's rivals' claims that he was educating the children to graphomania, to depreciate words and to become mere publicity hunters.

Korczak's enduring dialogue with his readers was one of his wonderful qualities as an editor. He was never afraid to apologize for mistakes, to admit his errors, to accept the responsibility of correcting himself, to ask for advice and treat it seriously, to allow his readers to participate in editorial work, which was sometimes hard and sometimes tiresome and even a little annoying, often exposing the human weaknesses of the editor and his staff. Yet the encounter was always sincere and real.

Thus, before he left for summer camp with his protégés, taking a long leave from his editorial work, he wrote to his readers:

> Having thanked you for everything, I must now also apologize, for "Mali Pshgelund" has mortified many readers and I did not wish to aggravate anyone. Anyone can fail, even if he tries his best. My conscience is clear, however, for I have not missed one issue and was never late, although I have made various mistakes or forgotten things when my head ached or I wished to sleep. Sometimes I did not feel like writing at all, but I said: "It is hard—the readers are waiting, I cannot suffer in peace. And that week's issue was not so interesting, and was catarrhal or sleepy. Well, I ask you again, please do not be angry with me."[22]

The children's newspaper was a great success, and its reputation spread far and wide. Theaters, cinema houses, and organizers of sports competitions habitually invited the young reporters to various events, so that they would report them in the children's newspapers. The young reporters interviewed persons of renown—famous directors and important authors, and the newspaper urged the young to actively participate. The newspaper itself was mainly read by Jewish children, although there were a minority of Polish boys who also read the paper. The Jewish tone was very evident in the newspaper. One of the mottos of the paper was: "A periodical for children must protect children: a periodical for Jewish children must protect those children who were born Jews and who suffer on account of their origin."[23] Many of the children did not hesitate to write to the editorial board, to complain of exhibitions of anti-Semitism which they encountered, of the hostility of their environment, of the taunting of Christian boys on the streets, and of the harassment at school. One girl complained that her girlfriends said: "Jewish gang, Jews to Palestine" and recounted that the teacher once told a Christian girl: "You have a real Jewish character." One boy wrote:

> I am the only Jew in class. I am an unnecessary stranger. I am not a bad student and only have difficulties in drawing. I do not know what the fate of my letter will be, I only know that from this day, with the "Mali Pshgelund" I feel as if I have a new purpose and interest in life. There is no magic in my life at school.[24]

Korczak's affinity to Palestine was also very pronounced. He gave special emphasis to news from Palestine and displayed great interest in what went on there, in the situation of employment and security, the problems of the Jewish settlement and the like. He wished to establish ties with the children in Palestine, and he published letters appealing to the children in Palestine to contribute to the paper.

Their response to this appeal was very meager. Only the children of Ein-Charod, with whom Korczak had established personal ties, wrote to the paper. Other places did not respond at all. Korczak felt great pain and sorrow at this indifference, although he tried to explain this reaction to his readers by telling them that:

> Many of the Jews who left for Palestine have a grudge against Poland. They said that they had been slaves and now only wish to begin a new life and forget all that was before. It is probably because of this that they do not want to write to "Mali Pshgelund."[25]

After the children's paper had become well established, having been edited by Korczak for a period of nearly three years, he handed over the editorship to his student, Yaji Abramov, who edited it for over ten years, and only when the Second World War broke out in 1939 did the newspaper close. Abramov, who was not a Jew, changed the nature of the paper somewhat, and converted it into an instrument for the expression of progressive humanistically oriented youths. The newspaper became a large and thriving establishment that also sponsored study-circles, summer camps, sports competitions and the like.

Some of the scholars who researched Korczak's enterprise and a number of his biographers wondered why Korczak resigned from the newspaper when it had flourished so beautifully. Some claimed that he was offended by the struggles with his rivals, by the accusations directed at him that he was spoiling the children's tastes and fostering graphomania. Others thought that when the enterprise became well established he no longer felt his work to be a challenge and feeling that he had become stale, with nothing new on the horizon, had decided to relinquish his place to another. It is doubtful, however, whether either of these two reasons has any truth in them, for his biographer, Hana Mordetkovitz-Olatchkova, relates that he had dreams of expanding the scope of the newspaper. He wished to convert it from a newspaper intended for Jewish children to a newspaper intended for children all over the world. She claims that he was helped in this vision by a young Warsaw reporter who introduced him to two editors of one of the largest newspaper enterprises in Warsaw, who had hatched the idea of founding a large and illustrated newspaper for children. She wrote:

> Two hours before the time of the meeting, Korczak phoned and said: "madam, I am now at 'Beitenu' in Bialni. I am in the process of vacci-

nating the children against small-pox and am wearing my everyday
clothes. Is it obligatory that I appear before these gentlemen dressed in
great finery? For if so, I will immediately ring Krochlmane and an
orphan will come from the orphanage and bring my new clothes on a
stick to the editorial board, so that they will see that I have something
to wear." The shocked reporter managed to avert the danger of having
the garment brought on a stick, but the respected editors were somewhat aghast as they stared at the embarrassed, bespectacled and be-
draggled looking man with his threadbare sleeves and wrinkled
trousers.[26]

When the editors asked Korczak how he viewed the newspaper's image,
he answered:

I want this to be a newspaper which will be forbidden by the Ministe-
rium, banned by parents and educators, until none of the adults will
wish to buy it for the child, and the children will buy it themselves with
money they will collar from their parents.[27]

The editors failed to understand Korczak's words and did not perceive
that this was the only possible form of newspaper to which a child may
become attached.

28

One Home, Many Homes:
A Comparative View

Our aim is to create a man with steel thoughts and crystal feelings.[1]

When summarizing and assessing the educational theory and enterprise of Korczak, it is only fitting that we consider the long list of educational-social theories and educational enterprises stimulated by the schools of various educators such as Wieniken, Pestalozzi, Neill, Makarenko, and others. Only by comparing the various theories, their common points, and their differences will we be able to emphasize those characteristics that are unique to Korczak's theory and enterprise, both good and bad.

The Enterprise of Johan Heinrich Pestalozzi

Korczak deeply appreciated the educational enterprise of Pestalozzi (1746–1827). In his book, *How to Love Children*, Korczak noted that "The letters of Pestalozzi from the time of his stay in Stanaz, are the most beautiful writings of a practical educator."[2] Korczak felt a spiritual proximity to Pestalozzi and one can point out quite a few similarities between the life works of both educators, for both of them devoted their lives to the care of poor, neglected, and unfortunate children.

Among the pantheon of great social educators, Pestalozzi appears as a greatly suffering figure who has known much pain and sorrow. He is the manifestation of the man of great new ideals, who finds it hard to formulate them, and harder still to effect them in practice. Pestalozzi's nature did not favor the creation of a complete and consistent method. He was a great educator, but had nothing of the well formulated scientific-educational method, and none of the consistency of the researcher. He was, however, a man of wonderful intuition, with a deep understanding for the soul of the child, and an endless store of love. And, by virtue of this intuition, understanding, and love, he managed to perceive the very essence of the educational problem and instigate change in the education-

297

al methods current in his time. In this he was very much like Korczak. Though Korczak was equipped with a greater number of more perfect scientific tools than Pestalozzi and his knowledge was greater and far deeper, he, too, never formulated any ordered and complete educational method, and his pedagogical intuition and great love of the child were always the guiding force in his educational theory and practice.

Pestalozzi, like Korczak, placed love at the very center of his theory and educational enterprise. He devoted his entire life to the poor and the sons of the peasants. His life was a constant struggle, in which bitter and harsh failure often figured, while the joy of achievements was rarely come by. Pestalozzi was a man of educational action, the classic figure of the teacher and educator. It was not some abstract educational theory that filled him and his life, but the educational act, the actual educational experience, the pedagogical love and care, the constant companionship of children in educational institutions, the task of the father and educator at one and the same time. His educational theory was based more on emotion, enthusiasm, and pedagogical pathos than on restrained and carefully deliberate intellectual analyses. In similar fashion, Korczak's educational theory also grew out of educational empiricism, for he, too, placed the educational experience at the center, and, like Pestalozzi, he stressed the necessary combination of the father's task with the educator's role. Pestalozzi claimed that institutional education must absorb the merits of family education and that it must serve as a kind of family for the child.

Korczak adopted the exact same approach in his own institutions when he attempted to instill them with a family atmosphere, to create father and mother substitutes, and to provide a sense of intimacy based on trust, love, and mutual respect. He, too, claimed that by fulfilling the needs of daily life, by responding to the child's wishes, and providing him with a sense of confidence and security, one can liberate the child's injured personality and create a possibility and willingness to become educated.

Pestalozzi was instrumental in changing the entire educational method of his time.[3] He placed the child at the center of the educational process and was thus one of the founders of the individualist concept in education, a concept that Korczak also upheld. Pestalozzi stressed that the educator who wished to develop a harmonious personality must see the child in his entirety. Rather than the development of intellect or emotion alone, the issue is the education of the whole child. Pestalozzi stressed that one must remember that the life circumstances of every person are different, that the needs of every individual are different, and that the customs of people are different, as are their inner motivations, and their spiritual strengths. Education must be directed at each individual and tailored to every person. Korczak wholly accepted this view and always stressed the education of each individual according to his psychological needs, his potential, and his life circumstances.

We can also discern a certain similarity between Korczak and Pestalozzi in the religiousness of the two persons. Pestalozzi was not a believer in the orthodox sense, but was a man of deep religiousness, and an internal and profound faith. He considered love to be the essence and source of real worship for God. Pestalozzi believed that each man sees God as a figure he likes, but that the great man rises above the dust that God leaves behind him in passing, above the ritual of God's image, until he attains that most faithful of all forms of worship—love. Pestalozzi wrote that it is not by means of words that a man helps his fellow man come closer to God, but through action:

> If you help the poor so that he can live like a man—then you shall show him the face of God, and if you educate the orphan, as if you were his father—then you shall teach him to know his Father in Heaven.

There are many Christian motives in Pestalozzi's approach that do not directly concern us in this comparison. However, it is only proper that we emphasize Korczak's deep religiosity, his belief that the way of love leads man to transcend himself, and his recognition of the value of religious experience.[4]

Pestalozzi stressed the obligation of education to provide every man with a chance for happiness in the context of his social position. He was of the opinion that one should not educate the poor to riches, but rather prepare them for a respectable life as befits their station. For this reason, the preparation of children for their future lives was directed toward their class affiliations, and the options possible within the limits of their status were considered. In his institutions, he initiated the teaching of crafts, and the children were employed in weaving, spinning, and agriculture. In his essay, "Linehard and Gertrud," he stressed that menial labor must accompany the work of the mind. Besides its economic value, work constitutes an important means of clarifying concepts, of teaching concentration, of preserving what has been learned in memory, and of learning through concrete experience. In this, Pestalozzi placed the first foundations for the concept of a school of work, a working school. He noted that the school must provide the child with a knowledge of the appliances and working tools available to him as well as the methods of observation, the calm deliberation, and the ability to always improve his working tools.

Korczak, too, attributed great importance to work and its educational value. He stressed that the process of work might become a social factor and foster important personality traits. The protégés in his institutions were given duties in various services and thus acquired practical working knowledge in diverse areas. The committee responsible for coordinating the work usually provided every protégé with special roles that took account of his physical prowess and the time available to him. The achievements of work were publicized and encouraged. Korczak stressed that one can educate for work only through work itself. In order to stress the importance of work Korczak wrote:

> At the orphanage we have taken out the broom and the mop from their hiding place under the stairs and posted them not only for show, but as a mark of respect, at the main passage to the dormitory. And it was strange to see how in the clear light of day, these lowly objects seemed so noble, as if they had donned some spiritual image which caused them to caress the eye in their aesthetic beauty—when we realise that the value of a well-wiped table is equal to the value of a well-written page in the child's notebook—so long as we take care not to view the children's work as a substitute for the work of servants, but rather as an educational work which can shape their personalities—it is our duty to invest a great deal of thought-effort in this matter.[5]

There is a world of difference between the views of Korczak and Pestalozzi on this matter, for the latter was bent on the training of his children for the future demands they may encounter in life and wished to provide them with occupational training, while Korczak wished to foster an attitude that viewed work as a value in and of itself, and, therefore, encouraged the educational possibilities inherent in work, but did not ascribe any importance to actual occupational training.

In contrast to Korczak, who viewed the welfare of the child as the single most important issue and thus did not direct his attention to the possible improvement of society and did not adopt the kind of educational thinking orientated toward effecting some hoped-for social change, Pestalozzi was constantly aware of this issue of changing society and believed that the only way to rectify the state was by rectifying man, and that the rectification of man can only be effected through education.

Pestalozzi viewed Rousseau's injunction to return to the "natural condition" as a total mistake. For he considered that it is from this very condition that man fled when he established the social condition. Pestalozzi presented a third condition—the moral condition. All of man's attempts in the two previous conditions have indicated the baseness of his animal nature and caused him to acknowledge the demands imposed by morality. At this point in his argument, Pestalozzi once more transferred the focus to the life of the individual. He wrote:

Morality bears the stamp of individuality. It does not exist between two people, no man can feel it in my stead: I exist. No man can feel in my stead: I am moral. We must live a social life together, with no faith in the morality which exists between one person and another; rather, in the midst of this distrust my need for morality is born, and my soul transcends to the sensation that I can make myself into a more noble creature than can nature and the human race make me in the form of no more than a bestial and social creature.

Pestalozzi believed in the possibility of rectifying society by mending its members, and viewed education as the instrument with which to effect the great social amendment, and enable humanity to progress toward perfection and happiness.

Korczak, too, was deeply troubled by social injustices. At the very beginning of his career, he was influenced by the leading left-wing agitators of his time, and even believed that the capitalist regime was bound to fall. Like Pestalozzi, he believed that to mend the world one must first mend education and redeem the child, but unlike Pestalozzi, Korczak only staked out this little plot of caring for his protégés and did not wish to step beyond these boundaries into the realm of economic speculation and the development of educational approaches aimed at improving the face of society.

Weiniken's Enterprise

Gustav Weiniken, who is considered to be one of the founders of the German Youth Villages at the beginning of the twentieth century, was the father of a number of very important ideas in the realm of social education. He founded a youth village in Weikesdorf, which later served as a model for other youth villages. In many respects, there are similarities between the philosophy and enterprise of Weiniken and those of Korczak.

Weiniken stressed that childhood is not merely a preparatory period, but rather has a value and beauty of its own, and hence a right to an independent existence and the chance to develop its own special character. Korczak was of the same mind when he stressed the self-worth of childhood and youth, and the importance of this period in its own right and not as a preparatory period for adulthood.

Weiniken devoted much thought to the "Culture of Youth." He noted that the youngster wishes to shape his own life, independently of the demands and conventions of adult society. Weiniken's school shied away from political education and did not wish to endow the children with occupational training. The aim of the school, according to Weiniken, was to send the youngster into the world, not only equipped with a strong will to progress and make his own way but also with the ability to discern the good and the beautiful and with an unbiased love for the truth.

Korczak was guided by similar assumptions in his own institutions. He gave no consideration to occupational training, to providing the child with some profession, or to preparing him for political life and citizenship; rather, he viewed his main task to be the world of the child in the immediate present, his psychological needs, his wishes, and his interests. He wished to endow his protégés with the principles of the good and the beautiful, to instill in them a love of truth, and to base the relationships among them on respect, mutual trust, and a truth that recognizes no compromise.

Weiniken stressed that one must coordinate the requirements of culture and society with the rights of youth.

> School must recognize the right of youth to an independent life, while youth must recognize the value of cultural work. It must be a reconciliation between the nature of youth and the knowledge of culture, between play and work, the young generation and the old. Here, a youngster can be active in his acquisition of the values of culture. Only in such a school will it be possible to realise the culture of youth (which is actually a special way), and the youthful lifestyle which befits its nature.[6]

Weiniken's point of departure was a cultural one, his stress on the "Culture of Youth." Korczak's point of departure was an individualistic one—the welfare and perfection of the individual. Korczak was rarely preoccupied by any sense of cultural continuity. Governing Weiniken's institution was a general assembly of students and teachers. The assembly was directed by the institution's manager, and was empowered to discuss all those areas that concern their economic lives and the problems of culture. There was no parliament in this institution, nor were elections held. The entire community made the decisions. Over time, however, a committee was eventually elected, the function of which was to provide the manager and the community with proposals and suggestions. The members of the committee were elected from among the higher classes, and each member took a number of students from the lower classes under his wing. This idea of sponsorship or guardianship was also applied in Korczak's institutions where it fulfilled an important educational role as an instrument for the socialization and the introduction of new protégés into the life of the institution.[7]

When compared to Weiniken's institutions, Korczak's institutions were far more democratic. The greater part of the self-administration was in the hands of the protégés themselves, and the teachers had no such central leadership role as in Weiniken's institutions. Although the teachers in Korczak's orphanages did have an advisory, guiding, and supportive role, the actual government was in the hands of the protégés themselves.

Weiniken was the living spirit at a large congress of youth that took place in October 1913 on Mount Maisner, and in which about three thousand youngsters participated. This congress laid some of the main foundations of the German Youth-Movement, which proclaimed that youth wished to shape its life through self-decision, self-responsibility, and an inner truth. It seems that Korczak, too, at the beginning of his work as an educator, was close to the idea of a youth movement and a youth culture. Hanna Mordetkovitz-Olaczkova relates:

In 1908, Korczak published an article on school life and suggested summer camps with tents and flags which would depart to the villages and towns and include various games and sports activities, the offering of assistance to the local inhabitants, lectures on matters of hygiene, and more. This was before the founding of the Scout movement which was to quickly realize a part of this plan, and leave the rest for other ideational organizations of youth in our times.[8]

Korczak attempted to put some of these ideas into practice in his summer camps.[9]

In his writings about the youth movement, Korczak stressed that it must differ from school. Boys do not gather within it to study, but in order to seek answers to questions that cannot be found in books. He wrote:

We gather in a youth movement in order to seek the truth, we gather in order to recognize our young truth about man and about the world— in order to learn to read life as it is and as we would like it to be. . . . Each one of us knows different things, and knows them in a different way. And when ten of us are together and each one of us is ten years old, then the sum of our knowledge is like that of a hundred year old man, of whom we think as having a great deal of experience, acquired over his many years of life. Our truth is young, different—it is ours. Each one of us has seen and heard different things and met different people. Each understands according to his own way, presents questions in a different way and answers them differently as well.[10]

Makarenko's Enterprise

Makarenko (1888–1939) occupies a central place in the history of Russian education after the revolution. In his enterprise and philosophy, one can find a crystallization and solidification of some of the most important principles of Russian pedagogy, which have become the legacy of Russian education to this very day. Makarenko viewed his educational enterprise as his mission in life. He knew how to devote himself to this enterprise and become so deeply involved in his educational work as to forget himself. In this Makarenko can be closely compared with Korczak, for both of them devoted their entire lives to their educational work, both were seen to be excellent educators with an influential educational personality of great personal charisma; both served as constant personal models for the child; and both had a great deal of trust in the child. On the other hand, there is a world of difference between Korczak's figure that had an element of gentleness, almost of femininity—a personality full of love for the child and belief in the child's need for freedom and happiness, and the figure of Makarenko that had a great deal of strictness and severity about it, as well as adherence to external ideals and a fanaticism in realizing them. Korczak opposed those who wished to shape the child in their own strict form and image, and who wished to force their concepts on him. Makarenko, in contrast, began the social education of the child and his political shaping from a very early age.

Makarenko objected to the adoption of preformulated pedagogical theories in the actual practice of education, and viewed pedagogical theoreticians with great cynicism. He wrote:

> How many thousands of years does it (the science of pedagogy) exist! Under what names. What brilliant thoughts: Pestalozzi, Rousseau, Nathrope, Blonsky! How many books, how much paper, and prayer! And despite all this—an empty void, total zero. Faced with one single thug, no discussion is possible, no method, no instrument, no logic—absolutely nothing, just a put-on![11]

Korczak, too, was greatly suspicious of all ready-made pedagogical theories, and was unwilling to apply accepted psychological principles to his educational practice. Rather he preferred educational experience, the constant experience gained in the educational institution to the most rich theoretical knowledge. He was widely read in the pedagogical literature but refused to accept its assumptions if they were not borne out by his daily experience. In his practical work, too, he never subscribed to fixed principles but was always open to change and the crystallization of new methods out of the concrete situation which is always different for every individual case.

Korczak's educational approach was essentially pedocentric, i.e., the focal point of the educational process was the existence of the child and his experiences. The child is at the center, and the role of education, in Korczak's opinion, is but to create the best possible conditions for his development and growth. In his educational work, his point of departure and his goal in education are identical: the full development of the child, without giving any real consideration to the society within which the child will be obliged to grow, nor to its advancement and development. Moreover, Korczak did not take care of children over the age of fourteen. So long as the child was in the institution, he did his best to fulfill his needs, to make his days as pleasant as possible, and to provide him with a taste of the happy childhood of which he was deprived. However, once the protégés were obliged to leave the institution and go out into life, their encounter with real life was often very difficult, as Korczak did not prepare them for this meeting which often turned out to be a severe head-on collision.

The exact opposite may be said of the youth settlements of Makarenko. His educational viewpoint was not pedocentric but clearly a totalitarian social one. His approach did not focus on the child but on society and the political conceptions in the image of which he strove to shape his protégés. He shifted the focus of attention and the educational authority from the individual to society. According to his social-political conceptions, Makarenko believed that the aim of society was to empower the educator to act in its behalf and to guide his work. The main purpose of education was not to provide for the interests or pleasures or happiness of the child. Rather he believed that through integration into the social fabric, the child will achieve happiness. Accordingly, he did not perceive learning to be an experience, but a social and civil duty. Pointing to the figure of the desirable student he stated:

Our schools must produce energetic comrades with a strong consciousness of socialist society, who will be always capable, at any moment of their lives and without hesitation, of finding the right criterion with which to judge a personal act, and at the same time will be capable of demanding from others that they also behave correctly. Our student, whomsoever he may be, cannot but appear first of all as a member of his collective, as a man of his society, who not only bears the responsibility for his own actions but also for the actions of his comrades.[12]

As a direct consequence of this conception, education, according to Makarenko, is conducted by means of indoctrination based on propaganda and censorship. In this way, education becomes a part of the permanent self-justifying propaganda of society.[13]

In contrast to this indoctrination, and to the authoritarian, totalitarian shaping of children, Korczak's educational position is based on the protégé's absolute freedom, his right to shape his own belief and opinion system according to his own convictions, to decide his way in life for himself, to live a life of liberty in a free democratic society. No contrast is more stark than that which can be found between the words of Makarenko and those which Korczak wrote down in his diary but a few months before his martyred death:

> I wish to die knowingly, fully and clearly aware. I do not know what I would have said to the children in parting, I would wish to tell them, though, that they have total freedom in choosing their way.[14]

Both Korczak and Makarenko ascribed a great deal of importance to the early education of the child and the education provided within the framework of the family. This, however, is the full extent of the similarity. Makarenko stressed that children are the future shapers of the state and of society, that they are the future parents and teachers and that the fate of the nation and the country is therefore dependent on them. Parents must be constantly aware of their great responsibility. It is a responsibility not only toward their son as an individual but also for the fate of their entire society. As a consequence each family must first of all determine the goals of its education, the ideal in which it wishes to educate its sons, and the image that it would give them. Family education of the Makarenko brand is authoritarian education. The true educational authority of the parents derives from their fulfillment of their civic duties, from their recognition of their responsibility toward society in the education of their children, from the actual knowledge and help they provide to their children, and from their personal living example. Although, Korczak, too, stressed the importance of family education and frequently emphasized the central role of the parents' personal example, he totally disregarded any civic responsibility that the family might have, and rather stressed the therapeutic role of the family, the right of the child to respect and free development and an appreciation of his life in the present.

As for the desired figure of the educator, both Korczak and Makarenko did not lay any great store by the educator's theoretical pedagogical training, and rather stressed his devotion and excellent practical work. Both noted that the work of the educator must be carried out in close proximity to the students and in friendship. Makarenko noted a long list of forms of contact with the protégés, which can help the educator get closer to his students, such as participation in their work, in the farm committees, in outings, in circles, in editing the bulletin, in dances and in mutual reading, parties, etc. This constant contact brings the protégé closer to his educator and effects him beneficially. The educators at Makarenko's settlements worked very hard. Besides their regular educational work, they had three additional duties that they carried out by rotation: 1) Duty from five o'clock in the morning until the bell for studies; 2) work duty; 3) dormitory duty. Korczak, too, imposed similar chores on his educators. They were busy with many duties, participated in all the work of the institution, were involved in the social lives of the students, did menial and cleaning jobs, and fully devoted themselves to the life of the orphanage.[15]

From the point of view of the internal organization of life in their institutions, one can discern a certain similarity between the two educators, besides their obvious differences. Both Korczak and Makarenko emphasized the students' self-administration. The main instrument of self-administration in Makarenko's institutions was the general assembly of the institution's protégés. All the members of the collective participated in the general assembly and were allowed to express their opinion. The decisions of the general assembly were to be taken seriously. Both the management of the institution and every other body were required to view the decisions of the general assembly as the decisions of the entire institution. It was, therefore, sometimes desirable to make special preparations in order to prevent undesirable decisions that might be taken by the general assembly. Such intervention through propaganda, the take-over of centers of influence and programmed guidance, was absolutely nonexistent in Korczak's institutions. Despite the external similarities between the institutions of self-administration in Makarenko's and Korczak's institutions, there is one essential and basic difference between the two. Makarenko's institutions were noted by their tendentiously political character. They were based on a social ideal and received inspiration from such party institutions as the Comsomol. Korczak's institutions were independent and democratic in character.

If Korczak was somewhat remiss in his attitude to social ideals, Makarenko was greatly remiss in his approach to the individual and to the individual differences between persons. On the other hand, if Korczak was not very successful in preparing his protégés to face life, Makarenko worked very hard to prepare them for their encounter. Morever, in his institutions, Makarenko did not establish isolated educational islands cut off from life, but rather combined education and life into one single essence.

A. S. Neill's Enterprise

A. S. Neill is one of the most prominent proponents and actual practitioners of pedocentric education. He stressed that one must not obscure the uniqueness which is to be found in every child and must not require him to adjust to the accepted and constraining patterns of social life. Conformity eventually leads to uniformity and defaces the individual value of the person. Education must provide the best conditions for the development and growth of the student. It must respond to the requirements of every individual child and fulfill the demands posed by his talents, interests, and unique needs.

Neill evinced an attitude of uncompromising respect toward life and freedom with complete negation of coercion and the use of force. His school at Summerhill was based on the provision of full freedom to the children in the belief that children who grew up free will develop within them the qualities of wisdom, love, perfection, and courage that are also the goals of classic Western humanism.

Neill criticized modern society and claimed that the man we are developing is a creature of the multitudes, that our society is no longer sane and that most of our religious customs are a sham. Neill believed in internationalism and stressed that the willingness to make war is a barbaric atavism of the human race. Rather than an attempt to educate children to fit into the present order of things, he made an effort to raise children who would grow to be happy adults.

Many have discussed and criticized the freedom in Neill's institutions. In the context of social relationships, this freedom expressed itself as a total lack of authority on the part of adults. In Neill's institutions, adults were not entitled to order children about, and had equal rights and duties. In their assemblies, children were entitled to call the adults to trial, to vote against them, and to castigate their actions and criticize them if they deemed that the adults had acted against the principles of equality, freedom, and justice. The principles of freedom, mutuality of relationships, and mutual respect prevailed in Korczak's institutions as well, where adults had no special rights and they certainly had no right to command or coerce. In the orphanage regulations, Korczak noted that children must obey the binding rules rather than the staff. The adult members of the staff must know the rules and act accordingly. Special dispensations and rights could be gotten only through application to the protégés' self-administration. The self-administration was entitled to reject the staff's applications. Like Neill, in Korczak's institutions one could call the educators to trial before a court of protégés, and Korczak himself was put on trial from time to time.[16]

On the other hand, many have been mistaken in their opinion that the freedom in Neill's institutions has bordered on lawless anarchy. Neill continually reiterated that freedom does not mean anarchy, and that respect for the individual must be mutual. He even published a special book titled *Freedom—Not Permissiveness*,[17] in which he noted that many have a rather obscure idea of the meaning of the term "freedom." They do not understand that freedom is something one gives and takes. They confuse freedom with permissiveness, which is, according to his definition, trespassing on the freedom of others. Neill emphasized the need for self-control that he saw as the capacity to respect the rights of other people.

Neill instituted a student self-rule at Summerhill. This rule was democratic in form. Everything pertaining to the social life, the life in the group—including punishments for social transgressions—was determined by way of free election at the school's general assembly, which was held on Saturday nights. Each of the members of the teaching staff and each child, regardless of his age, had one vote. Neill noted that the function of the self-rule at Summerhill was not only to pass laws, but also to discuss the social issues of the community. At the beginning of each term a vote was held about the rules of going to bed. There were also questions of general behavior. The assembly elected a sports committee and a dancing committee, a theater committee, sleep officers, and city officers whose duty it was to notify of any shameful behavior beyond the school boundaries.[18] There is a great similarity between the principles of self-rule in Korczak's and Neill's institutions, though Korczak's democratic government was more bounded and structured by a system of rules, regulations, and established procedures, while affairs were more flexible in Neill's case and more easily changed and reshaped. At the same time, there is no doubt whatsoever that Korczak would have certainly agreed with Neill when he said:

> A school that does not have self-rule—cannot be called a progressive school. That is a school of compromise. One cannot have freedom unless the children feel themselves to be totally free to run their own social lives.[19]

An essential difference between Neill and Korczak can be found in their attitude to work. Korczak ascribed a great deal of educational and formational importance to work, he took care that children and staff participate in all the work of the institution, and wished to foster an attitude of respect for the sanctity of work. Neill was also concerned with this issue, and at first there was a community rule at Summerhill that stipulated that every child over the age of twelve and every member of the teaching staff must work on the school grounds at least two hours a week. The pay was token—five pennies an hour. Anyone who didn't work was fined ten pennies. Some, among the members of the staff, preferred to pay the fine. Most of those who did work belittled the whole matter as a chore to be gotten rid of and kept looking at their watch the whole time. Eventually this rule was abolished by the children and Neill stressed: "My personal opinion is that a clear minded civilization will not ask children to work before, at least, the age of eighteen."[20]

Neil and Korczak have a similar opinion of play. Both of them ascribed to play an important role in the development of the child and the life of the educational institution. At Summerhill, the six-year-olds played all day long. Neill emphasized that for children of this age fantasy and reality were very close to each other, and that the adult attitude to play as a waste of time was too arbitrary. Neill wrote:

> Behind the attitude of negation or lack of satisfaction with play, lies some foggy moral concept, a hint that it is not so good to be a child. This hint is revealed in the reproach which is often directed to young adults: "don't be childish." Parents who have forgotten their childhood longings—have forgotten how to play and how to fantasize—will not make good parents. When a child loses his ability to play, he is psychically dead and constitutes a danger to any other child who comes into contact with him.[21]

Korczak, too, stressed the importance of play in the child's normal development. He called to parents and teachers to allow children to run about, make a noise, run wild, and revel. He said: "Most children love movement and noise. Their physical and moral development depends on their freedom of movement."[22]

Korczak and Neill ascribed similar importance to theater and dramatic play in the education of the child and in the life of the educational institution. Both Korczak and Neill preferred plays written by the children, and stressed the importance of creative drama. In this respect, Neill was far more radical than Korczak, and only plays that were actually written at Summerhill were presented at the institution. A play written by a teacher was presented only if there was a shortage in plays written by the children. The participants in the play prepared their costumes with their own hands. Neill placed a great emphasis on creative drama and would give his protégés various tasks such as:

> Put on a coat which exists only in your imagination; take it off and hang it on a hook. Take a bouquet of flowers and discover a thorn inside it. Open and read a telegram in which you are notified that your father or mother have died. Eat a quick meal at a railway restaurant, constantly fearful lest the train leave without you.[23]

The spontaneous play, the mimes, the pantomime, and the movements were sometimes even accompanied by words.

Korczak, by comparison, was more eclectic in his choice of playwrights, and he often wrote short sketches for presentation at the orphanage. He recognized how deeply children love dramatic expression, the play, and the mutual theatrical experience, and devoted a respectable place to dramatic activity in his institutions, both to plays staged by the children and to the viewing of theater performances outside the orphanage.

Both Neill and Korczak ascribed little importance to pedagogical literature. Yoseph Arnon, who visited Neill's institution and was tempted to compare the two educators, wrote:

It was not only the external appearances which evoked comparative associations, but also many of Neill's opinions, hints and mottos, which put me back twenty-five years to Korczak's room in the attic of the orphanage at Krochlmane St. There (with Korczak) I had heard the idea: Books? Textbooks? These are worthless if you seek wisdom. For every three hundred pages you will find one idea, which it is worth your while to preserve in your soul, and that idea—was not expressed by the writer of the book, but came from within you, it is your idea. . . . Here, [with Neill] I heard the speech of the man of action: 'I don't read pedagogical periodicals, and there are hardly any scientific pedagogical books either. Neil stresses: "Psychology is very dangerous; thus, for example, I had some psychologists working for me who had the mark of the university stamped into their foreheads rather than their hearts." These came, and on entering the gates of Summerhill lifted their hands and cried: Freedom to the child! But after two months of work they ran away for they did not understand the child. One must not seek psychology, but the child.[24]

Korczak was far more moderate than Neill. He struggled for the child, but his struggle was not directed at social change, rebellion against social frameworks, and negation of adult cultural values. Korczak contented himself with fostering his own institutions. He noted that in his educational method he aspired:

To base the children's organization on mutual affection and justice and to keep them away, for awhile, from the evil that can be found in adult affairs; to allow them a few years of quiet, peace and clarity in which to grow and mature; not to oppress, not to burden, not to neglect, not to deprive—I claim I did it for the few at the orphanage. Despite the harsh conditions: This is a desert oasis, which to my sorrow is now covered by the evil sands of the surrounding desolation.[25]

Neill was far more revolutionary. He opposed the entire value system of adult society, was dead set against conventional lies in all areas of life, and in the name of love-of-life rebelled anarchically against all the accepted moral frameworks of society. Erich Fromm summarized this well when he wrote:

Neill's essential goal is to raise children who are *alive*, who deep within themselves are active people rather than passive observers and consumers. In this respect, education has but one goal: To Live. And life has no purpose but one—to live . . . what Neill wished to create was a *good* man. A good man is a live man, a man in harmony with life, in harmony with fellow men, in harmony with nature, in harmony with the rhythm which pervades the entire universe.[26]

29

The Dream and the Disillusion: An Attempt at Summary and Assessment

And the hour shall come when a man will know himself and respect and love, and the hour shall come in history's clock when man shall know the place of good, the place of evil, the place of pleasure, the place of pain. The hour shall come when energy shall reveal its secrets, as shall movement and warmth and light. The life of matter and the life of the soul after death shall, join into one harmony, a good order, happiness and spring.[1]

Many have tried to characterize Korczak, some with great emotional involvement and love and others through long observation and acquaintance. Igor Neverly, who knew Korzak over a period of sixteen years, describes him as "a dreamer with a poet's heart, sensitive and loving, and at the same time a man of intensive thought (according to his nature or habit), who poses more and more questions as to essence and purpose—and who, because he saw so deeply, could not, despite the goodness of his heart, observe the world with optimism, but rather received it with belated skepticism."[2]

Korczak had that blend of heart and mind, of penetrating vision and a scientific affinity with great love and full devotion to his educational work. He had his own views regarding the world, society, life, and the universe, but he did not have any unified or uniform philosophy, and certainly no pre-prepared responses. He always stressed, "I pose questions for human beings [babies, elderly people]. In the face of facts, events and fates, I am not carried away by the ambition to provide answers, but rather strive for further questions."

As we re-examine and reread Korczak's books and inspect his life and educational enterprise, we encounter his wonderful image which wins us over with its great sincerity, its deep spiritual honesty, and above all its great love for the child and for man. Every station in his life, beginning with his early childhood years, through his rich years of enterprise and culminating in his last journey, illuminates him with a brilliant light. There are many facets to Korczak's enterprise, and each one of them

313

reflects the nobility of his spirit and his sacrifice for his fellow human beings—a physician who wishes to succor the miserable and the oppressed, who forgoes recognition and wealth and only seeks to alleviate their pain; an educator who devotes his entire life to the child, who lives the lives of his orphans twenty four hours a day at the orphanage boarding school, is always involved in the lives of his protégés and gives them his entire soul; and an author and editor who aspired to give his readers all the goodness and light that were in his soul.

Korczak never ceased contemplating and observing the children, and devoted the whole of his time to deepening his acquaintance with them, and all with a great measure of humbleness and lack of ostentatiousness, in recognition of the fact that there are no limits to the understanding of the child and that one must never speak of a child in the future tense, but only in the past and present tenses. Korczak wrote:

> I have read interesting books. I am now reading interesting children. Never say "I already know." I read the same child a first, second, third and tenth time and still I know very little. For the child is a big and wide world which has existed for a long time and shall exist forever. I know a little of what was, a little of what is, but what of the future?[3]

Anyone who came into contact with Korczak carried his image in his heart for a long time. His many students frequently told of his wonderful qualities and his total devotion to his enterprises. Thus, in his memoirs of the great educator, with great excitement, Moshe Zertal described Korczak at the orphanage:

> I have seen the "doctor" among the children. The nonexistence of any formal barriers between himself and the orphans was clearly evident. I saw him sitting naturally on a small bench, close to a child who read a book. I have seen him listening to a lively conversation among children, or encouraging and directing a "brutal" fight between two rivals who had lost their heads. Many times I have seen him kiss the back of a small or weak child's hand. In the bowing of his head one could see his respect and reverence for the young child who makes his way in the hostile world of the adults.
>
> His walk, his speech and his manner when among children indicated that this was his life. It is here that he breathed fully and deeply, here that he could create at his best, here that he learned the secret of life and attempted to teach the rules of life.[4]

Another admirer of Korczak, Ida Marzashan, describes his life at the orphanage in the newspaper *Falks Stime* (The people's voice):

During the last years he lived in an attic. He slept on a simple iron bed, covered with a blanket, and always kept another bed in his room for a weak or disturbed child who found it hard to adjust to the life of the group, or for a child whom Korczak wanted to keep track of or talk with, because he found special interest in his life and history. The children often visited him in the attic. The little sparrows were also permanent guests; food was always waiting for these little birds.[5]

Ida related how she was injured in the ghetto and brought to the orphanage where Korczak and Stefa cared for her with great devotion. One day, during a severe bombing, she was seized with a terrible fear. She lay on her bed, alone in her room, and the explosion made the blood freeze in her veins. In her fright, she jumped out of bed and ran into the corridor. There she bumped into Korczak and told him of her fear and sorrow, and he answered, "God, and who is not sad now. The whole world is wrapped in a great sadness."[6]

And, indeed, Korczak drank the bitter cup of sorrow in those terrible days in the ghetto. Yet he had known sorrow long before then and sadness was his constant companion throughout his life: in his painful childhood under the shadow of his father's mental illness, in his work in the poor quarters of Warsaw; in his nursing of children on their death beds in hospitals; in the death of his mother; in the morbid thoughts that repeatedly besieged him; in the sorrow of the orphaned children; and in the shattering of many of his dreams as the bestial side of man waxed stronger and the ugly visage of the Poles and the monstrous face of the Nazi animal were exposed.

This sad man did not succumb to his sorrow, but rather, in his encounters with people, in his guidance of teachers, and in his acts among the children, he knew how to check his sorrow, put on a smiling face, and win the hearts of all.

Moreover, he excelled in his well-developed sense of humor, in his literary creations, in his witty lectures, and in his work with the protégés of the orphanage. His acquaintances related how he knew hundreds of jokes which were always at his fingertips on all occasions.[7] His jests often carried an undertone of pain, as can be discerned from his own wonderfully picturesque definition: "Laughter is sometimes born of the tears of a sad and lonely doctor."[8] He himself commented on the macabre sense of humor characteristic of doctors who daily look into the face of death. He wrote:

> The joke is the doctor's morphine . . . the jokes especially flourish among military doctors stationed in hospitals close to the battle fields, where one must sew members together and try to assemble a human

being . . . the joke is the antiseptic capable of combatting the infection of the heart and the soul.[9]

Humor can be seen throughout his literary oeuvre. It permeates his writing for children and can even be found in his writing for adults. Even among the nightmares of *The Senate of Madmen* we can discern a great deal of humor, such as in snatches of a mad conversation concerned with the establishment of urinal clubs.[10]

With his special brand of humor he knew how to cope with the intolerable difficulties of the orphanage in the ghetto when the institution was almost on the verge of starvation. Even in the proclamation which he published in the *Nash Pshgelund*, and in which he wished to stir the hearts of the Jews to aid his institution, he makes use of his subtle, pained, self-directed humor, which might perhaps help melt their hearts.

> It is bad to be old, but it is even worse to be an old Jew.
> Can something be worse?
> Oy, Oy, Oy,—And if the old Jew is penniless?
> And if he is not only penniless but also unresourceful?
> Is that not the worst of all?
> No. And if the unresourceful old Jew, bears the heavy burden of a large group of children, and his heart aches, and not only the heart but also the legs and the hips, and his eyes can see that his strength has ebbed?[11]

Even in the face of approaching death, he sought laughter and smiles, even the smile which is no longer amused. In the final passages of the diary which he wrote in the ghetto, one small passage, almost a report, sticks out in its "Korczakness":

> A cloudy morning. The time is five thirty.
> A seemingly normal beginning of another day. I said to Hanna:—Good Morning!
> She looked at me uncomprehendingly.
> I asked:
> —Smile.
> There are certain smiles which are sickly, pale and tubercular.[12]

This sad-happy man was unassuming and modest in all his ways. He did not wish to stand in the limelight, elbow his way forward, or call attention to himself. Ada Hageri-Poznansky wrote that:

> At first glance he made no impression whatsoever. He was a man of medium stature, balding and with a small goatee. Dressed in simple

clothes, his speech was quiet and his sentences were short and fragmented. Only those who encountered his gaze, a uniquely penetrating gaze of singular quality, will never forget him.[13]

And at the same time, a great deal of criticism can be directed at Korczak's educational teaching. He was a great educator, but he did not establish any coherent and consistent educational method. He excelled in his pedagogical intuition and in the depth of his understanding for the soul of the child, but he was not an investigator obligated to distance himself from the subject of his investigation and study the phenomena from the proper perspective. He collected facts and documents, impressions and notes of the child, but his conclusions were drawn intuitively rather than through any scientific discourse based on his findings. His psychological diagnoses are not sufficiently precise. His distinctions between childhood, adolescence, and adulthood are blurred. In discussing children psychologically, the poet, the warrior, and the great lover within him usually had the upper hand over the sharp and discerning researcher. In this area, he was even sometimes given to a certain rash and unfounded extremism, belittling the scientific value of psychology and stressing the importance of direct personal experience. He noted that he preferred to hand a child over to a woman who raised chickens during a period of five years, rather than to an intelligent lady with a diploma. He was so contemptuous of the science of psychology that in his opinion the educational value of the old nursemaid was greater than that of the psychologist Charlotte Beihler. In a letter to Joseph Arnon he wrote:

I view Freud as a dangerous monomaniac, but anyone who, thanks to him, has understood his subconscious, the unknown deeps of his mind, and become reconciled with the impossibility of ever knowing them— must be very very grateful to him.[14]

Korczak rejected the psychological approach of monistic thinkers and for this reason also rejected Jung and Adler. Even though there were certain similarities between himself and Adler, especially as regards their care for the status of the individual in society and their wish to establish an equilibrium between the weak young child and his society, Korczak feared the generalizations of established psychological methods, which in the way of all generalizations were, in his opinion, both false and dangerous. Moreover, such generalizations are, by nature, limited to a theoretical level while his own orientation was the empirical assessment of each individual, unfettered by any a priori theoretical psychological truisms. Korczak's strongest objections were directed at psychology's authoritarian, self-assured attitude and its generalizations. He stressed:

It is not the actual technique of psychology which is irritating, but the cocky, taunting self-assurance. Generalizations can only be achieved through a series of many observations and their comparison, and by means of a thorough assesment of special cases.[15]

Korczak considered the precise, meticulous, and detailed observation of every child as an individual to be the main requirement. Ada Poznansky-Hagery told of her work with Korczak, and how he repeatedly demanded from all educators at the orphanage that they conduct such observations of their protégés. She wrote:

Korczak devoted many hours to teaching the importance of observing the child. He taught us to write down simple facts, whose value we always discovered after a time. We had to be honest when noting down our observations and to admit when we saw nothing, or did not pay attention—on account of tiredness or absent-mindedness. We slowly learned to pay attention to the tiny details which make up the entire picture. To this very day my psychological work is based on such precise observations. I have learned to perceive a glance, a change in tone, a sudden paling—and all this thanks to Korczak's teachings.[16]

Most of Korczak's commentators and researchers tended to view his enterprise and his teachings in glowing colors, and were rarely critical of him. Outstanding, in this respect, is Akiva Ernest Simon, who, in his pamphlet, "Pestalozzi and Korczak—Pioneers of Social Education," raised some justified points of criticism against Korczak in three areas: psychological, pedagogical, and sociological. In the area of psychology, Simon contested Korczak's entire theory of childhood:

Any theory of childhood, which ascribes to it complete internal autonomy—such as Korczak's theory—does not take sufficient account of the great desire of this very age to grow and emulate the adult in order to become him.[17]

Korczak, who wished to base the whole educational process and the approach to the child on the child's personality and needs in the present, failed to perceive that the "Child's Present" always encapsulates the dimension of the future, which is enfolded within the child as the plant is enfolded within the seed or the sapling. The child does not aspire to perpetuate his condition; quite the contrary, he aspires to become an adult, and as soon as possible, and this aspiration to adulthood becomes an integral part of the child's inner world. These dreams of growing-up are evident in the child's games, such as "Mummy-Daddy" games or role games in which the child imagines himself to be a doctor, a teacher, a soldier, a driver, etc. Thus, Korczak's disregard of the child's wish to grow up is a weak link in his concept of the age of childhood.

In the area of pedagogy, Simon stressed that a teacher who has a family, in contrast to Korczak, "The Pioneer Monk," has an additional perspective on the whole educational process, which the unmarried educator lacks.

A teacher who has a home of his own, daily sees that children do not grow of themselves, but must be raised through the directed effort of adults within the society of adults and oriented to that society.[18]

Korczak, who never raised a family, lived an artificial, experimental life, and as a consequence distorted some of the truths about the world of the child. His attitude to the child was sometimes abstract, for he did not see him as part of the family circle, nor did he contend with social questions or with the child's problems of social adjustment—which are the essential problems of the entire family.

In the area of sociology, Simon claimed that Korczak's concept of social stratification was mistaken, for the stratification prevalent in modern society is not age-determined, as it was in primitive societies, but class determined, and this holds true for the age of children as well. "The application of the class principle to the area of the generational gap, blinded Korczak's eyes from seeing social reality as it is." Thus Korczak failed to address the main issue in modern society, which is not the struggle between members of various age groups, but between members of different classes and social strata. Particularly, as these differences of class, status, and strata are also evident among the children themselves. Korczak did not contend with these problems, and his mistaken perception failed to grasp the sociological reality of our society, simultaneously detracting from the importance and power of his educational struggle. We have already stressed that Korczak's educational approach was an essentially pedocentric one, wherein the child is placed at the center of the educational process, and the role of education is to provide the best possible conditions for the development and growth of the protégé. In the course of his educational activity, Korczak never set himself any educational goal external to the child. The essence and goal of his education were identical: the child. In his version of childhood, the child was portrayed as lacking any social ideals, with nothing to guide him forward, nor any standard against which to choose his way. Care was only taken of the child's present, of his full development, and no consideration was given to the society in which the child will have to grow, nor to the progress and development of that society.

Moreover, wishing to protect his orphans, Korczak bottled them within the orphanage and created a different planet, shut off from the outside world. The orphanage had no substantial ties with outside children, apart from school contacts, and was separated from the world of children and youth that lay beyond its walls.

Leon Harari was a *Mali Pshgelund* reporter, who frequently met Korczak during editorial conferences and at the editorial meetings that took place on Thursday evenings. He felt, when he visited the orphanage, that Korczak, too, was a different man when on the "inside" than he was on the "outside" of the institution. He wrote:

> In our meetings with Korczak at the orphanage yard, there was also a kind of strangeness between us and him. Somehow, this Korczak—I accuse him of nothing—was different. This was Korczak of the orphanage. He was hospitable, he invited us to sit down and join in "court" sessions and listen to readings of the newspaper, yet he always sat beyond this, beside the table. It is very possible that we too sought some affinity between ourselves and the children of the orphanage, but Korczak did not contribute to the encounter. I have worked with immigrant youth in Israel. The first thing I did was to acquaint them with the members of the kibbutz. I do not understand why Korczak did not do so. We were young and we did not analyze or consider the psychological problems, but why did he not do it?[19]

Harari stressed that this sense of strangeness, of part superciliousness, part inferiority, of non-mediation in the relationship, could also be felt in meetings with orphanage protégés who chanced into town on various errands. They seemed to carry the protective armor of the orphanage even when they were outside it. Orphanage protégé Sverin Nutkevitz said similar things about the orphanage:

> The educator—in my opinion—must have some goal. I want to educate the child to integrate with society; I think that this was Makarenko's aim. But there was none of this with Korczak. The great fight between Palska and Korczak, if there was such a fight, before their ways parted, was because Palska wanted to integrate the children from the Bialinska home with the environment surrounding the institution, and the environment from which the children originally came. Korczak did not agree.
>
> Our orphanage was a house with a high wall and a closed gate, so that we only saw the school and the orphanage. We had no contact whatsoever with the external world. We were raised in a greenhouse. When we left the oprhanage, the wind was so cold that it could often break us. But it seems that the effect of Korczak's education was so

strong that few broke. It is this great secret—how this could have happened—that I am trying to decipher without success.[20]

Korczak did not take care of boys over the age of fourteen. While the child was at the institution, he did his best to fulfill all of his needs, to make his days as pleasant as possible, and to provide him with a taste of the happy childhood of which he had been deprived. Once the children left the institution and encountered life, this meeting was very difficult for many of them. One of the protégés said: "So long as you are with Korczak, you have everything: Cups, spoons, napkins, curtains—and when you finish school, you get a kick in the ass—and out onto the street!"

In a conversation that centered about Korczak, Sverin Nutkevitz told the following story of his weekend leave from the orphanage and of his later life experiences when he left the orphanage:

On that Friday, while I was still a new boy (and you remember, how we then got the equipment with the satchel and the coat), I was very happy to go out—there was no school, one doesn't have to be home at a certain time. I can wander about the "Kretzlen" (The Flea Market). You know what fun it was to run about that place on a Saturday afternoon!

I wondered about for an hour, two hours. I was hungry. I had a few pennies, because I worked. Evening came, where do I go? I have no home, I really have no home, no such thing exists for me. It was a great crisis for me. My sisters were forced to leave the apartment because they did not pay the rent for more than two years. Well, I had once heard Korczak say that one can sleep in a park or under a bridge. I went under the bridge and I slept well. I wish I could sleep so well all my life. Suddenly I heard a shout "Get Up!" It was a policeman and he asked: "What are you doing here?" "I have no home and I am sleeping here," I answered. "Go away!"—He shouted. And I was totally shaken.

While with Korczak, I was used to everything being based on rules, for he built everything in the framework of orderly laws, both permissive and demanding. All the clauses in the children's constitution were written in a forgiving spirit because the child "did but not on purpose." There was self-administration, there was a parliament, etc.

And here I was, just out, and facing a policeman. I was shocked: "Mr. Policeman, sir, I have no father and mother, perhaps you can, find me a place to sleep?" "Go away or I'll thrash you" was the policeman's reply and he added many more words which the censorship will not allow one to put to paper. I thought: How can this be? I am not a criminal; I just want to pass the night. Then I thought: This does not correspond to Korczak's laws, and since that time I have never stopped thinking of the gap between what went on at the orphanage and what took place in its surroundings.

It seems that the sensation that "something was amiss" became so deeply ingrained within me, that many years later—(about 20 years), when after the war I again returned to Krochlmane st. and saw the ruined building, I looked at it and felt no kinship. This house held no meaning for me. I did not cry that my "parent's" house had been ruined. I looked at it very objectively as a place where I had spent a number of my childhood years.

I left the orphanage, and matters arranged themselves and at first I began working in a factory for cardboard boxes where my role was to get rid of the waste. On Friday the proprietor called me and said: "Go to Bialinska st., to the 'Novoshszi' theater and buy me two tickets at 5 zluti." A messenger boy—after finishing work. I told him: "Boss, I should be paid for my work." "I don't have the money today, you will get paid on Monday"—he replied. I exploded: "What? You have enough for the theater and you don't have enough to pay my salary?!" Of course, he gave me the money, but I was full of shame and mortification. When I came to my sisters and told them the story in tears, they burst out laughing and told me something which has since been deeply engraved in my memory: "Life is not Korczak's home! Here everything seems a little different. Take it into account!"

I look on this [Korczak's] paradise critically, for it was based on a detached reality which did not prepare us for real life. Korczak built a republic of children![21]

We hear the very same accusations from the mouth of another orphanage protégé, Ytzchak Belfer (Ytchu), who says:

In retrospect, the arrangements at the orphanage now seem to me to have been largely utopian, i.e. as an unrealistic society. It was a house full of goodness and justice. It was the "land" of children, in which everything was well understood and prepared for the child.[22]

Korczak himself was aware of this weakness in his enterprise, and even tried a number of times to rectify it by instituting a harsh, sober, and realistic regime. But he quickly reneged, for by his very nature he could not educate otherwise, and thus, to the bitter end, he continued to pamper the children, to provide illusions through fables and thrilling stories, to lull them to sleep by weaving dreams and to stress that:

The role of the educators is to educate, to protect under the wings of love and experience. To guard against the danger with warmth and peace, to preserve, to wait until they grow up, develop, accumulate enough power for independent flight.

Although Korczak and the educators defended their protégés at the institution and shielded them under the wings of love and experience, they did not prepare them for life in competitive, achievement-orientated, complex adult society based on hypocrisy, lies, pretense, and the trampling of others.

The fate of the protégés of the Jewish orphanage was even harsher, for they encountered prejudice in addition to the difficulties, frustration, and bitter disappointments. Gdalia Alkoshi understood this well when he noted:

At every turn they encountered the alien society's hate of the Jew, and their human suffering was further aggravated by the special suffering of the Jew. The institution at which they grew up did not educate them to fully identify with their people, nor with their national culture or their historic land. Their Jewish consciousness was thus not deep enough to help lighten their suffering as Jews and endow their special plight with meaning. It is no wonder then, that many of the graduates of the Jewish orphanage on Krochlmane st., felt themselves bewildered, disappointed and embittered when they left the institution.[23]

Aware of this weakness in his enterprise, Korczak attempted to increase the orphans' contact with life outside the institution by sending them out to study at the various schools in the city. Although he bitterly criticized existing schools and was well aware of their many and serious faults, he, nevertheless, did not wish to found a school within his institutions, for he wanted his protégés to come in contact with the external world, get to know it, live through the experiences it offers, and learn how to cope with it. Only during the last period, when it was no longer possible to send the Jewish protégés to a city school, did he begin to teach them in his own institutions. At the same time, the encounter with the external world did not change the essence of the introverted, protected, and loving world of the orphanage.

During the Saturday night conversations that Korczak had with the Burse protégés and the educators, many bitter questions were posed in regard to this issue of the orphanage's seclusion. Jacob Zuk, who was one of the Burse protégés, recorded Korczak's attempt at a reply:

"Are the protégés who leave the institution ready for the battle of life? What benefit do the protégés accrue from their stay at the institution, except for nutrition, improved health, a bit of knowledge and the like? . . . We educate our protégés to an advanced form of social life, to a life of order and discipline; while what is required in real life are strong and forceful elbows. Will they survive? . . ." Confronted by these life-questions, the doctor would think aloud, as if conversing with himself, and wonder; "Perhaps . . . do I know? . . . Perhaps you are right? . . . I am not a young man, I have set myself a most modest goal, to provide a hundred children with a roof and shelter over their heads and food to satiate their hunger, to ensure their growth and to protect them from the dangers and temptations of the street. I do my best for these children aged 6–14. Moreover, let others be envious, let them continue our enterprise and care for the young. . . . I, I have not succeeded, perhaps fate will be kinder to you, perhaps you shall get to live in a better, more progressive, more just world . . . perhaps. I do not know? Are you right?"[24]

At the same time, it would be false to present Korczak as admitting his failure on this issue out of a feeling of helplessness. Korczak understood that there was almost no parallel between the dictates of society and life and the very essence of his concept of education as it was intended to care for the child's requirements and fulfill his spiritual needs. He believed that those years of childhood and adolescence until the age of fourteen, which the child spent at his institution in an atmosphere of freedom and protection, might foster a free and open personality and make the child a free person who would later know how to cope with the new reality he was to enter. Korczak understood one important psychological issue, which most of the critics of the "greenhouse conditions" ignored, that the main role of the educational institution is to build the personality of the protégé, to try to rectify the severe defects that life has left in his personality, to make up for the maternal deprivation that many of the protégés had experienced, and so on. In his conversations with the educators, the instructors, and the Bourse protégés, he emphasized that the children who came to the orphanage bore within them a severe familial deprivation, a deficit of warmth, love, physical proximity, pampering, attention, intimate relationships, and stable affection.

Korczak wished to make up for this deficit. He believed that it was possible that the love, warmth, and attention that he provided the children might not be an immediate practical guarantee that they will get along in life, or know how to cope with a cruel reality, sly persons, and various oppressive laws; but, that, on the other hand, this large helping of

love worked something important and deep on their personality and prepared them to acquire a positive and social attitude toward life instead of
closing themselves against it and rejecting it. It seems that this infusion of
love and intimate human contact acts directly on the shaping of the personality; they instill it with that reservoir of spiritual confidence and positive
regard that, in the long run, also provide it with the strength to overcome
the disappointments and the failures so characteristic of the encounter
with the external world. Although Korczak knew the grave dangers that
faced his protégés when they went out into life, and was aware that many
of them might break, be injured, and suffer, he nevertheless considered
that if education were to become a compromise and a surrender, there
was no chance whatsoever to ever begin the process of liberating the
child, and thus, in the long run, effecting a change of the whole of society. In great sadness and sobriety, Korczak emphasized:

> To guarantee that the development of all children be free and corre-
> spond to their full mental capacities, to fully realise their hidden poten-
> tial powers, to educate them to respect the good, the beautiful and
> freedom. . . . You the naive, try. The public has given you a young
> savage for you to shape his image and prepare him to be easily digest-
> ible. And it is waiting—the state is waiting, the church, the future
> employer—demanding, waiting and guarding. The state demands
> sovereign patriotism, the church—episcopal belief, the employer—
> honesty and decency, and all of them together demand mediocrity and
> submission. They shall break the stronger one, trample the quiet one,
> occasionally bribe the capricious and always bar the way of the
> unfortunate.[25]

Korczak viewed his institutions as most important. His devotion was to
the child alone. He did not attempt to cope with the general problem of
educating the children of the poor. He wished to concentrate on his therapeutic work, to be constantly concerned with the empirical daily reality
of his institutions, and he never found the time or the justification to
make generalizations or to attempt to formulate therapeutic procedures.
Nor did he try to make his institutions a place where many educators
dealing with orphans and neglected children could learn. His pedagogical
method was inseparably connected with his personality, his special character and way of life, his pedagogical intuition and his personal aura, and
so on; and it is, therefore, almost impossible to emulate his methods or
translate them into practical procedures applicable to other institutions.
Although he faithfully guided the Burse protégés in their educational
work and instructed pedagogical courses, he never took the trouble to

formulate consistent and methodical conclusions based on the enormous experience he had accumulated, and he refused, on principle, to expand and direct himself to general educational problems. Moshe Zertal (Silbertal) quotes Irena Chamilanska who testified:

> He [Korczak] kept difficult, sick or defective children away from the orphanage and was bent on ensuring that the children's group shall be as responsive as possible to education, organization and social life. The efforts of the educators were also directed to this end, as was the complex internal constitution of the orphanage with its many chapters and clauses. When Korczak was requested to provide help outside the home, he defended himself by saying: "I cannot give everything to all children," and if he could not give to all children, he wanted to give all that was in his power—at least to his own protégés.[26]

Harsh testimony, though it only happened once, of his focus on the welfare of the entire group to the point of disregarding the disturbed individual, demanding that such an individual be expelled from the institution, can be found in the notes of his diary. He wrote of an aggressive child, Museik, who, for a period of three years, made the lives of thirty kindergarten orphans very miserable:

> I wrote an article for the "Pedagogica Specialna" about him, in which I mentioned penal colonies, and even capital punishment. For he is young! He will run wild and torture others for fifty consecutive years! The beloved Ms. Maria, with a shy smile:—You were joking of course? Not at all. How much injustice, how much pain, how many tears. . . . If so, you do not believe that one can correct—I am not Adler—I answered angrily.[27]

An additional example in this context was raised by orphanage protégé, Sverin Nutkevitz, who related:

> There was a lad called Srulek in the Korczak home. He was a very ugly boy with horse teeth, one crooked eye and bald. I assume that being so ugly he was as prickly as a porcupine, and his barbs were always ready. He was in the fourth grade. He was put on trial every Saturday and finally received the 1000 clause. We were sort of friends because it is hard to call it friendship. I knew how to play with him. He was calm when he was with me and treated me gently. I was never struck by him even though he beat up everyone else. Before he left, when he got the 1000, he told me that he had nowhere to go. At home he had a step-

father who did not want him. What should he do? Korczak created his republic but did not have a solution for all the difficult children. This is a further test of Korczak's method. But I am no judge.[28]

Joseph Arnon wrote of Korczak's position on this issue:

My powers can hardly extend to one hundred, one hundred and ten children. I wish to give them at least a certain period of life, in which they will obtain a spiritual charge which might last them for their lives in future. I know, that there are hopeless children. At any rate, within the limits of my actions I will not be able to surmount their difficulties and therefore won't be able to help them.

Why should such a child occupy the place of a child whom I might be able to help?[29]

This open-eyed realism forced Korczak to make cruel decisions, although this happened very rarely. On the other hand, there are very many examples of instances in which Korczak devoted a great deal of thought to the care of one small and narrow segment of the educational-therapeutic front of orphaned and poor children, of difficult children, wherein his main key to their world was always the key of understanding, lots of attention and love.[30]

Had we wished, in concluding our discussion, to answer the questions: What has Korczak bequeathed us? What are the durable elements of his teaching—our list would be very long indeed. All that is left to us is to attempt to distill his contribution in a kind of quick synopsis of his whole teachings.

Michael Verblovsky, of the Korczak Association in Stockholm, Sweden, who was an instructor at the Jewish orphanage run by Korczak, summarized his teachings in ten main points,[31] and although we shall extend this list and double it, we will not be able to encompass more than a tiny fragment of his great contribution to education:

1) A humane and human in-depth vision of man.
2) Perception of the child as a person from his earliest childhood, and not as a scaled-down adult.
3) A thorough examination of the possibilities and limitations of education.
4) An in-depth evaluation of the question of freedom in education.
5) Belief that a change of conditions, such as the creation of an educational environment, is capable of effecting great positive change in man.

6) Rejection of all types of educational labels, a priori definitions of the role of education and the perception of education as shaping the child.

7) Organization of the children's group as a true democratic society based on laws, obligations, and rights, self-rule, avoidance of the imposition of decrees from above and of tyranny.

8) Trust in the child, which is expressed in action and in the provision of responsibility rather than in declarations or empty speeches.

9) Respect for the child, which develops his faith in his own powers and in the possibilities open to him, which have been affirmed through experience.

10) The construction of a large-scale model of children's self-rule in which adults and children cooperate in a single democratic society.

11) Basing the training of educators on constant involvement in educational practice, observations, monitoring, and ceaseless experience.

12) Aversion to bookish learning and customized advice, and the basing of education on action and on response to the needs of the individual.

13) An individualistic concept, of education, in which man is the focus of education and the fulfillment of his needs and the response to his unique world are the main issues. Yet the very concept of *man*, in its human aspects and its connections with human society, does not allow education to be dragged from individualism to egocentricity or anarchy.

14) An important emphasis on the realization of the individual in the social context, on his right to pray, to dream, to creatively express himself, to keep silent.

15) Recognition of the importance of literature, reading, listening to a tale, creative writing, and personal expression in educational work.

16) A strong emphasis on the personality of the educator and on personal example.

17) Reformulation of educational methods, avoiding all forms of humiliating punishment.

18) Combining the activities of education and of therapy into one cohesive whole, the merging of medicine and education, and viewing the school as a human clinic that, contributes to man's mental hygiene, his physical health, and his spiritual fitness.

19) Emphasis on the role of nature in education, the importance of the outing as an encounter with landscapes and views, and as a meeting of man with himself and his God. The importance of leaving the stifling city for the country and its wide spaces.

20) And above all the place of love in education.

Despite the justified criticism that might be directed at Korczak's educational teachings, his figure shines out to us in a radiant mirror, and we see a great-hearted and loving educator, who devoted his entire life to the education of the child and who carried the flag of life through the gates of death and on to eternity. His name shall continue to be a source of light to those who dream the dream of a more beautiful world.

Notes

Chapter 1. Life As a Calling

1. Stephania Nei, "On Janusz Korczak," translated by Biniamin Tene in *A Gesture to Korczak*, (Tel-Aviv: Beit Lochamei Hagetaot, Korczak Association in Israel, Hakibbutz Hameuchad Publications, 1985), 30.

2. Quoted by Ytzchak Perlis in his book, *A Jew from Poland* (*The Life and Enterprise of Janusz Korczak*) (Beit Lochamei: Hagetaot and Hakibbutz Hameuchad Publications, 1988). The excerpt was taken from *Mali Pshgelund* 3.12.1926. The material is kept at the Korczak archive at Beit Lochamei Hagetaot.

3. Quoted by Alexander Guterman in his article, "The Jewish Roots of Janusz Korczak," in Adir Cohen, Aden Shevach, and Yatziv Reuven, eds. *Studies in the Legacy of Janusz Korczak*, vol. 1 (Haifa, University of Haifa Publishing House, The Janusz Korczak Association in Israel, and Beit Lochamei Hagetaot, 1987), 41–84.

4. Ibid., 61–62.

5. Ibid., 66.

6. Ibid., 66–67.

7. Janusz Korczak, *From the Ghetto*, translated by Zvi Arad (Tel-Aviv: Hakibbutz Hameuchad, 1972), 80–81.

8. Paulina Apanshlak, *The Doctor Stayed*, translated by H. S. Ben-Abraham (Jerusalem: Kiryat Sefer, 1946), 30.

9. Ibid., 30–31.

10. And see Yerachmiel Weingarten, *Janusz Korczak—The Tormented Jew* (Tel-Aviv: Bronfman, 1979), 176.

11. The prayer is quoted in Apanshlak Paulina's book, *The Doctor Stayed*, 46.

12. See also his childhood memories in his book, *From the Ghetto*, 155–56.

13. Ibid., 157.

14. Janusz Korczak, "When I Shall be Little Again," in *Pedagogical Writings*, Translated by Dov Sadan and Shimshon Meltzer (Tel-Aviv: Hakibbutz Haemuchad, 1962), 87.

15. Ibid.

16. Quoted by Yehuda Cahana in his article, "Janusz Korczak and School," in *Studies in Education*, edited by Adir Cohen, vols. 43–44. (March 1968): 88.

17. Korczak, *From the Ghetto*, 132–33.

18. Ibid., 151.

19. Yerachmiel Weingarten, *Janusz Korczak* (Tel-Aviv: Ministry of Security, the Publishers, Tarmil Library, 1982), 34.

20. Korczak, *From the Ghetto*, 160.

21. Ibid., 156.

22. Ibid.

23. Igor Neverly, "Chapters of Childhood and Youth," in *Mibefnim*, edited by Perlis Ytzchak and Meirovitz Aharon (Tel-Aviv: Beit Lochamei Hagetaot and Hakibbutz Hameuchad Publications, 1980), 21.

24. Alicja Szlazakowa, *Janusz Korczak*, translated by Edmund Konowicz (Warsaw: Wydawnictua Skolne i Pedagogiczme, 1978).

25. Perlis, *A Jew from Poland*, 13–14.

26. Gedalia Alkoshi, *Janusz Korczak in Hebrew* (Tel-Aviv: Hakibbutz Hameuchad, 1972), 15.

27. Igor Neverly, "The Testament of the Old Doctor," translated by Joseph Arnon, *Education* 3–4 (1978), 113–27.

28. Korczak, *From the Ghetto*, 190.

29. Perlis, *A Jew from Poland*, 18.

30. Korczak, *From the Ghetto*, 124.

31. Ibid., 125.

32. Janusz Korczak, *With the Child*, translated by Zvi Arad (Tel-Aviv: Beit Lochamei Hagetaot and Hakkibutz Hameuchad Pulbications, 1974), 142–343.

33. Hana Mordetkovitz-Ohlatczkova, *The Life of Janusz Korczak*, translated by Zvi Arad (Tel-Aviv: Hakkibbutz Hameuchad Publications, 1961), 35.

34. Janusz Korczak, *How to Love Children*, translated by Jacob Zuk (Tel-Aviv: Hakibbutz Hameuchad Publication, 1960), 87.

35. Janusz Korczak, "Moshekim, Yosekim, Srulekim," in *With the Child*, 51–128.

36. Quoted by Perlis in his book, *A Jew from Poland*, 37–38.

37. Quoted in Ada Poznansky-Hageri's article, "Korczak as an Educational Model," in the appendix to Hana Mordetkovitz-Ohlatczkova's book, *The Life of Janusz Korczak*, 203.

38. Korczak, *From the Ghetto*, 105.

39. Ibid., 127–28.

40. Quoted by Weingarten in his book, *Janusz Korczak—The Tormented Jew*, 105.

41. David Zilber, "In the Presence of Janusz Korczak," *Molad* 8 (1980), 39–40, 213.

42. Janusz Korczak, *The Child's Religion*, translated by Dov Sadan and Zvi Arad (Tel-Aviv, Beit Lochamei Hagetaot and Hakkibbutz Hameuchad Publications, 1978), 257.

43. Korczak, "How to Love Children," 396–97.

44. Joseph Arnon, *Janusz Korczak's Educational Method* (Tel-Aviv: Otzar Hamoreh, 1972), 102.

45. Quoted by Perlis in his book, *A Jew from Poland*, 62.

46. David Zilber, "In the Presence of Janusz Korczak," *Molad* 8 (1980), 215.

47. Weingarten, *Janusz Korczak—The Tormented Jew*, 145.

48. Ytzchak Greenbaum, *The Wars of the Polish Jews* (Tel-Aviv: Haverim Publications, 1941), 112.

49. For a more extensive discussion, see the chapter on the orphanage.

50. Avraham Lewinson, *The History of Warsaw's Jews* (Tel-Aviv: Am-Oved, 1943), 305–6.

51. Weingarten, *Janusz Korczak—The Tormented Jew*, 185.

52. Ibid., 187.

53. Korczak, *Pedagogical Writings*, 194.

54. Ibid.

55. Quoted by Perlis in his book, *A Jew from Poland*, 106.

56. Ibid., 107.

57. Arnon, *Janusz Korczak's Educational Method*, 76.

58. Ibid., 77.

59. See also Ada Poznansky-Hageri, "The Influence of Janusz Korczak and Stefa Vileczinska on the Children of the Kibbutz," *The Communal Education* no. 27, 95 (1978), 64–71.

60. Korczak, *The Child's Religion*, 69–70.

61. Mordetkovitz-Ohlatczkova, *The Life of Janusz Korczak*, 125.

62. Weingarten, *Janusz Korczak—The Tormented Jew*, 282.

63. Ibid., 304.

64. Korczak, *Pedagogical Writings*, 185.

65. Zartal Moshe, *In the Presence of Janusz Korczak* (Merchavia: Sifryat Poalim, 1962), 31–37.

66. Korczak, *The Child's Religion*, 113.

67. Ibid., 85–86.

68. Ibid., 109.

69. Ibid.

70. Ibid., 114.

71. Zartel, *In the Presence of Janusz Korczak*, 34.

72. Arnon, *Janusz Korczak's Educational Method*, 81.

73. Korczak, *Pedagogical Writings*, 195.

74. Ibid., 196.

75. Ibid.

76. Ibid.

77. Ibid.

78. Ibid.

79. Ibid., 199.

80. Ibid., his letter of 30 March, 1937.

81. Ibid., 199, his letter of 23 May, 1937.

82. Ibid., his letter of 30 March, 1937.

83. Gilaad Zrubavel, "Conversations and Meetings," in Mordetkovitz-Ohlatczkova, *The Life of Janusz Korczak*, 191.

84. Ibid., 190.

85. Ibid., 190.

86. Ytzchak Greenbaum, *In Days of Destruction and Holocaust* (Tel-Aviv: Haverim Publications, 1946), 187–89.

87. Korczak, *Pedagogical Writings*, 78.

88. Korczak, *From the Ghetto*, 179.

89. Ibid., 113.

90. Arnon, *Janusz Korczak's Educational Method*, 95.

91. M. Lansky, *The Life of the Jews in Ghetto Warsaw* (Jerusalem: The Holocaust Library, n.d.), 39–40.

92. Quoted in Perlis's article "The Last Chapter—Korczak in the Warsaw Ghetto," in Korczak's book, *From the Ghetto*, 25–26.

93. D. Gotsporecth, H. Hadary, and A. Reichman, eds., *The Book of Liberty* (Tel-Aviv: Hakibbutz Hameuchad, 1947), 464.

94. Jona Buchian, "I Shall Remember . . . ," *Mibefnim* 24, no. 4 (Ellul, 1962): 420–28.

95. Korczak, *From the Ghetto*, 129–30.

96. Quoted by Perlis in his book, *A Jew from Poland*, 195.

97. Quoted in Weingarten, *Janusz Korczak—The Tormented Jew*, 327.

98. And see Adam Czerniakov, *The Warsaw Ghetto Diary*, edited by Nachman Blumental, A. Tratkover, N. Ak, and Y. Karmish (Jerusalem: Yad Vashem, 1969), 179.

99. And see Emanuel Czerniakov, *Writings from the Ghetto*, Jewish Historical Institute, *Jewish Book* (Warsaw [in Yiddish]: 1961), Book 1, 7, 263, 277.

100. John Ouerbach, "Korczak," translated by Avraham Yavin, *Mibefnim* 29, no. 4 (Tamuz, 1972), 252–53.

101. Ibid.

102. Korczak, *From the Ghetto*, 76–77.

103. Korczak, *From the Ghetto*, 88.

104. Mordetkovitz-Ohlatczkova, *The Life of Janusz Korczak*, 160.

105. Korczak, *From the Ghetto*, 160.

106. Quoted in Sarah Nishmit's book, *The Struggle of the Ghetto* (Tel-Aviv: Culture and Education, 1968), 132–33.

107. Various testimonies quoted by Ytzchak Perlis in his article "The Last Chapter—Korczak in the Warsaw Ghetto", in Korczak's book, *From the Ghetto*, 25–26.

108. Quoted by Weingarten in his book, *Janusz Korczak—The Tormented Jew*, 341.

109. Nachman Blumental, "Janusz Korczak and the Nazi Authorities," in *Yad Vashem*, Anthology of Research on Events of the Holocaust and the Bravery Vol. 7 (Jerusalem: Yad Vashem, 1961), 155–56.

Chapter 2. *With God I Shall Converse*: Religion and Religious Education in the Teaching of Korczak

1. Janusz Korczak, *With God I Shall Converse—The Prayers of Those Who Do Not Pray*, translated by Yehushua Markovitz (Jerusalem: Kiryat Sefer, 1979), 16–17.

2. Yosef Arnon, *The Educational Method of Janusz Korczak* (Merhavia: Sifriat Poalim, 1962), 80.

3. Janusz Korczak, *The Senate of Madmen*, translated by Uri Orlev, in *Studies in the Heritage of Janusz Korczak*, edited by Adir Cohen, Sevack Eden, and Reuven Yatziv (The Association of Janusz Korczak in Israel, Beit Lochamei Hagetaot and the Hakkibutz Hameuchad Publications, 1979), Vol. 2.

4. Quoted in Mordetdovitz-Ohlatchkova's book, *The Life of Janusz Korczak*, translated by Zvi Arad (Tel-Aviv: Hakibbutz Hameuchad, 1961), 80–81.

5. Presented by Perlis in his Introduction to Janusz Korczak's book, *From the Ghetto*, translated by Zvi Arad (Tel-Aviv: Hakibbutz Hameuchad, 1972), 54.

6. Janusz Korczak, "Rules of Education," translated by Itzchak Perlis, in *Mibefnim*, 1962, 24, 417–19.

7. Ibid., 11–12.

8. Ibid., 13–14.

9. Ibid., 14.

10. Ibid., 8.

11. Ibid., 5.

12. Ibid., 5.

13. Ibid., 55.

14. Ibid., 32–33.

15. Ibid., 33.

16. Ibid., 43.

17. Ibid.

18. Erich Fromm, *And You Shall Be as Gods*, translated by Yoram Rosler (Jerusalem: A. Rubinstein, 1975).

19. Korczak, *With God I Shall Converse*, 46.

20. Adir Cohen, *Love and Hope—Education in the Sane Society* (Tel-Aviv: Reshafim, 1985), 126.

21. Korczak, *With God I Shall Converse*, 24.

22. Ibid., 25.

23. Ibid., 23.

24. Quoted by Yoseph Arnon in his article, "The Faith of Janusz Korczak," *Studies in Education*, 19 (June 1978), 8.

25. Korczak, *With God I Shall Converse*, 19–20.

26. Ibid., 21.

27. Erich Fromm, *Psychoanalysis and Religion*, translated by Shmuel Shichor and Rachel Ravid (Tel-Aviv: Daga Books, 1964), 58.

28. Arnon, "The Faith of Janusz Korczak," 12.

29. Janusz Korczak, *From the Ghetto*, translated by Zvi Arad (Beit Lochamei: Hagetaot and the Hakibbutz Hameuchad Publications, 1972).

30. Janusz Korczak, *The Drawing-Room Kid*, translated by Arie Buchner and Avraham Berles (Tel-Aviv: Yesod, 1973), 32.

31. Mordetkovitz Ohlachkova, *The Life of Janusz Korczak*, 163.

32. Korczak, *Pedagogical Writings*, 140.

33. Korczak, *The Senate of Madmen*, *Studies in the Heritage of Janusz Korczak*, Vol. 2, 29.

34. Yerachmiel Weingarten, *Janusz Korczak* (Tel-Aviv: The Ministry of Security Publications, Tarmil Library, 1982), 19.

35. Ibid., 55.

36. Ibid., 97–98.

37. Ibid., 122.

38. Ibid.

Chapter 3. To the Sun: The Summer Camps

1. Janusz Korczak, "Moshekim, Yosekim, Srulekim," in *With the Child*, translated by Zvi Arad (Tel-Aviv: Beit Lochamei Hagetaot and Hakibbutz Hameuchad Publications, 1974), 127–28.

2. Ibid., 98.

3. Ibid., 90.

4. Janusz Korczak, *How to Love Children*, translated by Jacob Zuk (Tel-Aviv: Hakibbutz Hameuchad Publications, 1960), 99.

5. Ibid., 106.

6. Ibid., 114.

7. Ibid., 119–20.

8. Ibid., 143.

9. Ibid., 144.

10. Ibid., 129.

11. Ibid., 145–46.

Chapter 4. To Be a Home: The Orphange as a Home and a House of Education

1. Janusz Korczak, *With the Child*, translated by Zvi Arad (Tel-Aviv: Beit Lochamei Hagetaot and Hakibbutz Hameuchad Publications, 1974), 183–84.
2. Ibid., 393.
3. Ibid.
4. Ibid., 394.
5. Korczak, *How to Love Children*, 7.
6. Korczak, *With the Child*, 395.
7. Ibid., 399.
8. Janusz Korczak, "The Child's Right to Respect," in *Pedagogical Writings*, translated by Dov Sadan and Shimshon Meltzer (Tel-Aviv: Hakibbutz Hameuchad, 1962), 12.
9. Janusz Korczak, "Rules of Education," translated by Ytzchak Perlis, in *Mibefnim* 24 (September 1962): 417–19.
10. Ibid.
11. Ibid.
12. Joseph Arnon, *Janusz Korczak's Educational Method* (Tel-Aviv: Otzar Hamore, 1972), 32.
13. David Zilber, "In the Presence of Janusz Korczak" (memoirs), *Molad* 8, no. 39–40 (1980): 213–14.
14. Weingarten, *Janusz Korczak—The Tormented Jew*, 106.
15. Anat Cohen-Ronen, *Janusz Korczak, His Personality, Theory and Educational Enterprise* (stencil) (Ein-Charod: Hakibbutz Hameuchad), 27.
16. Quoted in Weingarten, *Janusz Korczak—The Tormented Jew*, 139–40.
17. Korczak, *How to Love Children*, 52.
18. Ibid., 54.
19. Korczak, *Pedagogical Writings*, 34.
20. Zuk Jacob, "Working with the Doctor," in *Janusz Korczak—Educator to the Last*, edited by Perlis Ytzchak and Meirovitz Aharon (Tel-Aviv: Beit Lochamei Hagetaot and Hakibbutz Hameuchad Publications, 1980), 38.
21. Ada Poznansky-Hageri, "Janusz Korczak and Stefa Vileczinska in the Eyes of Their Protégés," *Education and Its Environment* (Tel-Aviv: Seminar Hakibbutzim 1982–1983).
22. Israel (Staszek) Zingman, *Janusz Korczak among the Orphans* (Tel-Aviv: Sifryat Po'alim, 1979), 62–63.
23. Ibid., 81–82.
24. The Letter is produced in Zvi Sherfstein's book, *Great Educators of Our People* (Jerusalem: Reuben Mas, 1964), 272.
25. Poznansky-Hageri, "Janusz Korczak and Stefa Vileczinska."
26. Zvi Kurzweil, *The Educational Teaching of Janusz Korczak* (Tel-Aviv: Culture and Education, 1968), 37.
27. Ada Poznansky-Hageri, "Likes and Dislikes Among Children in Institutions," *Megamot*, 8 (October 1957), no. 4: 419–29.
28. Ibid., 420.
29. Ibid., 422–23.
30. Ibid.
31. J. Bowlby, *Maternal Care and Mental Health* (Geneva: WHO, 1950 [Engl.]).

32. Quoted in Arnon, Joseph, *Janusz Korczak's Educational Method* (Tel-Aviv: Otzar Hamore, 1972), 51.

33. Ibid.

34. Ibid.

35. Janusz Korczak, "The Orphanage", in *How to Love Children*, in the volume *With the Child*, translated by Zvi Arad (Tel-Aviv: Beit Lochamei Hagetaot and Hakibbutz Hameuchad Publications, 1974), 418–20.

36. Ibid., 454.

37. Ibid., 458.

38. Ibid., 413.

39. Korczak, *From the Ghetto*, 166–67.

40. Jacob Zuk, "In the Presence of Janusz Korczak and Stefania Vileczinska," Vol. 4 *Ofakim* (Merchavia: Sifryat Po'alim, November, 1955, Year 9), 340.

41. David Zilber, "In the Presence of Janusz Korczak" (memoirs), *Molad* 8, no. 39–41 (1980): 213–18.

42. Korczak, *Pedagogical Writings*, 57.

43. Korczak, *How to Love Children*, 67.

44. Ibid., 22.

45. Ibid., 62.

46. Ibid., 76.

47. Arnon, *Janusz Korczak's Educational Method*, 31.

48. Orna Freidman-Diller, "The Figure of Janusz Korczak," Vol. 3, *Ofakim* (Merchavia: Sifriat Hapo'alim, November, 1955, Year 9), 348.

49. Korczak, *How to Love Children*, 15.

Chapter 5. The Child is Father to the Man: The Concept of the Child as the Focus of the Educational Process

1. Janusz Korczak, "The Spring and the Child," in *The Child's Religion*, translated by Zvi Arad (Tel-Aviv: Beit Lochamei Hagetaot and Hakibbutz Hameuchad Publications, 1978), 249.

2. Korczak, "Rules of Education (Conversations with Instructors)," 302.

3. Janusz Korczak, "The Child's Right to Respect," in *Pedagogical Writings*, translated by Dov Sadan and Shimshon Meltzer (Tel-Aviv: Hakibbutz Hameuchad, 1962), 13.

4. Ibid., 16.

5. Korczak, "When I Shall Be Little Again," 86.

6. Korczak, "Rules of Living," 52.

7. Janusz Korczak, from the introduction for the adult reader in "When I Shall Be Little Again," *Pedagogical Writings*, Vol. 2, 2d ed. (Tel-Aviv: Hakkibutz Hameuchad Publications, 1945).

8. Korczak, "Humorous Pedagogy," 69.

9. Janusz Korczak, "How to Love Children," in *With the Child*, translated by Zvi Arad (Tel-Aviv: Beit Lochamei Hagetaot and Hakibbutz Hameuchad Publications, 1974), 187.

10. Ibid., 187–88.

11. See our discussion on "Between a Pulse and a Heart—Korczak's concept of medicine and education."

12. Korczak, "How to Love Children," 187.
13. Korczak, "The Spring and the Child," 75.
14. Ibid., 75–76.
15. Joseph Arnon, "Lights and Shadows in Education in England," *Ofakim* 4, 8th year, 28 (November, 1954): 408.
16. See Adir Cohen, *The Educational Teaching of Martin Buber*, in the chapter "Buber's Theory of Dialogue as the Basis of His Educational Teaching" (Tel-Aviv: Yachdav, 1976), 53–70.
17. Martin M. Buber, "Epilogue to the I-Thou Book," in *In The Secret of Conversation, Of Man and His Stance Before Existence* (Jerusalem: Mossad Bialik, 1963), 99.
18. Ibid., 101.
19. See note 16. The chapter: "Martin Buber and Change in Modern Education" 365–72.
20. Janusz Korczak, "The Child's Right to Respect," translated by Dov Sadan, *A Childhood of Respect* (Tel-Aviv: Beit Lochamei Hagetaot and Hakkibutz Hameuchad Publications, 1977), 223.
21. Ibid.
22. Janusz Korczak, "The Child in the Family," in "How to Love Children" in his book *With the Child*, 239.
23. Ibid., 257.
24. Ibid., 328.
25. Korczak, *The Religion of the Child*, 305.

Chapter 6. The Growth of Spring: *Rules of Living*

1. Janusz Korczak, "The Spring and the Child," in *The Child's Religion*, translated by Zvi Arad (Tel-Aviv: Beit Lochamei Hagetaot and Hakibbutz Hameuchad Publications, 1978), 250.
2. Ibid., 241–42.
3. Janusz Korczak, "Rules of Life," in *Pedagogical Writings*, translated by Shimshon Meltzer (Tel-Aviv: Hakibbutz Hameuchad publications, 1962), 20.
4. Ibid., 21.
5. J. Bowlby, *Maternal Care and Mental Health*, WHO, Geneva, 1950, (Engl.)
6. Janusz Korczak, "Rules of Life," 30.
7. Ibid., 32.
8. Ibid., 34.
9. Janusz Korczak, "The Child in the Family," in "How to Love Children" in *With the Child*, translated by Zvi Arad (Tel-Aviv: Beit Lochamei Hagetaot and Hakibbutz Hameuchad Publications, 1974), 226.
10. Ibid., 227.
11. Ibid.
12. Ibid., 231.
13. Ibid., 228.
14. Ibid.
15. Ibid.
16. Weingarten, *Janusz Korczak—The Tormented Jew*, 205.
17. Korczak, *Pedagogical Writings*, 51.

Chapter 7. Between a Pulse and a Heart: Korczak's Conception of Medicine and Education

1. Quoted by Ya'akov Rottem in his article "Janusz Korczak as a Physician," Adir Cohen, ed., *Janusz Korczak, Proceedings of the International Congress Celebrating His Hundredth Anniversary* (University of Haifa and University of Tel-Aviv, 1979), 130.
2. Janusz Korczak, *How to Love Children*, translated by Jacob Zuk (Tel-Aviv: Hakibbutz Hameuchad Publications, 1960), 87.
3. Janusz Korczak, "The Special School," in *The Child's Religion*, translated by Zvi Arad (Tel-Aviv: Beit Lochamei Hagetaot and Hakibbutz Hameuchad Publications, 1978), 255.
4. Ibid.
5. Korczak, "How to Love Children," in *With the Child*, 172.
6. Ibid., 170–71.
7. Ibid., 175.
8. Ibid., 166.
9. Korczak, *From the Ghetto*, 189.
10. Korczak, *How to Love Children*, 84–85.
11. Ibid., 90.
12. Korczak, *With the Child*, 209.
13. Ibid., 186.
14. Ibid.
15. Ibid.
16. Korczak, *How to Love Children*, 16–17.
17. Korczak, *Pedagogical Writings*, 142.
18. Weingarten, *Janusz Korczak—The Tormented Jew*, 212–13.
19. Korczak, *With the Child*, 159.
20. Weingarten, *Janusz Korczak—The Tormented Jew*, 213.

Chapter 8. To Touch without Burdening: On the Educator's Image

1. Janusz Korczak, "The Spring and the Child," in *The Child's Religion*, translated by Zvi Arad (Tel-Aviv: Beit Lochamei Hagetaot and Hakibbutz Hameuchad Publications, 1978), 243.
2. Ibid., 270.
3. Ibid., 270–71.
4. Israel Scheffler, *The Language of Education* (Springfield, Ill.: Thomas Publications Corporation, 1966 [Engl.]).
5. Korczak, *The Child's Religion*, 271.
6. Ibid., 273.
7. Korczak, *How to Love Children*, 33.
8. Ibid., 34.
9. Ibid., 31.
10. Ibid.
11. Ibid., 14.
12. Ibid., chap. 5.

13. Ibid., 14.
14. Janusz Korczak, "The Child's Right to Respect," in *Pedagogical Writings*, translated by Dov Sadan and Shimshon Meltzer (Tel-Aviv: Hakibbutz Hameuchad Publications, 1962), 12.
15. Korczak, *How to Love Children*, 40.
16. Korczak, *Pedagogical Writings*, 13.
17. Hana Mordetkovitz-Ohlatczkova, *The Life of Janusz Korczak* (Tel-Aviv: Hakibbutz Hameuchad Publications, 1961).
18. Korczak, *How to Love Children*, 40.
19. Mordetkovitz-Ohlatczkova, *The Life of Janusz Korczak*, 97.
20. Korczak, *Pedagogical Writings*, 137.
21. Korczak, *How to Love Children*, 8.
22. Korczak *The Child's Religion*, 308.
23. Ibid.
24. Ibid.
25. Ibid.
26. Ibid., 252–53.
27. Ibid., 73–79.
28. See Adir Cohen, *Free Education* (Tel-Aviv: Reshafim, 1984), 49–62.
29. A. S. Neill, *Summerhill, A Radical Approach to the Raising of Children*, translated by Rephael Elgad (Tel-Aviv: Yehoshua Chichik, Undated), 29.
30. Korczak, "On the Educational Seminary," 74.
31. Ibid.
32. Ibid., 78.
33. Ibid.
34. Korczak, "6 × 5 (Thirty Years of Thinking about the Child)," in *The Child's Religion*, 297–98.
35. Ibid., 298.

Chapter 9. To Be a Light: On Educational Teaching

1. Janusz Korczak, "Rules of Life," in *Pedagogical Writings*, translated by Dov Sadan and Shimshon Meltzer (Tel-Aviv: Hakibbutz Hameuchad, 1962).
2. See Alfred North Whitehead, *The Goals of Education* translated by A. C. Brown (Jerusalem: The Hebrew University School of Education, published by M. Neuman, 1958), and see also Adir Cohen, *A Revolution in Education* (Tel-Aviv: Reshafim, 1983).
3. Ibid., 12.
4. John Dewey, *The Child and the Curriculum: School and Society*, translated by Chaim Braver (Tel-Aviv: Otzar Hamore, 1960), 8.
5. See Cohen, *A Revolution in Education*, 13–46.
6. Richard Livingstone, *Education in a Preplexed World*, translated by Nava Illan (Jerusalem: The Hebrew University School of Education, 1960), 68.
7. Janusz Korczak, *Pedagogical Writings*, translated by Dov Sadan and Shimshon Meltzer (Tel-Aviv: Hakibbutz Hameuchad, 1962), 136.
8. Ibid.
9. Ibid., 42.
10. Ibid., 43.
11. See Cohen, *A Revolution in Education*, 152–80.
12. Ibid., 101–48.

13. Ibid., 183–209.
14. See Adir Cohen, *Free Education* (Tel-Aviv: Reshafim, 1984), 147–78.
15. Ibid., 71–104.
16. Ibid., 107–42.
17. Presented by Yehuda Cahana in his article "Janusz Korczak and the School," *Readings in Education*, edited by Adir Cohen, vol. 43–44 (March 1968): 85–98.
18. Cohen, *A Revolution in Education*, 159.
19. Paul Goodman, *Compulsory Miseducation* (New York: Penguin Books, 1971), 25.
20. Cahana, "Janusz Korczak," 91.
21. Korczak, *Pedagogical Writings*, 43.
22. Ibid., 43.
23. Korczak, *The Child's Religion*, 75.
24. Ibid., 243.
25. Korczak, *Pedagogical Writings*, 77.
26. Ibid., 47.
27. Ibid., 63.
28. See the chapter "A Hundred Rebellious Ideas" that deals with punishment in education.
29. Korczak, *Pedagogical Writings*, 78.

Chapter 10. A Hundred Rebellious Ideas: On Punishment in Education

1. Janusz Korczak, "The Boarding School" in *How to Love Children*, translated by Jacob Zuk, in the book *With The Child* (Tel-Aviv: Beit Lochamei Hagetaot and Hakibbutz Hameuchad Publications, 1974), 311.
2. Korczak, *Pedagogical Writings*, 57.
3. Janusz Korczak, "The Spring and the Child," in *The Child's Religion*, translated by Zvi Arad (Tel-Aviv: Beit Lochamei Hagetaot and Hakibbutz Hameuchad Publications, 1978), 233.
4. Janusz Korczak, *How to Love Children*, translated by Jacob Zuk, in *With The Child* (Tel-Aviv: Hakibbutz Hameuchad Publications, 1960), 41.
5. Korczak, *Pedagogical Writings*, 201.
6. Ibid. note 4, 45.
7. Ibid., 48.
8. Ibid., 51.
9. Ibid., 13.
10. Ibid., note 1, 307.

Chapter 11. Youth—That Is Madness: On Sexual Education

1. Janusz Korczak, *The Drawing Room Kid*, translated by Arie Buchner and Avraham Berles (Tel-Aviv: Yesod, 1973), 54.
2. Janusz Korczak, *How to Love Children*, translated by Jacob Zuk (Tel-Aviv: Hakibbutz Hameuchad Publications, 1960), 21.

3. Korczak, *The Drawing Room Kid*, 54.
4. Korczak, *Pedagogical Writings*, 76.
5. Ibid., 75.
6. Ibid., 71.

Chapter 12. Free Will and Coercion: Janusz Korczak's Literary Creation

1. Janusz Korczak, *With God I Shall Converse*, translated by Yehushua Markovitz (Jerusalem: Kiryat Sefer, 1979), 56.
2. Korczak, *From the Ghetto*, 155.
3. Ibid., 141.
4. Ibid., 77.
5. Korczak, *Pedagogical Writings*, 169.
6. Ibid., 169.
7. Korczak, *From the Ghetto*, 140.
8. Korczak, *With God I Shall Converse*, 56.
9. Ibid.
10. Ibid., 57.
11. Ibid., 58.
12. Ibid.
13. Ibid., 60.
14. Yerachmiel Weingarten *Janusz Korczak* (Tel-Aviv: Ministry of Security—The Publishers, Tarmil Library, 1982), 26–65.
15. Korczak, *From the Ghetto*, 119.
16. Ibid., 120.

Chapter 13. *The Drawing Room Kid*

1. Janusz Korczak, *The Drawing Room Kid*, translated by Arie Buchner and Abraham Berles (Tel-Aviv: Yesod, 5733), 19.
2. Presented by Yerachmiel Weingarten in his book, *Janusz Korczak—The Tormented Jew* (Tel-Aviv: Bronfman, 1979), 171.
3. Korczak, *The Drawing Room Kid*, 16.
4. Ibid., 23–24.
5. Ibid., 27.
6. Ibid., 25.
7. Ibid., 40.
8. Ibid., 31.
9. Ibid., 115.
10. Ibid., 99.
11. Ibid., 113.
12. Ibid., 117.
13. Ibid., 165.
14. Gedalia Alkoshi, *Janusz Korczak in Hebrew* (Tel-Aviv: Hakibbutz Hameuchad, 1972), 17.
15. Korczak, *The Drawing Room Kid*, 147–48.
16. Ytzchak Perlis, *A Jew from Poland* (*The Life and Enterprise of Janusz*

Korczak) (Tel-Aviv: Beit Lochamei Hagetaot and the Hakibbutz Hameuchad Publications, 1986), 22.

Chapter 14. *When I Shall Be Little Again*

1. Zvi Kurzweil, *The Educational Teaching of Janusz Korczak* (Tel-Aviv: Culture and Education, 1968), 64.
2. Martin Buber, *In the Secret of Conversation*, 2d ed. (Jerusalem: Mosad Bialik, 1963), 257–58.
3. Janusz Korczak, "When I Shall Be Little Again," in *Pedagogical Writings*, translated by Dov Sadan and Shimshon Meltzer (Tel-Aviv: Hakibbutz Hameuchad, 1962), 90.
4. Ibid., 91.
5. Ibid., 101.
6. Ibid., 113.
7. Ibid., 106.
8. Ibid., 82.
9. Ibid., 96.
10. Ibid., 86.

Chapter 15. *Bobo*

1. Janusz Korczak, "Bobo," in *With the Child*, translated by Zvi Arad (Tel-Aviv: Beit Lochamei Hageta'ot and Hakibbutz Hameuchad Pulications, 1974), 129–50.
2. Ibid., 131.
3. Ibid., 132.
4. Ibid., 133.
5. Ibid., 134.
6. Ibid., 135.
7. Ibid.
8. Ibid.
9. Ibid., 138.
10. Ibid., 139.
11. Ibid.
12. Ibid., 146.
13. Ibid., 150.
14. Ibid., 142.

Chapter 16. *The Senate of Madmen*

1. From a review published in "Wiadonsci Literackie," Issue no. 41, 1931. Reprinted in the book: Alicja Sclazakowa, *Janusz Korczak*, translated by Edmund Konowic (Warszawa: Wydaawnictwa Szkolne i Pedagogiczne, 1978), 106. (Engl.)
2. From a review published in *Robotonic*, issue 347, 1931. Reprinted in Sclazakowa, *Janusz Korczak*, 106.

3. From an interview published in "Gloss," Issue 293, 1931. Reprinted in Sclazakowa, *Janusz Korczak*, 108.

4. Janusz Korczak, *The Senate of Madmen*, translated by Uri Orlev, in Cohen Adir, Aden Shevach, and Yatziv Reuven in *Studies in the Legacy of Janusz Korczak* (The Janusz Korczak Association, Beit Lochamei Hagetaot and Hakibbutz Hameuchad, 1988), vol. 2.

5. Ibid.

6. Ibid.

7. Ibid.

8. Ibid.

9. Ibid.

10. Ibid.

11. Ibid.

12. Ibid.

13. Ibid.

14. Ibid.

15. Ibid.

16. Ibid.

17. Ibid.

18. Ibid.

19. Ibid.

20. Ibid.

21. Ada Poznansky-Hagery, "The Reconciliatory Period of Janusz Korczak's Life," in *Studies in Education* 37–39 (September 1984): 280.

22. Korczak, *The Senate of Madmen*.

23. Ibid.

24. Ibid.

25. Ibid.

26. See translation of his letters, *Mibefnim* 4, no. 1 (June 1937): 132.

27. Moshe Zartal, "The Voice of Conscience," in *Stage* 15 (Autumn 1965): 51.

Chapter 17. From the Ghetto

1. Korczak, *From the Ghetto*.

2. Ibid., 77–78.

3. Ytzchak Perlis, Ibid, "The Last Chapter/Korczak in the Warsaw Ghetto," 12.

4. Simon, Akiva Ernst, *Pestalozzi and Korczak–Pioneers of Social Education* (Tel-Aviv: Urim, 1949), p. 58.

5. Korczak, *From the Ghetto*, 82.

6. Ibid.

7. Ibid., 106.

8. Ibid., 133.

9. Ibid.

10. Ibid., 134.

11. Ibid., 135.

12. Ibid., 136.

13. Ibid., 168–69.

14. Yona Buchian, "I Shall Remember . . ." in *Mibefnim* 24, no. 4 (September 1962): 420.

Chapter 18. The Miracle Worker: Janusz Korczak's Books for Children

1. Janusz Korczak, "The Spring and the Child" in *The Child's Religion*, translated by Zvi Arad (Tel-Aviv: Beit Lochamei Hagetaot and Hakibbutz Hameuchad Publications, 1978), 251.
2. Ibid., 234.
3. Korczak, *Pedagogical Writings*, 120.
4. Ibid., 52.
5. Ibid.
6. In this matter, see Adir Cohen, *Methods of Teaching Poetry* (Tel-Aviv: Akad, 1973), 24–27.
7. Korczak, *Pedagogical Writings*, 66–67.
8. Janusz Korczak, *King Matia the First*, translated by Uri Orlev (Jerusalem: Keter, 1979), 9.
9. Janusz Korczak, *The Stubborn Boy—The Life of Louis Pasteur*, translated by Shimshon Meltzer (Jerusalem: Adam, 1978), 5.
10. Korczak, *Pedagogical Writings*, 67.
11. Janusz Korczak, "The Tale and the Child," translated by Chava Verba *Hed Hagan*, Teachers Union 1948, year 10, vol. 3–4, 21–23.
12. Ibid.
13. Ibid., 50.
14. Korczak, "The Child in the Family," 240.
15. Janusz Korczak, *Stories For Children*, collected and edited by Zrubavel Gilad (Tel-Aviv: Hakibbutz Hameuchad, 1958), 42.
16. Janusz Korczak, *The Prayer*, translated by Arie Buchner (Tel-Aviv: Yesod, 1970), 106.
17. Korczak, "The Child in the Family," 272.

Chapter 19. King Matia

1. Janusz Korczak, *King Matia on the Desert Island*, translated by Uri Orlev (Jerusalem: Keter, 1979), 196.
2. Janusz Korczak, *King Matia the First*, translated by Joseph Lichtenbaum (Tel-Aviv: Nishversky, 1966), 96.
3. Gedalia Alkoshi, *Janusz Korczak in Hebrew* (Tel-Aviv: Hakibbutz Hameuchad, 1972), 25.
4. Korczak, *King Matia the First*, 55.
5. Janusz Korczak, *King Matia the First*, translated by Uri Orlev (Jerusalem: Keter, 1979), 17.
6. Ibid., 45.
7. Ibid., 23.
8. Korczak, *King Matia on the Desert Island*, 49.
9. Ibid., 147.
10. Korczak, *King Matia the First*, translated by Uri Orlev, 184.
11. Korczak, *King Matia the First*, translated by J. Lichtenbaum, 100.
12. Ibid., 130.
13. Korczak, *Pedagogical Writings*, 69.
14. Korczak, *King Matia the First*, translated by Uri Orlev, 127.

15. Ibid., 203.
16. Ibid., 211.
17. Korczak, *King Matia on the Desert Island*, translated by Uri Orlev, 63.
18. Ibid., 44.
19. Ibid.
20. Ibid., 45.
21. Korczak, *Pedagogical Writings*, 9.
22. Korczak, *King Matia on the Desert Island*, 70–71.
23. Ibid.
24. Korczak, *King Matia the First*, translated by J. Lichtenbaum, 228.
25. Korczak, *King Matia the First*, translated by Uri Orlev, 126.
26. Korczak, *King Matia on the Desert Island*, 78–79.
27. Ibid., 79–80.
28. Ibid., 80.
29. Ibid., 86.
30. Ibid., 91.

Chapter 20. *The Stubborn Boy*

1. Janusz Korczak, *The Stubborn Boy—The Life of Louis Pasteur*, translated by Shimshon Melzer (Jerusalem: Adam, 1978), 5.
2. Gil'ad Zrubavel, "Conversations and Encounters," in Anna Motrdetke-vitzch Olachkova, *The Life of Janusz Korczak* (Tel-Aviv: Hakkibutz Hameuchad, 1961), 191.
3. Janusz Korczak, *The Stubborn Boy—The Life of Louis Pasteur*, translated by Shimshon Melzer (Tel-Aviv: Mordechai Neuman, undated), 49–50.
4. Richard Livingstone, *Education in a Bewildered World*, translated by H. llan (Jerusalem: Hebrew University School of Education, 1960), 55.
5. Janusz Korczak, "Louis Pasteur," article in the publication "In the sun" reproduced in his book *The Child's Religion*, translated by Zvi Arad (Tel-Aviv: Beit Lochamei Hagetaot and the Hakkibutz Hameuchad Pulications, 1971), 343.
6. Korczak, *The Stubborn Boy* (Neuman), 9.
7. Ibid., 82.
8. Ibid., 99.
9. Ibid., 89.
10. Ibid., 17.
11. Ibid., 5.
12. Ibid., 35.
13. Ibid., 20.
14. Ibid., 122.

Chapter 21. *Little Jack*

1. Janusz Korczak, "Rules of Living," in *A Childhood of Dignity*, translated by Shimshon Meltzer (Tel-Aviv: Beit Lochamei Hagetaot and Hakkibutz Hameuchad Publications, 1977), 299.
2. Janusz Korczak, *Little Jack*, translated by J. Frieshman, 3d ed. (Tel-Aviv: Hakkibutz Hameuchad, 1967).

3. Ibid., 18.
4. Ibid., 20.
5. Ibid., 23.
6. Ibid., 27.
7. Ibid., 6.

Chapter 22. *Yotam the Magical*

1. Janusz Korczak, *Kaitoch the Wizard*, translated by Uri Orlev (Tel-Aviv: Am Oved, 1987), 5.
2. Janusz Korczak, *Yotam the Magical*, translated by Joseph Liechtenbaum (Tel-Aviv: Am Oved, 1969).
3. Ibid., 17.
4. Ibid., 28.
5. Ibid., 27.
6. Ibid., 171.
7. Ibid., 172.
8. Ibid.
9. Ibid., 82.
10. Korczak, *Kaitoch the Wizard*, 139–40.
11. Ibid., chap. 11, 110–19.
12. Korczak, *Yotam the Magical*, 60.
13. Ibid.
14. Korczak, *Kaitoch the Wizard*, 83.
15. Ibid., 107.
16. Ibid., 174.
17. Ibid., 26.
18. Ibid., 126.
19. Ibid.

Chapter 23. *At the Summer Camp*

1. Janusz Korczak, *At the Summer Camp*, translated by Arie Buchner (Tel-Aviv: Niv, 1965). This work appeared in another Hebrew translation entitled "Mushekim, Yosekim, Serulim" (translated by Zvi Arad), in the book *With The Child* (Tel-Aviv: Beit Lochamei Hagetaot and the Kibbutz Hameuchad Publications, 1972), 51–128.
2. Korczak, *At The Summer Camp*, 5.
3. Ibid., 7–8.
4. Ibid., 14.
5. Ibid., 131.
6. Ibid., 143–44.
7. Ibid., 144.
8. Ibid., 137.
9. Ibid., 126.
10. Ibid., 85–86.
11. Ibid., 48.

Chapter 24. *An Unlucky Week*

1. Janusz Korczak, "An Unlucky Week—From the Life of the School," translated by Uri Orlev, in *Studies in the Legacy of Janusz Korczak*, edited by Adir Cohen, Aden Shevach, and Yatziv Reuven (Beit Lochamei Hagetaot, The Janusz Korczak Association in Israel and the University of Haifa Publications, 1987), vol. 1, 119–44.
2. Janusz Korczak, "The Dormitory" from "How to Love Children," in the book *With The Child*, (Tel-Aviv: Beit Lochamei Hagetaot and the Hakkibutz Hameuchad Publications, 1974).
3. Korczak, "An Unlucky Week," 119.
4. Ibid., 120.
5. See Adir Cohen, "The Culture of the Beaten and the Hungry", *Gazit*, The 200th Issue, Vol. 17 (Kislev-Adar, 1960), 123–26.
6. Korczak, "An Unlucky Week," 120.
7. Ibid., 125.
8. Ibid., 126.
9. Ibid., 129.
10. Ibid., 141.
11. Ibid., 139.
12. Ibid., 143.

Chapter 25. "Fame"

1. Janusz Korczak, "The Legend and the Child," translated by Chava Varba, *Hed-Hagan*, 1960, 10th year, vol. 3–4, 21–23.
2. Janusz Korczak, *Fame*, translated by Arie Buchner (Tel-Aviv: Yesod, 1970).
3. Ibid., 86.
4. Ibid., 87.
5. Korczak, *From The Ghetto*, 90.
6. Korczak, *Fame*, 37–38.
7. Ibid., 19.
8. Ibid., 10.
9. Ibid., 77.
10. Ibid., 98–99.
11. Ibid., 57.
12. Ibid., 66.
13. Ibid., 88.
14. Ibid., 106.
15. Ibid., 58–62.
16. Ibid., 7.

Chapter 26. "People are Good": Korczak's Short Stories for Children

1. Janusz Korczak, *Stories for Children*, collected and edited by Zrubavel Gil'ad (Tel-Aviv: Hakkibutz Hameuchad, 1958).

2. Janusz Korczak, *People Are Good*, translated by Aire Buchner (Tel-Aviv: Niv, 1967), 15–28.

3. Ibid., 31–71.

4. Ibid., 39.

5. Ibid.

6. Ibid., 50.

7. Ibid., 71.

8. Korczak *Stories for Children*, 15.

9. Ibid., 16.

10. Ibid., 25.

11. Ibid., 42.

12. Ibid., 26.

13. Ibid., 19.

14. Ibid., 60–61.

15. Gdalia Alkushi, *Janusz Korczak in Hebrew* (Tel-Aviv: Hakkibutz Hameuchad, 1972), 82.

16. Ibid.

17. Korczak, *Stories for Children*, 60.

18. Ibid., 46.

19. Ibid., 49.

20. Janusz Korczak, "The Scar," in *The Child's Religion*, translated by Zvi Arad (Tel-Aviv: Beit Lochamei Hagetaot and Hakkibutz Hameuchad, 1978), 344–46.

21. Adir Cohen, *Encounters—To Touch Words, To Live a Poem*, vol. IV (Tel-Aviv: Am-Oved, 1985), 37–39.

22. Dvora Kubovy, *Therapeutic Teaching* (Jerusalem: The Hebrew University School of Education, 1970), 143–45.

23. Ibid., 143.

24. Korczak, *Stories For Children*.

25. Ytzchak Yatziv, "Without Barriers" in Mordetkevitz-Olatchkova, Hanna, *The Life of Janusz Korczak* (Tel-Aviv: Hakkibutz Hameuchad, 1968), 177.

26. Janusz Korczak, "There Are Four Rooms in the Heart," in Adir Cohen, *Encounters—To Touch Words, To Live a Poem*, vol. II (Tel-Aviv, Am-Oved, 1986), 144.

Chapter 27. To Children, by Children, for Children: About the Children's Newspaper

1. From Korczak's article in the *Mali Pashgelund*, 3 September, 1936, reprinted in his book *The Child's Religion*, translated by Zvi Arad (Tel-Aviv: Beit Lochamei Hagetaot and Hakibbutz Hameuchad Publications, 1978), 356.

2. Janusz Korczak, *The School Newspaper*, translated by Arie Buchner (Tel-Aviv: Niv, 1958).

3. Ibid.

4. Ibid., 147.

5. Ibid.

6. Ibid.

7. Ibid., 144.

8. Ibid.

9. Ibid., 352.

10. Yerachmiel Weingarten, *Janusz Korczak—The Tormented Jew* (Tel-Aviv: Bronfman, 1979), 251–52.
11. Ibid., 381.
12. Ibid., 400.
13. Ibid., 401.
13. Ibid., 383–85.
14. Ibid., 411–13.
15. Ibid., 372.
16. Ibid., 373.
17. Ibid., 374.
18. Ibid., 392–95.
19. Ibid., 394.
20. Ibid., 394–95.
21. Ibid., 421.
22. Ibid., 368.
23. Ibid.
24. Ibid., 378, and see also the chapter "To Be Jewish."
25. Hana Mordetkovitz-Olatchkova, *The Life of Janusz Korczak*, translated by Zvi Arad (Tel-Aviv: Hakkibutz Hameuchad, 1961), 113.
26. Ibid.

Chapter 28. One Home, Many Homes: A Comparative View

1. Janusz Korczak, "The Child's Religion," in *The Child's Religion*, translated by Zvi Arad (Tel-Aviv: Beit Lochamei Hagetaot and Hakibbutz Hameuchad Publications, 1978), 237.
2. Janusz Korczak, *How to Love Children*, translated by Jacob Zuk (Tel-Aviv: Hakibbutz Hameuchad Publications, 1960), 35.
3. See Adir Cohen, *Pestalozzi the Man and His Educational Method* (Jerusalem: Published by Zionist Federation's Department of Youth and Pioneering, 1963).
4. See the chapter "With God I Shall Converse."
5. Joseph Arnon, *Janusz Korczak's Educational Method* (Tel-Aviv: Otzar Hamore, 1972), 54.
6. Shevach Aden, *The Educating Community*, Chapters in Social Education (Tel-Aviv: N. Tvarsky, 1951).
7. See the chapter "To Be a Home."
8. Mordetkovitz-Ohlatczkova, *The Life of Janusz Korczak*, 134.
9. See the chapter "To the Sun."
10. Janusz Korczak, "We Are Not Known" (Conversations with Instructors). translated by Perlis Ytzchak—*Mibefnim*, Winter 1973, Vol. 38 (February 1973), 136–37.
11. A. S. Makarenko, *The Pedagogical Poem*, translated by Avraham Shlonsky (Merchavia: Sifryat Poalim), 98.
12. A. S. Makarenko, *On The Education of Youth*, translated by Pesach Ben-Amram (Tel-Aviv: Hakkibutz Hameuchad, 1961), 64.
13. See Adir Cohen, *Makarenko the Educator* (Tel-Aviv: Gomeh, 1972).
14. Korczak, *From the Ghetto*, 161.
15. See the chapter "To Be a Home."

16. See the chapter "A Hundred Rebellious Ideas."

17. A. S. Neil, *Freedom—Not Permisiveness*, translated by Ofra Burla-Adar (Tel-Aviv: Joshua Chichik, undated).

18. A. S. Neil, *Summerhill*, translated by Rephael Elgad (Tel-Aviv: Joshua Chichik, undated), 43–52.

19. Ibid., 49.

20. Ibid., 56.

21. Ibid., 59.

22. Korczak, *How to Love Children*, 36.

23. Neill, *Summerhill*, 63–64.

24. Joseph Arnon, "Lights and Shadows in English Education," *Ophakim*, eighth year, d (28) (November, 1954), 407.

25. Korczak, *Pedagogical Writings*, 260.

26. See the anthology *Summerhill: For and Against* (Tel-Aviv: Joshua Chichik, undated), 188. And see: Adir Cohen, *Free Education* (Tel-Aviv: Reshaphim, 1984), 11–69.

Chapter 29. The Dream and the Disillusion: An Attempt at Summary and Assessment

1. Janusz Korczak, *The Child's Religion*, translated by Zvi Arad (Tel-Aviv: Beit Lochamei Hagetaot and Hakibbutz Hameuchad Publications, 1978), 237.

2. Igor Neverly, "Chapters of Childhood and Youth," in *Janusz Korczak Educator to the Last*, edited by Perlis Ytzchak and Meirovitz Aharon, (Tel-Aviv: Beit Lochamei Hagetaot and Hakibbutz Hameuchad Publications, 1980), 19.

3. Janusz Korczak, "Rules of Education," translated by Perlis Ytzchak, 24 (September 1962): 417–19.

4. Moshe Zertal, *In the Presence of Janusz Korczak*, 2d expanded ed. (Merchavia: Sifryat Poalim, 1962), 9.

5. Ida Marzaszan, "The Educator and Teacher," translated by Meir Weil, *Education* 30, issue 5.

6. Quoted In Ada Hagery-Poznansky's article, "The Influence of Janusz Korczak on Educators," in *Studies in the Legacy of Janusz Korczak*, edited by Adir Cohen, Aden Shevach and Yatziv Reuven (Tel Aviv: Beit Lochamei Hagetaot, the Janusz Korczak Association, and the University of Haifa publications, 1987), vol. 1, 153.

7. Weingarten, *Janusz Korczak—The Tormented Jew*, 206.

8. Ibid.

9. Ibid.

10. Korczak, "The Senate of Madmen," translated by Uri Orlev.

11. Weingarten, *Janusz Korczak—The Tormented Jew*, 322.

12. Korczak, *From the Ghetto*, 172.

13. Hagery-Poznansky, "The Influence of Janusz Korczak."

14. Korczak, *Pedagogical Writings*. 205.

15. Korczak, *The Child's Religion*, 269.

16. Hagery-Poznansky, "The Influence of Janusz Korczak," 155.

17. Akiva Ernest Simon, *Pestalozzi and Korczak—Pioneers of Social Education* (Tel-Aviv: Urim, 1949).

18. Leon Harary, "On Janusz Korczak," *The Communal Education* 27, no. 95 (1978), 48–56.

19. Presented in the articles of Joseph Arnon, "The Meeting of an Educator with His Ex-protégés in Korczak's Orphanage," *The Communal Education* 27, no. 95 (1978), 8–19.

20. Ibid.

21. Ibid.

22. Ibid.

23. Gedalia Alkoshi, *Janusz Korczak in Hebrew* (Tel-Aviv: Hakibbutz Hameuchad, 1972), 66.

24. Jacob Zuk, "In the Company of Janusz Korczak and Stefania Vilesczinska," *Ofakim* (November, 1955), year 9, issue 2 (32), 340–41.

25. Korczak, *How to Love Children*, 15.

26. Moshe Silbertal, "About Janusz Korczak," *Ofakim* (November 1955), year 9, issue 3 (32), 333–34.

27. Korczak, *From the Ghetto*, 86.

28. Arnon, "The Meeting of an Educator."

29. Ibid.

30. See the chapter "To Be a Home."

31. Michael Verbulusky, "Janusz Korczak as I knew Him," in *Studies in the Legacy of Janusz Korczak*, edited by Adir Cohen, Aden Shevach, and Yatziv Reuven (Beit Lohamei Hagetaot), vol. 1, 159–62.

Bibliography

Aden, Shevach. *The Educational Community—Chapters in Social Education*. Tel-Aviv: N. Tversky, 1951.

Alkoshi, Gdalia. *Janusz Korczak in Hebrew*. Tel-Aviv: The Y. Katznelson Beith Lochamei Haggetaot, Hakkibutz Hameuchad Publications, 1972.

Apanshlak, Paulina. *The Doctor Stayed*. Translated by H. S. Ben-Abraham. Jerusalem: Kiryat Sefer, 1946.

Arnon, Joseph. *Janusz Korczak's Educational Method*. Merchavia: Sifryat Poalim, 1962.

Beiner, Friedheem. "Korczak's Theory of Educational Dialogue—Thoughts on Its Application In Teaching at Schools." Translated by Chanita Rozental. In Adir Cohen, Aden Shevach, and Yatziv Reuven, eds., *Studies In the Legacy of Janusz Korczak*, 1:31–40. Haifa: University of Haifa Publishing House, The Janusz Korczak Association in Israel, and Beit Lochamei Hagetaot, 1987.

Bergson, Gershon. *Korczak The Children's Author*. Tel-Aviv: Sifryat Poalim, 1978.

Cohen, Adir, ed. *Janusz Korczak—The Discussions of The International Congress On His Hundredth Birthday*. Haifa: University of Haifa and University of Tel-Aviv, 1979.

Cohen, Adir, Aden Shevach, and Yatziv Reuven (eds.)—*Studies in the Legacy of Janusz Korczak*. Vol. 1. Haifa: The University of Haifa Publishing House, The Janusz Korczak Association in Israel, and Beit Lochamei Hagetaot, 1987.

Cohen-Ronen, Ada. *Janusz Korczak—His Personality, Teaching and Educational Enterprise*. Ein Charod: Hakkibutz Hameuchad Publications, 1968 (in stencil).

Gilad, Zrubavel. *An Unfinished Conversation*. Tel-Aviv: Hakibbutz Hameuchad Publications, 1965.

Greenbaum, Ytzchak. *In Days of Destruction and Holocaust*. Tel-Aviv: Haverim Publications, 1946.

Hyams, Joseph. *A Field of Buttercups: The Story of Janusz Korczak and the Orphanage*. London: F. Muller, 1969.

Kopland, Steven. "Education to Realistic Idealism According to Janusz Korczak—Readings in The Consciousness of Despair and Hope." Translated by Chanita Rosenblatt. In Adir Cohen, Aden Shevach and Yatziv Reuven, eds., *Studies In the Legacy of Janusz Korczak*, 1:7–27. Haifa: University of Haifa Publishing House, The Janusz Korczak Association in Israel, and Beit Lochamei Hagetaot, 1987.

Korczak, Janusz. "The Child and The Legend." Translated by Chava Verva. In *Hed Hagan*, 10th Year, no. 3–4 (Tel-Aviv, 1945): 23–31.

———. *A Childhood of Respect*. Translated by Dov Sadan and Shimshon Meltzer. Tel-Aviv: Beit Lochamei Haggetaot and Hakkibutz Hameuchad Publications, 1977.

————. *The Child's Religion*. Translated by Dov Sadan and Zvi Arad. Tel-Aviv: The Ytzchak Katznelson Beit Lochamei Haggetaot and Hakibbutz Hameuchad Publications, 1978.

————. *The Drawing-Room Kid*. Translated by Arie Buchner and Avraham Berles. Tel-Aviv: Yesod, 1973.

————. *Fame*. Translated by Arie Buchner. Tel-Aviv: Niv, 1958.

————. *From the Ghetto (1939–1942)*. Translated by Zvi Arad. Tel-Aviv: The Ytzchak Katznelson Beit Lochamei Haggetaot and the Hakkibutz Hameuchad Publications, 1972.

————. *How to Love Children, The Boarding School, The Summer Camps*. Translated by Jacob Zuk. Tel-Aviv: Hakibbutz Hameuchad Publications, 1960.

————. *Kaitoch the Wizard*. Translated by Uri Orlev. Tel-Aviv: Am Oved, 1987.

————. *King Matia The First*. Translated by Joseph Lichtenbaum. 6th ed. Tel-Aviv: N. Tversky, 1960.

————. *King Matia The First*. Translated by Uri Orilev. 2 vols. Jerusalem: Keter, 1979.

————. *King Matia On The Desert Island*. Translated by Uri Orlev. Jerusalem: Keter, 1979.

————. *Little Jack*. Translated by Y. Frishman. Tel-Aviv: Hakibbutz Hameuchad Publications, 1944.

————. *The Newspaper at School*. Translated by Arie Buchner. Tel- Aviv: Niv, 1958.

————. *Pedagogical Writings*. Translated by Dov Sadan and Shimshon Meltzer. Tel-Aviv: Hakibbutz Hameuchad, 1962.

————. *People are Good*. Translated by Arie Buchner. Tel-Aviv: Niv, 1967.

————. *Plays*. Translated by Arie Buchner. Tel-Aviv: Niv, 1958.

————. *The Senate of Madmen*. Translated by Uri Orlev. In Adir Cohen, Aden Shevach, and Yatziv Reuven, eds., *Studies in the Legacy of Janusz Korczak*. The Janusz Korczak Association in Israel, Beit Lochamei Haggetaot and Hakkibutz Hameuchad Publications, 1988, no. 2.

————. *Stories For Children*. Collected and edited by Zrubavel Gilad. Tel-Aviv: Hakkibutz Hameuchad, 1958.

————. *The Stubborn Boy: The Life of Louis Pasteur*. Translated by Shimshon Meltzer. Tel-Aviv: M. Neuman, 1969.

————. *At the Summer Camp*. Translated by Arie Buchner. Tel-Aviv: Niv, 1965.

————. "Three Streams." Translated by Miryam Akavia. In Adir Cohen, Aden Shevach, and Yatziv Reuven, eds., *Studies in the Legacy of Janusz Korczak*, 1:145–46. Haifa: University of Haifa Publishing House, The Janusz Korczak Association in Israel, and Beit Lochamei Hagetaot, 1987.

————. "An Unlucky Week—From The Life of School." Translated by Uri Orlev. In Adir Cohen, Aden Shevach, and Yatziv Reuven, eds., *Studies in the Legacy of Janusz Korczak*, 1:119–44. Haifa: University of Haifa Publishing House, The Janusz Korczak Association in Israel, and Beit Lochamei Hagetaot, 1987.

————. *With God I Shall Converse—The Prayers of Those Who Do Not Pray*. Translated by Yehushua Markovitz. Jerusalem: Kiryat Sefer, 1979.

———. *With the Child*. Translated by Zvi Arad, with introduction and notes by Ytzchak Perlis. Tel-Aviv: The Ytzchak Katznelson Beit Lochamei Haggetaot and Hakibbutz Hameuchad Publications, 1972.

———. *Yotam the Magical*. Translated by Joseph Liechtenbaum. Tel-Aviv: Am Oved, 1964.

Kurzwell, Zvi. *The Educational Teachings of Janusz Korczak*. Tel-Aviv: Culture and Education, 1968.

Lansky, M. *The Life of the Jews in The Warsaw Ghetto*. Jerusalem: Holocaust Library, n.d.

Levin, Alexander, ed. *Janusz Korczak, Bibliografia 1896–1942*. Warsaw: Agentur Dieck, 1985.

———. "The Unique in Korczak's Legacy." Translated by Eva Aharonson. In Adir Cohen, Aden Shevach, and Yatziv Reuven, eds., *Studies in the Legacy of Janusz Korczak*, 1:25–30. Haifa: University of Haifa Publishing House, The Janusz Korczak Association in Israel, and Beit Lochamei Hagetaot, 1987.

Levinson, Abraham. *The History of Warsaw's Jews*. Tel-Aviv: Am Oved, 1953.

Marzashan, Ida. "Janusz Korczak's Last Journey." Translated by Aharon Yatziv. In Adir Cohen, Aden Shevach, and Yatziv Reuven, eds., *Studies in the Legacy of Janusz Korczak*, 1:163–67. Haifa: University of Haifa Publishing House, The Janusz Korczak Association in Israel, and Beit Lochamei Hagetaot, 1987.

Mordetkovitz-Olatchkova, Hanna. *The Life of Janusz Korczak*. Translated by Zvi Arad. Tel-Aviv: Hakibbutz Hameuchad, 1961.

Nishmit, Sarah. "On The Diaries of Children and Youth." In Tsizling Neria and Lahad Ezra, eds., *Readings in Memory of Janusz Korczak*, 39–49. Tel-Aviv: Beit Lochamei Haggetaot, 1986.

Perlis, Ytzchak. "The Decisive Test." In Janusz Korczak, *The Child's Religion*, translated by Ziv Arad, 6–66. Tel-Aviv: Beit Lochamei Haggetaot and Hakibbutz Hameuchad, 1978.

———. "Janusz Korczak—Jewish Fate As A Choice." In Adir Cohen, ed., *Janusz Korczak*, Discussions of the International Congress on His Hundredth Anniversary, 69–76. Haifa: Universities of Haifa and Tel-Aviv, 1979.

———. *A Jew From Poland (The Life and Enterprise of Janusz Korczak)*. Tel-Aviv: Beit Lochamei Haggetaot and Hakibbutz Hameuchad Publications, 1986.

———. "The Last Chapter—Korczak in the Warsaw Ghetto." In Janusz Korczak, *From the Ghetto*, 9–71. Tel-Aviv: Beit Lochamei Haggetaot and Hakibbutz Hameuchad Publications, 1972.

———. "The Question of Janusz Korczak's National Identity." In Tsizling Neria and Lahad Ezra, eds., *Studies in Memory of Janusz Korczak*, 27–37. Tel-Aviv: Beit Lochamei Haggetaot, 1986.

———. "The Way To The Child." In Janusz Korczak, *With The Child*, 9–50. Tel-Aviv: Beit Lochamei Haggetaot and Hakibbutz Hameuchad Publications, 1972.

Perlis, Ytzchak, and Meirovitz Aharon, eds. *Janusz Korczak: Educator to the Last*. Tel-Aviv: Beit Lochamei Haggetaot and Hakibbutz Hameuchad Publications, 1980.

Poznansky-Hageri, Ada. "How He Told And Wrote For Children." In Perlis Ytzchak and Meirovitz Aharon, eds., *Educator to the Last*, 39–47. Tel-Aviv: Beit Lochamei Haggetaot and Hakibbutz Hameuchad Publications, 1980.

————. "The Influence of Korczak on Educators." In Adir Cohen, Aden She-vach, and Yatziv Reuven, eds., *Studies in the Legacy of Janusz Korczak*, 1:153–58. University of Haifa Publishing House, The Janusz Korczak Association in Israel, and Beit Lochamei Hagetaot, 1987.

Rotem, Ya'akov. "Janusz Korczak as a Physician." In Adir Cohen, ed., *Janusz Korczak* (Discussions of the International Congress on His Hundredth Anniversary), 127–32. Haifa: Universities of Haifa and Tel-Aviv, 1979.

————. "Janusz Korczak in the Eyes of A Doctor." In Perlis Ytzchak and Meiro-vitz Aharon, eds., *Janusz Korczak Educator to the Last*, 79–93. Tel-Aviv: Beit Lochamei Haggetaot and Hakibbutz Hameuchad Publications, 1980.

Rozen, Zvi. "The Problem of Alienation and Its Overcoming in Korczak's Teaching." In Adir Cohen, ed., *Janusz Korczak* (Discussions of the Interna-tional Congress on His Hundredth Anniversary), 53–62. Haifa: Universities of Haifa and Tel-Aviv, 1979.

Sartel (Silbertal), Moshe. *In the Presence of Janusz Korczak*. Merchavia: Sifryat Poalim, 1962.

Singerman, Israel. *Janusz Korczak Among the Orphans*. Tel-Aviv: Sifryat Poalim, 1979.

Sokolov, Florian. *My Father—Nachum Sokolov*. Translated by Esther Blumenzweig. Jerusalem: The Zionist Library, 1970.

Szlazakowa, Alicja. *Janusz Korczak*. Translated by Edmund Ronowicz. Warsaw: Wydawnictwa Szkolne i Pedagogiczne, 1978.

Tczerniakov, Adam. *The Warsaw Ghetto Diary*. Edited by Nachman Blumental, A. Tratkover, N. Ak, and Y. Karmish. Jerusalem: Yad Vashem, 1969.

Verbolvesky, Michael. "Janusz Korczak as I Knew Him." Translated by Eva Aharonson. In Adir Cohen, Aden Shevach, and Yatziv Reuven, eds., *Studies in the Legacy of Janusz Korczak*, 1:159–62. Haifa: University of Haifa Pub-lishing House, The Janusz Korczak Association in Israel, and Beit Lochamei Hagetaot, 1987.

Waldeik, Kis. "Korczak's Realism and It's Importance in The Instruction of Education." Translated by Orna Silberman. In Adir Cohen, Aden Shevach, and Yatziv Reuven, eds., *Studies in the Legacy of Janusz Korczak*, 1:101–6. Haifa: University of Haifa Publishing House, The Janusz Korczak Association in Israel, and Beit Lochamei Hagetaot, 1987.

Weingarten, Yerachmiel. *Janusz Korczak*. Tel-Aviv: Ministry of Security—The Publishers, Tarmil Library, 1982.

————. *Janusz Korczak—The Tormented Jew*. Tel-Aviv: Bronfman, 1979.

Wolins, Martin, ed. *Selected Works of Janusz Korczak*. National Science Founda-tion, Washington D.C. by the Scientific Publications Foreign Cooperation Cen-ter of the Central Institute for Scientific, Technical and Economic Informa-tion, Warsaw, 1967.

Zuk, Jacob. "Working with the Doctor." In Ytzchak Perlis and Aharon Meiro-vitz, eds., *Janusz Korczak: Educator to the Last*, 35–38. Tel-Aviv: Beit Lochamei Haggetaot and Hakibbutz Hameuchad Publications, 1980.

Zylberberg, Michal. *A Warsaw Diary, 1939–1945*. London: Valentine, Mitchell, 1969.

Subject Index

Author Index

Pasteur, Louis, 243–48
Perla, Joshua, 65
Perlis, Itzchak, 26, 28, 191, 214
Pestalozzi, Johan Heinrich, 125, 214, 297–301, 304
Piotrovsky, Ian, 47
Postman, Neil, 165
Proust, Marcel, 178, 179

Razimowsky, W., 36
Rousseau, Jean-Jacques, 121, 123, 125, 156, 214, 300, 304

Shaw, George Bernard, 207
Shimanska, Zufia (Rosenblum), 58
Shlangel, Vladislav, 65–66
Shuller, Friedrich, 133
Simon, Akiva Ernest, 214, 318–20
Slonimsky, Anthon, 203
Spock, Benjamin, 140

Tolstoy, Leo, 125, 214

Verblovsky, Michael, 327–28
Vileczinska, Stefania, 35–36, 44, 56, 58–60, 65, 93, 95, 101, 115, 116

Weingarten, Yerachmiel, 17, 22, 39, 42, 47, 79, 81, 95, 97, 136, 144, 182, 185, 290
Weingartner, Charles, 165
Wieneken, Gustav, 297, 301
Whitehead, Alfred North, 161

Yatziv, Ytzchak, 283

Zeromasky, Stephan, 179
Zertal, Moshe, 314, 326
Zilber, David, 34, 94, 116–17
Zingman, Israel, 100–101
Zuk, Ya'akov, 99, 115, 323–24